Hacking Digital Ethics

Hacking Digital Ethics

Andréa Belliger and David J. Krieger

Anthem Press
An imprint of Wimbledon Publishing Company
www.anthempress.com

This edition first published in UK and USA 2022
by ANTHEM PRESS
75–76 Blackfriars Road, London SE1 8HA, UK
or PO Box 9779, London SW19 7ZG, UK
and
244 Madison Ave #116, New York, NY 10016, USA

First published in the UK and USA by Anthem Press in 2021

Copyright © Andréa Belliger and David J. Krieger 2022

The authors assert the moral right to be identified as the authors of this work.

All rights reserved. Without limiting the rights under copyright reserved above,
no part of this publication may be reproduced, stored or introduced into
a retrieval system, or transmitted, in any form or by any means
(electronic, mechanical, photocopying, recording or otherwise),
without the prior written permission of both the copyright
owner and the above publisher of this book.

British Library Cataloguing-in-Publication Data
A catalogue record for this book is available from the British Library.

Library of Congress Control Number: 2021934704

ISBN-13: 978-1-83998-588-1 (Pbk)
ISBN-10: 1-83998-588-7 (Pbk)

Cover image credit: James Felton Keith

This title is also available as an e-book.

CONTENTS

Series Editors' Introduction — vii

Introduction: Ethical Hacking and Hacking Ethics — 1

Chapter One The Exploit — 9
   1.1 We Do What We Are and Not What We Ought to Do — 9
   1.2 Systems Theory — 14
      1.2.1 Principles of Systemic Order — 17
      1.2.2 Communication — 21
      1.2.3 Consequences of Luhmann's Theory of Communication for Morality and Ethics — 23
      1.2.4 Cognitive and Normative Expectations and the Problem of Double Contingency — 27
      1.2.5 Symbolically Generalized Media and Functional Differentiation — 31
      1.2.6 Consequences of Functional Differentiation — 35
      1.2.7 The Function of Morality in Modern Society — 39
      1.2.8 Can Society as a Whole Be Modeled as a System? — 44
      1.2.9 What Is the Status of Social Theory? — 60
   1.3 Actor-Network Theory — 65
      1.3.1 The Difference a Stone Makes — 68
      1.3.2 Information — 77

Chapter Two The Breach — 89
   2.1 The Philosophical Mythology of Humanism — 89
      2.1.1 The Philosophy of Information and Information Ethics — 89
      2.1.2 What Is Information? — 92
      2.1.3 Information Ethics — 98
      2.1.4 The Informational Self — 102
      2.1.5 Privacy — 113
   2.2 Social Science Critique — 125
      2.2.1 The Modern Constitution — 125
      2.2.2 Critique — 130
      2.2.3 Platform Society — 133
      2.2.4 Surveillance Capitalism — 142
   2.3 Media Scandalization — 160
   2.4 Civil Society Activism — 169

Chapter Three The Redesign 187
    3.1 Network Norms 187
        3.1.1 Connectivity 191
        3.1.2 Flow 192
        3.1.3 Communication 194
        3.1.4 Participation 194
        3.1.5 Transparency 195
        3.1.6 Authenticity 196
        3.1.7 Flexibility 199
    3.2 Network Governance 202
        3.2.1 The Three Disruptions 203
        3.2.2 Governance 204
    3.3 Design 213
        3.3.1 Attribution of Moral Agency and Responsibility 216
        3.3.2 Case Study: Google's Framework for Internal Algorithmic Auditing 234
        3.3.3 What Is Design? 240
    3.4 Digital Ethics 243

Bibliography 257
Index 265

SERIES EDITORS' INTRODUCTION
Hacking Digital Ethics

As lead editors, we are excited to write this introduction to Belliger and Krieger's *Hacking Digital Ethics*, the second authored volume in the Anthem Press Ethics of Personal Data Collection Series. We appreciate ongoing cooperation with the acquisitions editor Megan Greiving, whose initial communication with Colette inspired our cooperation after speaking with the publisher Tej P. S. Sood.

The series builds on a special issue of *Genocide Studies and Prevention* organized by Colette at the invitation of Professor Douglas S. Irvin-Erickson, School for Conflict Analysis and Resolution, George Mason University, Virginia, and Yasemin Irwin-Erickson, with funding for workshops at New York University provided by a grant from the Robert Bosch Foundation in Stuttgart, Germany. We are most grateful to Carolin Wattenberg, senior manager to the board of management, and Dr. Stella Voutta, program director, at the Bosch Foundation, as well as Anda Catharina Ruf, advisor for private foundations and philanthropy, Deutsche Gesellschaft für Internationale Zusammenarbeit (GIZ) GmbH (German Corporation for International Cooperation GmbH), for their helpful and timely assistance in Germany.

Belliger and Krieger have been at the bleeding edge of thought on ethics and technology for the past few decades. Our earliest memory relative to this series was Belliger's publication *On Networking: A Hermeneutics for the Digital Age* (2012). Our aim is to explore the ethics of personal data collection because we identify personal data as the most microscopic measure of our information state. More specifically, we understand data as the new matter. Our expectation is for a data point to be identifiable with every piece of physical matter. Via data we are identifying the essence of what we are. In their exploration of network theory during the 2010 decade, Belliger and Krieger had to examine the methodological interpretation of philosophical texts like those of ancient religions, including the Abrahamic beliefs.

James recalls becoming familiar with our coauthors after giving a talk at the Transhumanism and Spirituality Conference in 2010, sponsored by the Mormon Transhumanist Association at the University of Utah's Marriott Library. After a presentation titled "Integrationalism: Spiritual Disincentives for Humanity," James was approached by Common Ground Publishing to expand his paper into a book (published in 2012) and was directed to Belliger's paper. James considered that his and Belliger's thoughts overlapped, if only slightly, in her study of a hermeneutics for the digital era and his use of data science to examine both popular ancient theology and modern religious speeches to find a central objective of spirituality. In a word cloud, *connectivity* stood out among the rest of the concepts presented. Data based on the meaning of language used over the past five thousand years has yielded versions of the word *connectivity*. James studied spirituality to see if connections were incentivized by the spirit.

Throughout the decade, in technoprogressive communities like Humanity Plus, the Institute for Ethics and Emerging Technology, Lifeboat Foundation, Singularity University, the Future of Humanity Institute at Oxford, and many others, we all nurtured concepts like concluding the Information Age. As digital data became something that we discovered to be coupled with all things, and information became something that we understood existed via data, it would only be a matter of time until a new age of knowing arrived. The revolution heralds an era in which the intangible and even spiritual starts to come into view, via the network of humanity. We are excited to introduce the original research in this manuscript to the Anthem Press Series with familiar authors.

This specific volume is rare in the authors' effort to hack the typical methodological approach to ethics as a scientific sect. In the context of the Anthem Press Series, *Hacking Digital Ethics* expands the concepts defined in Kaliya Young's volume, *The Domains of Identity* (2020), which is rooted in a consideration of the many individuals and institutions that might enforce one's self-sovereignty. This volume further expands the series to consider the idea pioneered by Belliger and Krieger, which is that, in a fully digital world, it is necessary to consider the network's or the community's rights along with the individual's normalized human rights. In the context of the COVID-19 pandemic, we are reminded of the ethics of contact tracing and the paradoxical potential of a community's right to a safe space with self-sovereign individuals wearing masks. Belliger and Krieger's volume is a bridge between domains of identity and a forthcoming volume edited by Mazzucelli, Keith, and Hollifield, *The Ethics of Personal Data Collection in International Relations: Inclusionism in the Time of COVID-19*. It is a bridge between the 14 domains of managed identity that Kaliya Young presents and the redesign of 7 norms that Belliger and Krieger explain.

Personal data collection presents a unique dynamism that has not been acknowledged in the modern literature. The reality that individuals are at their best when they identify with a community is not at war with the reality that communities are at their best only when they identify all of their individuals. In that regard, we insist on translating the ethic of what Belliger and Krieger call *the informational self* with norms that networks-of-humanity demand, like flexibility, authenticity, transparency, participation, communication flow, and, of course, connectivity.

At the macro-level in which Belliger and Krieger reason, the ethical concerns we face require anti-surveillance protection of a legal nature to prevent indefensible surveillance and incessant accumulation of personal data. Only in this way will the growing power of states to control every facet of the lives of targeted communities be held in check. It is no longer enough to define human rights in terms of limits placed on arbitrary state power in defense of individual freedom, as liberals do. In the second decade of the twenty-first century, billions of people across the planet are interconnected in ways that are a matter of life and death. In a "post-pandemic world," the survival of the human species is dependent on connectivity, which is a core objective of spirituality. This second volume in the series asks readers to rethink ethics in the context of the fragile community, which is composed of individuals vulnerable to surveillance capitalism as well as what John Sexton identifies in *Standing for Reason* (2019) as "secular dogmatism," which contributes to the increasing polarization in societies. In thinking about the relevance of *Hacking Digital Ethics*, throughout our world today the macro- and micro-levels connect with considerable tensions in play: to counter the dangers of the surveillance capitalism Zuboff defines (2019), as Wu explains, "A little less knowledge is what will keep us free," whereas to address the pitfalls of secular dogmatism, only a great deal more awareness may safeguard the peace in community.

We look forward to developing network partnerships, drawing on the ideas presented by Anne-Marie Slaughter in her volume, *The Chessboard & the Web* (2017), with the Institute for Communication & Leadership in Lucerne, Switzerland, where the authors of *Hacking Digital Ethics* hold key positions. By developing projects with colleagues within the BMW Foundation Herbert Quandt Responsible Leaders Network, the contributors to this series intend purposefully to exchange ideas and propose initiatives that speak to various themes first introduced by Kaliya Young in her timely analysis.

Colette Mazzucelli, New York University, United States
James Felton Keith, Keith Institute, New York, United States

INTRODUCTION: ETHICAL HACKING AND HACKING ETHICS

There are ethical hackers. Usually they work for the security industry or as independents who find it rewarding and honorable to discover bugs and just plain bad code in the prolific offerings of the commercial software industry. Many don't get paid for their efforts or are even exposed to intimidation and threats by the software vendors whose sloppy and irresponsible work they uncover. What motivates them is usually pride in their ability to discover what others have overlooked. Some are interested in enhancing their reputation. Still others prefer to remain anonymous. Anonymity is often helpful because ethical hackers often make enemies on both sides. The criminals don't like them, because they spoil their profits, and the software industry doesn't like them, because they reveal their failures. Ethical hackers find themselves in a peculiar "outsider" position. Their activities oppose them to established regimes, whether legal or criminal. Explicitly or implicitly, they seem to stand in the tradition of anarchism, since any position beyond the confines of established power appears as radical freedom, independence, and creativity. Concerning the digital, this is a tradition that goes back to the early days of the Internet, where many envisioned a virtual world of freedom and uninhibited self-expression, of democracy and equality.[1] The famous *Hacker Manifesto* of McKenzie Wark, although published much later in 2004, derives from the early vision of a free and unrestricted Internet. It proclaims optimistically that hackers are inheriting the world since human creativity cannot be suppressed by any ruling class or oppressive regime.

Although Wark places hacking in the Marxist tradition of revolutionary and emancipatory labor, his definition of what hacking is and what it means to be a hacker goes beyond any ideology of class struggle. For Wark, hacking does not consist of merely breaking into computer systems or databases. More radically, hacking is the construction of meaning in any form whatever. Meaning, or information, is always opposed to mere redundancy. Hackers break into the status quo, established systems, taken-for-granted patterns, accepted forms of order, and unquestioned codes; change things; and create new forms out of the old. Hackers "produce new concepts, new perceptions, new sensations, hacked out of raw data" (Wark 2004, [002]). Breaking into established

---

1 See the Wikipedia article on hacker culture (https://en.wikipedia.org/wiki/Hacker_culture) and S. Levy's famous book *Hackers: Heroes of the Computer Revolution* (1984). See also the well-known distinction between white hat, black hat, and gray hat hackers (https://en.wikipedia.org/wiki/Grey_hat).

systems and creating something new are not limited to manipulating computer code. "Whatever code we hack, be it programming language, poetic language, math or music, curves or colorings, we are the abstractors of new worlds" ([002]). Wark sees hacking and hackers not as more or less sociopathic computer nerds. Instead, a hacker is anyone who works creatively. "Whether we come to represent ourselves as researchers or authors, artists or biologists, chemists or musicians, philosophers or programmers, each of these subjectivities is but a fragment of a class still becoming, bit by bit, aware of itself as such" ([002]).

Quite against his intentions, Wark's hacker looks less like Marx's proletariat and much more like Heidegger's authentic *dasein*. For Heidegger, *dasein* exists in two modes. The mode of the "they-self" (*das Man*) and the mode of authenticity (*Eigentlichkeit*). Both are rooted in *dasein*'s way of being as being thrown into a world for which *dasein* finds itself caring (*Sorge*) in many practical endeavors. In these endeavors, *dasein* can simply conform to ways of acting, thinking, and feeling that are already present in society and which more or less determine all its relations to itself and the world. It can simply do what is expected by tradition, by institutions, and so on. Or *dasein* can be "resolute" (*Entschlossenheit*) and can free itself from the expectations, habits, and clichés of everyday life and disclose a world that has been hidden behind what is already there. Resolute *dasein* is the famous "authenticity" of existentialism.

Authenticity throws *dasein* back upon itself as the originary source of meaning and value, whereby it must be emphasized that *dasein* has nothing to do with the autonomous rational subject of modern Western philosophy from Hobbes and Descartes to Husserl. *Dasein* is authentic precisely then, when it steps back from the sovereign self-determination of subjectivity, the inauguration of social contracts, and the Promethean heroism of revolution and lets truth occur in the appearance of beings as they are. Authentic resolution is not at all a sovereign act of will, a struggle for self-realization, or the constitution of an individual, but much rather "releasement" (*Gelassenheit*), or a letting-be of Being in its disclosure and its withdrawal. Heidegger was therefore always careful to point out that authenticity was not an ethical norm addressed to an autonomous rational subject, like Kant's categorical imperative, nor was it to be thought of as moral in any other sense of the word.

Finally, with regard to Nietzsche, *dasein* should not be understood as a pure willing of will and thus as a kind of "overman," beyond good and evil. There are two reasons for this. First, ethical norms are usually the way in which society expresses how it expects its members to behave. Norms, therefore, have little to do with what authentic existence is called to become. This is not because authentic *dasein* is asocial, but because participation in society cannot be reduced to fulfilling expectations. Second, ethics, whatever it might originally have been, has long ago become an academic discipline, a scientific and theoretical endeavor that has little to do with *dasein*'s original form of being-in-the-world as care (*Sorge*). To take a step back from practical engagement in life, put down one's tools, and take up an attitude of reflection upon duties and obligations is based upon the distinction between what is and what ought to be, as well as the concomitant distinction between subject and object of knowledge and action. In opposition to the traditional view of ethics and morality, *dasein*, and ethical hackers as well, seem to be primarily concerned with practice instead of theory and with what can be done instead of what ought to be done. The hacker, according to Wark, does what he or she is and not what he or she ought to do according to the expectations or rules of conduct laid down by any community.

It is interesting that for both Heidegger's authentic *dasein* and Wark's hackers, the primary concern is not to comply with any normative expectations. Neither authentic *dasein* nor ethical hackers are concerned with being good. This is because hacking, as well as authentic *dasein*, by its very nature does not comply with anyone's expectations. Artistic creativity is what it is, because no one expects it or even claims that in any moral sense of the word one "ought" to do it. Who says artists ought to be concerned with the well-being of all creatures, respect human autonomy, protect privacy, promote solidarity among all peoples, be subject to democratic accountability, contribute to social equality and justice, respect diversity and minorities, anticipate adverse consequences of what they do, work to make people responsible, ensure sustainability, and so on?[2] As Wark puts it, "To hack is to differ" ([003]), but not to do good. "Hackers create the possibility of new things entering the world. Not always great things, or even good things, but new things" (2004). This view of what hacking means seems to put hacking—as well as *dasein*—beyond good and evil, that is, beyond moral and ethical considerations. As it turns out, perhaps there are no ethical hackers after all. Maybe hacking has nothing at all to do with ethics. And yet ….

Can ethics be hacked? Can new and unexpected meaning be found in or behind established traditions of moral discourse? Does not the digital transformation challenge us to develop a digital ethics that is just as disruptive and transformative as the technologies it proposes to regulate? Would ethical hacking be the same as hacking ethics? This book attempts to answer these questions. The occasion for this attempt is the digital transformation, the advent of a global network society, the information age, knowledge society, datafication, and whatever other terms come to mind to describe our present historical moment.[3] In the face of this changing reality, ethics has attempted to become digital ethics. No area of personal or social life is not conditioned by the digital and everything that it stands for and everything it brings with it. Marx would probably have been overjoyed to learn that very soon there will be no more workers since robots will do the work; that everyone will own the means of production, that is, their own creativity and skills; and that a sharing economy will largely replace capitalism. But would he be happy about the prospects of a posthuman or even transhuman world in which not only intelligence but also agency and identity are distributed among heterogeneous networks of humans

---

2 The question is rhetorical. In fact, many do claim that art ought to be "ethical." The presuppositions of current discussions about the relation of art and ethics, however, are based on distinctions between aesthetics and ethics, and about what art is that neither Heidegger nor Wark would agree to. The norms mentioned are the 10 principles of the Montreal Declaration for the Responsible Development of Artificial Intelligence (2017) and reflect typical lists of the principles of digital ethics.
3 The idea of the digital transformation is central to this book. For those who would like a precise definition, see Section 3.2.1, "The Three Disruptions."

and nonhumans? Would he be happy at the prospect of a data-driven society in which decisions are made based on evidence and not intuition, gut feelings, cognitive bias, prejudice, experience, and inherited assumptions? Indeed, not only Marxism but practically no theory or worldview that has arisen within the modern period, including ethics, finds itself able to cope with the new digital world order. Instead, we are experiencing in all areas the defensive reaction of Western industrial society to the disruptive influences of digital technologies. The world is changing. Digital transformation disrupts traditional forms of order, whether it be the order of knowledge, the order of cooperative action in social organizations, or the self-understanding of human existence.

The world of Western modernity is disappearing and a new world, let us call it a global network society, is emerging in its stead. For established institutions and habits of thought, this is a threatening and highly uncertain situation. Facing up to this situation does indeed have an ethical dimension; it does call for ethics. But an adequate moral response to this situation is not and cannot be merely applying traditional values and norms to digital technologies. Nonetheless, the current discourse of digital ethics consists almost entirely of attempts to apply traditional normative ethics to the development and deployment of new technologies. The thesis of this book is that no amount of rights and duties, of moral norms and ethical imperatives, and no list of ethical guidelines or principles of good artificial intelligence (AI) or ethical big data are going to have the slightest effect if they do not leave the presuppositions, convictions, and traditions of Western industrial society behind and embark upon exploring a new world with new values and new forms of responsibility and accountability. This is the challenge of hacking digital ethics. The hack, from this point of view, consists of breaking into the codes of traditional moral discourse and redesigning things so that something like digital ethics can appear unconcealed from the outworn and concealing veil of modernity. Perhaps, despite all the publicity and attention; the hasty founding of institutes, centers, and departments for digital ethics; the activism of nonprofit organizations; and the flood of guidelines, declarations, and programs supporting ethical design, development, and deployment of technology, there currently is no such thing as digital ethics. There is only modern Western ethics, that is, ethics that arose within modern Western society, that is, within a no-longer-viable social order and a passing historical moment. It could be that a uniquely digital ethics is waiting for the hack to come into view for the first time. One could even go so far as to claim that ethics today is fundamentally dependent upon the hack and not the other way around. It is not hacking that needs ethics; it is ethics that needs hacking. Could such an endeavor be judged by the standards it leaves behind? Can the global network society be judged by the standards of Western industrial society? What new norms take the place of the old ones? And what does ethics become when it no longer answers the questions of the world in which it was formed, which defined what it was, and which, whether we like it or not, no longer exists?

Scanning the discourse of digital ethics for weaknesses, entry points, or possible exploits, what the hacker finds is that the discourse of digital ethics runs on an insecure "legacy" system consisting of four interdependent, mutually reinforcing components. The first component is a philosophical mythology of humanism, which tells the story of the autonomous rational subject and the inalienable, universal values, norms, and rights that derive from it. The second component is the tradition of social science critique, which is primarily concerned with uncovering abuses of power by political and business elites, denouncing injustice, and debunking ideology. The third component of the discourse of digital ethics is media scandalization. Locked into the economy of attention, the media rely upon the continuous production of moral outrage to capture the attention of information consumers. Without understanding how moral outrage generated by the scandalization of the new media by the old media functions to create and maintain a specific moral discourse about the digital, the current form of digital ethics cannot be adequately described. The fourth component is moral admonishing and lobbying by civil society actors, watchdog NGOs, and private as well as semi-private institutions that assume that they represent the interests of "the public" while speaking for themselves, that is, their own particular publics.

A further aspect of contemporary ethical discourse that is closely related to the four mentioned above can be termed "political opportunism." Moral discourse that is expressed as political opportunism consists of the reactions of politics to perceived public pressure usually generated by media scandals and civil society activism. Moralizing in this area is expressed through government-initiated investigations, widely publicized hearings, interventions, and the enactment of regulations. When government activity and the enactment and enforcement of laws and regulations arise from belief in the philosophical mythology of humanism, supported by social science critique, the lobbying of civil society actors, and media scandalization, this can be termed "opportunism" to the extent that chances for gaining and maintaining political power and legitimation are the primary motivating factors. We do not consider political opportunism a basic component of contemporary moral discourse; much rather, it is the typical and perhaps necessary form in which the political system operates. Politics is not concerned with truth or the morally good, but with the mechanisms by which power is obtained and maintained in the face of an ever-threatening opposition. Nonetheless, political opportunism does play a role in influencing, motivating, reinforcing, and legitimating the components of contemporary moral discourse we have identified. These components make up the legacy system upon which the discourse of digital ethics currently runs. This is what we are attempting to hack into.

We will take up the challenge of hacking digital ethics by first developing what in hacking circles is known as an "exploit kit" (Chapter 1). An exploit kit is a kind of toolbox with instruments, code, and practices that are able to identify vulnerabilities in computer systems and breach their security. These tools can be used, or "exploited," to reveal bad code, bugs, insecure processes, and so on. In our case, the exploit kit contains not code, but arguments, concepts, definitions, and theoretical strategies that reveal the vulnerabilities of current digital ethics as well as modern moral discourse in general. What happens to normative discourse when there is no longer a clear distinction between the "is" and the "ought" and between the "subject" and the "object"? What does it mean for ethics when social reality consists of neither autonomous individuals nor a homogeneous social whole? What does it mean for morality if agency and responsibility are distributed among hybrid networks of humans and nonhumans? And finally, what does it mean for digital ethics if information is by nature relational and therefore cannot constitute individual persons and groups and cannot be reduced to either public or private property? If the world consists of information, and information is not a thing that can be owned or isolated from other information, what happens to the foundational distinctions of Western society? Our exploit kit gives us the tools to show that many of the distinctions that lie at the basis of modern Western ethics and morality can no longer be assumed true and unquestionable. We will develop this exploit kit by examining the ethical implications of two contemporary theoretical programs. One is Niklas Luhmann's theory of social systems, whereas the other is Bruno Latour's actor-network theory. Systems theory and actor-network theory provide us with the exploits we will use to demonstrate the vulnerability of legacy moral discourse in its dependence upon the philosophical mythology of humanism, social science critique, media scandalization, and civil society activism. We claim that understanding social order and human existence at the beginning of the twenty-first century means leaving the myth of humanism behind and facing the challenge of envisioning a world based upon a relational ontology of information instead of substances and autonomous rational subjects.

Once we have assembled our exploit kit, we will attempt to "breach" the legacy system upon which the discourse of digital ethics runs (Chapter 2). We will begin with a critical appraisal of Luciano Floridi's philosophy of information and information ethics, which represent the most ambitious attempt to found a systematic digital ethics to date. We will begin by taking a close look at Floridi's proposal to meet the challenge of the digital transformation by developing a philosophy of information and a specific information ethics based upon it. As one of the few who have acknowledged the revolutionary character of the digital transformation and attempted to face the consequences, Floridi's important contributions to digital ethics will serve as a test of the extent to which current forms of digital ethics are able to overcome the humanist assumptions of traditional Western ethics. The purpose of this exercise is to lay bare and reconfigure the mythology of humanism behind present-day ethical thought and the ways in which it is expressed in social science critique, the publicistic and lobbying efforts of civil society actors, and media scandalization. We will show that the status of moral discourse at the beginning of the twenty-first century is uncertain with regard to the subject and nature of moral agency and deeply disrupted by the demise of humanism while at the same time attempting to carry on as usual and avoid questioning traditional values and norms. Our claim will be that since assumptions about human nature, free will, ontological individualism, and belief in the autonomous rational subject can no longer be taken for granted, the entire enterprise of ethics must be reconceived. Our hack will show that what has formerly claimed to be digital ethics has nothing to do with the digital but instead represents the defense reaction of modern Western social order to the digital transformation and the advent of a global network society. What the hack reveals is that despite all the talk in its name, there is no such thing as digital ethics. There is merely modern Western ethics attempting to reassert itself in the face of the emergence of a global network society.

We then go on to ask what are the values and norms that arise in a global network society and that are based on the digital transformation (Chapter 3). What the hack shows is that "we have never been modern"—following Latour—and that digital ethics must be "redesigned" on the basis of a non-modern morality that guides the work of constructing socio-technical networks of both humans and nonhumans. This inquiry is guided by the question of what values and norms are embedded in digital technologies. What norms can take the place of the outdated morality of Western modernity? To answer this question, it will be necessary to listen to what things, artifacts, and technologies that have become our most significant nonhuman others are telling us about who we are. The non-modern and unofficial morality that has always guided the building of networks and the activities of networking that construct social order is not based on assumptions of free will and the sovereignty of human agency but the "affordances" of things. The most significant of our nonhuman others are today subsumable under the concept of digital information and communication technologies (ICTs) in all their forms. If we wish to describe the norms guiding networking in today's digital world, we must look for norms and values arising from the affordances of these technologies. The digital transformation creates new norms and values that replace the norms and values of Western industrial society. What are these new "network norms?" They are connectivity, flow, communication, participation, transparency, authenticity, and flexibility. None of these norms is based upon any kind of privileged knowledge of human nature or the myth of the autonomous rational subject and the supposedly incontrovertible and inalienable rights derived therefrom. On the contrary, network norms are the principles guiding the construction of complex socio-technical networks, that is, the networks in which we live in today's world.

To the extent that new network norms guiding networking in today's world can be discovered and described at this early stage of the digital transformation, we go on to ask how the network norms can be expressed in regulative frameworks. Since we are no longer dealing with autonomous rational subjects as the bearers of moral accountability and responsibility, since ethics and morality must leave behind notions of good and evil, of praise and blame, which heretofore were addressed to human individuals and their deeds alone, and since traditional forms of regulation both moral and political have become dysfunctional, the very idea of the moral and the ethical must be redefined as an issue of "network governance." If there is to be a digital ethics at all, it cannot be an ethics based on modern Western conceptions of human nature and the legal as well as normative forms of regulation typical of industrial social order. The description of new values, new network norms that replace the traditional values and norms of humanism, leads us to the question of what forms of regulation are appropriate for complex socio-technical networks operating on a global scale. We will be concerned to show how new forms of governance step in when traditional hierarchical forms of moral admonishment and government regulation no longer prove effective.

We propose not only to base digital ethics on governance instead of government, but to reconceptualize moral agency as "design." Design is not an esthetic add-on to merely functional artifacts, and it is not something only "designers" do. Design, as we propose to understand the term, designates a fundamental form of agency, namely, that form of agency that constructs socio-technical networks. Latour speaks of "technical mediation," that is, activities of translating and enrolling actors into hybrid networks. We propose understanding design as a distributed and symmetrical agency undertaken by all actors that together construct a network. Design, therefore, becomes a foundational concept of digital ethics. Because they are the expression of design, complex socio-technical networks are morally responsible and accountable. Design can be either good or bad. Good design is how network governance is implemented. It governs networks by following the network norms that influence how networking is done in today's digital world. What does society look like when the hierarchies are gone; when nonhumans, as well as humans, are moral agents; and when moral responsibility and accountability are distributed throughout hybrid networks? To the extent that we can formulate at least a plausible answer to these questions, our hack will have been successful. The hack intends to disrupt the legacy system of moral discourse, which, although it calls itself digital ethics, has nothing to do with the digital but much rather with the attempt to reassert the norms and values of Western modernity in the face of the perceived threat of the digital transformation. The hack claims to be an ethical hack because it attempts to design an ethics that deserves to be called digital ethics.

A word of warning: We are concerned to emphasize that no pejorative connotations are intended. All the components of contemporary ethical discourse—that legacy system upon which current digital ethics is running—are linked together in many ways and mutually influence, reinforce, and condition each other such that there arises what can be termed "a specific discourse of digital ethics." The hacker intends to break into this system and change codes, forge new links, redirect trajectories of thought and practice, and generally redesign ethics so that it can function in the socio-technical environment of the global network society. This is not another exercise in the typically modern gesture of critique. The hacker does not aim to debunk, denounce, admonish, or blame anyone or any institution. The hacker exposes no moral wrongdoing, no abuse of power, no ideology, and no attempts to hide or disguise any of the above. The hacker makes no appeal to moral outrage. No scandal is staged. There is no intention of reasserting, legitimizing, or reinforcing anything that could be seen as the normative foundations of social order or the evolutionary achievements of Western culture. This book is not a critique; it is a hack. The hack follows its own rules and goals and refuses to be subsumed under the system it breaks into and attempts to change. Hacking digital ethics is to be understood in this book as an attempt to disrupt the complacencies, the traditionalism, the lack of imagination, and the vulnerabilities of present-day ethical discourse and raise questions that heretofore have not been adequately addressed. It attempts to be an ethical hack, even at the risk of having to take up an outsider position and making enemies on all sides. The intentions are noble. The work, however, is dirty and will undoubtedly offend many. But this is what ethical hacking is all about.

Chapter One

THE EXPLOIT

1.1 We Do What We Are and Not What We Ought to Do

We all know what we ought to do. We ought to quit smoking, stop drinking, eat less sugar, exercise more, lose weight, drop the party scene, not waste food, buy organic, switch to bicycling, drive electric, reduce the carbon foot print, vote, be civically responsible, give to charities, maintain a healthy work-life balance, spend more time with the family, turn off the television, refrain from speaking badly about others, obey traffic laws, keep promises, recycle waste, read serious books, improve our skills, not cheat on taxes, think positively, not steal anything, tell the truth, think of others first, not hurt anyone, lend a helping hand, do our homework, respect teachers, persons of authority, and institutions, be humble, trustworthy, and reliable, overcome our prejudices, avoid discrimination, support the needy, not waste time, clean the garage, and much much more. Some of the time, we do manage to do some of the things we ought to do. But mostly, we don't. And never will. Why not? Why can't we be what we ought to be? The answer is simple. Because we do what we are and not what we ought to do. No amount of ethics, moral reprimands, supervision, sanctions, rehabilitation programs, hard words, pangs of guilt, or social pressure will change this situation. Because it can't be changed without changing what we are.

What does it mean to be called upon to change what we are and not only what we do? This is a philosophical question and not merely a practical matter. How can something become other than what it is without losing itself along the way? If we try to imagine what kind of person we would be if we did do everything we ought to do, there would almost certainly be something strange about this person, something that does not belong to us. What is it like to be a saint? Surely, a burden of guilt and remorse would fall from our shoulders, but these would no longer be *our* shoulders. They would belong to a person we could hardly imagine. This is not because we cannot change our ways, as it were, turn around, which is the original meaning of the word "conversion." It is also not because we cannot be virtuous, that is, act on the basis of a good character. It is because even if we did change our ways, even if we did direct our activities to developing a good character, we would not become what we should be for the simple reason that we do not and cannot know what we should be.[1] We may know what we should do. Everyone is telling us. But we do not know what we should be. Of course, a greedy person could become generous.

---

1 For the attempt to base an ethics for the digital age precisely on the assumption of classical virtue ethics that human nature is characterized by "a basic moral psychology" from which "technomoral virtues" can be derived, see Vallor (2016). See also the blogpost "Can Networks Be Virtuous"? at http://interpretingnetworks.ch/can-networks-be-virtuous/.

But there are so many situations in which greed or generosity means different things to different people, has different intentions and different consequences, that it is impossible to know if either our own or another person's character has really changed or, even for that matter, changed for the better. The norms, rules, and expectations that we and others at any time have do not define who we are; they describe what a certain person, group, community, or culture at a particular time in history and in a specific situation thinks we are. Such interpretations, as history shows, are never exhaustive descriptions of human existence. And as history implies, they never will be. Historicity, or what Heidegger calls "facticity," means that what we are is nothing we can define, know in advance, complete, or fulfill; therefore, there is nothing we can ever make "perfect" (Latin *per-facere* = make complete). The historicity of human existence means that not only is every single human endeavor incomplete, but existence itself. Not only what we do but what we are is fundamentally imperfect, whereby the word "imperfect" does not imply a moral judgment. There is no end to what we have to do to do everything we ought to do. This is what we are—the paradoxical endlessness of finitude.[2]

Despite a seemingly fundamental imperfectability, ethics has always ignored this fact and insisted upon the perfectibility of human existence. Ought implies can. It makes no sense to tell people what they ought to do if they can't do it. To maintain the meaning and purpose of ethics, therefore, one must assume perfectibility, that is, a free will and knowledge of the good.[3] For Aristotle, the good life (*eudaimonia*) consisted of fulfilling the potential of human nature whose highest and most valuable faculty is contemplation. For Kant, the only unconditional good is the unconditionally good will, which becomes unconditioned the moment it chooses what pure reason dictates that it ought to choose, that is, the categorical imperative. No considerations of particular goods or advantages are allowed by the imperatives of universal reason. For utilitarianism, the good is the greatest amount of pleasure for the greatest number. This implies that one can know what is good for people, what makes them happy, and also that one can somehow quantify it. In all of these views and their many variations, it was presupposed that the human

---

[2] From the Heideggerian point of view (see *Letter on Humanism*), it would seem that ethics is the attempt to persuade people to be inauthentic, to conform to expectations, and in doing so to, in fact, renounce freedom. Ethics makes the same mistake as traditional theories of truth that suppose a correspondence (*adequatio*) between intellect and thing (*res*), since ethics supposes a correspondence between will and norm. The presupposition of both is that the norm and the thing (*res*) are present to knowing and willing. This ignores the withdrawal and concealment of Being in the unconcealment of appearances, that is, the facticity and historicity of Being. If Heidegger's notion of authenticity is to have an ethical dimension at all, then it would lie in the acceptance of the facticity of existence and the decision to preserve the openness of all beings to new meaning. For a discussion of ethics in Heidegger's early work, see Aggleton (2016), Webb (2009), and Reid (2019).

[3] "Kant held that we must believe in an undetermined free will because it is presupposed by our practical reasoning and our moral life. But Kant also believed that science and theoretical reason could not explain how an undetermined free will was possible. We had to believe it on faith" (Kane 2002, 19). For neuroscientific arguments against free will, see Caruso (2012), and for a critique of traditional notions of freedom as much too simplistic, see Willke (2019).

individual was free and therefore able to choose the good, and it was assumed that the good could be known, calculated, or derived from direct knowledge of human nature. Free will, at least in the modern period, has been a cornerstone of the ethical edifice, regardless of architectural variants. And the good has always been knowable and therefore attainable.

In modern Western thought, the bearer of free will is the individual subject. Subjectivity, however, was not composed of the faculty of the will alone, but more importantly, the faculty of reason. Indeed, since Descartes, the subject is essentially constituted by a specific form of reason, the certainty of itself expressed in Descartes's famous phrase *cogito ergo sum*. Interestingly, assenting to the truth of the *cogito* was for Descartes not a free choice. The truth of the *cogito* consisted in the fact that one couldn't choose otherwise. This is what certainty means. Clear and distinct ideas cannot be denied. It is impossible to deny that I am thinking when I'm thinking, try as I might. What freedom, we ask, is left to the will? To deny the *cogito* is unthinkable and therefore impossible. What could be denied, however, are the consequences of this newfound freedom. To accept the freedom of subjectivity, an act of courage was needed. As Kant put it, *sapere aude* (dare to know). Daring to make use of one's faculties of reason and judgment is not only enlightenment; it is the specific form of modern freedom. Free subjectivity lies in its courageous acceptance of reason. The subject is free because it determines itself, gives itself the law of reason. A thinking subject that denies that it thinks would cease to be a subject, since the very essence of subjectivity is self-reflection. Even if the *cogito* could and somehow did manage to deny itself, this would presumably only destroy the empirical, individual mind of a particular person, who had obviously lost their mind anyway, but not the Mind itself, which is by nature universal or "transcendental."[4] For Kant, it was only when the will of the individual chose transcendental or universal norms that it could be considered unconditionally good. The primacy of reason in ethics, however, does not end here. This is only the beginning.

Even the calculus of pleasure offered by utilitarianism was a choice for reason, since it was a mathematical exercise, even though what was being calculated was pleasure and pain. It would appear that Western ethics presupposes a free will that is only free when it wills something other than itself, namely, reason or at least those norms, rules, and standards that appear accessible to knowing and by nature universal. The founding assumptions of modern ethics are not only that people have a free will and the ability to know the good through reason but also that knowing the good is itself something good. Ethics was not a "value-free" science, but a morally praiseworthy form of knowing. Even when ethics claimed that the good resides in a different faculty of the soul than reason, for example, sensibility or the feeling of pleasure, it was considered more reasonable to

---

4 Despite claims for the universality and incontestability of reason that echo through modernity and accompanying convictions that one cannot live with contradictions, the history of religions and cultures shows that people have everywhere and at all times believed and assented to the most absurd nonsense. The empirical universality of contradictions, paradoxes, absurdities, and nonsense seems to rival if not exceed the logical universality of reason.

choose pleasure than pain and even more reasonable to choose more pleasure than pain. The uncertain and ambiguous relation between reason and will, which has characterized modern Western thought, was for Nietzsche a thorn in the flesh. For Nietzsche, the fact that the will must will something other than itself in order to be good amounts to slavery and not freedom. Truly free are only those who will freedom itself and nothing else. With this insight, all the norms and values that appeared so reasonable throughout the ages were with one sweep annihilated. The will to will is the will to power, which has come to be called nihilism. Not only was God dead, but godly reason as well. With this short review of modern ethics in mind, it would not be an understatement to say that the status of moral discourse at the dawn of the twenty-first century has become problematic in many ways.

At least since Plato, the history of moral discourse in the West has been based upon a view of human nature that distinguishes different faculties of the soul, such as reason, will, and sensibility or feeling, which enter into shifting relations of complicity, dominance, or servitude with one another. If for Plato and Aristotle, the person motivated by pleasure was the epitome of moral disorder, for Hume and the utilitarians pleasure was the basis of morality. Whatever position ethics took, it was based on a specific understanding of human nature. At the beginning of the twenty-first century, we are in the position where this "folk psychology" and the philosophical anthropology based upon it appear questionable. We now have reason to believe that there is no such thing as the bounded, unified subject or a soul consisting of various faculties. We have reason to believe that cognition is not something in the mind, whether empirical or transcendental, but something distributed in networks of human and nonhuman actors. We have reason to believe that free will is an illusion constructed by the distributed mind and that agency and identity cannot be attributed to any individual entity but are instead network effects. It is the results of contemporary psychology, sociology, cognitive science, neuroscience, and other disciplines that give us reason to believe that agency, identity, and cognition are not as centuries of folk psychology and philosophy have assumed. New technologies of artificial intelligence are producing machines that rival human cognitive abilities and can even claim to be social partners. Floridi has spoken in this regard of a "fourth revolution."[5] Galileo banned humans from the center of the cosmos, and Darwin dethroned humankind from its unique position within creation. Freud then deposed the proud Cartesian ego from being master in its own house. Finally, machines are threatening to rival humans in the one ability humans still claim as their own, namely, rationality. In addition to this, new philosophical assessments of being and meaning open perspectives for rethinking the foundations of Western thought.

The reaction of traditional ethics and moral discourse to these events has been either pure disregard or, when the advent of technological disruption cannot be denied, the attempt to develop "digital ethics." Digital ethics, in its present form, as we shall argue, is an attempt to carry over the ethical discourse of modern Western industrial society into the digital age. It's the same old story; only the names have changed. Is this reaction

---

5 See Floridi (2014).

adequate to the situation? What does the digital transformation mean for ethics? What kind of discourse is ethics, if there is no individual agent who possesses a free will capable of choosing the good, and if the good is unknown and perhaps unknowable, and if any knowledge claiming to know the good is itself suspect and of questionable social value? Do the ever more urgent calls to subject the global network society to ethics; to establish ethical guidelines for every profession; and to set up ethics commissions for every form of research, development, and technological innovation make sense? What lies behind the many attempts to set up ethical guidelines for the development and deployment of digital technologies? Is it not much rather the case that the digital transformation and all the theoretical advances surrounding and accompanying it have called ethics itself into question and changed the rules of the game in ways that traditional ethical discourse cannot understand or respond to? Maybe it is time for ethics to stop assuming that it is good, to stop attempting to tell people what to do, and to begin to ask how or in what way ethics under the conditions of the digital transformation is at all possible.

The present historical moment is not the first time that a need has been felt to ground ethics, to explain how it is possible and what forms of ethics are meaningful. This endeavor has come to be called metaethics. At least in the analytical tradition of philosophy, it is usual to distinguish between normative ethics, applied ethics, and metaethics, where the first two are involved with telling people what they ought to do and the last with explaining why this is at all possible, necessary, and meaningful. Applied ethics does not attempt to tell *everyone* what to do, but is primarily concerned with codes of conduct for certain people involved in certain areas of work, for example, medical professionals, computer programmers, researchers, businesspeople, journalists, legal professionals, teachers, and so on. Since the digital is not considered to be a fundamental condition of social order, meaning, and being, but a particular technology or social practice, among others, most of what currently goes under the label of digital ethics is nothing but established normative ethics merely being applied to digital technologies or practices. This is applied ethics. Applied ethics does not question its normative basis, but, as the name suggests, simply applies already established norms to particular situations and practices.

To say that digital ethics is applied ethics, for example, ethical guidelines for AI, or the Internet of Things, or big data, or robotics, or brain–computer interfaces, and so on implies that digital ethics does not question the presuppositions of current normative ethics. Standard normative ethics are the ethics of Western industrial society. Those who champion applied digital ethics do not consider any of the technologies or practices they subsume under the title "digital" to be transformative of society as a whole. Applied ethics does not attempt to ground its norms for their own sake and with regard to everyone and everything, but simply takes over given values, norms, and rules of society. Paradoxically, digital ethics, in its present form, makes no effort to ground its norms and guidelines in the transformed reality of the digital world.[6] This fact is not only astonishing and highly questionable; it is deeply problematic. For if there is a digital transformation at all, then all of ethics must be grounded in the digital. Insofar as digital ethics understands itself to

---

6   This claim will be grounded in the discussion of Floridi's work in the next chapter.

be applied ethics, we are dealing with a digital ethics that de facto denies the digital transformation. It may call itself digital ethics, but it has no idea what the digital means and is not even concerned with asking. Instead of questioning the foundations of contemporary social order, the forms and conditions of knowledge and cooperative action, and human self-understanding in the face of the digital transformation, we are presented with placative lists of norms and values unquestioningly taken over from the normative ethics of modern Western industrial society.[7] What is at issue when dealing with digital ethics is not the need to apply traditional ethics to new technologies. What is at issue is ethics itself and the status of moral discourse under the conditions of the emergence of a global network society. Adequately addressing this issue demands that we break into and disrupt long-established, unquestioned, and seemingly incontrovertible assumptions and forms of moral discourse. This is why our hack is needed. A good hacker proceeds carefully and must first develop the tools, the code, and the exploit that will be able to go behind the defenses of legacy systems of thought and allow the bugs and sloppy programming to be exposed, dismantled, and redesigned. In order to develop our exploit kit, we will use two current sociological theories: systems theory and actor-network theory (ANT). Our claim is that these theories offer the concepts, definitions, methods of thought, and perspectives that allow the hack to breach the legacy system of digital ethics as it is currently being practiced and to redesign ethics for the digital age.

1.2 Systems Theory

The sociological view of ethics implied in the question of what ethics is under the conditions of a certain form of social order goes back at least to Durkheim, who saw in morality the very stuff of social reality.[8] The rise of sociology signifies an important shift in perspective when dealing with ethics. With regard to the foundations of morality, ethics is no longer a normative discipline within the broad scope of philosophical anthropology. It is no longer itself a moral enterprise primarily concerned with telling people what they ought to do while at the same time supposing that this in itself is the right thing to do. It no longer bases its pronouncements in supposedly self-evident truths about human nature or natural law. And finally, ethics is definitively separated from individual norms that are good in themselves. Instead, ethics and morality become the object of a positive, value-free, empirical science and are understood as a certain "function" that must be fulfilled in all societies. Durkheim's primary concern was to demarcate and describe

---

7   A representative list would be, for example, human dignity, respect, equality, justice, responsibility, global mindedness, cultural diversity, freedom, privacy, tolerance, and democracy. Europe's identity crisis caused by the need to find its place in a global environment dominated by China and the United States has led to systematic attempts to list specifically "European" values. See, for example, the Standard Eurobarometer 77 Spring 2012—The Values of Europeans, https://ec.europa.eu/commfrontoffice/publicopinion/archives/eb/eb77/eb77_value_en.pdf, and the ongoing publications of the European Value Studies, https://brill.com/view/serial/EVS.
8   We follow here the interpretation of Durkheim by Karsenti (2012).

a domain of reality that could become the object of the new science of sociology. This domain was defined by the internal tension, that is, the unity and difference, of the one and the many. Society, as a specific object of scientific investigation, was defined as the unity of the difference between individual and group. The tension between the one and the many, to which the individual as person—a social construct—belonged in order to be an individual at all became visible and open to scientific investigation in certain phenomena that were considered to be "social facts" (*faits sociaux*). One significant social fact was morality.[9]

For Durkheim, morality was a social fact that is present in every form of social order. From the sociological perspective, morality is through and through a social phenomenon and cannot be derived from human nature or universal reason, or ascribed to an individual agent apart from society. At the heart of morality is the experience of obligation, the "ought." The ought commands obedience not because it has the form of a certain norm, value, or definition of the good, but because it obliges the individual to conform to rules that originate in something beyond the individual, something to which the individual owes unconditioned respect. The individual becomes aware of society in the experience of unconditioned obligation. Obligation functions to integrate individuals into society. This obligation, or ought, is unconditioned because it is not exhausted or canceled out by the fulfillment of any particular rules or duties. No matter how good we may be, we will always feel obligated to be better. Furthermore, despite obvious cultural and historical differences, the ought is constitutive of every society everywhere and at all times. Society transcends any individual as well as the particular rules or norms of particular, historic communities. Not only are moral norms and rules everywhere and at all times different, but one can never fulfill all the obligations that exist at any time or place. This is not because there are too many or because the will is weak, but because the social fact of obligation, the ought, transcends individual existence while at the same time conditioning it. It is at once manifest in the personal experiences of individuals as a "collective consciousness," or feelings of "solidarity," as well as in the common behavior of the group. For Durkheim, there can be only one thing that is capable of explaining the sense of obligation that lies at the heart of ethics and morality, and this is society.

Durkheim's sociological interpretation of ethics is close to Kant's notion of duty, with the exception that the source of the ought is experienced not only as a categorical and universal imperative but also as desirable and beneficial to the individual. Obligation addresses not only reason but also the will and emotions of real persons. Durkheim intentionally rejects the distinctions between reason, will, and feeling typical of traditional

---

9   Another social fact was the division of labor in society that makes individuals at once individual and dependent on others in society. Organic solidarity arises on the basis of functional differentiation. The individual had to fulfill a certain function in society, for which it itself was not the author and which depended on other functions being fulfilled. The baker needs the farmer to produce grain, the farmer needs many craftsmen to produce the tools he uses, and so on. Society as a whole constructs the functions, that is, the persons that it needs. Because social functions are not mechanical or even organic functions, persons had to be allowed a certain freedom of interpretation. Social rules were therefore not deterministic but normative.

notions of human nature. He claims that the ought is universal precisely because it addresses the whole person in their concrete historical and social circumstances and not merely the isolated individual or the purely rational faculty of the soul. The source of moral obligation is, therefore, not to be found in any faculty of the soul, whether reason, will, or sensibility. Morality is not a fact of psychology or even philosophical anthropology, but a social fact. For Durkheim, ethics and religion are very close together, since religion is nothing other than belief in a higher authority, both good and desirable as well as frightening and transcendent, an authority that commands obedience and respect. This is not to deny individual appropriation and expression of moral (or religious) rules or, as Durkheim has been accused, to glorify conformism. Instead, morality fulfills an essential social function; it integrates individuals into the social realm, for even in the modification or rejection of moral rules, their existence and influence are acknowledged. The fact that I *can* violate a rule is precisely what identifies the rule as normative in distinction to a deterministic law of nature, which I cannot "violate." I cannot violate the law of gravity, but I can rob a bank, even though stealing is morally prohibited.

Society, for Durkheim, is that domain of reality in which the unity of the difference between the one and the many becomes apparent and effective. It is morality that demands individual freedom while at the same time demanding obedience to the norms. The social is therefore the domain of reality that defines the ethical. Morality is no longer a set of norms and values, but a *function* that enables society, as well as the individual who is essentially a social being, to exist. Morality is a function that demands only that some norms are obligatory, but it does not prescribe which these are. As long as society exists, there are norms, and there is morality. But it is not the task of sociology, as it was for traditional ethics, to prescribe what these norms and values might be. The sociological view of ethics and morality is, at least in principle, value free. The sociological perspective introduces an entirely new understanding of morality. Traditional ethics had always supposed that knowing the good was itself morally good and the good that one knew was good in itself and not relative to other goods, values, or norms that fulfill similar functions. With the shift toward social science, ethics has become one social fact among others, a phenomenon known by objective, value-free science. At the time, few realized that the status of moral discourse had so dramatically changed.

The sociological transformation of ethics is upheld and radicalized by Niklas Luhmann.[10] Luhmann explicitly moves the discussion of the nature of society as well as ethics away from traditional assumptions about human nature and social order. He takes over Durkheim's functionalism but bases it on the principles of general systems theory.[11] Luhmann's radical reconceptualization of sociology rejects, as Durkheim before him, the

---

10 See above all *Social Systems* (1995) and *Theory of Society* (2012, 2013).
11 See Luhmann (1995, 2012, 13). Founding fathers of systems thinking are Ludwig von Bertalannfy, Norbert Wiener, Ross Ashby, Heinz von Foerster, Humberto Maturana, Francisco Varela, and all those who contributed to the discipline of cybernetics. Talcot Parsons introduced systems models into sociology and was a major influence on the development of Luhmann's thinking.

traditional foundations of ethics, but also, and more importantly, four fundamental and interrelated assumptions that have served as the basis of modern social theory. These are

(1) that society consists of actual people and relations between people
(2) that society is constituted or at least integrated by consensus among human beings, by concordant opinion and complementary purpose
(3) that societies are regional, territorially defined entities, so that Brazil as a society differs from Thailand, and the United States from Russia, as does Uruguay from Paraguay
(4) that societies, like groups of people and like territories, can be observed from outside. Luhmann (2012, 6)

These four assumptions are not only the pillars upon which modern social theory is erected and which still today inform our view of the world, but they are also fundamental assumptions of modern ethics. Rejecting these four assumptions, therefore, has consequences for the status of moral discourse. Once society no longer consists of human beings, there is neither the need nor the possibility to base norms and values on human nature. Once there is no longer a need for consensus on values and norms, every proclamation of universal and incontrovertible rights and duties is relative and subject to comparison with other such claims. Durkheim's question of what function morality fulfills in society becomes an open question again. Once society is no longer a kind of entity, an object with spatial boundaries, it can no longer be the object of value-free science. If society is not an object, it can only be known from within. The distinction between subject and object disappears. Furthermore, if society is no longer some kind of super substance, it must be understood as an ontological dimension *sui generis*, which, as we shall see, Luhmann (2012) describes as "meaning." This implies that knowledge of society, as well as knowledge of the good, is itself a social function. Society is all-encompassing and has no outside, no position from which it can be observed, described, or morally judged.

1.2.1 Principles of Systemic Order

Luhmann's rejection of the above-mentioned four assumptions and his proposal for a *theory of social systems* is based upon recent interdisciplinary theoretical developments that can be subsumed under the idea of a general systems theory. According to what can be called the paradigm of systemic order, or a general systems theory, order on all levels of reality, whether physical, biological, or social, is systemic. Ontologically speaking, there are systems, and nothing else.[12] Reality, and this includes social reality, consists of systems. What is a system? A system is a whole or a unity composed of elements that are related in such a way that the whole operates to achieve a particular goal. Although general systems theory describes any kind of system, whether physical, biological, or social, the model for systemic order is usually the living organism. Biological systems are considered to be autopoietic, self-referential, and operationally and informationally closed systems.[13]

---

12 Luhmann (1995).
13 See Maturana and Varela (1973, 1987).

Biological systems are first of all autopoietic; that is, they organize and (re)produce themselves according to their organizing principles, their DNA, which can also be called the "code" of the system. Generally, the code of a system has three functions: selection, relationing, and steering. It *selects* certain things from the environment to become elements in the system, which implies that all other things are excluded. Selection is at once a principle of inclusion and exclusion. Selection establishes a constitutive difference between the system and its environment. Without this difference, there can be no system. The principle of selection furthermore implies that there can be no system of everything. A system is always less than all there is. The environment, therefore, is always more complex than the system. Indeed, it is the overcomplex environment that motivates the creation of systemic order as a reduction of complexity. The second principle of systemic order is *relationing*. The system *relates* the elements that have been selected in certain ways so that specific operations become possible. If we consider a table as a system, then it can be said to consist of two elements: the top and the table legs. These two elements must be related to each other in specific ways; otherwise, there is no table, but something else, or merely a heap of materials. The tabletop and table legs are related in such a way that they make certain operations possible; for example, when properly related to each other, there appears a working space at middle body height. Selection and relationing imply that the operations of the system are *steered*. Steering is the third principle of systemic order. Steering directs the operations of the system toward achieving a goal, for example, in the case of the table, to make it possible to work on a surface while sitting.

In the case of living systems, the goal of system operations can be considered homeostasis. For living systems, the goal is to live, that is, to continue the organism's operations. This is self-production or "autopoiesis." Autopoiesis implies that the system must direct its operations toward itself. A lion, for example, eats in order to be able to keep on eating and not in order to reduce the population of zebras in the environment. Everything an organism does, it does to maintain its operations. This means that the operations of the system are directed toward the system and not toward the environment. When a system refers its operations to itself, it can be called "self-referential." Self-referential systems are therefore said to be "operationally closed." They direct their operations toward themselves. As we noted above with regard to lions and zebras, the goal of the lions is not to reduce the population of zebras, but to eat so that they can continue to live. Autopoietic, self-referential, and thus operationally closed systems are also "informationally closed." The system/environment difference excludes "communication" with the environment. The organism experiences only "perturbations" from the environment, out of which it constructs information on the basis of its organization.[14] A frog constructs

---

14 It is worth noting that this is also the model of cognitive science until today. Cognitive systems construct an inner model of the world out of undifferentiated stimuli. The model is not the world itself, but a model of the world. Its nature is therefore "mental," "virtual," "semantic," and so on. This implies that meaning is a realm somehow apart from the real that exists in the cognitive apparatus, that is, brains, of certain organisms or perhaps even machines endowed with artificial intelligence. We will return to this later when discussing Floridi's philosophy of information.

information only out of black spots moving quickly across the visual field and not out of music coming from a nearby house. This is known as "selective perception." Successful information construction can be observed as a viable adaptation to the environment. The model of autopoietic, self-referential, and operationally and informationally closed systems became for Luhmann the theoretical foundation of any adequate inquiry into society and morality.

It is important to note that in general systems theory order arises as the solution to a problem. The ontological foundations of general systems theory suppose that things do not merely exist or are what they are because they have a particular essence or nature. There is nothing that is simply given. Order exists as the solution to a problem. The problem that systemic order solves is chaos, that is, complexity and contingency. The equal probability of all events, or what can be called absolute complexity, must be reduced in some way or other for order or regularity of any kind to appear. The theoretical framework that systems theory provides replaces the age-old substance ontology of Western philosophy in which the world consists of things. Traditionally, each being, including human beings, have their nature, their "essence" that makes them into what they are. Systems theory presents us with a world made up of systems that function to reduce complexity, and which themselves are made up of functions. The functional nature of systemic order is derived from the fact that systems do not merely select elements from the environment but construct their elements to fulfill specific functions. A system is not an assembly of things around which one has drawn some kind of boundary, for example, groceries in a bag. Consider again the table. A table is a system consisting of two different types of elements: the legs and the top. Table legs and tabletops are not things that lie about in the environment waiting to be discovered by the table system. There may be wooden logs and stone slabs lying around in the environment, but it is the organizing code of the table that constructs these things to fulfill the functions of table legs and tabletop. Table legs and tabletops are, therefore, not things, but functions, which is why anything, whether it be wood or stone or glass or plastic or metal and so on, in almost endless forms and sizes, can become elements of a table. No matter what material they are made of or even what shape they have, whatever functions as a tabletop or as the legs of a table are elements of the table system. The same is true of living systems. The elements of a living system can be understood as the organs of an animal. Lungs, stomach, heart, liver, and so on do not lie about in the environment until some animal stumbles over them and incorporates them into itself. The organism constructs them to fulfill specific functions that it needs in order to live. This is why organs can be replaced; for example, someone receives a new heart from a pig or even a mechanical heart. The heart is a pump and can be exchanged for anything that functions appropriately. Systems are therefore made up of functions and not of things.

Systems select and construct elements, thus distinguishing themselves from an environment. They relate and steer their operations to achieve specific goals. Whatever the purpose may be, it is also always to reduce complexity, to bring order into chaos. To the extent that systems exist as solutions to the problem of complexity, which is also a kind of function, it can be said that systems theory rests upon a *functional ontology* instead of a substance ontology. The world does not consist of things; it consists of functions.

Understanding the world, therefore, does not come from understanding *what* things are, but *how* something functions. The functional perspective that Luhmann inherited from Durkheim and Parsons and radically extended and enriched on the basis of cybernetics, systems sciences, and similar developments changes the direction of questioning from attempting to describe *what* something is—this was the question guiding all of modern social theory—to attempting to describe *how* something is. How does a particular form of order solve the problem of complexity by functioning in a certain way? The functional ontology implied in systems theory is of great importance for understanding Luhmann's theory of society as well as his assessment of ethics and morality.

Despite the almost omnipresent biological metaphors in systems theory, Luhmann locates human beings and society on a higher level of emergent order than life, namely, on the level of *meaning*. Human beings and society are for Luhmann systems, just like everything else that exists, but they are neither physical nor biological systems; they are *meaning systems*. Furthermore, in order to make it clear that society, as well as morality, cannot be deduced from human nature, Luhmann distinguishes two different kinds of meaning systems: psychic systems, that is, human individuals characterized by perception and cognition, and social systems. Luhmann introduces a very unusual solution to the classical problem of social theory, namely, how to integrate individuals into society. He proposes that individuals are not part of society at all and instead be banned from the social system. A decisive theoretical advancement over traditional sociology is his insistence that social systems do not consist of human individuals and their actions. Contrary to Durkheim as well as almost all of modern social theory, including Weber and Habermas, society, for Luhmann, consists of communications and not of human beings. Recalling Aristotle's definition of the human being as a rational animal, Luhmann clearly assigns the animal part to the biological level of order and the rational part to meaning. In distinction to Aristotle, however, the two levels of order do not come together to form a human being. Human beings are either psychic systems or constructions of communication and not substances with a particular nature.

To say that meaning is a level of emergent order beyond the biological level, just as the biological level is beyond the merely chemical and physical level, has many important implications. Emergence is the appearance of a phenomenon that cannot be deduced or derived from what has preceded. On the one hand, the idea of emergence means that the coding of a higher level is more complex, variable, and inclusive than the level of emergent order below it. For this reason, biological coding is more complex and inclusive than physical or chemical coding. This is why biological systems can manipulate matter in ways that physical systems cannot. The same can be said for the level of emergent order called "meaning." Meaning is what Aristotle called "reason" (*nous, logos*) and which has been variously designated spirit, soul, reason, intelligence, mind and so on throughout Western history. For general systems theory, the code that constructs meaning can manipulate and change biological as well as physical order in ways that the physical or biological codes cannot. The greater complexity and variability of meaning explains why technology and genetic engineering are possible. In terms of the ability to solve the problem of complexity, meaning systems are more complex, more inclusive, and more powerful than biological systems, just as life is more complex, more inclusive, and more powerful than purely physical systems. On the other hand, emergence implies that there is no reason to assume that the mechanisms of the code on one level are the same on a higher level. The mechanisms that construct biological order, mechanisms of variation and selection that are reflected in the theory of evolution, need not apply for the construction of meaning. One could say that biological order is constructed by the evolutionary mechanisms of variation and selection. To say that meaning is a higher level of emergent order implies that the mechanisms of evolution need not apply to the construction of meaning. Meaning can be governed by other mechanisms than variation and selection, that is, by rules that do not apply to biological systems. This fact is often overlooked and has led to much confusion. Luhmann himself is no exception. As we shall see later in the discussion of ANT, the mechanisms operating in the construction of meaning can be understood as translation and enrollment instead of variation and selection. But let us not get ahead of our story. For the moment, it is important to note that the social system, for Luhmann, is a system within the emergent level of order that is called meaning.

1.2.2 Communication

Luhmann goes on to distinguish sharply on the level of meaning between cognition and communication. Beyond individual perception and cognition, there is the system of communications that constitutes society. "If reproduced autopoietically through recursions, communications form an emergent reality sui generis. Human beings cannot communicate; only communication can communicate" (Luhmann 2012, 57).[15] Since society is nothing other than cooperative action and cooperative action is only possible based on communication, Luhmann's surprising identification of society with communication is not as far-fetched as it might at first glance appear. Sociology, therefore, is concerned with answering the question of how communications self-organize into an autopoietic and operationally and informationally closed system and not with how individuals come together to form communities.[16] The claim that society does not consist of human beings but of communications is a far-reaching theoretical advance over traditional social theory and, as we shall argue, a game changer for understanding both society and morality in today's world.

---

15 As Heidegger puts it, language speaks.
16 That Luhmann still talks about individuals, on the one hand, and society, on the other, could be considered the dues he must pay in order to assert that he is offering a theory of "modern" society and not some other form of social order. One of the distinguishing characteristics of modernity is the distinction between individual and society and the ensuing problem of putting the two back together again. Luhmann seems to pursue a paradoxical strategy of integration by exclusion, maintaining thereby the parameters of modernity. This ambiguity is carried over into the theory of communication, as we shall see. Furthermore, it should be noted that even though meaning is an emergent phenomenon, this does not necessarily imply that it must be systemically organized. It could well be that meaning is organized not by selection, relationing, and steering, but by other "mechanisms." We will return to this possibility when discussing the advantages of ANT over systems theory.

For Luhmann, there is no longer any need to integrate individuals into society, which was the problem that Durkheim solved by means of morality. If morality no longer serves the function of solving the problem of the one and the many, what does it do, what function does it serve? From the perspective of a theory of social systems, the only thing that society needs to do is to make sure that one communication leads to another. According to Luhmann, the social system does this by constructing communication as a threefold selection: (1) the selection of information, or what is said; (2) the selection of a medium, or how the information is communicated; and (3) the selection of a further communication attached to the previous one, which Luhmann calls "understanding" or "acceptance."[17] Luhmann's theory of communication is fundamentally different from the usual understanding of communication as the transmission of a message from a sender to a receiver. Sender and receiver do not appear at all. There is only information that is communicated in some way with the effect of initiating further communication. Although the general model of communication that Luhmann uses still supposes someone saying something to someone, communication, as a threefold selection, must in some way lead to understanding the message by means of a response, which constitutes a further communication, thus ensuring the autopoiesis of communication. If the receiver merely receives but does not respond in some way, there is no communication. This burdens communication—and therefore society—with the problem of how to ensure that communication continues. Once communication begins to operate, it autopoietically continues its operations by linking one communication to another. If someone greets someone else on the street, they are greeted under normal circumstances in return. If someone says they'll take a hamburger with fries, they usually get a nod of acceptance or some other sign that their order has been taken. One communication leads to another in all directions with all media and about all things. This is society. It is important to note that the response could be anything or nothing at all. There is a unique form of contingency built into communication. There are no guarantees that communication will continue. Because of this uncertainty, not only the selection of information and utterance is required but also *motivation* for accepting and responding. The social system must solve the problem of motivating responses that lead to further communication. Otherwise, society could simply disappear.

Luhmann's concept of communication is interesting for many reasons, not the least of which are two significant consequences for understanding ethics in today's world. The first consequence could be seen in the way in which Luhmann's definition of communication "solves" the fundamental sociological problem of inclusion. Who is included in society, and who or what is excluded? For moral concerns, this question is fundamental, since moral norms, as Durkheim already clearly saw, are social rules and apply only to those who are part of society. The originary moral act is therefore the decision to include or exclude someone or something from society. Luhmann's theory of communication answers this question in a unique and innovative way, which has important consequences for morality and ethics. The second consequence of Luhmann's notion of

---

17 See Luhmann (1995, 137).

communication has to do with the fundamental opposition of individual and group, that is, the question of freedom versus social conditioning. How can there be free individuals on the one side of the social contract and demands that individuals conform to social norms on the other? Signing the social contract may well be the beginning of morality, but the norms and rules stipulated by the contract are what morality consists of. Let us first take a short look at what Luhmann's definition of communication means for the question of inclusion and then turn to the issue of individual freedom as opposed to social constraint.

1.2.3 Consequences of Luhmann's Theory of Communication for Morality and Ethics

Surprisingly, and vey importantly, Luhmann's definition of communication as a threefold selection no longer presupposes a human person who communicates. The selection of a medium, that is, speaking, singing, waving one's hands, dancing, and so on, may imply someone or something that initiates communication. Still, it doesn't presuppose anything about who or what is doing this. Although it may be helpful in most cases to ascribe communications to someone who communicates, this is not necessary. The fact that human individuals are banned from the social system implies that the question of who is communicating can be answered in many ways. This fact has enormous consequences for the question of social inclusion and therefore also for morality. The answer to the question of "who" communicates, no matter whether it is a human being or a nonhuman, is at the same time the answer to the question of who or what is to be included in society. If the ascription of communication to a human being is not a necessary selection in the processing of communication, then nonhumans could also be considered members of society. This explains why human beings have never hesitated in accepting nonhumans into their lives. People have always spoken to gods, demons, spirits, ancestors, animals, plants, and other so-called natural entities. Already today, we talk to artificial agents, or AIs, without any problem, and will do so even more in the future.[18] How often do people talk to their pets, and how often do they respond? Human beings generally have no problem with letting anything at all speak, that is, become a part of their social lives in some way or another.[19] Since the scope of moral obligation extends to all members of society, Luhmann's theory in fact, even if not in intention, broadens moral consideration to all beings.

---

18 This explains why people have no problem accepting social robots. Rosenthal von der Pütten et al. (2013) report that humans respond emotionally and express empathy toward robots even when they explicitly know that they are interacting with machines. A recent survey of 8,370 employees, managers, and HR leaders across 10 countries found that 64 percent would trust a robot as a boss rather than a human (https://www.roboticsbusinessreview.com/ai/study-says-64-of-people-trust-a-robot-more-than-their-manager/).

19 We will offer an explanation of this fact from the point of view of a theory of information when discussing ANT below.

As a system of communications instead of a group of individuals, society does not need human beings and can easily ban them into the environment. This does not imply that *attribution* of communication to some entity may not still be needed, but this entity is a social construction and need not be human. This remains so even if what is constructed by society, especially in the modern world, is usually a "person." The threefold selection that constitutes communication, therefore, does not imply the selection of a human being as the initiator of communication. Luhmann's theory is no longer anthropocentric or humanist. Indeed, we will argue that a consistent and radical social constructivism with regard to who is included in society is inevitably a "posthumanist" position. This marks a decisive theoretical advance in social theory at the beginning of the twenty-first century.[20] A posthumanist, non-anthropocentric theory of social order raises the question of what kind of ethics and morality are appropriate when human individuals are no longer the only possible moral agents, and when attribution of responsibility, praise and blame, and retribution no longer address human beings exclusively.[21] To the extent that humanism has been—and, as we shall see, continues to be—the foundation of ethics and moral discourse at least in the West, a posthumanist understanding of society carries with it the necessity for a radical revision of ethics.

The question of the ascription of communication and, therefore, of inclusion in society is important not only because it distinguishes society from what society is not, or from that which is somehow "outside" society, but also because the social boundary is the boundary of morality. As Levinas pointed out, the decision of whether we are dealing with a "who" or with a "what" is a decision of whether we are morally responsible or not.[22] Social inclusion is moral inclusion. The boundary of society is also the boundary of morality. For Luhmann (2008, 107), "morality [...] arises with implicit or explicit communication of respect" (translated by authors). Respect means that "ego and alter grant each other the possibility of earning respect" (ibid., translated by authors). Rules or norms constitute society only to the extent that they, in some way, always presuppose and communicate the conditions of mutual recognition. Respect (*Achtung*, usually translated as "esteem") is, therefore, the basis of the acceptance of the other as *alter ego*, an acceptance upon which communication, including the communication of norms, is based. The assumption is that we do not attempt to talk to those beings we do not consider to be like us. To accept the other as a being like ourselves, that is, *alter* as *alter ego*, is the beginning of social order and morality as well. Empirically, as we have noted, this assumption is hardly supported, since humans have always communicated with gods, animals, demons,

---

20 Of course, the entire postmodern critique of anthropocentrism, subjectivism, and humanism in all its forms must not be forgotten. With regard to digital ethics, see Gunkel (2012) for an argument on the basis of Levinas for accepting robots and nonhumans as social partners with accompanying recognition of their moral status.
21 We will return to these questions when discussing artificial moral agency, distributed morality, and the problems of moral attribution when dealing with complex socio-technical networks below.
22 For a recent discussion of Levinas in relation to the issues of digital ethics and artificial moral agency, see Gunkel (2012).

rivers, trees, things, and so on knowing quite well that they are different from us. Of course, Luhmann could argue that this is only possible because humans have somehow made these other beings to be "like" humans, which, however, presupposes that humans know who or what they are before they enter into communication with others. It could very well be that human existence is interpreted in dialogue with others and not a settled issue before all communication can begin. With this caveat in mind, basing morality on respect leaves the question open of who or what we choose to respect and to exclude. It also raises questions of the moral basis of such decisions. With what "right" is inclusion or exclusion decided? Could it be that there is an obligation to be open to communication with anything and everything? We will return to this question later when discussing ANT, distributed morality, and the extension of moral agency to nonhumans. For the moment, let us note that Luhmann does not base morality exclusively on respect. As we shall see below, morality is also based upon a specific *strategy of learning* that constitutes rules as moral norms. Before looking more closely at this other foundation of morality in Luhmann's theory of society, we turn to the second consequence of defining communication as a threefold selection.

The first implication of Luhmann's theory of communication leaves the question open of who is communicating. This leads directly to a posthumanist social theory since nonhumans can also communicate. It opens up the possibility of extending the moral domain far beyond humanity. The second implication of Luhmann's definition of communication is that no one can communicate alone, all by themselves, independent of others, as pure individuals. Luhmann's theory of communication is fundamentally anti-individualist. Whatever way one may answer the question of attribution, communication cannot be the act of an autonomous rational subject or a matter of free will. Despite how convinced I may be that I am an individual endowed with a fundamental right to "free speech," if others do not respond to what I say, I have said nothing. My freedom to speak, therefore, is conditioned by the willingness of others to *accept* what I say as meaningful communication, that is, communication that obliges a response. Just as Wittgenstein's concept of language, Luhmann's concept of communication is fundamentally "intersubjective"—leaving aside for the moment what is meant by the word "subject" apart from noting that we cannot be talking about individuals who have no place in Luhmann's social system.

The fact that communication depends on those who communicate accepting and responding to communications has very important consequences. Perhaps the most important of these is that the social system must somehow see to it that all must adjust their selections of information, utterance, and understanding so that they are "accepted" as communications to which a response is called for, needed, and indeed *obliged*. One can't say just anything one wants. In a complex and highly differentiated world, so many different things can be said in so many different ways that understanding has become improbable. Luhmann never tires of declaring that the success of communication, and therefore of society, is very improbable. This is because the problem that society must solve is not the integration of individuals into a social whole; it is the problem of aligning expectations and motivating acceptance of communications. Once society attains a certain complexity, there are so many different things that can be said in so many different ways by so many possible speakers that it is almost a miracle when somebody understands and responds to what others say. However, the chance of communications being accepted and understood is greatly increased if all have the same expectations about what is going on. As Wittgenstein might say, and as Goffman has demonstrated, if one doesn't know what language-game is being played, it is difficult to participate in social interaction. We will discuss this problem at length below under the concept of "double contingency." For the moment, let us emphasize that it is only when one communication leads to another that the autopoiesis of society as a system of communications is guaranteed.

A shared language alone is not enough. Language, by itself, does not reduce complexity but increases it. Language allows anything to be said and offers either acceptance or rejection of communication as equally possible. One is free to say either yes or no. One is free to say anything one wants. When society becomes so complex that an immense variety of possible selections must be reduced in every interaction, the need to make the links between communications more efficient and more reliable becomes crucial. The need arises to code communications in different ways with regard to the functions they fulfill in society. These are the "functional subsystems" that characterize modern society and which will occupy us at length in what follows. Functional subsystems are business, law, education, religion, politics, art, science, healthcare, and so on. Modern society, for Luhmann, is *functionally differentiated* because this is the only way the complexity of possible selections can be efficiently reduced. Functional differentiation brings with it a further problem, which we will discuss below, namely, the question of overcomplexity. Far from being a theory of integration, the theory of functional differentiation turns out to be a theory of disintegration. Society is fragmented into semi-autonomous subsystems, each with its own "rationality" and its own form of cultural reproduction and socialization. Sociology is left with the problem of explaining how the subsystems are integrated into society as a whole. One cannot assume society is a whole, a totality, in which everyone has their place. The fundamental question social theory must answer is: Wherein lies the unity of the social system?[23]

It is the imperative to ensure that communication does not cease and that one communication leads to another, thus guaranteeing the autopoiesis of society, which leads to the defining characteristic of modernity, namely, *functional differentiation*. Premodern societies were characterized by segmented and stratified forms of differentiation. In

---

23 For a short summary of functional differentiation, see Luhmann (1989). It is important to note that although systemic order arises as a solution to the problem of complexity, environmental complexity can only be reduced by building up internal, system complexity—see Ashby's law of requisite variety—which leads to the paradoxical situation that internal complexity tends toward equality with external complexity. Systems tend to become more and more complex until they become so complex that there is no longer a difference between the system and the environment. Functional differentiation therefore increases the complexity of society and leads not to integration but disintegration of the social whole. Either the system disintegrates into the environment, or the environment takes on systemic character. The only way out of this dilemma, we will argue, is to shift to a different theoretical model and speak not of systems, but of networks.

segmented differentiation, social units of similar kinds, for example, tribes or clans, were only loosely integrated into a social whole. They were all on the same level. Stratified, or hierarchical, differentiation, on the contrary, assigns levels, status, and positions on a hierarchical scale to different groups, professions, trades, persons, and so on. There are rulers and ruled, noblemen and serfs. In a stratified society, fixed social positions and top-down, command-and-control communication guarantee social unity. Functional differentiation arises when society becomes so complex that command-and-control communication cannot effectively reduce complexity and establish order. I may respond to a communication by reading a newspaper article, by writing a letter, by voting against a particular candidate, by buying a certain product, by taking notes for an exam, by commenting on a work of art, by praying, by calling the police or suing someone, and so on. Many of these options as well as the "freedom" that I experience by being able to choose among them were simply not available in premodern societies. What we moderns experience as freedom is the product of the functional differentiation that characterizes modernity. Even when modern social theory has come to believe that all "men" are born free, it is not DNA that gives people choices, but society. Although it may seem that I am free to respond as I wish, no matter how I communicate, communication is never the completely autonomous act of a free, self-determined individual. Communication is always embedded in and conditioned by a specific context, frame, or functional subsystem of society. Even artists, who claim the right of radical nonconformity, must successfully convince society that what they are doing is art and not madness or crime. If others are to be sufficiently motivated to accept my selections of information and utterance as a premise for their communication so that they respond in ways that allow communication to continue, we must all share certain expectations about what we are doing. Are we in an educational context, are we doing business, or are we attempting to gain political office, reach a legally binding decision, appreciate a work of art, pray to god, manufacture an automobile, or discover a scientific fact? As we will see, it is the shared acceptance of expectations—Wittgenstein would say shared knowledge about what language-game we are playing—that allows communication to run smoothly. Society, therefore, depends upon these shared expectations about what counts as meaningful communication. It does not depend on any transcendent obligation to somehow belong to a social group as Durkheim supposed. Regardless of who is communicating, that is, quite apart from the problem of inclusion in society, there is no society to be included in if one communication does not lead to another. This requires shared expectations. Where do shared expectations come from?

1.2.4 Cognitive and Normative Expectations and the Problem of Double Contingency

Let us now turn to the second source of morality in Luhmann's theory, namely, the norms and rules that make up the social contract. Despite the fundamental shift of focus from the problem of the one and the many to the problem of ensuring ongoing communication, and despite the posthumanist breach of humanist assumptions of social inclusion, Luhmann's account of the origins and function of morality begins, at least logically, with the distinction between "cognitive" and "normative" expectations and accompanying strategies of learning.[24] In order to illustrate this distinction, let us assume a human individual interacting with a complex and uncertain environment. Let us suppose a sort of Hobbesian state of nature from which not a social contract, but *adaptive learning* arises. Some forms of behavior prove to be successful; for example, I see an apple, I eat it, or I see a wolf, I run. These experiences are selected by memory. Many similar experiences are related to each other and generalized by cognitive processes. There arise specific expectations; namely, when I eat apples and run from wolves, I will stay well-fed and alive. Such expectations are what Galtung and Luhmann refer to as *cognitive expectations*. Cognitive expectations can become rules. Because humans are social beings whose existence depends on successful cooperation with each other, cognition becomes communication.[25] Reason abstracts and generalizes from the experience of one individual, packs this abstraction into a sign of some kind, and then uses this sign or symbol to communicate with others. The individual no longer speaks merely of "I," but of "you" and eventually "everybody." A rule is born that says, "Whenever you see an apple, eat it" or "Whenever you see a wolf, run." This rule can and must be communicated and shared in the group so that the "you" becomes generalized to "everybody." The group now follows specific rules of behavior that, in turn, work upon the group to constitute social order. People are told that it is "good" to eat apples and "bad" not to run from wolves. Those who do eat apples and run from wolves live to tell about it, so communication, which according to Luhmann is what society is made of, continues. Social order, therefore, arises from adaptive learning, which reduces the complexity of the environment. Some things or events become "relevant" in the sense of triggering specific constructions of information—"apples are good to eat," "wolves are dangerous and must be avoided"—which lead via communication in the form of rules to viable behavior for everyone in the group. Everyone survives by eating apples and running from wolves, and their survival is a result of communication, which is the very substance of social reality.

Those who do not eat apples or run from wolves do not survive. They simply vanish, which means that rules of this sort cannot be considered moral rules. Moral rules can be violated without necessarily paying for this with your life. Morality, for this reason, cannot be understood on the basis of adaptive learning. Indeed, for Luhmann, moral rules are characterized by *explicitly refusing to learn*. This is the distinguishing characteristic of *normative expectations*. Within the scope of adaptive learning, when someone violates the rule, and does not vanish, this could lead to a change in the rule. For example, the rule could now say, "When you see a wolf, try to domesticate it so that it looks after your goats instead of eating them." This is adaptive learning, which is the basis of cognitive

---

24 Luhmann takes this distinction over from Galtung's psychology. See Luhmann (2008, 36). Since it is only human beings who have expectations, the implication is that the theory of morality is a theory of human interaction. We will argue that this need not be so.

25 Luhmann describes the relation of psychic systems to social systems as one of "interpenetration," or also "structural coupling," which means that two systems become interdependent upon each other much as mutually adapted organisms in an ecosystem. The mechanism of interpenetration for individuals and society is language. See Luhmann (1995).

expectations. At the same time, it shows that running from wolves is not a *moral prescription*, since even though some people violated the rule and didn't run, they nonetheless did the "right" thing. The point of moral rules is not the success you may have by violating them, but the fact of the violation itself, despite whatever success you might have. This was pointed out by Plato speaking through Socrates in his debates with the sophists. The sophists were champions of adaptive learning. They claimed that success speaks for itself or, in short, might makes right. The birth of morality lies precisely in negating adaptive learning and substituting some other kind of rules and some other kind of expectations and a different strategy for reducing complexity than that of adaptive learning.[26]

Luhmann's explanation of how morality—and also society!—comes into being relies, therefore, not on behavior that is directed toward things and events in the environment, such as the advantages of eating apples and running from wolves, which are matters of pragmatic success or failure and subject to cognitive expectations and adaptive learning. Instead, morality is based on normative expectations and a strategy of refusing to learn. Refusing to learn means that the rule must be upheld no matter what experience teaches. Such rules are beyond the vicissitudes of history. They are necessarily universal and transcendent, since no matter what happens, one must acknowledge their truth and legitimacy. Stealing is wrong, no matter how successful I may be at it. For Luhmann, as well as all modern social theorists, this kind of expectation and learning strategy can only be applied when dealing with other people. I cannot steal an apple from a tree. The tree cannot accuse me of stealing, at least so long it is not considered to be a social partner and included in society. I can only steal from another person. Interactions between people are of an entirely different nature than interactions between people and things or animals. Unlike apples and wolves, people are assumed to have the freedom to do whatever they like. They do not have to do what you expect them to do.[27]

Not only do you know that others do not have to accept your expectations, but you also know that they know this about you, namely, that you do not have to do what they

---

26 As noted above, Luhmann (2008, 107) does not rely exclusively on the refusal to learn as the primary characteristic of morality, but bases morality also on "respect" (*Achtung*), which arises from ego's acceptance of *alter* as an *alter ego* and vice versa. Not only does this reveal a residual humanist legacy in Luhmann's theory of society—society arises not out of communication, but from a pre-communicative, pre-social empathy or ability to put oneself in the position of the other—but it also blurs the distinction between morality and other expectations and rules for behavior that are subject to adaptive learning, such as customs, habits, and more or less shared assumptions about how things are "normally" to be done. This is the area of morality that is investigated by so-called relational sociology following the symbolic interactionism of G. H. Mead. See Abbott (2020) for an overview.

27 Of course, this is also true of apples and wolves. The ontological distinction between things and human beings, which underlies and enables the distinction between cognitive and normative expectations, and also legitimates the two strategies of either adaptive learning or refusal to learn, is based on modern assumptions, the ontology of substance, and humanism. Here the ambiguity in Luhmann's theory between a radically new theory of society based on meaning and communication instead of the traditional problem of the one and the many and commitments to fundamental assumptions of Western modernity becomes apparent.

expect of you. Furthermore, neither you nor they know what expectations the other has. *Ego* and *alter* both expect that both have expectations and that these expectations can be disappointed. The freedom to do whatever one wants and to have whatever expectations one wants is called "contingency." Contingency means that expectations and actions can be surprising and are, in principle, uncertain. Since contingency is there for both parties, this situation is called "double contingency." The point of this is that double contingency is a problem that must be solved if cooperative action, that is, society, is to be possible. *Ego* must somehow come to an agreement with *alter* about what they both can expect of each other. Otherwise we are faced with Hobbes's war of all against all in which life is nasty brutish and short. For Parsons (1951), who introduced the idea of double contingency as a foundational concept of social theory, the solution to this problem lies in the fact that *ego* and *alter* actually do communicate. If *ego* and *alter* are able to communicate and if they take the time, and the risk, to talk instead of fighting, they can come to an agreement about what they expect from each other and how as well as why they should fulfill these mutual expectations. These then become *normative expectations*. For Parsons, the possibility of agreement lies in the fact that to be able to communicate, *ego* and *alter* must use a *common language*. Despite all their difference, they do have something in common.

This common stock of symbols, signs, and rules that language presupposes constitutes something higher or greater, something that prescribes to both *ego* and *alter* certain ideas about reality and about themselves. Hobbes spoke of reason. Parsons calls this "culture" (1951, 105). Without culture, there would be no possibility of communication, even if one supposes that it is through communication that culture first arises. Culture, and all that it implies in the form of language, customs, shared values, worldviews, institutions, and so on, therefore becomes an empirical but a priori condition of the possibility of social order. This, of course, is a tautology that claims that society arises from society. The question then becomes how this tautology can be "de-tautologized," that is, broken up into different entities that are not the same. Traditional social theory attempts to solve the problem by distinguishing between the one and the many. This distinction sets the stage for social theory to appear as an answer to the question of how individuals can be *integrated* into the social whole. For Durkheim, the answer to this question lies in morality. The unconditioned obligation that individuals experienced and that was expressed in moral imperatives represented the unity of the difference between the one and the many and thus the solution to the problem of double contingency. Moral norms are universal and transcendent and were to be upheld regardless of experience. No matter how successful one may be in crime, it is still crime and must be morally condemned. Only so, Durkheim argued, could the contingency of human behavior be aligned with social expectations and life in society become possible.

Luhmann's solution to the problem of double contingency, in distinction to Durkheim's, lies in functional differentiation, which not only constitutes society as a system comprising many subsystems but also leaves society as a whole, as we shall argue, without systemic unity. In other words, society is at once a system and not a system. Instead of a tautology, Luhmann offers a paradox. This has consequences for the status of moral discourse. One of which, as we shall see below, is that normative expectations have no place in society and no function. In a world in which being is function, to have no function amounts to ontological suicide. We will later see what we mean when we say that in Luhmann's theory morality has no function. We will be concerned to propose a solution to resolve the paradox without falling back into a tautology by appealing to ANT. As we shall see, this will have consequences for understanding what ethics and morality can be. But again, let us not get ahead of our story. For the moment, let us focus on Luhmann's solution to the problem of double contingency and its consequences for ethics and morality.

1.2.5 Symbolically Generalized Media and Functional Differentiation

The assumption that allows double contingency to be perceived as a problem that is solved by the emergence of society is that the world consists of autonomous individuals whose actions are contingent. At the same time, these individuals are not autonomous but conditioned, influenced, perhaps even "constructed" by language and culture. There is a paradox of freedom and order at the heart of modern social theory.[28] This was the situation that Hobbes described as the state of nature or a war of all against all. In Hobbes's state of nature, the complexity of double contingency was reduced by violence, even if it were the violence of the sovereign legitimated by the social contract. For Luhmann, however, the reduction of the complexity represented by double contingency, that is, the construction of social order, does not depend on the light of reason persuading otherwise irrational, egoistic, and reckless individuals to enter into a social contract, to lay down their weapons, and to submit to an absolute monarch or, as Durkheim would say, the transcendence of society. Furthermore, the solution to the problem of double contingency for Luhmann does not rest upon the assumption of an always already dominating culture or tradition, as Parsons supposed. Finally, since society does not consist of human beings anyway, but of communications, autonomous individuals cannot be presupposed. This forces Luhmann to define contingency otherwise than as the result of human freedom.[29]

---

28 Although Luhmann projects this situation into a kind of originary "beginning" of social order, the society at issue is the functionally differentiated society of Western modernity, which alone has constructed autonomous rational subjects or free individuals in the sense that is presupposed by the situation of double contingency. No one in a premodern or non-modern society would come up with the idea that they were free to do whatever they wished. See Luhmann (1995, 137). Freedom, let it be noted here, is not a given, that is, something human beings are "born" with, but a social construction. One is not born free; one is born into a society in which certain forms of freedom are available and others not. For a recent discussion, see Willke (2019).

29 See Vanderstraeten (2002) for a discussion of Luhmann's unique interpretation of contingency not as individual freedom, but as the openness of possible meaning. See also Luhmann (1977, 509): "Contingency means that being depends on selection which, in turn, implies the possibility of not being and the being of other possibilities." The important point is that it is the social system that makes the selection and not individual human agents. Only communication can communicate!

In Luhmann's scenario, the contingency of communication, that is, the possibility of noncommunication, can be reduced by *motivating ego* to accept *alter*'s selections. If this is not to be left to arbitrary feelings, attitudes, interests, and goals, then some mechanism must ensure that communications are accepted and responded to in such a way that the autopoiesis of the communication system continues. Language alone, according to Luhmann, does not suffice since it offers for every communication without distinction or prejudice the possibility of "yes" or "no." It is a 50/50 proposition. Whether communication will be successful or not is a matter of equal probability of all events, which can be compared to chaos. Based on language alone, therefore, successful communication becomes highly improbable. Consensus on culturally transmitted values is also not reliable since the disintegration of the premodern religiously anchored world left society in a condition of value pluralism and moral fragmentation. Picking up on a suggestion made by Parsons, Luhmann proposes to solve the problem of double contingency by reference to "symbolically generalized media."[30] For Luhmann (2012, 190), symbolically generalized media are "a functional equivalent to the usual normative safeguard of social cohesion." They do not serve to "safeguard expectations against disappointment" (ibid.), but to address "the problem of the improbability of communication" by "assuming the function of rendering expectable the acceptance of a communication in cases where rejection is probable" (ibid.). With regard to the role that moral norms were thought to play in solving the problem of double contingency, Luhmann claims that "symbolically generalized media [...] are a functional equivalent of morality, conditioning the likelihood of acceptance or rejection" (192). What are symbolically generalized media, and how can they replace normative consensus as the basis of social order?

If symbolically generalized media are to be a "functional equivalent" to normative consensus, they must be able to reduce the complexity of communication or, in other words, align expectations among all participants in communication. Since communication is a threefold selection, including not only the selection of a medium (utterance) but also the selection of information (what is communicated) and the selection of a response (the acceptance of communication), symbolically generalized media must reduce the complexity of all three selections. They must limit not only the enormous amount of possible ways of communicating but also the overload of information as well as the innumerable possibilities of acceptance or rejection. How do they accomplish this daunting task? The medium that does this work is "symbolic" because it is social; that is, it is a sign that is shared and understood by all participants to communication. It is "generalized" because it applies to many similar situations and is not limited to just one occurrence or one communicative event. Luhmann often cites the example of money. Money is a symbolically generalized medium. When someone takes money into their hand, they, and

---

30 "Classical social theories have answered the question of what makes social order possible by reference to normative conditions: to natural law, the social contract, or consensual morality. This has also been true for sociology, for Durkheim, and for Talcott Parsons. However, Parsons pointed the way to an alternative, which is not, however, unchecked but assigned to the still normative meaning of codes and shared symbolic values. It lies in the theory of symbolically generalized media" (Luhmann 2012, 190).

everyone else, know that it is a matter of buying or selling something. Taking money into your hand is the selection of the medium. What is to be bought or sold with the money is not just anything but is reduced to being "property." What you don't own, you can't sell, and if you buy something, you assume that it is now your property. This is the selection of information. All other communications, for example, whether an action is legal or illegal, whether it has to do with certifying skills in an educational program, whether it is art or not art, whether it is research in science or not, and so on, are automatically excluded when one chooses the medium of money, which of course does not mean that one doesn't pay for legal services, educational programs, an so on. The payment in these cases is not the legal judgment, the educational certification, the scientific research, or the gaining of political power. Buying and selling is not a communication within any other subsystem than business.

Furthermore, once the medium is chosen, one cannot do just anything with it; one buys and sells, even when what one sells is one's labor. Finally, one buys and sells not only once but also in many similar situations. One buys and sells to continue to buy and sell. As Luhmann puts it, "That communications are accepted therefore means only that their acceptance is taken as the premise for further communication" (193). One business transaction motivates acceptance by leading almost automatically to others. If you buy a new car, you have to sell your labor to be able to pay for it. If you sell your car, you have to buy a bus ticket or a bicycle or do something else with the money. In this way, "the achievement of these media [...] can therefore be described as the ongoing enablement of a highly improbable combination of selection and motivation" (ibid.). The medium of money is symbolic because it represents buying and selling property and is generalized to apply to anything that can be bought or sold. A symbolically generalized medium such as money enables the functional differentiation of a specific social subsystem that can be called business or the economic system.

Although it is said that everything has its price, communications that fall under other symbolically generalized media, such as power for the political system, legality in the legal system, certification in the educational system, and truth in the science system, cannot be bought and sold. At least it is considered "wrong" to legally disqualify political opponents, bribe judges, buy university degrees, or politically influence scientific research, and so on. This means that the moral attributes of good and evil, or right and wrong, come to have a very different meaning in functionally differentiated societies than in premodern society. In functionally differentiated societies, the problem of double contingency is solved by a selection of a symbolically generalized medium that functions as that higher power instead of God or tradition that makes expectations of expectations predictable and cooperative action without recourse to violence possible. Premodern appeals to norms and values sanctioned by God, or nature is replaced in modern functionally differentiated societies by the values inherent in the symbolically generalized media and the functional subsystems arising from them. The higher power that before was responsible for social cohesion and which Parsons still subsumed under the unitary concept of "culture" is broken up into many powers, each with its specific definition of the "good." Good business, good education, good science, or good art is no longer understood with reference to religious truths, or human nature, or any other criteria than what the functional subsystem defines as a necessary condition of its operations. This functional understanding of morality holds not only for the subsystems but also for society as such. The social system is only concerned with the autopoietic replication of communication and no longer with what is being said or with any concrete definition of the good. From the point of view of the social system as a whole, the "good" consists in the *amount of communications* society can generate.[31]

If the problem of double contingency is solved, as it were automatically, by the symbolically generalized media and the functional subsystems arising from them, what does this mean for morality? All significant cooperative action in society is subsumed under one or another of the functional subsystems. Whatever we do of any importance is either business, education, law, science, art, politics, religion, and so on. The codes of the functional subsystems prescribe what is to be considered good business, good education, good politics, good science, and so on. This kind of good is pragmatic and the result of adaptive learning. It is not universal but limited to a particular subsystem. It is therefore not moral or normative. What function is left for morality? It would seem that morality is no longer needed to integrate people into social structures, nor to guide their choices. Does morality still have a place in modern society? Obviously it must since modern philosophy and social theory from Hobbes to Nietzsche is almost obsessively preoccupied with ethics and morality. No modern thinker worth his/her salt has not proposed an ethics. How is this almost obsessive concern of modernity with ethics to be explained? Modernity's concern with ethics and morals could be interpreted as a symptom of a deeper malaise, namely, the unsettling paradox of a society that has disintegrated into semi-autonomous subsystems but is unable to free itself from the nostalgia for premodern unity. Freedom is everywhere demanded but attainable only under the law. The paradox of autonomy supposes radical freedom of choice but only if one subjects oneself to the law, just as the problem of double contingency presupposes free individuals who can enter society only by submitting to the dictates of a higher power. The solution to this typically modern problem is autonomy; that is, the law is not imposed from outside the self, which amounts to heteronomy, but one gives oneself the law. The law that the autonomous rational subject must give itself in order to be free while at the same time a member of society is not its own to dispose of as it wills. The law that the autonomous rational subject must give itself is beyond merely "subjective" whim. Arbitrary decision making, as Wittgenstein pointed out in his argument against the possibility of a private language, is no decision making at all. It is chaos.

Just as the word of God in premodern society, modern society retains a higher authority but demands that it serve a function. For Hobbes, it is reason that motivates individuals to enter into the social contract. For Kant, reason has become "pure," universal, and transcendental and therefore able to bind individuals to universal moral norms. But modernity seems thereby to have forgotten that the function of the achievements

---

31 This marks a shift from a qualitative to a quantitative measure of the good. Floridi, as we shall see below, offers a similar definition of the good as the amount of information in the "infosphere," which is his word for what Luhmann calls the social system.

of the symbolically generalized media and the subsystems arising from them already settle the issue without recourse to reason, whether it be pure or not. From the ashes of normative integration, there emerges the problem that the disintegrating dynamic of functional differentiation must somehow be countered and absorbed by the integration of the subsystems into a social whole. After all, the functional subsystems must, in some way, make up a unified society. Territorial boundaries, as Luhmann shows, cannot define society, since the functional subsystems expand globally. Business is subject to the same organizing principles no matter where in the world it takes place. And because the organizing principles of business are not territorially binding, business is global. This holds for all the functional subsystems. There is only one "world society," which is defined alone by the limits of communication. What then constitutes the unity of society as a whole? The "world" of business is not the world of science, and the world of science is not the world of politics. Nonetheless, all these globally extended worlds must somehow make up one society. The problem of the one and the many returns but on the level of functional subsystems within the social system. The paradox of autonomy, which is the paradox of individual and society—how can they be the same and yet different—is repeated on the level of system integration. The obsession of modernity with ethics could be understood as a response to the increasing disintegration of society introduced by functional differentiation. The modern obsession with ethics could be seen to arise from the specifically modern need to conceptualize the whole whose integrity God can no longer guarantee.[32] Whether it be Hobbes's social contract, or Kant's categorical imperative, or Habermas's rational discourse, there is no question that Western modernity can be characterized by a specific moral discourse. This discourse, however, is defined by the threat of radical functionalism on the one side and an equally radical attempt to maintain a kind of premodern wholistic unity on the other. Here is where morality comes in. What is the status of this uniquely modern moral discourse in a world where only that which fulfills a function has any raison d'être? Guided by this question, our hack attempts to use Luhmann's theory as a kind of "exploit" to break into the legacy system of modern moral discourse and show its vulnerabilities.

1.2.6 Consequences of Functional Differentiation

Although much as already been said about functional differentiation, we must take a closer look at what this modern form of social order means for morality and ethics. To understand the status of moral discourse in Luhmann's theory, it is necessary to understand what it means to define society as a functionally differentiated system of communications and not as a unified group of human individuals. As we shall see, from the point of view of a system whose existence depends upon ongoing communication, moral

---

32 Habermas's theory of the "life-world" (1984, 1987, 1996) as the basis of social cohesion via rational discourse is perhaps the last serious revival of the modern belief in one world. See the critique of Habermas in Willke (2019, 242). Willke characterizes Habermas's idea of a unitary life-world governed by rationality as a "mythos" (244).

communications that are based on the refusal to learn pose a problem rather than a solution. Luhmann's verdict on morality turns out to be rather harsh. It will not please those who are busy drawing up ethical guidelines for all kinds of human endeavors, including, of course, digital ethics. In short, the learning strategy of refusing to learn is a strategy that maintains the rightness of rules and the wrongness of transgressions, regardless of empirical outcomes and, thus, regardless of concrete, historical conditions. Normative expectations refer necessarily to universal and absolute truths, for only what is universally true for all time can claim to be derived from a higher power independent of pragmatic concerns. The strategy of refusing to learn typical of normative expectations, according to Luhmann, causes more problems today than it solves. This is not only an empirical observation but a theoretical exigency, since for Luhmann, the higher power that solves the problem of double contingency and ensures social interaction can be neither the values and norms of tradition nor an absolute monarch, but the self-organization of the social system itself. What is contingent in social interaction is not the freedom and autonomy of individuals, which must be somehow limited by being brought under moral or legal control, but whether or not communication will continue, society does not depend upon integrating willful, reckless, egoistic, or even criminally inclined individuals into groups capable of cooperative action, but upon making sure that one communication leads to another and so on without rupture, break, gaps, or blockages. When communication stops, society disappears. This implies that society requires neither consensus on values dictated by either God or pure reason nor authoritarian government, as modernity has always supposed regardless of how government is legitimated. Society requires only that communication communicates. This is why Luhmann (2008, 266) claims that the task of ethics today, ethics understood as the scientific theory of morality, is actually to warn society against morality. Why must society be warned against morality? How does morality threaten the autopoiesis of the social system? In order to answer these questions, we must delve more deeply into Luhmann's theory of a functionally differentiated society, which is the society in which we moderns live.

Functional differentiation means that society is no longer a whole into which independent parts (e.g., the socially constructed persons of Durkheim's division of labor or Habermas's rational speakers) must be integrated in order to ensure the possibility of cooperative action. In a premodern, stratified society, people were born into fixed and well-defined "positions" or identities, such as nobleman, servant, handworker, or farmer. Every activity and position was always already integrated into an ahistorical, religiously interpreted world order. There was no problem of integration because identity was given by birth, and one's position in the social order determined who one was and what one could and could not do. There were no autonomous rational subjects, no free individuals who could follow Kant's appeal for Enlightenment and dare to use their powers of judgment to criticize tradition; there were no self-evident and inalienable human rights based upon an abstract human nature in which all were somehow equal. In distinction to this premodern world, in which the idea of individual freedom played no constitutive role, the modern world is defined by the disintegration of the religious world order into semi-autonomous subsystems. These social subsystems exclude each other and organize their respective communications according to internal and independent codes. Every functional subsystem of society is itself an autopoietic and operationally and informationally closed system constituted by banning every communication that is not coded according to its own unique guiding distinctions (*Leitdifferenzen*) into the environment. The legal system, for example, codes any relevant activity as either legal or illegal. The binary code allows only a positive or negative value and excludes all other possibilities. The economic system codes all relevant things as property that is either sold or bought for profit or loss. The educational system codes only those communications that serve the certification or noncertification of competences and skills for potential jobs. The science system codes everything as either true or false. The political system codes only what contributes to attaining and maintaining power, that is, control over offices and institutions. The religious system codes all events as either immanent or transcendent. The media system codes everything as either news or not news. The healthcare system codes only sick or healthy.[33]

Each code is at once exclusive and universal. It is universal since everything in the world can be coded in its particular way but exclusive because all that is not coded in its specific way is banned into the environment of the system. There is nothing, for example, that cannot be bought or sold, used to gain votes, used to establish legality or illegality, and so on. But at the same time, one cannot buy and sell legal judgments or political office or educational certifications. Each of the social subsystems not only includes everything but also excludes everything that is not coded by its particular binary distinctions. Because there is nothing that cannot be bought or sold, business opportunities are everywhere. Nothing holds the economic system within territorial borders. The world of business is global, as are all other functional subsystems. This is why society cannot be identified with any territorial or national borders. As Luhmann never tires of saying, there is only one "world society." But each functional subsystem pays a price for its universality. Each subsystem is universal only because it excludes everything that does not fall under its specific code. What cannot be bought or sold, for example, passing an exam at school, winning a case before a court, being voted into political office, and so on, simply does not enter the world of business. *At least it shouldn't!* The same is true of the political system. There is nothing that cannot help my candidate or party gain power, except paying for votes or judicially condemning the opposing candidate. There is practically nothing that cannot become relevant to judging whether some action is either in conformity with the law or opposed to it, except bribing the judge, passing or failing an exam, or being voted into office. People born into a functionally differentiated society have no position, no essential determination given to them by birth. They can be and do practically anything, anywhere, at any time. A functionally differentiated society needs people who can participate in all of the various subsystems. To be modern means that one can be anything and everything and therefore one must be free to choose. Modernity condemns its members to freedom.

Modern individuals, as opposed to their premodern counterparts, must continuously choose which identity to perform in which subsystem. They must decide what work they

---

33 For an overview, see Luhmann (1989).

do, what kind of education they get, where they live, who they marry, and so on almost indefinitely. The modern world is a world of freedom, self-determination, and individual subjectivity. It is, therefore, a world that would appear desperately in need of ethics. There are so many decisions and possible actions that need the guidance of norms. But it is a world in which concrete moral imperatives are no longer universal, no longer everywhere applicable, and no longer shared by everyone. It is precisely at that historical moment when freedom demands the most moral guidance that one is also free to choose one's values and norms. In this situation, moral norms can retain their universality only by becoming increasingly abstract and increasingly removed from concrete life. Modern life is played out in so many different and incommensurable situations that concrete norms have only local application. Since God is no longer available to guarantee values and norms for everyone, everywhere, and in all circumstances, modernity has assigned this task to transcendental reason or intuitive and incontrovertible knowledge of human nature. Functional differentiation solves the problem of double contingency and social order by means of adaptive learning and leaves morality with its strategy of refusal to learn without anything left to do, except to become so abstract and unspecific that it can indeed be applied anywhere, but what this may mean is so vague and underdetermined that it has no effect on action or behavior. On the one hand, modernity presents us with a situation of almost unlimited freedom, which seems to desperately call for universal, unquestionable, normative regulation, while on the other hand, whatever norms address the whole of society are so empty and unspecific that they have no effect. Kant's categorical imperative, as well as so-called universal human rights, illustrates very well this peculiar condition of modern moral discourse.[34]

It may well be that every social act, that is, every communication, can be coded as either good or bad, but do specifically moral communications have any place in a functionally differentiated society? Let us recall that moral attribution of praise and blame is not subject to adaptive learning. Ethical principles are not supposed to adapt to historical circumstances or change on the basis of empirical success or failure. Lying is wrong, no matter how much success it might bring and regardless of whether it is done in business, science, politics, law, or any other functional subsystem. But what constitutes honesty and dishonesty in business is different from what this may mean in politics or science or education. And what about art? Does art lie? Religious truth is different from scientific truth. Legal truth is different from political truth. What function does a universal coding of communication as either good or bad still have when ongoing communication has been effectively secured by the symbolically generalized media of the functional subsystems of society? The question is justified because it would seem that there is no activity in any of the subsystems, whether it be business, politics, science, education, law, or whatever, that cannot *also* be morally praised or blamed. The attributes "good" and "bad" can be applied to all actions *in addition to* whether they are profitable, legal, and politically useful; serve scientific research;

---

[34] Weber and Habermas have continued this tradition of saving morality via abstraction.

contribute to educational certification; and so on. It appears that morality in modern society could be understood as a kind of supersystem that encompasses all the other social functions by adding moral praise or blame onto economic, political, educational, and other success or failure.

From this point of view, it can be said that the functional differentiation of society creates the possibility, even the necessity, of a specifically modern form of moral discourse characterized, on the one hand, by universal normative ethics and, on the other hand, by applied ethics. The universal code of good and evil is, therefore, necessarily so abstract that it can be recoded and "applied" in every subsystem. There arises business ethics, ethics for scientific research, ethics for education, and ethics for professions such as lawyers or doctors. Indeed, functional differentiation means that the businessman, the politician, the lawyer, the researcher, the software developer, or the educator can all be praised or blamed not merely with regard to their system specific actions, but with regard to moral norms that are valid beyond the borders of any of the functional subsystems. Moral norms, as we saw, must be universal and unchanging, above the vicissitudes of history. Applied ethics, as the name suggests, is nothing other than universal normative ethics "applied" to the functional subsystems. However, it is only applied *ethics* because the norms it applies are valid for all no matter in what subsystem of society they may be active. As Luhmann (1991, 894) puts it, morality addresses the "whole person," and not the various functional roles the person may be playing:

> I understand by morality a special form of communication which carries with it indications of approval or disapproval. It is not a question of good or bad achievements in specific respects, e.g. as an astronaut, musician, researcher or football player, but of the whole person insofar as s/he is esteemed as a participant in communication.

From the point of view of Luhmann's functionalist theory of society, norms that address the whole person must address *society as a whole* because they are valid for all the various activities a person has in all the different subsystems in which the person is involved. But it is precisely the functional differentiation of modern society that places universal norms in question. In a world in which functionality is the only legitimation for existence, the question of what function universal norms fulfill becomes crucial. According to Luhmann's theory, if there is any moral imperative that could claim to address society as a whole, it is the imperative to reduce the complexity of communication and thus ensure the autopoiesis of society. Does morality do this? What is the function of morality in the functionally differentiated society of Western modernity? In the following, we will examine various possible answers to this question.

1.2.7 The Function of Morality in Modern Society

One possible answer to the question of the function of morality in modern society could be to claim that morality is an attempt to coordinate and steer the reactions of the various subsystems to each other. This claim not only usurps the function of the political system, which consists in steering society by means of collectively binding decisions, but would also incite many conflicts about the normative foundations of politics.[35] It would also position morality on a level above the functional subsystems. On this supposedly "universal" level, the transcendence of moral norms would be ensured while at the same time explaining how morality contributes to maintaining and supporting communication within the subsystems. Within a functional subsystem, such as business, good business not only would be profitable, measured by the internal code of the economic system, but also should be morally right, measured by a moral code applicable to society as a whole. Communication that is ethically good in business, that is, for example, communication about buying and selling that is truthful, fair, socially responsible, and so on, is the same as what would be considered morally good communication in the political system, in education, in law, in science, in religion, or in art. If morality is to bridge the gap between the various functional subsystems and society as a whole, the attributes of moral goodness must be the same no matter what social subsystem they are applied to. Morality, according to this explanation of its role in society, must not only *disturb* the functional subsystems and hope that they construct the wished-for information about what they ought to do themselves but must also *inform* them, guide them, and steer their operations. It must do this in the same way for all subsystems. Such a task could only be accomplished by a code that is at once external and internal to the various subsystems. Is the moral code good/bad able to fulfill this requirement? Can any code whatsoever be at once inside and outside a system?

In terms of the relations between the economic system and the political system, for example, if everyone could agree that it is morally right to redistribute wealth by means of social welfare programs or that state intervention in the free market is morally wrong, this would probably soften the conflict potential and dangers of systemic failure and social disintegration. If everyone could agree that political influence upon the judiciary is morally wrong, conflicts arising from the separation of powers could be avoided. Apart from the fact that there is no agreement on these issues, and that modern society is characterized by inherent value pluralism, it could still be argued that the fact that communications coded by one system are dysfunctional within another system shows that this dysfunctionality indicates the violation of a moral norm. For example, attempting to buy or sell votes within the political system or legal verdicts within the judicial system is dysfunctional and, therefore, immoral. Actions that are foreign to the specific code of the system in which they attempt to operate are perceived to be in some way "inadmissible" or "condemnable." But are they also immoral? The functional subsystems have their own ways of prohibiting or sanctioning dysfunctional communications. The attempt to buy a legal judgment assumes that legal judgments can be handled as property and can be bought or sold. This assumption and the offer to buy or sell a judicial verdict simply cannot be processed by the legal system. In many cases, such attempts are clearly prohibited by law. If they do take place, then the system has its own rules to sanction such

---

35 Willke (2016) assumes that modernity has completely dissociated itself from a normative regulation of society and that politics, as the steering function of society, relies on cognitive expectations alone.

communications. From the point of view of morality, the claim is that in addition to being dysfunctional, communications proper to one system would also be immoral in another system. Is this moral add-on necessary at all? Does it help to de-escalate system conflicts? As Luhmann observes, and as Helmut Willke (2009) with regard to globalization has convincingly shown, whenever morality is brought in to try to accomplish the task of system integration within society as a whole, it creates more conflict than it solves.[36] Far from having the effect of integrating the individual into society as Durkheim supposed, and far from integrating the functional subsystems as would be expected to be a desideratum in Luhmann's theory, morality contributes to the disintegration of the social system.[37] This makes moral discourse in modern functionally differentiated societies dysfunctional.

The thesis of the dysfunctionality of morality is not based merely on the empirical observation that moral communication mostly leads to conflicts. There is a theoretical basis as well. Conflicts in society need not be a bad thing. Conflicts may lead to further discussion, more communication, extended negotiations, and so on, but they may also lead to the collapse of communication and the outbreak of violence. The ability and willingness to learn, as Willke (2017) has pointed out, is a fundamental presupposition of the autopoiesis of the communication system that modern society is. Morality, however, necessarily refuses to learn. Without following the strategy of adaptive learning, at least one side to the discussion will refuse to learn and end up stubbornly repeating what it has claimed to be true, its truth, its moral rule, its norms, its values.[38] From the perspective of the theory of communication, simply repeating what one has already said is redundant and contains no information.[39] Endless redundancy reduces the informational content of the message to zero, thus disrupting the communicative process. When no information is selected by a communicative act, the other two selections necessary for communication

---

36 "Moral hat […] eine Tendenz, Streit zu erzeugen oder aus Streit zu entstehen und den Streit dann zu verschärfen. Moral ist polemogener Natur. […] So können Steppenbrände entstehen—und Erfahrungen, die Europa seit dem Hochmittelalter mit religiös aufgezogenen Aufständen und Unterdrückungen, mit den Schrecken der Inquisition, mit Kriegern um moralisch verbindliche Wahrheiten und mit aus Empörung entstandenen Revolten gemacht hat, sollten eigentlich beim Stichwort Moral immer gleich dieses Problem vor Augen führen" (Morality has the tendency to produce conflict or to arise from conflict and to exacerbate conflict. Morality is conflictual in nature. […] In this way brushfires can occur—since the late Middle Ages Europe has experienced religiously inspired uprisings and oppression, the terrors of the Inquisition, wars in the name of morally binding truths, and revolts arising from indignation—and, therefore, when one speaks of morality, one should keep this in mind) (Luhmann 2008, 280–81; translated by authors).
37 Theoretically, for Luhmann, it must be noted that integration is nothing other than the more or less "viable" adaptation at any time of the subsystems to each other. Strictly speaking, there is no such thing as integration in society as a whole any more than it can be said that an organism is "integrated" into its environment. Phenotypically, there is only adaptive learning or, genotypically, the at-any-time more or less viable adaptation to the environment, which can also be called evolution.
38 This approach to truth can be termed "fundamentalism." See Jäggi/Krieger (1991).
39 We will deal at length with the concept of "information" below.

to occur are blocked. Someone may be loudly talking, but when they continuously repeat themselves, what can one say in response? What possible consequent communication can link up to a message that is simply repeated again and again?

Stubbornly repeating the moral norm and claiming that it is a universal and unquestionable truth and that, therefore, nothing more can be said amounts to demanding that all discussion be dropped. There is no room for attempts at dialogue, appeals to reason, or offers of compromise. The demand is that the other simply "convert" to the truth of the moral norm. The learning strategy of morality, we recall, is the refusal to learn. As even Habermas admitted, and as every religious prophet knows, there is no argument against absolute truth. In the face of truth that is contrafactually upheld, there are only two possibilities, either martyrdom or apostasy to one's old beliefs and conversion to a new absolute truth.[40] Moral communication, which pursues the strategy of refusing to learn, must necessarily address the whole of society and it must address society from the standpoint of absolute truth. When communication attempts to address society as a whole, it seems to be attempting to revert to a premodern undifferentiated social order informed by a religiously anchored worldview. In the context of functionally differentiated society and a multicultural and multireligious global society, the problem of different ethical norms and conflicting fundamental values has become acute. The strategy of refusing to learn, which lies at the basis of moral discourse, would seem to have become hopelessly dysfunctional. Far from integrating the fragmented social systems into a whole, morality introduces a further divisive factor.

Let us recall that what we are looking for is a purpose, a function for morality in the modern world. If morality does not serve to integrate people or even functional subsystems into a social whole, what does it do? What other possible functions does morality offer? Moral codes, as we saw, primarily and necessarily address the whole of society and not any specific functional subsystem.[41] It is for this reason that applied ethics, whether in business, scientific research, software development, and so on, is always based on generalized normative ethics. What is morally good or bad in business is so because it is good or bad in itself, as such, everywhere and at all times.[42] Moral norms are rules addressing everyone, or as Luhmann would say the "whole person" and not just the lawyer, the doctor, the researcher, or the businessman. The difficulty with the conception

---

40 See Krieger (1991) for a critique of Habermas and a communication theoretical discussion of the concept of "conversion."
41 Railton (2019, 74) lists the defining characteristics of moral evaluations as (1) cognitive; (2) opinion independent; (3) nonparochial, that is, applicable to all regardless of social position or function; (4) authority independent, or applicable even when not enforced; (5) nonhypothetical, or independent of external incentives; and (6) directed toward the good, the meaning of which all agree to.
42 This explains the often noted vagueness, generality, and lack of specific applicability of applied ethics and the many ethical guidelines for technologies such as AI, or IoT, or Big data. Although ethics are called upon to regulate activities in specific areas, values and norms remain abstract, vague, and unspecific. This can also be seen in the fact that ethical guidelines are almost identical despite the many different areas, medicine, scientific research, business, education, law, politics, and so on in which they are supposed to apply.

that moral norms necessarily address society as a whole, that is, their function lies in the constitution or the communicative realization of society as such, arises from the fact that to do this morality must be decoupled from any functional description. Functional entities are, by definition, open to comparison with other solutions that may function better. If the heart is nothing but a pump, then perhaps some different kind of pump would work better. Functional subsystems have one specific purpose, goal, or function within a whole. The economic system is responsible for the material reproduction of society. It is because material reproduction is a function that it can be asked if capitalism could not be replaced by a form of economic organization that functions better. The current educational system functions to certify skills and competencies for jobs. It can be asked if some other educational system might not fulfill this task better. But what is the function of society?

There is a conceptual problem with applying functionalism to the social whole. Society as a whole, it would seem, has no specific purpose other than to reduce the complexity of communication in such a way as to ensure its autopoiesis. Communication communicates, and that is all it does. If there is a moral imperative that could be derived from this situation, then it would say, "Thou shalt communicate!" And nothing more. It may well be that modern society does this through functional differentiation. But how can functional differentiation be functionally compared to other forms of society to judge the viability of this form of social order in comparison to others? Could another kind of society that was not functional "function" better? How could this be known without presupposing what is in question? This would amount to asking Descartes if he could not come up with some other way of knowing he was a thinking being than by thinking. Can the presupposition of functional comparison itself be functionally compared to other possible forms of order? What alternative to communication is there, and even if there were such an alternative, how could it be communicated? The difficulty of understanding how any kind of communication can be addressed to society as a whole and thereby fulfill a function can be taken as an indication that morality is not merely dysfunctional but also and, more importantly, *afunctional*.

In general systems theory, with its functional ontology, nothing can be without a function. If it should turn out that moral discourse is dysfunctional because it is afunctional, this could be the "exploit" we have been looking for. The state of moral discourse in Luhmann's theory can serve as an exploit by which we can break into the legacy system upon which modern moral discourse runs and show its vulnerabilities, its bugs, its inability to address the issues confronting a global network society. We will attempt to do this by noting that morality is not only dysfunctional because it endangers the autopoiesis of communication, as Luhmann noted, but also and more importantly, and this Luhmann does not explicitly say, because it serves no purpose whatsoever. We shall argue that it is precisely because morality is afunctional and serves no purpose that it can be understood to be dysfunctional. The relation between afunctionality and dysfunctionality is based on answering the theoretical question of how society as a whole is capable of being addressed by any kind of communication. Is society as a whole coded as a system in the same way as the functional subsystems? Can any binary distinction, such as good/bad, be used to select, relate, and steer communication on the level of society as a whole? And if so, what kind of distinction is this? What kind of communication does it code and enable? This question marks not only a critical point concerning morality and ethics but also a central problem of Luhmann's theory. Could it be that the model of systemic order may well be able to describe functional subsystems within society, but not society as a whole? Could it be that society can achieve ongoing communication only by itself becoming something other than a system? Would this imply that the dynamic of communication could be conceived in a quite different way than Luhmann does in terms of the operations of an autopoietic, self-referential, and operationally as well as informationally closed system? What would society be if it is not a system? And what consequences could this have for ethics and morality, that is, for the question of what function morality plays in society?

1.2.8 Can Society as a Whole Be Modeled as a System?

If moral coding necessarily orders communication on the level of society as a whole, with regard to both inclusion in society and the normative expectations regulating social interaction, it is important to know what we are talking about when speaking of the social as such. The first question that needs to be answered concerns the nature of society. Can society be modeled as a system? When not, how can society be theoretically conceived? This leads to a discussion of the meaning of meaning, since the social system arises on the emergent level of order that is called meaning. The second question that will occupy us concerns the status of the theory that describes society? Are we still doing sociology? Does Luhmann remain within Durkheim's program of a social science, or are we doing something entirely different? If so, what is the moral status of this knowledge? Is it still "value-free" as both Durkheim and Luhmann maintain social science must be? Or do age-old claims that knowledge of the good is not only universal but also itself good return in a different form? Let us begin with the first question. What does it mean to speak of society as a system? We will examine several possible answers. First, if society exists on the level of meaning, can society be adequately described as an autopoietic, self-referential, and operationally and informationally closed system in the same way as biological systems? This leads to the comparison between society and an organism. Can the unity and totality of society be compared to the unity of a biological system? Finally, if society is not like an organism, perhaps it is like a community of organisms existing within an "ecosystem." When we speak of society as consisting of interdependent functional subsystems, are we talking about something that is like an ecosystem?

As long as society was conceived of as a kind of thing, an object with territorial limits, it could be tolerated that different societies have different norms and values. The famous doctrine of tolerance that was supposed to put an end to religious wars in Europe was based on the territorial exclusion of "heretical" societies. As soon, however, as society became a system of communications no longer bounded in space and time, but existing on the level of the emergent order of meaning, society ceased to have physical boundaries and, indeed, no boundaries at all. As a system of meaning, society must have boundaries, as all systems must, but these are "virtual" boundaries, boundaries of a unique kind. The question arises as to whether these boundaries are capable of constituting a unified whole that could be coded by systemic operations of selection, relationing, and steering. Can meaning be modeled as a system? Ultimately, the question we will be asking in what follows is whether or not general systems theory, which is rooted in the cybernetic modeling of biological order, can become an adequate theory of meaning. Posing the question in this way is necessary because Luhmann has replaced the distinction between individual and society with the distinction between communication and noncommunication, meaning and non-meaning. As a system of meaning, society can no longer be understood to be one domain of reality among others, not even as a domain of communication as opposed to noncommunication.

The social system operates by constructing meaning through communication. Since there is nothing that is not meaningful—even what is meaningless is processed as a certain kind of meaning—the social is all-encompassing. Outside of communication, there is not mere silence; there is nothing; and actually, there is not even nothing since nothing is something we can talk about. As Wittgenstein put it, the limits of my language are the limits of my world. Just as society can no longer be territorially bounded, the social in Luhmann's theory ceases to become a kind of thing that could be an object of science. Instead, society becomes the at-once transcendental and empirical condition of meaning. Or, as Luhmann put it, society can be observed only from within.

Society is the empirical condition of meaning since any direct, intuitive, introspective access to pure reason or privileged access to Truth or to God's Word must now be mediated with reference to communication within historical societies. This is what Heidegger refers to as "being-in-the-world" or "historicity" or "facticity." Society becomes the transcendental condition of meaning because the founding distinctions of sociology are no longer society/nature and individual/society but meaning/non-meaning. Sociology ceases to be what Durkheim supposed it to be, that is, one science, among others, but instead, it becomes a general theory of meaning, and such a theory has a very special status for there is nothing at all outside meaning. We will return to this below.

Let us recall that selection, relationing, and steering are fundamental principles of systemic order and not exclusively human processes of cognition or communication. For Luhmann, when processes of selection, relationing, and steering order human conscious experience and social communication, they are principles of *meaning*. Meaning is the level of emergent order upon which psychic and social systems come into being. Theorizing meaning as a level of emergent order would seem to support the distinction between society as a meaning system and other kinds of systems, for example, biological systems or physical–chemical systems in nature. If the same principles constitute order on the physical, biological, and social levels, all can be considered systems. However, once meaning has emerged as a level of order beyond the physical and biological levels, the code organizing meaning, whatever this code might be, swallows, so to speak, the levels of order beneath it. There is no longer any direct access to the physical or the biological world since they are integrated into the world that is henceforth constituted by meaning. And there is no guarantee that the principles that constitute biological order are the same as those that constitute meaning. It could be that selection, relationing, and steering are done quite differently on the level of emergent order that is meaning than on the biological level. Perhaps, once meaning emerges, we are playing an entirely different game that has its own rules and demands to be understood on its own terms. In other words, it could turn out to be more meaningful not to model society as an autopoietic, self-referential, and operationally and informationally closed system.

This option is offered by the theory itself. Just as biological coding assimilated and used physical processes for its purposes and in its own ways, so can meaning assimilate and use physical and biological forms of order for its purposes and in its own ways.[43] To understand society as a whole and not any specific function within society, it is therefore necessary to understand meaning. To say that society can be observed only from within means that there is no nature out there beyond the city walls, and there is no state of nature in which asocial individuals somehow roam around outside of meaning involved in a war of all against all until they "rationally" decide to enter into a social contract. The boundaries of society are not physical boundaries, but boundaries set by meaning. It is for this reason, and not merely the global extension of the functional subsystems, that Luhmann rejects the traditional assumptions of society as one object among others as well as something territorially bounded. The implication is that society becomes coterminous with what the Western philosophical tradition has called "Being." Luhmann's sociology inevitably leads to a discussion of the theory of meaning.

What is the function of meaning? Where does meaning come from? What are the limits or boundaries of meaning? We realize that the reader may find these questions an unnecessary detour. We started out asking about the nature of society, and now we are led into the theory of meaning. Instead of seeing this discussion as a detour, we prefer to think of it as a shortcut, a shortcut that goes directly to the point at which we will later break into the legacy system of moral discourse our hack is aiming at. In order to understand the status of moral discourse at the beginning of the twenty-first century, it would seem that one must answer the question of meaning and not merely the question of social inclusion and the good.[44] For Luhmann (1990, 21–79), despite repeated claims to have gone beyond traditional European positions, it is still the case that the concept of meaning is primarily derived from human conscious experience, the essential characteristics of which he derives from Husserl's phenomenology. According to Husserl, every object of intentional consciousness appears against a horizon of other possible contents and thus refers to or is associated with other possible intentional objects. If I see a tree, then I can be aware of only the tree because I have the possibility of looking up to see the sky or down to see the earth or looking beyond to see the forest, and so on without end. Despite the (co)-presence of all these things, indeed, of the whole world as a "horizon" of any intended object of awareness, meaning is constituted in the act of conscious intentionality. The choice of human conscious experience, whether it be the experience of an individual or a transcendental subject, as the primary source of meaning, can be seen as a humanistic legacy in Luhmann's theory. Even when he later emphasizes in a Hegelian manner a logic of differences as the foundation for his theory of meaning, Luhmann

---

43 See Krieger (1996) for a discussion of the theory of evolutionary systemic order.
44 As we will see in the next chapter, this move leads to the significance of the concept of "information" for founding ethics and morality.

never completely frees himself from locating meaning primarily in human individuals, their big brains, and their linguistic abilities, just as he always assumed communication must be ascribed to persons.

In his later work, Luhmann (2012, 19) modifies this subjectivist basis of his theory of meaning by relying more on a logic of difference based on Spencer-Brown's *Laws of Form* (1969) and the "poly-contextural" or "transclassical" logic of Gotthard Günther.[45] The system of meaning begins to look more and more like Hegel's Spirit. Nevertheless, Luhmann never completely overcomes the assumption that constructing meaning is something humans do and non-humans do not do. "All communication is structurally coupled with consciousness. Without consciousness, communication is impossible. Communication is *totally* dependent (in *every* operation) on consciousness" (Luhmann 2012, 56; emphasis in original). From the point of view of the logic of difference, what humans do by means of consciousness is to "introduce distinctions."[46] This meaning-constructing operation Luhmann calls "observation."[47] Observation is done by means of negation. I know that the animal I see is a dog because I know that dogs are *not* cats, *not* trees, *not* horses, and so on, and more importantly, I know that I am *not* the dog, and the dog is *not* me. I know this because the observation of something introduces distinctions not only between what is observed and what is not observed, and therefore what could be observed, but also always between self and other. Self-observation distinguishes the observer from the observed. Following Spencer-Brown (1969), Luhmann calls this "form." Form is a distinction in which two sides come into being, one of which is designated, indicated, or named and the other represents everything else that is not named, but could be. Here we find again Husserl's intentional object, which comes into view only against a horizon of other possible states and objects. When I see a dog, I don't necessarily see everything else in the world at the same time, but I know that I could also look to see where the cat is hiding. Succinctly, "observing means simply distinguishing and indicating" (Luhmann 2012, 34). Form, in short, is a difference with a name. And there

---

45 See https://de.wikipedia.org/wiki/Polykontexturalit%C3%A4tstheorie and https://en.wikipedia.org/wiki/Gotthard_G%C3%BCnther.

46 As Spencer-Brown (1969, 3) declares, "Draw a distinction." The question of who carries out this command and how the command is carried out will become important in our discussion of ANT below.

47 "Psychic and social systems shape their operations as observational undertakings, which allow the system itself to be distinguished from its environment—even though (and I must add because) the operation can take place only within the system. In other words, they distinguish between self-reference and other-reference. For them, boundaries are therefore not material artifacts but forms with two sides" (Luhmann 2012, 19). This double distinction, one between observed and other potential objects and the other between observer and observed, Luhmann, following Spencer-Brown, describes as "re-entry," that is, the reentry of a distinction into itself. In other words, the distinction between self and other is not out there in the environment but takes place within the system, or one can also say, the outside is inside. This is a unique characteristic of meaning that the physical and biological levels of order do not share, even though they also are constituted by a distinction between system and environment. Only in their case, this "distinction" is not logical but physical.

is no name without a difference. Form becomes a name when it "re-enters" into itself as a name *for me*, as self-reference and other-reference.

It is important to note that for Luhmann, form is based on *negation* and not *relation*. Negation makes distinguishing and indicating possible. It is a cognitive act of a human being with a big brain that commands the use of language. I don't *do* negation, I *say* it, even if only to myself. If I say it to others, then this is an operation of the social system. Negation is different from relation. When I am walking the dog, this is a relation and not negation. I may be thinking about something entirely different than what I am doing, but I am still walking the dog. The dog is also actively participating in his own way. The dog and I are in a relation. We are what we are and do what we do because both of us are participating, both of us are doing something, and we are doing it together. We will return to this important distinction later when discussing ANT. Practices such as walking dogs, working with a hammer, or wielding an ax are not Luhmann's preferred examples of meaning. The paradigmatic acts of meaning construction for Luhmann are thinking and saying. These are either mental states, that is, operations of an individual psychic system, or communications that take place as operations of the social system. Of course, what is happening is always in some way both together. The question of how psychic systems and social systems are different is a difficult issue in Luhmann's theory, to which we will return. At the moment, suffice it to say that meaning is defined as a distinction, a difference that is constructed by negation. As we will see, this implies that meaning can be equated to information, since information is also defined as a difference. Indeed, the selection of information is one of the three necessary selections that every communication must make. Without information, communication would be meaningless. The construction of information in communication constitutes the social system. This is an important principle that we will pursue in later discussions of ANT and the philosophy and ethics of information. We will argue that information need not be constituted by negation but instead by relation. For Luhmann, however, information is always in some way syntactically organized and thus must be understood as semantic meaning. But, we ask, does meaning necessarily imply semiotic coding? Must meaning be semantic, that is, linguistic in nature? We will return to the question of the nature and origin of information in terms of relation instead of negation and in terms of networking instead of observing when discussing the network model of order below. For the moment, let us focus on the implications of Luhmann's theory of meaning for understanding the social system.

For Durkheim, society as a whole manifests itself in moral obligation. Morality functioned to integrate individuals into society. For Luhmann, morality no longer fulfills this function. On the contrary, morality has become dysfunctional because it disrupts communication rather than furthers it, and this because it attempts to address society as a whole, that is, to apply the moral code to all communications whatsoever in the same way. Quite apart from the empirical issue of whether morality supports or disrupts communication, the question that must be asked on the theoretical level is whether the theory of functional differentiation allows for any communications to be addressed to society as a whole. What is the relation between the functional subsystems and the society that they make up? We are not merely rephrasing the question discussed above, whether moral communication integrates the functional subsystems into the social whole. We are now asking if there can be such a thing as the social whole at all. Is society anything more or anything other than the relations of the subsystems among themselves? And if not, how do these relations constitute an autopoietic and informationally and operationally closed system that we could call *the* social system. If there is such a thing as *the* social system, what function does it fulfill? What communications does it consist of and how are they coded? If we are not talking about a whole that is made up of parts, that is, if we are no longer dealing with the traditional problem of the one and the many, what are we talking about when we speak of society as such and not merely of social subsystems such as business, education, law, science, and so on? If we are talking about a position within society from which we attempt to address all the subsystems together, what, or where in society, is this position and how would such communications be coded? Can we exist in society but not in any of the subsystems of which society is composed? If we are more or less "distributed" among the subsystems, for example, religious on Sunday, economic at work, political in the pub, educational in school, and so on, what is the unity of the socially constructed person? What is the unity of society? What, if anything, makes society into a unitary bounded system?

These questions lead to still further questions: Does the functionally differentiated society Luhmann describes as typically "modern" not entail the fragmentation of identity and disunity of the person as well as the disintegration of society, as postmodern critique has argued? Could it be that just as ethics represent a nostalgia for the lost unity of society, individuality, freedom, and autonomy are so important for modern Western culture, precisely because the socially constructed person of modern society is not an autonomous rational subject, a free individual, but much rather fragmented into many identities among which we must constantly choose? We moderns must choose our work, our partners, our friends, our homes, which toothpaste we buy, whether we take the bus or the car, how we dress, and so on. We experience this social reality as freedom, autonomy, and self-determination and assume this freedom to constitute human nature and to be acknowledged and guaranteed by our unique democratic form of government.[48] But, in fact, the compulsion to be free and the many identities functionally differentiated society produces are social constructions of modernity. What is this modern society in which, on the one hand, almost everything demands a free choice, while on the other hand, it is not clear who is making these decisions and what values and norms guide them? Could it be that the autonomous rational subject, the individual, as well as the idea of a unitary social whole, are myths? Could it be that Luhmann's theory is more radical than he himself supposed, since shifting the sociological perspective away from the problem of the one and the many leaves modernity with neither bounded individuals nor a social whole? If so, contemporary ethical discourse, including the discourse of digital ethics, is based upon an outworn mythology.[49] This makes current normative as well

---

48 See Willke (2020) for a discussion of the problems modern notions of freedom and democracy are facing with the emergence of a global network society.
49 The terms "myth" and "mythology" are not meant in a pejorative sense, but refer to the narrative construction of social order. For a discussion, see Belliger and Krieger (2016).

as applied ethics vulnerable for hacking. It discloses fundamental "bugs" that lead to the demand to redesign moral discourse for a global network society.

In view of all these open questions, we must ask what does the concept of the "social" mean from the perspective of a general systems theory?[50] It is interesting to note that despite all of Luhmann's claims to the contrary and despite the entire trajectory of his theory, society as a whole can hardly be modeled as a system. If there is one thing that general systems theory can't give us, it is a theory of society as a whole. There are many reasons for this. First, as a whole, society cannot fulfill the requirements of operational and informational closure. Operational closure implies the distinction between system and environment. A system can direct its operations only toward itself, if it can distinguish itself from all that it is not, that is, the environment. But what is outside society? As long as society was understood to be a kind of thing, a substance, it could be observed from without. It had clear limits. Outside society was, for example, nature. And as long as societies were territorially bounded, outside the city walls were perhaps other societies. As an operationally closed system of communications, society must be self-referential in that it must be able to refer one communication to another, and not to something other than communication. It must know what communication is and what it is not. Here again, how can society know what is not communication, when this distinction itself must be communicated? Furthermore, society must be informationally closed. Informational closure implies self-reference because the environment cannot "inform" the system; it can only "disturb" it. Informationally closed systems construct system relevant information out of perturbations coming from the environment. There is no communication between system and environment, but if there is nothing other than communication, nothing at all comes from the environment. It is a general principle of systems theory that systems are constituted by exclusion. But what does society as a whole exclude? As a system of communications, it could be argued that society excludes noncommunication. But as Watzlawick, Beavin-Bavelas, and Jackson (1967) noted, one cannot not communicate.[51]

---

50 The anomaly that no communication can address society as a whole was recognized already in the 1990s (see Fuchs 1992). Instead of being allowed to challenge the systems theory paradigm, however, the problem was dealt with in Ptolemaic fashion by generating ever more theoretical epicycles. Luhmann (2012, 40) attempts to address this issue by distinguishing between three levels of analysis: "(1) general systems theory and, within it, the general theory of autopoietic systems; (2) the theory of social systems; (3) the theory of the societal system as a special instance of social system." This merely pushes the question back to the social system, since society as a whole is a "special instance" of the social system. Luhmann attempts to resolve these issues by describing the operational closure of communication. The social, regardless of level of generality, is nothing other than communication. The concept of communication, however, depends on a theory of meaning that leads to a tension in Luhmann's theory between meaning and society, which we attempt to exploit for purposes of our hack.

51 Luhmann, on the contrary, holds on to "the definiteness of the external boundary (= the distinguishability of communication and noncommunication)," which he claims "enables the operational closure of the world society system" (2012, 87). However, this is difficult to reconcile with the statement that "world society is the occurrence of world in communication" (87),

The distinction between communication and noncommunication must itself be communicated. The only resistance that communication can experience is communicative resistance. It could be argued that since society is a meaning system, it excludes everything that is meaningless. The binary distinction between meaning and non-meaning, however, is paradoxical, since even non-meaning must have some kind of meaning in order to be used by the meaning system as a boundary at all. Even the distinction between information and noise must itself be information and not noise, since it is a difference that makes a difference.

Social systems understood as meaning systems represent a very unusual kind of system. They are all-encompassing, thus violating the principle of selection, which demands exclusion. They are not operationally closed since self-reference depends on distinction from something other and there is no other. They are not informationally closed, since there are no undifferentiated perturbations coming from outside that could serve as the stuff out of which information is constructed. Could it be that meaning is not a systemic phenomenon but must be modeled by other principles of order than selection, relationing, and steering? Could it be that although the functional subsystems can be modeled as systems, the society of which they are subsystems is itself not a system?

Luhmann argues that such things as physical reality, chemical and organic processes, and even neurophysical and cognitive phenomena constitute the environment of society.[52] We have cited Luhmann's remarkable exclusion of human beings from society often. But this claim disregards the fact that all these apparently noncommunicative phenomena are constructed in communication and endowed with meaning. Otherwise, we couldn't talk about them and describe them in any theory. The fact that supposedly extra-communicative phenomena are constructed by communication means they could be constructed otherwise or not at all. An organism cannot do this. If an organism does not construct information that is "viable," it vanishes. It must adapt to the constraints of the environment or perish. The social system has no environment in the sense that organisms do or even in the same sense in which the functional subsystems do. In distinction to the social system, the codes of the functional subsystems exclude themselves. The distinctions between profit/nonprofit, legal/illegal, certified/noncertified, true/false, and so on cannot code themselves. These distinctions are not themselves either profitable or legal or true or certified; they are what makes it possible to decide what is profitable or not, legal or not, certified or not, and so on. The codes of the functional subsystems construct the borders, the limits of the subsystems, and because these are system boundaries, they do not fall within these subsystems. Also, the subsystems effectively ban all other forms of communication than those that can be coded by their binary distinctions. The

---

since it is impossible to imagine where the world stops and non-world begins, and it is equally impossible to say it.

52 "The thesis of self-production by communication postulates clear boundaries between system and environment. The reproduction of communications from communications takes place as society. All further physical, chemical, organic, neurophysiological, and mental conditions are environmental conditions. Society can substitute for them within the limits of its own operational capabilities" (Luhmann 2012, xiii).

functional subsystems do not allow information to come from outside system boundaries. The different functional subsystems can *function* precisely because they are operationally and informationally closed systems. They are confronted by perturbations coming from an environment consisting of communications that are coded differently, that do not make "sense" within their constitutive borders, and to which they must adapt by means of internal information construction. To speak of a social system beyond the functional subsystems implies that these are somehow integrated into a social whole, a supersystem. How is this possible?

Following the organic analogy, one could suppose that society constructs the subsystems as "organic" functions much like an organism constructs a cardiovascular system or a central nervous system or a digestive system. On the biological level, the various organs of the body are dependent upon the organizing principles, the DNA of the living system, such that it can be said that the whole is more than the sum of the parts and indeed something entirely different. But what is the DNA, the "code" of society that determines what functional elements it should construct? For society, there is no analogous code. And there are no analogous environmental constraints that would "force" the construction of any particular function. An organism must take up energy by eating, it must acquire oxygen by breathing, and some kind of circulatory system must see to it that nutrients and oxygen are distributed throughout the body. But what does a meaning system have to do other than create meaning? And who or what is to say how this is to be done or not to be done? Of course, meaning does not exist independently of the physical and biological levels of order from which it emerged. There are real constraints. But what they are and how they may influence the order of society is not given. The force of gravity, it might be objected, constrains not only physical and biological systems but also meaning systems. But does it? Has society not found different ways to "defy" gravity? What technologies of the future may bring we can only speculate. As history demonstrates, society is infinitely variable, and the future is open. The biological analogy seems unconvincing.

As opposed to organisms, meaning systems, and therefore society, do not achieve closure by means of exclusion, but by means of inclusion. Any distinction that could be made between the social system and its environment necessarily falls within the system, that is, within society. Business is not politics. But society is society. Where or what is the environment? Nature, as well as persons, are social constructs. This makes it impossible to describe the operations of the social system in terms of function, that is, in terms of viability or adaptation to an environment. An organism with an appropriate sensory-motor system, central nervous system, and so on can be judged viable if it constructs information out of perturbations coming from the environment such that it can continue its autopoiesis. If lions hunt zebras instead of butterflies, this is because their principle of organization, their code, or DNA allows them to construct appropriate information out of everything that is moving in the environment. If this code functions properly, the lions will find zebras and eat them and will survive. Society is not like a lion that lives in a certain environment to which it must adapt or perish. Society is not confronted with restraints on what is good to communicate and what not. The autopoiesis of society is the communicative construction of meaning. If this stops, then no one is there to tell the story. If it continues, there is no way of judging whether this or that way of communicating is functionally better or worse than any other. Even if every religion, worldview, and ideology claims it knows the answer to this question, there is no way to know or decide whether a particular society is viable or not, except, of course, after the fact. Civilizations, history teaches, rise and fall. Religions and philosophies are founded, flourish, and then disappear. Apart from always premature judgments about history, who can say which culture, worldview, language, religion, nation, or people is more meaningful, more communicable, and therefore more viable than another? A pessimist or perhaps a realist would say history decides. This is indeed so, but until history makes its judgment, assuming those coming later are in a position to appreciate it, what environmental constraints, conditions, limitations, or resistance does communication have to conform to in order to be viable?

There is no criterion of viability for meaning systems since there is nothing that they can be said to adapt to. Lions have adapted to zebras. What is society adapted to? What is the environment of society? Of course, the entire ecological discussion can be interpreted as a question of the viability of a particular kind of society within a particular interpretation of the natural world. Nevertheless, we are not dealing directly with nature, but with different interpretations of nature, that is, different communications. If nature didn't have its advocates and did not "speak," there would be no ecological issue. Ecology and what it stands for is a conflict within the domain of meaning and not a conflict between society and an otherwise mute nature. If the outside is inside for systems of meaning, then perhaps questions of adaptation to an environment are misplaced. These questions are nonetheless important because they show that society cannot be modeled as a system. If society cannot be modeled as a system, then even if society consists of communications, these communications cannot be described as operations of an autopoietic and operationally and informationally closed system. Without boundaries, without clear self-reference, which depends on reference to the other, no communication could be addressed to society. This makes morality, understood as the attempt to address society as such, impossible. Indeed, Luhmann would agree. He assumes that the code of morality, the distinction between good and evil, cannot be considered a necessary code of society because it is itself neither good nor evil. Moral discourse has always assumed the opposite, namely, that distinguishing between good and evil was itself good. This assumption reflects the self-appraisal of modern moral discourse as coterminous with the social as such. But Luhmann has shown the destructive consequences of this claim and that ethics should therefore warn society against morality.

Let us return to the question of the environment of the social system. Luhmann insists that society does exclude an environment. For Luhmann, the most important environment of the social system is human individuals. He attempts to answer the question of the relation of society to this environment by explaining the social construction of persons in terms of the ascription of communicative actions (2012, 42). When communication happens, who is doing the talking? The distinction between utterance and information implies the existence and the action of someone who says something. The selection of utterance is thus interpreted by the social system as an act of a person, that is, an entity constructed by communication in order to further communication. Who is this person, and where do persons come from? Whatever persons are, they are not individual human beings. Individual human beings are not elements of the social system. They make up the environment of the social system. To what extent the social system depends on or is constrained by the "operational fictions" (42)[53] of acting and speaking persons is a question that Luhmann proposes to answer by introducing the concept of "structural coupling."

The admittedly "difficult question" of "how the system of society relates to its environment" (Luhmann 2012, 54) is answered by a concept taken over from the biologist Humberto Maturana (1973, 1987). The concept of "structural coupling" is designed to describe what is usually referred to as the "adaptation" of an organism to its environment. Organisms that are not able to adapt to changes in the environment simply disappear. Those that are, are so because they have built up internal structures allowing them to continue their autopoiesis under certain environmental conditions. Supposing that those environmental conditions are relatively stable, one can speak of them as "structures" of the environment. The relatively constant population of zebras in certain areas of Africa are an environmental structure relevant for lions. It can, therefore, be said that lions and zebras are structurally coupled. For Maturana and Luhmann, this means that the structure of the organism and the structure of the environment are so tuned to each other that the organism is viable in that environment. Maturana, however, does not speak of lions and zebras. He cites the example of the muscular system of the body and Earth's gravity. Gravity is a remarkably constant feature influencing all life on Earth. Gravity selects for bodies with certain muscular capabilities. Those organisms that do not adapt to the force of gravity do not survive. Viability or adaptation on Earth is the result of structural coupling between organisms and gravity. Carried over into the theory of social systems, this allows Luhmann to claim that communication and consciousness are structurally coupled. "Without consciousness, communication is impossible. Communication is *totally* dependent (in *every* operation) on consciousness" (Luhmann 2012, 56; emphasis in original). Let us look more closely at this analogy.

To begin with, when we are talking about consciousness and communication being structurally coupled, we are not talking about specific relations between two different things. The force of gravity and the muscles of living beings are different kinds of entities. Structural coupling explains how one reacts to the other. Over the course of hundreds of millions of years, organisms of all kinds developed muscular systems that were adapted to the force of gravity. How does this situation apply to the social system and its environment, that is, individual cognitive systems? What are the "structures" that are supposedly coupled? According to Luhmann, the structures that are coupled in the case of the social system and consciousness is language.[54] Consciousness and communication, although they are two entirely distinct systems, each with its own constitutive operations,

---

53 "The identification of utterance as 'action' is the construct of an observer, that is, the construct of a communication system observing itself" (Luhmann 2012, 45).
54 "The regular structural coupling of consciousness systems with communication systems is made possible by language" (Luhmann 2012, 60).

both construct meaning by means of the same semiotically coded differences.[55] On the one side, we have thinking, which is a kind of private language, and on the other side, we have communication. The difference and relation of the private languages or thoughts of individual conscious minds and the public language of communication is not clearly explained. If they are structurally coupled, then they are related to each other as the muscles of the body to Earth's gravity. Nevertheless, there is no convincing reason why what I may be thinking about my boss and what I am actually saying to him, although different, are not part of the same social situation, encoded in the same language. Indeed, we can't imagine it otherwise.

It is difficult to imagine how language for individual cognitive systems and language for social systems are as different as muscles in an organism and the force of gravity in the environment. Are we talking about two structures that are coupled or just one that is in some way both private and public, mental and social?[56] The idea of structural coupling excludes a mutual determination of the structures of the system and the environment. A direct determination of the one by the other would violate the principles of operational and informational closure. We know that consciousness and communication somehow fit together, but we don't know why or how. For Luhmann, however, it is clear that consciousness can think but not communicate. "Human beings cannot communicate; only communication can communicate. [...] There is no nonsocially mediated communication from consciousness to consciousness and there is no communication between the individual and society" (Luhmann 2012, 57–58). Are we to imagine that thinking exerts a kind of force upon communication, much like the force of gravity upon the muscles of the body? Are we to assume that communication somehow reacts to this force such that what is thought and what is said are structurally coupled, even though thinking and communication in no way communicate with each other and indeed, must be as different as gravity and muscle? Does Descartes say the *cogito* or merely think it? Would he still be certain of his existence if he said it, but didn't think it? Does the idea of structural coupling explain why and how individuals must be banned into the environment of the social system while at the same time reconstructed as persons or speakers

---

55 Luhmann (2012, 117) explains this by means of the distinction between medium and form. There is a pool of words in any language that can be combined in various ways. As pool, the words are "loosely coupled"; this is medium; when they are "strictly coupled" or combined into sentences, this is form. "A medium consists of loosely coupled elements, whereas a form joins the same elements in strict coupling" (118). Apart from the fact that "loose" and "strict" are very vague concepts that can be applied in many different ways to many different situations, it could still be claimed that this pretty well covers semantics and syntax. But the binary distinction between medium and form leaves out of account the third dimension of language, namely, pragmatics, or what Wittgenstein calls "use." If meaning is use, as Wittgenstein argued, medium and form are useless for a theory of meaning.
56 The "linguistic turn" in Western philosophy in the twentieth century above all personified by Wittgenstein is based upon precisely the insight that a private language is not possible and that cognition is essentially social.

within the social system? One must ask if it would not be more efficient from a theoretical point of view just to do away with human individuals altogether.[57]

Returning to the analogy of muscles and gravity, which is the source of Luhmann's notion of structural coupling, it is clear that the force of gravity represents an external resistance to the activity of muscles and that this resistance sets the environmental constraints to which organisms must adapt. But if there is any "resistance" to communication, however, it must come from communication itself. How is this possible? It must be admitted that the operations of psychic systems, be they thinking, perception, or cognition do not resist communication but constitute communication. The idea that cognition somehow resists or constrains communication amounts to saying that the muscles of the body could only experience the weight of things on earth by means of opposing muscles. It is not the stone that is heavy; it is muscles in the body that push down on those muscles attempting to lift the stone. The fact that for meaning systems, as we noted above, the environment is not something outside the system, but is constituted by the system within itself, makes the very idea of adaptation and, therefore, also of structural coupling problematic. In addition to these difficulties, it should be noted that the question of whether there might be other "things" in the environment of the social system that could somehow condition communication is not even considered. This is apparent in the admission that the relation of the social system to its environment is actually a structural coupling of two kinds of systems—society and consciousness—and not a structural coupling between a system and general environmental conditions such as gravity, climate, geography, altitude, rivers, mountains, oceans, forest, animals, things, artifacts, technologies, and so on.

Of course, external reality does perturb the nervous system of the organism, but it is the organism that constructs information out of these undifferentiated perturbations. From an epistemological point of view, Luhmann's theory is thoroughly Kantian and thus constructivist.[58] It is interesting that Luhmann uses the concept of structural coupling, which was designed to describe the relation of an organism to its environment, exclusively for the relations between systems. Importantly, he uses it not only to explain the relation of the social system to psychic systems but also to explain the relations of the social subsystems to each other. The legal system, for example, is said to be structurally coupled to the economic system, which is structurally coupled to the political system and the educational system, and so on. How can the same mechanism constitute at once the unity of a system (the social system made up of functional subsystems) and the difference between the system and its environment, that is, adaptation? Does the circulatory system "adapt" to the central nervous system, the digestive system, the skeletal system, the respiratory system, and so on? Finally, if there is nothing outside of communication—here we must think of communication in the broad sense including language and meaning—that conditions it, then there is no outside at all and the system/environment difference that is necessary to constitute a system collapses. It would appear, as we suggested above, that it is very difficult to model society as a system.

---

57 We interpret Luhmann's theory for this reason as basically posthumanist.
58 For Luhmann's own discussion of his relation to Kant, see Luhmann (2013, 167).

The idea that morality has the function of integrating individuals into society is not only empirically false, as Luhmann claims, but also theoretically impossible. The theoretical impossibility comes not alone from the fact that individuals are excluded from society but also from the fact that society as a whole is not a system. There are no elements that could be measured by their success in fulfilling certain functions or be compared to other possible ways of fulfilling this or that function. How can we decide if a certain form of legal system functions viably? This can be decided with regard to living systems. If the heart doesn't pump blood, we die. We can survive if we replace the heart with something else that functions as a pump. If the legal system doesn't settle conflicts by means of law, then we organize society differently, perhaps without coding communications as legal or illegal. How do we know that the capitalist economic system is viably adapted to the legal system, or to the educational system, or to religion, or even to society as a whole? Ever since Marx, much social theory is convinced that it is not. The theory of functional differentiation leads to paradoxical results. If the various "subsystems" of society are not analogous to organs within a living being, and society cannot be understood as a whole that is more than the sum of the parts, how are we to understand the relation between the functional subsystems and society? Do they have a relation to society at all, or only to each other? And does the sum of their relations constitute a social whole that is greater than the sum of the parts?

Luhmann's radicalization of Durkheim's functionalism leads not only to the conclusion that morality is dysfunctional since it does not integrate either individuals or subsystems into society but also to the conclusion that a radically functionalist theory of society runs into limits when society as a whole comes into view. Morality is not only dysfunctional but also afunctional, since (1) it appears that there are no communications addressed to society as a whole, and therefore, morality, which is concerned with what is good and bad for everyone, everywhere, and at all times, has nothing to say, that is, no function whatsoever, and (2) society as a whole does not offer a functional solution to any problem. There is no functional alternative to meaning. If there were, then one would have to be able to say what it was and thus turn it into meaning again. As Wittgenstein might say, that of which we cannot speak, thereof we must be silent. This leads us to the question: If society is not a system, what is it? We are thrown back to the "what" question because the question of "how" society operates presupposes that it has a function. This is precisely what cannot be the case if it is impossible to make functional comparisons.

But perhaps we are not yet at an end. Perhaps it could be argued that if anything, society as a whole resembles more an open *ecosystem* than any of the closed functional systems that admittedly are theoretically modeled as organisms.[59] If we follow the analogy of the ecosystem instead of the analogy of the organism, could this be a way out of our problem and an answer to the question of what it means to speak of society as a system? According to this view, it is not the organism, but the ecosystem that models the relations of the functional subsystems to society and thus describes the social whole. The (semi)-autonomous functional subsystems are much rather like individual organisms operating

---

59 Interestingly, for Luhmann (1989), there can be no "ecological" communication.

more or less independently within an ecosystem. If society is more like an ecosystem than like a single organism, then it could still be modeled by systems theory. Is society an ecosystem?

The comparison with an "ecosystem" seems at first glance helpful when it comes to understanding what function society as a whole could be said to fulfill. In an ecosystem, organisms—in the case of society, we are talking about functionally differentiated social subsystems—achieve operational closure and self-reference by banning all other organisms, as well as all natural conditions, into the environment. Each organism is operationally and informationally closed to every other organism and to the natural elements in the ecosystem. Of course, all systems are open to the exchange of matter and energy, but this does not, as in the case of the force of gravity, affect operational and informational closure. With regard to the relations between organisms and the environment, all the environment can do is *disturb* the organisms and thus motivate information construction. Disturbances, or "perturbations," are not information.[60] Perturbations are not communications. They do not contain information. They are that out of which the organism constructs information. Informationally closed systems construct information from undifferentiated perturbations coming from the environment. If the information they construct allows them to react such that they can continue their operations, their autopoiesis, then for an observer, it appears that they have adapted successfully to the environment. In ecology, they are said to inhabit a "niche" in the environment. When a system operates such that it can continue its operations in a particular environment, this can be called adaptive learning.

Applying this analogy to society, since society continues to exist, we can assume that the social subsystems are more or less able to viably reduce the complexity that they create for each other and thus adapt to the perturbations in the environment that they represent for each other. The relative stability of the relations of the social subsystems to each other is for Luhmann a sign of structural coupling of the subsystems. But if anything changes too much, this can destabilize society. This is why political regulation of business activity is fraught with danger. It could be that the economic system cannot absorb the perturbances coming from the political struggle for power and legitimation and becomes in the face of costly and unrealistic regulations dysfunctional. This is also why business interests in maximizing profits can destabilize the political system. Laying off too many workers creates social unrest and problems that the political system is supposed to solve. As long as the autopoietic activities of the various subsystems do not disturb each other too much, it appears that society is stable, just as an ecosystem can appear stable—one speaks of "sustainability"—when no organism uses too much of scarce resources. Is society anything more than a balanced ecosystem?

As attractive as this solution may seem, it should be noted that in ecology, we do not have stable environments. Organisms can be as structurally coupled as possible, but

---

60 See Maturana and Varella (1987) for a discussion of informational closure. The concept of information will occupy us in detail below. For the moment, only the distinction between information and perturbation is of importance.

the environment changes anyway and often in unexpected, unforeseeable, and even catastrophic ways. The ecosystem itself is not adapted to anything and not in any way concerned to maintain any particular constellation of matter and energy, plants and animals, water and forests, and so on. Furthermore, the ecosystem, just as society, knows no boundaries, no limits, no constitutive difference to anything beyond or outside of itself. What function, if any, can the ecosystem have? Did, or does, the ecosystem of Earth function to keep any form of life viable? What would the dinosaurs say? This raises the question: can an ecosystem actually be a "system" in the proper sense of the word? Could it be that the concept of an "ecosystem" is an oxymoron, a contradiction in itself?

An ecosystem, despite the name, is not a system at all. It is not bounded. It is not coded. It has no specific operations. It is not operationally and informationally closed. And it is not autopoietic. The term "ecosystem" was coined in order to describe a "community" of organisms and their interactions within a geographically and temporally limited "ecotope." The systemic character of this construction came from the feedback loops with regard to the exchange of matter and energy that could be described within an ecotope. The closure of the ecosystem was an arbitrary construction of the observer. In fact, in nature, there are no such closures. Everything in some way affects everything else. There is no stability, no homeostasis. There are no limits, no borders, no difference between system and environment. An ecosystem consists of organisms in an environment and, therefore, cannot itself be considered a system unless it is distinguished from a more encompassing environment, which itself can only be seen as a system in distinction to a still more encompassing environment and so on into infinity.

An ecosystem cannot be a system because it contains everything, and no system can contain everything. This would violate the principle of selection. Who can say where the borders of an ecosystem are? The pond in the forest could be considered an ecosystem, but it is influenced by everything that happens in the forest, which may be near a city, which is located on a certain continent, which itself is influenced by shifting tectonic plates, which are related to many other factors including influences from the Moon, the Sun, cosmic rays, and so on. Who can say what the specific purpose of the pond is, let alone the forest, or even the city? The same is true of society modeled as a system of meaning. It includes everything, even the negation of itself. Society as a whole is much closer to the philosophical conception of "world" (e.g., in Heidegger) than to the concept of a system.[61] The very concept of an ecosystem is, therefore, self-contradictory. The object of ecology cannot be a system.[62] Just as the object of sociology cannot be

---

61 More precisely, Heidegger (1996, §14) speaks of "Being-in-the-World" as the way of being of *dasein* to which "worldhood" (*Weltlichkeit*) as the referential interconnectedness of all things belongs. It is the world that makes possible the thematic actualizing of any particular object of intentional consciousness against an infinite background of possible references and distinctions. For Heidegger, world is the condition of the possibility of meaning and not the cognitive or communicative act of introducing a distinction as in Luhmann's theory of meaning. For Luhmann's discussion of world, see Luhmann (2012, 83).
62 We will see below that what is being talked about in ecology is much rather a network than a system.

a specific domain of reality among others called society but encompasses everything. The whole of reality does not bring itself autocatalytically into being by selecting certain elements from an environment, relating them in certain ways for fulfilling specific purposes. The whole has no environment. It is the environment as well as the system. It cannot even be said to be the unity of the difference between system and environment since this could not be a systemic form of unity, and there is no other option. Order, as general systems theory claims, is systemic. On the one hand, an ecosystem always includes its environment; whereas, on the other hand, a system must always exclude the environment. "Environment" and "ecosystem" are paradoxically identical in meaning even though, according to systems theory, a system is constituted by distinguishing itself from an environment. The subject of ecology is a continuum and not a bounded unity. Systems may exist in a continuum, but they cannot exist as a continuum. Systems are necessarily bounded unities. We can summarize the comparison of society to an ecosystem by saying that although much of social life can be modeled as a system, and Luhmann has brilliantly demonstrated this, the society in which such functional subsystems operate cannot. Where does this leave sociology and the sociological theory of morality?

1.2.9 *What Is the Status of Social Theory?*

It would seem that the moment sociology becomes a universal theory, its specific object, society, disappears. Society disappears because there is nothing from which it can distinguish itself. The moment we begin talking about meaning, we are on a different level, perhaps what one could call a "metaphysical" level. As a system of meaning, society can no longer be a part of reality but becomes coterminous with everything that can exist. This can be called "world." The world cannot assume an even greater and more complex world in which it comes to be by means of selection and reduction of complexity. The world is not an island of order, somehow swimming on an ocean of chaos, even if this distinction might come in handy in certain circumstances. The difference between order and chaos is not given but is constructed by the system. What is more complex than the world? What is beyond the world which could serve as its environment? Within the systems theory paradigm, the environment of the social system, therefore, becomes a kind of Kantian *noumena* whose only raison d'etre is to disturb or stimulate the meaning-making operations of society, that is, communications. The question arises: Are we still talking about society and is sociology the right way to do this?

If we are not at this point to embark upon the same road traveled by German idealism in the attempt to come to terms with the question of how society can create itself by positing its own opposite, its own negation, then we must accept the fact that society as a whole cannot be modeled as a system. The difference between communication and non-communication must be drawn by communication within communication, and therefore, it is no difference between the system and a possible environment. With regard to physical systems, such as a table, or organic systems, such as frogs or lions, we know what the system/environment difference distinguishes since we observe both sides of the difference. The environment is not within the system. This changes the moment we are dealing with society as a whole, with communication, or with meaning. What does it mean for meaning to distinguish between meaning and non-meaning? One might as well ask: What is the purpose of the universe? Does the universe itself exist within something still greater? Why is there Being instead of nothing? The obvious difficulties that arise with questions such as these suggest that we must shift the theoretical perspective. Luhmann (2008, 74) claimed that his theory was a universal theory—he even speaks of a "super theory," which is much closer to the self-understanding of philosophy than Durkheim's vision of a positive and empirical science of social facts.

A universal theory claims to be able to explain everything, including itself, while at the same time not succumbing to the temptation to posit an absolute truth resistant to adaptive learning. Absolute truth, as we saw, is not science, but morality. Universal theories walk a thin line between science and morality, between the "is" and the "ought." It could be said that universal theories are a kind of morality in their own way. They could also be called "moralizing" theories because they claim to articulate the conditions of social existence. This is what Luhmann criticizes about traditional morality, which attempts to set conditions for social inclusions and proclaim normative expectations that no longer, or perhaps never did, correspond to social reality. Our hack will use this critique of morality to break into the current discourse of digital ethics and show its bugs and vulnerabilities. With regard to sociology, however, Luhmann nonetheless argues for the validity of sociology as a science with universal scope. But if we are talking about everything, this has consequences for morality, which heretofore has always been concerned to address only a specific domain of reality. Let us recall that morality begins at the same moment society comes into being, that is, at that moment when *alter* is respected (*Achtung*) as *alter ego*, thus creating the problem of double contingency, which can only be resolved by normative rules. If there is indeed nothing that cannot be communicated, and it is impossible not to communicate, it would seem that society in Luhmann's theory becomes coterminous with Being. The consequence is that everything, be it things, animals, and so on, gains moral significance. If everything is a "part" of society, it is a small step to suppose everything is a social "partner." The scope of morality extends suddenly far beyond the human and includes nonhumans as well. This would explain why Heidegger's pursuit of the question of Being has always been understood to have an ethical dimension, even though it has been equally clear that ethics must then be understood in an entirely different manner than what is traditionally understood by the term.

Apart from all the uncertainties the status of sociology as a theory of communication and meaning presents, one thing is certain: human nature, which in one way or another was the basis of ethics and morality since the ancient Greeks, can no longer have any effect on society and can no longer serve to ground or prescribe ethical norms. Neither social structures nor values and norms can be deduced from human nature. What is said to be human nature is a social construction, a way of communicating, which arises and also disappears on the basis of functions that it fulfills in the internal organization of the system of communications, which is society.[63] Values such as freedom and autonomy, privacy, security, well-being, equality, dignity, and the "human rights"

---

63 See Etinson (2018) for the controversy of human rights as natural or social.

expressed by them have been the subject of many declarations, national constitutions, and regulations. Despite all claims to the opposite, they are neither historically nor philosophically universal, but arose within modern Western industrial society and are based on a certain conception of the human individual and the social whole that is peculiar to this particular form of social order.[64] No matter how convinced we may be that Western values are singular achievements of cultural evolution that we must protect, it is undeniable that the evolution of society toward functional differentiation and beyond that toward a global network society has changed the meaning and function of the individual. Society no longer needs to integrate individuals into a group, nor does it need to preserve a pool of sufficient contingency and complexity by protecting the freedom and autonomy of principally asocial individuals. Durkheim's problem of the one and the many vanishes. This not only signals the end of humanism but also opens up the possibility that humans are not the only actors in the social system and not even the free individuals they thought they were. If communication seems to throw the baby out with the bathwater, everything, the baby and the bathwater as well, returns through the back door of meaning. Even though Luhmann never explicitly draws this conclusion, it can be argued that whatever communicates, and that can be not only humans but also some animals, extra-terrestrials, and currently AIs, and, as we shall see in the discussion of ANT below, everything, is a full-fledged member of society.[65] But when everything is included in society, then society, whatever it might be, cannot be a system and the theory of society cannot be scientific knowledge.

What is the status of Luhmann's theory within the society that the theory describes? Luhmann's super theory is at once a way in which the functional subsystem of science attempts to code all possible communications by means of the binary difference of true/false, while at the same time relying upon the more general distinction between meaning/non-meaning. Can this double coding work? The two codes are not on the same level. What is false is not true, but what is meaningless does have a meaning. The distinction between true/false is neither true nor false, but the distinction between meaning/non-meaning is—and must be!—meaningful. This leads to ambiguity with regard to the object domain of the theory as well as the status of the theory itself. Are we talking about society, that is, a particular domain of reality distinct, for example, from nature, or are we talking about something that extends beyond the domain of the social, indeed, beyond all

---

64 See Luhmann (2008, 236). Current attempts to anchor what is called "European values" in legal and political institutions, constitutions, laws, and regulations can be seen as trying to freeze the historical development of Western society at the industrial level and thus prevent social evolution and change. The rest of the world, it would seem, may continue at their own risk into the future, but Europe must stay the same.

65 As we noted above, Luhmann's theory can therefore be understood as "posthumanist," which also opens up the possibility to consider moral obligations not only toward humans but also toward nonhumans, which has become an influential aspect of current discussions on ecology. See Latour's work on Gaia and climate change (Latour 2017). On AIs as members of society, see the EU Parliament Initiative for an "electronic personality" (http://www.europarl.europa.eu/doceo/document/A-8-2017-0005_EN.html).

the current domains or divisions of reality, and addresses reality as a whole? What is the status of the theory that attempts to describe the social when the social becomes the all-encompassing reality? Society as the realm of communication and world as the realm of meaning are coterminous. If we are dealing with sociology and not with metaphysics, the theory must restrict its object domain to a specific, well-defined, and delimited area of reality. In addition to this, under the conditions of the functionally differentiated society of Western modernity, the theory must locate itself within the functional subsystem of science, at least if it wishes to offer us knowledge and not a new religion. This particular form of knowing would seem to extend only as far as the borders of the functional subsystem of science. The fundamental distinction between true/false codes only those communications as meaningful that function within the subsystem of science, even if the informational and operational closure of this system reconstructs potentially everything within its borders and thus legitimates a certain kind of claim to universality. But this only extends to what can be either true or false and does not cover what can be profitable, or legal, or educational, or morally obligating, and so on.

Admittedly, there is nothing that cannot be scientifically investigated. But science is not all there is to society. The distinction between true/false itself is not a part of the system, but a border of the system. It itself is neither true nor false, but a condition of the possibility of scientific meaning, which is constituted by a particular form of selection, relationing, and steering of communications. This implies that meaning means something else in every functional subsystem. A legal decision is neither true nor false; it makes no sense as scientific communication. One cannot decide the outcome of a scientific experiment in a courtroom, but only in the laboratory. Functional differentiation allows for a specific kind of universality that is paradoxically very limited, indeed, not universal at all. If you don't find science meaningful, then you can study law or go into business or politics. Meaning is coded differently in every subsystem, which amounts to saying that (1) there are many different kinds of meaning and many different kinds of communication, and (2) they are all on the same level. You can move laterally from one to another, but you cannot move up or down. Social space, to take a phrase from Latour (2005, 165), is flat. The super theory, therefore, is only super in relation to other scientific theories, but not in relation to society. Society is once again segmented, but all the segments are different. Hierarchies are possible only within subsystems, but not among them. This is why not even politics can claim the ability to steer the other functional subsystems. It can only create disturbances in the social environment that hopefully, but mostly do not, lead to de-escalation of systemic conflicts.[66] Theoretically, it is difficult to understand how the political system, or any subsystem at all, could steer society as a whole. There is no communication between system and environment. One organism in an ecosystem is as good or bad, functional or dysfunctional, viable or not on an equal footing with every other organism.

---

[66] On the failure of the political system, which is still territorially organized within the borders of nation-states, within the global network society, see Willke (2017).

It would seem that within the framework of Luhmann's theory, the question of meaning itself, what constitutes the meaning of meaning, what can be said truly about meaning, must be meaningless, at least as long as it is understood to be a question that can be meaningfully posed and answered only within a particular subsystem, for example, in Luhmann's case, within the functional subsystem of science. Indeed, Luhmann proposes a theory of meaning that intends to be scientifically true. In order to be coded scientifically, statements about the meaning of meaning must either be true or false. But if they are false, they are still meaningful. A theory of meaning cannot be falsified. Judgments about coherence, inclusivity, differentiatedness, complexity, heuristic value, and so on are more or less plausible and consensual, but that is all. What this shows is that at the level of the universality Luhmann claims for his super theory, the binary code of science, true/false, cannot be implemented. What methods and falsification procedures can be applied to statements about meaning? How could we decide whether or not Luhmann's theory is true or false? Whatever it might be, the super theory is not a *scientific* theory. This raises the question of where in society, that is, in what functional subsystem, the theory itself is communicated. If it is not in any of the functional subsystems, what function does it have? Does the super theory demand a super system whose communications it codes? Just as with morality, the moment communication is addressed to everyone beyond the limits of any subsystem, it becomes not merely dysfunctional, but afunctional, which only means that universal theories have a special status that must be clarified. They are similar to morality in that they communicate universal truths but are dissimilar in that they—presumably—are open to revision and adaptive learning. What kind of discourse is this? And what does this discourse have to do with moral discourse? Are universal theories somehow "good" in themselves, as traditional ethics has always claimed for itself? It was always considered good to know and proclaim the good. But what kind of "good" is being talked about when experience can revise definitions of the good and force the theory to adapt to changing circumstances? Or are super theories the end of ethics, that which must replace ethics, if it should turn out, as Luhmann claims, that morality has no function and must therefore be avoided?

If we interpret Luhmann's super theory as a theory of meaning, and we furthermore assume that meaning is not merely theoretical knowledge, but, as Heidegger proposed, a way of disclosing Being, then it could be claimed that what we are dealing with is neither theory nor practice, but an originary mode of existence that must be considered on its own terms. Meaning is not a "social fact" in Durkheim's sense; neither is it a functional code in Luhmann's interpretation of society as a specifically modern, functionally differentiated system. When meaning becomes the basic concept of sociology, sociology becomes something other.[67] But there is no functional subsystem to which this unique

---

67 Luhmann (1990, 24) explicitly positions the concept of meaning beyond any reference to a particular system, whether it be psychological or social. This does not imply, however, that textuality and inscription automatically become fundamental concepts of sociology. Luhmann's system of meaning is not to be equated with the postmodern concept of "discourse" and "text" or with the well-known "linguistic turn" in modern philosophy.

kind of communication can belong. If this kind of knowing is part of society at all, then the social cannot be fully understood exclusively in terms of functional differentiation and on the basis of the general principles of systemic order. In no way, however, does this imply that we must return to Western metaphysics and modern humanism. Whatever this special way of knowing that must somehow take account of everything may be—later we will attempt to describe it with the help of the concept of "design"—after Luhmann it cannot be the same as it was before. Luhmann's theoretical advances cannot be undone or disregarded.

Luhmann's theoretical achievement is not only to make traditional ethics, which was a philosophical discussion based on what was understood to be human nature, obsolete but also to shift the sociological perspective away from a science of society to basic concepts such as meaning and information. This comes aptly at the dawn of the "information" age and should perhaps be taken as a signal to reinterpret the question of the social as well as modern Western humanism in terms of information and explicitly as a theory of meaning. Why is there information instead of noise? What does it mean if humans are informational beings along with everything else? How is information constructed and communicated? How does the foundational concept of information relate to the new information and communication technologies that have initiated a digital revolution and therefore raised the issue of digital ethics? Is a new ethics of information needed? In order to attempt to answer these questions, we must look for a theoretical approach that does not fall behind the advances Luhmann has made, that is, a clearly posthumanist standpoint coupled with a disturbing uncertainty with regard to the status of traditional moral discourse, while at the same time opening up the possibility of understanding ethics and morality on different terms within a global network society and with regard to fundamentally new forms of knowing and acting. We suggest that what we are looking for could be found in ANT.

1.3 Actor-Network Theory

Let us go back to the beginning, that is, to adaptive learning. Luhmann told the story of how an individual, through variation of behavior, came to select certain experiences and generalize them into rules. After many times of having a similar experience, for example, "I saw a wolf and ran," "I saw a wolf and ran," "I saw a wolf and ran," and after noticing that I am still alive to tell the story, then I generalize to the "you." I would tell my brothers, my wife, my son or daughter: "Whenever you see a wolf, you ought to run." The "I" becomes a "you." The "is" becomes an "ought." I now say, "You ought to run."[68] Whatever you and I do, others could and perhaps should also do. We then tell others and thus generalize to "everyone." A rule is constructed, which itself constructs a group as the

---

68 The "is" becomes an "ought" only when the "you" appears. As Wittgenstein pointed out in his famous private language argument, there is no generalization or rule for one consciousness alone. Rules are necessarily intersubjective (https://en.wikipedia.org/wiki/Private_language_argument).

collective of all those who obey the rule. Adaptive learning is a process of selecting some aspects of experience and relationing them so that behavior can be steered in a certain way. Since adaptive learning is pragmatic and success oriented, it does not explain moral rules, which are oriented toward neither interactions with the environment, that is, with nonhumans, nor learning from experience. Moral rules, for Luhmann, arise to coordinate interactions between human beings in a situation of double contingency. Once the other is acknowledged and respected as an *alter ego* with his/her expectations and expectations of expectations, double contingency can only be reduced by a higher power that guarantees the normative validity and application of the rules. The rules hold regardless of what my experience might try to teach me; therefore, they require nonadaptive learning, that is, refusal to learn. What is morally good or bad is so regardless of what experience might teach us. Unlike laws, moral rules or norms cannot be changed whenever some ways of behaving seem to be more successful than others. When a rule is "true" regardless of what experience might try to teach us, then we may speak of this rule as absolute truth. Absolute truths are valid for everyone, at all times, and at all places. They necessarily address the whole of society and presuppose, therefore, that society is a bounded unity, a totality. Universal truth implies totality and not infinity. From the point of view of communication, absolute truths can only be repeated but not discussed. Redundancy, however, reduces their informational value to zero, which blocks all discussion. Saying the same thing over and over again in all situations is pure redundancy and leaves no room for further communication. Since for Luhmann, society is a system that consists of communications, anything that blocks discussion or threatens to stop communication is bad for society. For this reason, Luhmann concludes that morality is not good for society and that ethics, the theory of morality, should warn society against morality. This is Luhmann's story. In this story, the traditional roles of both individual and society, as well as morality, have become questionable and uncertain. What is society made of? Persons or communications? What constitutes the unity and boundaries of society? Who or what is included in society, and how are these actors to be normatively regulated? In order to answer these questions, and to complete the assembly of our exploit kit, we turn to ANT.

Bruno Latour tells a very different story than does Luhmann. Latour is known as one of the founders of ANT.[69] Latour does not begin with the interactions of a human individual with its environment. He does not project the mechanisms of biological adaptation onto the level of meaning. Consequently, meaning cannot be modeled as the autocatalytic emergence of a particular form of systemic order. Meaning is not an autopoietic and operationally and informationally closed system, whether it be psychic or social. For Latour, there can be no *system* of meaning. Instead, meaning emerges from the mutual and symmetrical actions of humans and nonhumans, or more correctly, protohumans and nonhumans, since the construction of meaning, information, and rules goes much farther back than *Homo sapiens*. Meaning emerges not as a system on the level of human

---

[69] For an overview, see Wikipedia (https://en.wikipedia.org/wiki/Actor%E2%80%93network_theory). For an introduction from Latour himself, see Latour (2005).

consciousness, cognition, and linguistic communication but as a *network* that may include but does not presuppose human beings.[70]

From the point of view of ANT, there are indeed systems, but these are to be understood as a certain kind of network. The autopoietic and operationally and informationally closed systems Luhmann describes as functional subsystems of society can be understood as particular forms of network order. They are functional networks that have become solidified into "black boxes." Black boxes are networks in which the relations between the actors have been reduced or subsumed to functions that result in standard input/output operations. The many internal constitutive links, relations, and associations have become invisible. We perceive only an external input and output, which seems almost automatic. For Latour (2005, 37) this means that the actors in the network have become "intermediaries" instead of "mediators."

> An intermediary, in my vocabulary, is what transports meaning or force without transformation: defining its inputs is enough to define its outputs. For all practical purposes, an intermediary can be taken not only as a black box, but also as a black box counting for one, even if it is internally made of many parts. Mediators, on the other hand, cannot be counted as just one; they might count for one, for nothing, for several, or for infinity. Their input is never a good predictor of their output; their specificity has to be taken into account every time. Mediators transform, translate, distort, and modify the meaning of the elements they are supposed to carry. (Latour 2005, 39)[71]

What Luhmann's theory of social systems describes are not fundamental forms of order but much rather black boxes within networks. The concept of "system" can, therefore, not be equated to the idea of "order." There are more fundamental forms of order than systems. We do not have systems on the one side and chaos on the other; what we have are more or less chaotic networks in which some have become rigid, standardized, and functionalized and where mediators have been turned into intermediaries. Systems, or black boxes, are a form of order in which information has been reduced to a high level of redundancy and the ongoing process of the construction of meaning has become channeled and slowed down giving the appearance of durability, fixed order, and structure against volatile agency and its unforeseeable vicissitudes.

---

70 We note that Latour himself does not explicitly propose a theory of meaning. Terms such as meaning, information, and even communication do not play important roles in his theoretical work. Nonetheless, we allow ourselves the liberty of interpreting ANT as a theory of meaning in order to compare it better to Luhmann, Heidegger, and other thinkers who have made both meaning and communication central concepts of twenty-first century thought. Latour's aversion to the concept of meaning comes from his critique of postmodernism as a theory of "discourse" based on signs and semiotics. All the world is a text, but where then are the things, the artifacts of which the world is made of? We need not accept the postmodern version of semiotics or hermeneutics. Our understanding of meaning is not primarily linguistic or semiotic, but explicitly includes things and the part they play in constructing meaning.

71 We will return to the all-important concept of "mediation" below when discussing networking.

From the point of view of ANT, Luhmann's social subsystems are black boxes. In contrast, society as a whole, which, as we argued above, cannot be modeled as a system anyway, is best understood as a network. For example, in the case of the legal system, redundancy is enforced by state power and the application of the binary code of legal/illegal. Redundancy in the science system is constructed by applying the binary code true/false by means of established research methods and programs. In the case of morality, redundancy is based on refusing to learn and the repetition of absolute truths. It is these regularities that we call rules, norms, methods, laws, and institutions or, generally, social structures.[72] For Durkheim, these structures were social facts. Luhmann speaks of social systems. From the point of view of ANT, social structures and social systems, as well as morality, are located on a level below or subsidiary to the originary process of the construction of meaning, which is a network process and not a system process. The fundamental processes of systemic order, as we saw, can be said to be selecting, relating, and steering. These processes of systemic order express themselves on the level of emergent order, which Luhmann calls meaning by means of cognition and communication. The cognitive and communicative operations of the systems of meaning Luhmann describes then construct the "actors" as either conscious individuals or communicating persons. From the point of view of network order, actors can be anything, both human and non-human, and meaning is constructed by operations other than cognition and communication. The fundamental processes of network order—or "networking," as we may say—Latour describes as "translating" and "enrolling." What are these processes?

1.3.1 The Difference a Stone Makes

To answer this question, let us go back in history before the appearance of human beings.[73] According to the current state of the archeological record, *Homo sapiens* appeared about 300,000 years ago. The first use of stone tools, however, goes back to almost 3.3 million years. In this period, known as the Paleolithic Age, hominins lived in groups and used stone, wood, and bone tools for hunting, scavenging, and whatever other purposes they might serve. Considering that this technology was used during the entire prehistory of *Homo sapiens*, that is, about three million years, it can be said that the stone ax is the most significant technological innovation of (proto-)human history. Since toolmaking is often considered a distinctive characteristic of culture and civilization, what does it mean that

---

72 Latour does not speak of social systems to describe the black boxes that law, religion, business, politics, and so on appear as; rather, he considers these to be "modes of existence." See Latour (2012) for the theory of modes of existence.

73 Meillassoux (2008) speaks of the "ancestral" in order to designate a realm beyond the "correlationist" presupposition of modern Western subjectivism, especially since Kant, and as exemplified in Husserl and Phenomenology. The assumption he questions with the idea of the ancestral is that Being—and therefore meaning—is necessarily correlated to human conscious experience. Correlationalism is a modern phenomenon arising from the strict distinction between subject and object and the necessity of then somehow putting them together again, since the one cannot exist without the other.

hominins were making and using tools several million years before *Homo sapiens* came on the scene? Indeed, what does it *mean* to use a stone ax? How did hominins acquire this technology, whereas the apes never developed the non-episodic use of tools?[74] Our story, as well as the investigation into ethics in a posthuman world, begins with this question about meaning in a prehuman world.

It should be noted that what is being described here is neither an adaptation of an organism to its environment nor a phenomenological description of human conscious experience. What is being described is a relation or "association" of certain things in the environment into certain kinds of behavior of the organism such that this behavior cannot be ascribed to the organism alone, but is a product of a specific kind of *cooperation between both organism and thing*.[75] In the case of the stone ax, it is a cooperation between a hominin and a certain type of stone. The activity of the hominin is not a "reaction" to an environmental stimulus. It is not a purely internal construction of information. It is a unique kind of cooperation between protohuman and nonhuman actors. It would be more appropriate not to speak of organism and environment at all, since strictly speaking, in this world, there is no system and no environment. Concepts such as "system" and "environment" carry the weight of a long history of theoretical development. They are inappropriate when attempting to describe what it means for a hominin to use a stone ax. How then are we to understand this specific cooperation between protohuman and nonhuman in creating and using a stone ax?

Let us suppose that a certain hominin picked up a particular stone that had a certain shape, weight, size, and so on, all of which suggested, offered, nudged, and proposed that it be held in the hand in a certain way and swung by the arm in a certain manner such that an animal was killed, an enemy frightened off, a piece of wood split, and so on. Other stones didn't do this. Different ways of holding the stone and of swinging the arm didn't do this. This particular stone, and others like it, had certain "affordances" that together with certain needs, anatomical structures, and abilities of the hominin over many hundreds of thousands of years of acting upon one another created something that did not exist before, namely, a "hunter," or a "warrior" who wielded a stone "ax." Although Latour does not use the term "affordance," it is a helpful term when attempting to describe the agency of nonhuman actors.[76] Gibson (1979, 129) writes:

---

74 Simian tool use is characterized by its "episodic" nature. See Donald (1991, 149), who describes the "culture" of apes as "episodic." "In fact, the word that seems best to epitomize the cognitive culture of apes [...] is the term episodic. Their lives are lived entirely in the present, as a series of concrete episodes and the highest element in their system of memory representation seems to be at the level of event representation."

75 "We can never understand and infer the nature of the 'cognitive function' responsible for the creation and use of a tool without first recognizing that the various processes responsible for the transformation of raw material to tool, as well as the tool itself, actively and reciprocally participate in the co-construction of what counts as 'cognitive function'" (Malafouris 2013, 163).

76 Latour does not use the term "affordances" for the contribution of humans or nonhumans to an actor network. Instead, he speaks of "programs of action" or "propositions" (Latour 1999, 309). A proposition is what "an actor offers to other actors" (309). Also, it should be noted

> An affordance is neither an objective property nor a subjective property; or it is both if you like. An affordance cuts across the dichotomy of subjective objective and helps us to understand its inadequacy. It is equally a fact of the environment and a fact of behavior. It is both physical and psychical, yet neither. An affordance points both ways, to the environment and to the observer.

Not only did this unique and exceptional cooperation between certain stones and hominins change the being, the identity, and the behavior of the hominins; it changed the behavior and identity of the stones as well, which were no longer mere stones, laying about on the ground, but "axes." The ax is not a mere stone, and a hunter wielding an ax is not a mere hominin. The ax and the hunter mutually enable and condition each other. There would be no hunter without the ax and no ax without the hunter. Together they build what could be called an "actor-network," that is, a mutual conditioning of protohuman and nonhuman—and later human and nonhuman—that makes both into something that neither was before. This mutual conditioning, which is where we locate the construction of meaning, Latour calls "technical mediation." What happens in technical mediation?

Latour (1994) describes technical mediation as a process of translating and enrolling actors into programs of action. Latour is careful to point out that the concept of the "technical" has many meanings and that he is using the word in a special sense. "Technical […] designates a very specific type of delegation, of movement, of shifting, that crosses over with entities that have different timing, different properties, different ontologies, and that are made to share the same destiny, thus creating a new actant" (Latour 1994, 44).[77] The word "technical" refers to the fact that human action is always associated and interwoven with nonhumans and their affordances. The agency of nonhumans that the term "affordance" designates is not understood as technological determinism. On the contrary, it is only the network of humans and nonhumans that together as a socio-technical ensemble constitutes the actor. The (pre)human hunter is a mere ape without the stone ax, and the stone ax is merely a stone without the hunter. It is the network that is the actor even when humans and nonhumans play out specific roles within a network What describes these roles and coordinates them can be called a "program of action."[78] As Latour (1992, 233) puts it, "Parts of a program of action may be delegated to a human, or to a nonhuman." Again, the network is the actor. "Action is a property of associated entities" (Latour 1994, 35). With regard to Luhmann's description of systems as dynamic problem-solving entities, it should be noted that for Latour also, technical mediation is a

---

that an affordance is not merely a "constraint," but an *active contribution* to the construction of information.

77 Further, "Technical skill is not uniquely possessed by humans and reluctantly granted to nonhumans. Skills emerge in the zone of transaction, they are properties of the assembly that circulate or are redistributed among human and nonhuman technicians, enabling and authorizing them to act" (Latour 1994, 45).

78 See Callon (1991, 136). Programs of action are usually formulated as narratives. See Belliger and Krieger (2016) for a discussion of the narrative construction of social order.

form of practice, a problem-solving activity. But this is as far as the similarity goes. The actors who are doing the practice are not exclusively humans. And the networks they construct through their activities of translating and enrolling are not closed systems. This becomes apparent when we see what translation and enrollment mean. How are these terms to be understood? What is translating? What does enrolling do? Who or what are actors? And what is a program of action? To answer these questions, we will take a small detour through the development of Latour's thought.

In distinction to Luhmann, whose theoretical concepts are derived from the principles of general systems theory, for Latour, basic concepts arise out of empirical description. Latour's method is ethnological description, namely, the ethnology of scientific work. Latour is considered one of the major contributors to science and technology studies (STS).[79] One of his first important publications was called "Science in Action" (Latour 1987), and another bore the title "Laboratory Life" (Latour and Woolgar 1979). The question guiding research in this area can be traced back to the sociology of knowledge in general and specifically to STS. For these disciplines, scientific knowledge, apart from whatever claims made for it by the philosophy of science and epistemology, is a social construction. Scientists work in social organizations called universities and laboratories. These organizations depend upon many other organizations and practices to exist and to operate. Science in the making is therefore not merely concerned with coding all communications in terms of truth or falsity but also with peer-reviewed publication; government funding and regulation; business applications; trial-and-error manipulation of substances and instruments; forms of documentation, inscription, and modeling; conferences and demonstrations; institutional policy decisions; and so on. Scientific research, therefore, cannot and should not be understood as a closed system coding all communications according to an exclusive binary distinction. Science also cannot be understood from the philosophical perspective as a disembodied, asocial, value-free, and pure knowledge of so-called objective facts.[80] Science is not a disinterested, objective knowledge, but an activity of construction of meaning in which both human and nonhuman actors are involved. It is nothing less than the traditional understanding of science together with its accompanying commitments to a reality divided into subjects and objects, society on the one side and nature on the other, which STS and ANT call into question.

With the self-critical observation and description, which is typical of ethnological fieldwork, Latour meticulously followed the activities of scientists in their day-to-day work in laboratories. He soon discovered that the idea of science as a closed system in Luhmann's sense, a domain which is clearly distinguished from other social areas, did not stand up to scrutiny. What the ethnologist investigating laboratory life and science in the making sees is

---

79 See the Wikipedia article on STS for an overview (https://en.wikipedia.org/wiki/Science_and_technology_studies).
80 See the famous characterization of science by Merton (1973).

visits by a lawyer who has come to deal with patents, a pastor who has come to discuss ethical issues, a technician who has come to repair a new microscope, an elected official who has come to talk about voting on a subsidy, a "business angel" who wants to discuss the launching of a new start-up, an industrialist concerned about perfecting a new fermenting agent, and so on. (Latour 2012, 30)

To assume that all these people do not communicate with each other but only disturb each other, as Luhmann's theory would have us believe, is, no matter how much "structural coupling" we might assume, hardly credible. The scientists themselves insist that all these people and concerns are necessary to the success of the laboratory, and they are not at all interested in drawing boundaries or excluding everything that is supposedly not "science." On the contrary, they actively seek and maintain associations with these and many other different social activities. The functioning of the laboratory depends on communication and close cooperation with many others, for example, educational programs at the university, which are not directly concerned with constructing scientific proofs, but with certifying skills, or with business investors who are concerned with knowledge transfer and innovation. This implies that Luhmann's view of society consisting of autonomous functional systems or domains must be rejected. Society on the ground and in practice resembles an open network much more than an assembly of structurally coupled, operationally and informationally closed systems.

The ethnologist also soon discovers that scientific experimentation itself cannot adequately be described as verification or falsification in the sense that the supposed objects under investigation, for example, bacteria or molecules, are passive objects deterministically reacting to the activities of researchers. Careful observation shows that the objects of inquiry also have something to "say" about the conditions under which they manifest themselves and the roles that they play. The actual work of experimentation is more like a set of challenges in which the objects of study are enabled to act in specific, and often unexpected, ways by going through many "mediators," such as microscopes or measurement devices or various forms of inscription and documentation. The results of an experiment are never merely deterministic and immediately apparent, and no matter how often they are repeated, they could always change. It is precisely the characteristic of "objectivity" that the object does not deterministically do what is expected of it or what it is "told" to do. Experimentation is, therefore, rather like a process of negotiation by which roles are discovered and assigned among human and nonhuman actors, negotiations in which both sides set conditions, show activities, demonstrate appearances of certain kinds, and "mediate" their communication in many different ways. For this reason, Latour suggests that the traditional self-understanding of science as active subjects capable of a pure knowing of passive objects or so-called facts does not do justice to the empirical reality of scientific work.

Far from being a closed system processing only communications that can be either true or false, science in action looks much more like an open network of heterogeneous and hybrid actors pursuing different and often conflicting goals. The laboratory is not defined as scientific by means of excluding everything legal, educational, economic, and so on but by including actors that are scientific *and* legal *and* economic *and* educational *and* religious, and so on. These actors are not merely human but also nonhuman, not only mental or communicative but also material and technical. The network does not operate self-referentially as does a closed system but expands and retracts in all directions at once, depending on changing needs and purposes. In distinction from systems, networks are principally open in all directions and tend, therefore, toward increasing rather than reducing complexity. The methodological rules Latour and his coworkers arrived at to accurately describe such a network were, first of all, to strictly and without presuppositions "follow the actors," whereby it should not be assumed in advance who the actors are. Anything and everything could play a part in establishing the outcome. This meant, secondly, that with regard to agency, "methodological symmetry" was to be preferred.[81] Methodological or "generalized symmetry" means that it cannot be presupposed that only humans act or do something in the process of constructing meaning. What or who actors are is a result of the relations they enter into when constructing a network. Therefore, the activities of building the network must be described in terms that apply to both humans and nonhumans equally, or "symmetrically." Modern philosophy of science and epistemology assumes disinterested knowing subjects confronting a passive and determinate nature. The traditional assumption is that actors are humans operating within a realm of freedom, whereas objects are facts that exist within a realm of necessity. These assumptions, Latour claims, cannot guide an understanding of how science works. Generalized symmetry with regard to agency and the imperative to follow the actors became the cornerstones of what has since come to be called "actor-network theory," or ANT.

The process by which human and nonhuman actors exercise their different forms of agency to negotiate some kind of stable and communicable result, what in science is usually summarized as the "discovery of facts," can be understood as "translation" and "enrollment." To explain what translation and enrollment mean, we return to our prehuman and the stone ax. Stone tools can be dated back to about half a million years before the genus *Homo* arose and almost three million years before *Homo sapiens* appeared. So-called Mode 1 tools come from the "Oldowan Industry," that is, sites found at the Olduvai Gorge in Tanzania.[82] These tools go back to 2.6 million years. They were made by hammering oval-shaped stones found in riverbeds into forms with sharp edges on one end by breaking away flakes, whereas the other end was round and could thus be easily held in the hand. This primitive stone ax, also called the "hand ax," is undoubtedly one of the first and even the longest-used tools in protohuman as well as human history. In many ways, it prefigured later technologies and can be considered a simple model of what it means to use tools or what technology is. When we consider that tool use is often said to be that which distinguishes humans from other animals and thus an important aspect of culture, the question of technology could lead to a deeper understanding of human existence

---

81 "To be symmetric, for us, simply means not to impose a priori some spurious asymmetry among human intentional action and a material world of causal relations" (Latour 2005, 76).
82 See https://en.wikipedia.org/wiki/Stone_tool.

than can be attained by beginning with full-blown linguistically mediated conscious experience as does modern philosophy as well as Luhmann's systems theory.[83]

What distinguishes technology from animal uses of "tools" is that for animals, when they pick up a stone or a stick and use it to break open a coconut or to forage for food, they drop it again and move on. Animal use of tools is characterized as "episodic." The stone ax may also have been left behind from time to time, but there was something else "holding" on to both protohuman and a particular stone that made a difference. Paradoxically, it can be said that the moment a hunter wields a stone ax, quite literally, "things have gotten out of hand."[84] In other words, the stone or the stick is no longer a tool for the moment, that is, only for as long as it is held in hand. Even when we are not holding it, the stone ax stays with us. It does not disappear the moment we are no longer using it. Technological mediation changes everything. We do not return to what we were before we used the stone ax. We remain a "hunter" or a "warrior" even when not holding the stone. The ape drops the stone when its purpose has been achieved. Nothing has changed. Neither the animal nor the stone has become something other than they were before. Stone and animal do not define each other. The purpose of the stone ax, however, is different from any single episode of its use. It is not merely a stone being used for some purpose foreign to it. It is bound up with the hunter or warrior as he/she is with it beyond the moment of episodic use. Something holds on to us when we are no longer using the stone as an ax, and we hold on to the stone, even when no longer holding it in hand. It is when "things get out of hand" that they take on a life of their own and remain with us. What do we hold onto when we put our tools aside? Or instead, what is it that is holding on to us?

In order to answer these questions, it is helpful to recall what Heidegger said about how *dasein* interacts with things. For Heidegger, the primary or original relation of humans to things is that of *practical use* or practical engagement with the world. *Dasein* is not primarily a disinterested observer of objects, but a user of tools. Things first appear not as passive objects, but as tools "ready to hand" and involved in practices or, as Latour would say, programs of action. The hammer, to cite Heidegger's famous example from *Being and Time*—an example that is not too far away from our stone ax—is primarily given in its many practical uses and not as a mere object of disinterested knowing. We do not originally encounter the hammer as a mere thing, a substance with specific attributes, such as shape, weight, color, material consistency, and so on. We encounter the hammer as "ready to hand," or involved in practices and various kinds of use, for example, building, crafting materials, and so on. The hammer is not a mere object, but something that makes us into what we are as "builders" or "carpenters." As a carpenter using a hammer, we are involved with many other things, such as a workbench, nails, a saw, wood, and also a purpose, the "what-for" of the work, that for which we are using

---

[83] It should be noted that with regard to scientific plausibility, Latour's story is much more credible than Parsons's and Luhmann's mythology of the originary encounter of double contingency. See, for example, the material engagement theory of Malafouris (2013), the mirror system hypothesis of Arbib (2012), and Corballis (2003, 2017) on the origins of language.

[84] See Belliger and Krieger (2016, 29).

these tools, such as the table we are building. *Dasein* is primarily engaged in many different practices, all of which arise from "caring" (*Sorge*) about oneself and the world. The hammer is an active participant. It contributes to its "usability." Not just anything can be used as a hammer. Not just any way of using the hammer functions properly. The use that the hammer allows for makes a particular type of work or a certain kind of practice possible. What is primary, what comes first, what stands at the beginning of human engagement with the world and therefore of meaning is not an autonomous rational subject of objective knowledge, but *practice*. This form of existence is a form of "knowing" in its own right. It is that form of knowing that constructs meaning. It is practice that discloses the hammer, the wood, the table, carpentry, the shop, the many things that can be made, the many things that can be done with them, as well as the others who play different roles in making and using things. Practice in this sense is not what modern philosophy calls "action." Practice is not something a human being alone can do. The carpenter is disclosed by the hammer, by the wood, by the table to be built, and by other things in the context of a certain practice. Just as knowing is not the act of an individual with a big brain, cognitive abilities, and linguistic skills, so is practice not the act of an individual, a free agent, or an autonomous subject. Practice as originary construction of meaning is something both humans and nonhumans participate in. As Latour would say, it is a process in which actor-networks are formed. Instead of practice, one could speak of *networking*. What networking does is to construct relations or references. Heidegger speaks of a "referential context" (*Verweisungszusammenhang, Bewandtnisganzheit*). *Dasein* discovers itself and, at the same time, the world primarily not as an autonomous rational subject facing mere things but as an actor in a network, a network in which all things are in many different ways related and involved with each other.

> The work which we primarily encounter when we deal with things and take care of them—what we are at work with—always already lets us encounter the what-for of its usability in the usability which essentially belongs to it. The work that has been ordered exists in its turn only on the basis of its use and the referential context of beings discovered in that use. (Heidegger 1996, 66)

Latour's idea of technical mediation resembles in many ways Heidegger's understanding of the meaning of Being and of *dasein*'s mode of existence as being-in-the-world. In his later work, Heidegger moved away from *dasein* and the humanistic implications embedded in the common understanding of *dasein* as human existence. Not only *dasein* but every being exists as an issue for itself. Not only humans but also language speaks. Indeed, everything has a voice and something to say, that is, a meaning. This is the view proposed by philosophical hermeneutics as opposed to textual hermeneutics. We need not pursue this further other than to note that Latour's notion of actor-networks can be interpreted in a way that is close to Heidegger's ideas about how practically dealing with things discloses a world of meaning.[85] Although Latour never explicitly proposed a theory

---

85 See Krieger and Belliger (2014) for a detailed comparison of philosophical hermeneutics and ANT. Although Heidegger is seldom listed as one of the influences in the development of

of Being or a theory of meaning, Heidegger did. This short reference to Heidegger is intended to support our interpretation of ANT as a theory of meaning and not merely as an empirical method for studying how scientists work or for doing ethnology in one's own backyard. With this in mind, let us return to Latour's notion of technical mediation.

Technical mediation is not "technical" in the usual sense of the word, which describes the workings of a machine or its engineering. Technical mediation describes how meaning is constructed. It is what Luhmann would call the operation of a meaning system, except we are no longer talking about "observation" or systemic order. Network order is the result of what may be called "networking."[86] Networking is what happens when things seem to "get out of hand," and an actor-network comes into being that associates humans and nonhumans in practical activities, such as using a hammer or a stone ax. Meaning is that which is still holding on to us when we drop our tools. When speaking of technical mediation, the word "technical" refers to practical activities with things in the world, whereas the term "mediation" refers to what makes such activities possible. Both are necessary. Both things and activities are needed for there to be meaning. Meaning is not a cognitive act, somehow added on to something and independent of it. Meaning is not signs that stand for things. Things not only "have" meaning, but they "are" meaning.[87] Technical mediation, as we noted, consists of processes of "translation" and "enrollment." In order for any tool to be used as a tool in a certain activity, a series of relations has to be established between the person using the tool and the tool itself, as well as between the tool and what it is supposed to work upon. The stone ax, for example, works upon an animal or a piece of wood. To do this, three elements—the hand, the stone, and the animal, or wood—have to be related to each other in specific ways.[88] Latour (1994, 32) speaks of a "detour" that must be taken by someone who wants to work upon something by means of a tool. In the case of the stone ax, one of our very distant relatives wanted to kill an animal or split a piece of wood. Since they couldn't do this very well with their bare hands, they had to take a detour via the stone ax. Latour calls this detour "translation."

> Translation does not mean a shift from one vocabulary to another, from one French word to one English word, for instance, as if the two languages existed independently. Like Michel Serres, I use translation to mean displacement, drift, invention, mediation, the creation of a link that did not exist before and that to some degree modifies two elements or agents. (Latour 1994, 32)

Latour's work, there are important insights to be gained from the comparison to Heidegger. For Latour's intellectual development, see Wieser (2012).
86 See Belliger and Krieger (2016) for a discussion of networking.
87 This is the idea behind what has come to be known as material semiotics, or material culture. See Law (2019).
88 Floridi (2014) calls this a "first order technology" in which someone uses a tool to work upon something.

Translation is a relation that transforms what it relates. It is not merely a matter of placing two already existing things into a relationship with each other, whereby the relationship is something added on to the things but does not change them. Translation is relating that transforms the related things into something new and unexpected. The hominin, who before had only their bare hands to work with, is now a being that can kill animals or split wood by wielding an ax. The stone is no longer something lying in a riverbed but has become an ax, a weapon held in the hand of a "hunter" or a "warrior." Furthermore, it should be noted that the animal that is killed or the wood that is split also contributes to this activity, because only some animals can become game and only some pieces of wood can be cut, and this only in specific ways. Finally, they can only be killed or split if the stone is worked upon by other stones so that one end is sharpened. The stone must learn that it must be sharp and not blunt. What is essential in this account is that all actors are equally, or "symmetrically," involved in constructing the activity of hunting or chopping. Symmetrical agency means that they have been "enrolled" into an actor-network. Translation has associated or linked them to each other in a way that enrolls them into a network that can do certain things. Actors are translated and enrolled into a program of action, that is; translation and enrollment construct them as actors with specific roles to play. The actor-network constructs what it means to be a hunter or a warrior or a builder. These are programs of action. The hunter has different goals than the warrior or the builder. They hold different things in their hands and wield them differently. The network and the possibilities that it creates did not exist before the work of translation and enrollment. When an ape picks up a stone and uses it to crack open a coconut, he drops it again, eats the coconut, and moves on. He has not become a hunter or anything other than he was before. The stone that is used and dropped has not changed and become something that it was not already. Nothing is there to hold on to the ape or the stone after the episodic use, or at least not enough is there to form an actor-network.[89] When an actor-network appears, however, something remains, something is there to hold on to all actors in the network, even when they move on to do other things. Something has come into being that was not there before. What is this something that has come into being that did not exist before? What is holding on to the actors and transforming them into something new, something that does not disappear the moment the activity ceases?

1.3.2 Information

Let us note at the outset that we are not talking about mental states, cognitive acts, and linguistic or communicative coding since we find ourselves at a point in time several million years before the appearance of *Homo sapiens*. Nonetheless, we are also not denying that some form of cognitive ability is needed. Indeed, it can be argued that activities of

---

[89] The use of tools by animals is well-documented and exhibits extraordinary similarities to human tool use. This seems to imply that we are not dealing with a radical discontinuity, but much rather with a case of emergence in the same way life emerges from matter.

translation and enrollment laid the foundation for the evolutionary advantages for big brains and language. What we are talking about is that actor-networks are the result of the translating and enrolling activities of different kinds of actors, the prehuman and nonhuman. In distinction to Luhmann's theory of meaning, we are talking about nonhuman actors who are involved in the processes of translating and enrolling just as much as the prehuman. This description is quite different from the usual interpretations of tool use. Nevertheless, we are still talking about relations and meaning. The implication is that meaning can no longer exclusively be attributed to human individuals or social systems. Meaning is not reducible to what we know but is the condition for the possibility of knowing. It is because the world is meaningful that we can know it and after millions of years of evolution even come to talk about it, and not the other way round.[90] It is because the world is meaningful, that having big brains and the command of language can prove an evolutionary advantage. We humans do not give meaning to the world; the world allows us to participate in and actively contribute to the meaning that it is. Let there be no misunderstanding. Big brains and language are important. They enable networks to be scaled up almost indefinitely and move quickly through uncountable links. Big brains and language make it possible to integrate many more links and relations into a network than would be possible with more limited cognitive abilities or none at all. Nevertheless, human cognition alone does not account for meaning, nor is it the source of meaning.[91] As the story of the stone ax shows, meaning was there long before *Homo sapiens*. It is, therefore, not *observation* (Luhmann) but *mediation* that constructs meaning. It is not the logical operator of negation but the construction of relations that make meaning. As mentioned above, we could say with Heidegger that not *dasein* alone but every being exists as an issue for itself. This is not because all beings are somehow endowed with intentional consciousness, but because all beings have the capacities of translation and enrollment; that is, all beings are potential mediators. How is this possible? What does mediation mean? What kind of relations does an actor-network consist of?

Let us take a closer look at technical mediation. For the stone to become a stone ax, it must be linked to a hand in the right way. Not every hand can hold or wield a stone. Only certain animals have the anatomical prerequisites for this. Not only the hand must hold the stone properly, but also the arm must wield it in specific ways. How the hand and arm hold and swing the stone are not innate or automatic; they must be learned, and it is the stone that teaches them. The stone *links* hand and arm to specific ways of holding and wielding it. Its size, consistency, shape, and weight suggest, encourage, even demand that hand and arm behave in certain ways and not others. But this is only one side of the link. The stone also *links* itself to individual animals and pieces of wood. Not all animals can be killed, or logs split with the stone. Just as the stone instructs hand and arm, so do certain animals, and certain pieces of wood guide the stone. It must have a certain

---

90 This marks the departure of Latour's theory from modern subjectivism in the line from Descartes and Kant to Husserl.
91 This is Latour's answer to the problem of correlationalism and modern subjectivism. It allows for an interpretation of ANT as a nondualistic posthumanism. See Krieger and Belliger (2014).

sharpness, an edge that can cut. This leads to the stone being worked upon by other stones so that a pointed end becomes a cutting edge. For a stone ax to appear, all actors in the network participate in their own ways and do things. Agency is not an attribute of a single entity but can be said to be "distributed."[92] Not only is agency distributed; it is distributed symmetrically; that is, there is no qualitative difference between the agency of the hominin and the agency of the stone, or animals, or wood. All do the same thing.[93] What the various actors in a network do is construct links, relations, or interfaces. These links connect certain stones not only to certain hands and certain animals and pieces of wood but also to all other stones, hands, animals, and wood that do not participate in constructing the actor-network of the stone ax. Knowing which is the right stone and the right way to hold and wield it means knowing which stones are not suitable and how not to hold and wield the ones that are. Following Floridi (2014, 35), these links or relations can be called "interfaces" because they face primarily in two directions. They are two sided because they are relations that "translate" in two directions, the direction of stone to hand, hand to stone, and then of stone to wood and wood to stone. What constitutes or constructs the actor-network is, therefore, a set of links or interfaces. It is important to note that it is not any of the things in themselves, the stone, the wood, or the hand, that is important. It is the relations or interfaces that create something that did not exist before. These relations are at once the result of the activities of all actors in the network as well as that which constitutes them as actors. Once relations appear, it is the relations that "hold" on to all the actors that are constituted by them and bind the actors together so that they remain what they have become, even after the stone ax is no longer being used and hands are busy doing other things.

Constructing links, interfaces, or relations to create an actor-network is quite different than what systems do when they construct elements as specific functions. The systemic organization of a table, for example, constructs certain things to be legs and a top. Tabletops and table legs are not things that lie about in the environment waiting to be stumbled over and then put together. They are constructed by the system to fulfill specific purposes or functions. The tabletop is not a thing; it is a function. This is why almost anything, whether stone, wood, glass, plastic, metal, and so on, can become a tabletop, that is, if it functions in the right way. The same can be said for the organs of an animal. They are functional entities constructed by the organizing principles of the

---

92 For a recent discussion of "distributed agency," see Enfield and Kockelman (2017). Summing up research that has come to be called the "new materialism," Iovino and Oppermann (2014, 3) write: "Agency assumes many forms, all of which are characterized by an important feature: they are material, and the meanings they produce influence in various ways the existence of both human and non-human natures. Agency, therefore, is not to be necessarily and exclusively associated with human beings and with human intentionality, but is a pervasive and inbuilt property of matter, as part and parcel of its generative dynamism." Instead of agency or action, we follow Gibson (1979) and speak of "affordances," but we interpret these to be operations of "translating" and "enrolling" of actors into networks, which, in turn, we define as information construction.

93 We return to these two fundamental characteristics of agency—distribution and symmetry—below when discussing how moral agency in digital ethics is to be defined.

biological system. Lungs, kidneys, and hearts don't lie around in the environment until an organism stumbles upon them and integrates them into itself. They are constructed by the organism whose organizing principle, DNA, requires certain functions to be fulfilled. Although the stone ax and the hunter are similar in that they also are not merely present in the environment but are constructed by the actor-network, the network is not a system. The actor-network that is the hunter with a stone ax is not a whole that is somehow greater than the sum of its parts. The actors in a network are not "parts" integrated into a whole. Although they work together to achieve specific goals, they remain independent. They can, at any time, do other things, suggest other relations, expand the network in unexpected ways, or even subvert the network and transform it into something completely different. Stone axes have been found that appear not to have been used for hunting or fighting at all, but for rituals, prestige, social status, or even advantages in finding a mate.[94] In the terminology of ANT, every actor in an actor-network is a "mediator," that is, capable of independent activities of translation and enrollment, and not merely an "intermediary," that is, a functioning part subsumed under the organizing principle of the whole.[95]

Just as the scientist in the laboratory that Latour studied links up to lawyers, politicians, businesspeople, and students in order to make the laboratory function properly, all actors in a network can enter into unexpected and "heterogeneous" relations. This implies that the relations that construct networks are not the same thing as the operations of selection, relationing, and steering that organize the operations of a system. In Luhmann's theory of meaning systems, cognitive and communicative operations introduce differences or distinctions. The logic of differences that Luhmann finds at the foundation of meaning is a process of inclusion and exclusion. This leads, as we have seen above, to organizing meaning in the form of a closed system, since the operations of the system cannot be directed toward continuing its own operations (autopoiesis) unless the system can distinguish itself from the environment. The system is constituted by constructing its own elements internally and excluding everything else into the environment. In a closed system, the "agency" of the elements is completely subsumed under or reduced to the functions they fulfill in the operations of the system. The lungs or the stomach of an animal, for example, cannot suddenly start doing things other than that for which they were constructed, that is, as long as the animal continues to live. The construction of links that create an actor-network, on the contrary, lead to open networks, in which relations are constantly being renegotiated by all actors.

Network relations cannot be reduced to the operations of the whole. The whole, that is, the identity or trajectory or program of action of the network, can at any time change on the basis of the mediating activities of the actors involved in it or by taking up

---

94 See Kohn and Mithen (1999).
95 See Latour's principle of "irreduction," which says that no being can be reduced to another or reduce others to itself. This form of reduction is precisely what systems do when they reduce environmental complexity by selecting, relating, and steering system operations. Of course, networks can be constructed as functional systems, but such black boxes can always be opened up and the network reconfigured.

new actors. The assumption that the whole is greater than the sum of the parts may be helpful for understanding biological forms of order but does not help us understand what is going on in society and on the level of meaning. In the realm of society and meaning, it is the actors who construct the network and not the system that constructs the actors.[96] In networks, the sum of the parts is always more than the whole and not less, since every actor potentially can expend the network in unexpected ways. The "powers" of the stone ax to ensure victories over enemies, food from the hunt, or advantages in woodworking could also build links to gods, demonstrate social prominence and "political" power, or identify warriors, craftsmen, hunters, and farmers each with its own special knowledge and well-protected secrets. For this reason, networks, in distinction to systems, can serve multiple goals at once, flexibly change goals, and indefinitely expand or scale down depending on the networking activities of the actors involved.

Constructing the links that make up an actor-network is not easy and not done quickly. The stone ax did not come into being overnight. On the contrary, we can imagine a process of uncountable trials and errors, of losing the connections and finding them again, that went on over hundreds of thousands, if not millions, of years. Gradually and little by little, however, the links became stronger, the relations were stabilized—which can primarily be attributed to the stability and durability of stones and wood—and they were repeated, learned, and passed on to others until there arouse a no longer bridgeable gap between the hunter with his stone ax and the ape who also used stones in episodic ways. In retrospect, this gap can be described as the emergence of a new order of being. Luhmann speaks of the emergence of meaning systems in the form of human consciousness and society. From the network perspective, we may also speak of the emergence of meaning, but not in the usual sense of the emergence of human cognition and linguistic communication. Meaning is not a form of being exclusively reserved for human actors and their social relations. Instead, the world of meaning emerges long before *Homo sapiens*, big brains, language, and what we call society. Meaning emerges as a network of relations created by the practical activities of both (pre)human and nonhuman actors. We propose defining these relations, the links that, as Heidegger would say, "gather things together" as *information*. Information is not a thing. It is not a mental state or the result of a cognitive act. Information is not, as Luhmann proposes, "observation," that is, binary distinctions founded upon negation, as Luhmann's logic of difference would have us believe. Furthermore, information is not what is talked about in communication. And finally, as we will see in Chapter 2 when discussing Floridi's philosophy and ethics of information, it is not an operation that applies syntactic rules to data.

Information is a form of being *sui generis*. It consists of relations and nothing else. On this level of being, there are only relations, and what exists does so *because* it is related by means of the mediating activities of both (pre)human and nonhuman actors, who

---

96 We are not proposing a new form of liberalism in which society is seen as the result of the activities of individuals by means of an "invisible hand," since not only human individuals are involved in the process but nonhumans as well and because the transformative effect of networking cannot support any kind of "egoism."

themselves can only perform such activities because they are taken up by relations. This is what "emergence" means. Phenomena appear that cannot be derived from anything other than themselves. Information can only come from information, just as for Luhmann, communication can only come from communication. Certain stones relate themselves to certain hands and to certain animals and wood but not to others, and it is *because* of these relating activities of translating and enrolling that Latour calls "technical mediation" that there are a stone ax and a hunter and not merely an ape that uses a stone episodically. Let us note that information as we define it is not a special kind of thing. Information is not a substance with attributes. *Information is a process;* one could say, *the process of networking.* We cannot hold information in our hands or even on a page of paper or in a database. We do not *have* information; we *do* it, or rather, it does something with us, and it is through information that we become what we are. We could also say, with Floridi, that we *are* information, but it must be noted that the meaning of "being" in this phrase, what it means when we "are" something, depends on what information is and not on traditional ontologies of substance. Information is not a new name for substance. Information must not be interpreted on the basis of Western metaphysics. It is as information, or more correctly, the ongoing construction of information, that humans, together with nonhumans, come to be what they are and do what they do. Information emerges not as mental states or linguistic acts, but as actor-networks. It is at once material and "mental," at once human and nonhuman, at once given and constructed. Indeed, all of these usual distinctions are not helpful and probably even misleading when it comes to defining information. This situation is not new.

The ontological status of information is notoriously uncertain. Wiener's (1948) famous definition that information is information and not matter or energy says more about what information is not than about what it is. Floridi (2014, 35) describes information as a kind of interface between the organism and the world.[97] When it comes to defining the concept of information, we suggest using Latour's principle of "irreduction." The principle of irreduction says that "nothing is, by itself, either reducible or irreducible to anything else" (Latour 1993a, 158). In other words, being is relational. Whatever is, it exists because it is a mediating mediator. What technical mediation does is to construct information. But not as something that comes after or as a kind of product of an activity. Instead, information emerges as the mode of being *sui generis*, which transforms the actors constructing it, elevating them, as it were, onto a new level of order that integrates all levels of order below itself, that is, the physical and biological levels. Perhaps we must face up to the fact that hardly any of the traditional concepts we use to define information adequately describe what information is. Information is what we are.[98] We, as

---

[97] We will discuss Floridi's philosophy of information below.
[98] Floridi (2014) speaks of humans as "inforgs" instead of cyborgs. Inforgs are beings that exist as information in a world that is also information, an "infosphere." Floridi's concept of information, however, is different from what we are here proposing. We are equating information with meaning. It is only very much later in the history of information when under certain circumstances it becomes useful to distinguish information from meaning, for example, when studying animal communication or developing a mathematical theory of information.

well as everything else in the world, are information and nothing else. Where Luhmann proclaims, "There are systems," Latour declares, "There are networks." Both of these contemporary theories talk about meaning and information but in entirely different ways. It makes a difference if information is produced by the autopoietic operations of an operationally and informationally closed system or by processes of networking.

It is not only the traditional and omnipresent distinction between subject and object, the mental and the material that ANT invites us to leave behind but also the accompanying distinction between society and nature. At least since Aristotle, things were classified as either self-made or made by human hand. Natural entities, such as stones or also animals, were self-made, whereas tools and whatever could be constructed with them were made by human hand; this was *techné*. Technological artifacts, which comes from the Greek *techné*, are products of *poiesis*, of making by another. *Poiesis* was distinguished from knowledge or what Aristotle called theory. In recent times the "question concerning technology" has moved to center stage. It has become apparent to everyone and has also become an issue of concern as well as puzzlement that human life in all aspects is now mediated by technology. Ever since Marx, opinions on the meaning and influence of technology have swung between technological determinist or social determinist positions. We need not review this discussion here.[99] The advent of digital information and communication technologies (ICTs) has put the entire debate on a new basis, since, as Floridi (2014) has pointed out when speaking of a "fourth revolution," technologies such as artificial intelligence have made it apparent that machines are not mere tools, but social partners rivaling human actors in cognitive abilities and the construction of social order. From the point of view offered by ANT, technologies were never mere tools, but actor-networks encompassing both the material and the cognitive. Indeed, the stone ax wielded by a hominin three million years ago cannot be understood in terms of free individuals using tools for good or evil in a domain of culture over against a determinate natural world of facts. These are distinctions that have their proper home in modern Western industrial society and cannot be applied to the origins of meaning.

The common distinction between culture or society, on the one side, and nature, on the other, is based on Descartes's distinction between *res cogitans* and *res extensa*, that is, thinking beings who were free and immaterial, on the one side, and natural beings that exist under the rule of determinate causality, on the other. This distinction grounded the distinction between the natural sciences and the social sciences. Sociology, as it was conceived at the end of the nineteenth century, was, therefore, a science concerned with free subjects who enter into relations with one another to build a world of culture, a world that does not obey the determinate laws of nature, but its own specific cultural laws. These were the laws that Durkheim, for example, claimed to be discoverable by the science of sociology. Whatever laws society might obey, they are what the social sciences, in the wake of Hegel, Marx, and Spencer, have been looking for ever since. The story of the stone ax and the idea of the actor-network allows us to leave aside this whole

---

99 For an overview, see the corresponding Wikipedia articles: https://en.wikipedia.org/wiki/Technological_determinism and https://en.wikipedia.org/wiki/Social_determinism.

set of assumptions and conceptual distinctions and go directly to a different conception of society and sociology. Even for Luhmann, the realm of nature, and also technology or artifacts of all kinds, are not part of the social system. Luhmann was careful to maintain the fundamental distinction between society and nature, or even society and technology. To be sure, for Luhmann, all these things are part of the social system, but only insofar as they are the subject matter of communication. For Latour, however, meaning is constructed not by communication, but by networking or, as he calls it, technical mediation. Furthermore, meaning is not in any sense of the word a realm somehow distinct from matter or from things. Actor-networks consist of both (pre)humans and nonhumans. They are always already "social," because they are constructed by relations, that is, "associations" among "actors." They are always already natural, because meaning is being and being is relational. There is no nature "out there" conceived of as a realm of objective facts governed by determinate causality and ontologically distinct from society as a realm of freedom, subjective opinions, cultural artifacts, and historically changing institutions.

From the actor-network perspective, there is no distinction between nature and culture, even if typically modern networks use this distinction. Actor-networks are always at once natural and cultural. The stone is part of the actor-network that constructs hunters with stone axes, and there would be no hunters or builders if stones were not involved. To mark the fundamental difference between the actor-network view and traditional sociology, Latour speaks of "associology," that is, a theory of the *associations* of humans and nonhumans that make up the world of meaning. As Latour (2005, 5, 9) puts it:

> Even though most social scientists would prefer to call "social" a homogeneous thing, it's perfectly acceptable to designate by the same word a trail of associations between heterogeneous elements. Since in both cases the word retains the same origin—from the Latin root socius—it is possible to remain faithful to the original intuitions of the social sciences by redefining sociology not as the "science of the social," but as the tracing of associations. In this meaning of the adjective, social does not designate a thing among other things, like a black sheep among other white sheep, but a type of connection between things that are not themselves social.

This implies that the science of sociology cannot define itself in opposition to the natural sciences, nor can the natural sciences continue to assume they are discovering objective facts of nature independent of all social concerns. It can be said that ANT extends and completes the universalization program of sociology that began with Durkheim and was continued by Luhmann but at the cost of acknowledging that sociology is no longer a science of society in distinction from nature or that such ontological domains even exist. Things, artifacts, and nature are no longer excluded from the realm of the "social" understood as everything networked and thus constituted by information. Nevertheless, the distinction between thinking and being with which Descartes laid the foundation of modern Western thought continues until this day to cause problems of all kinds. Within the parameters of theorizing set by these and other related distinctions, it is almost impossible to find a way out. Latour suggests in a provocative and radical statement that we should acknowledge that "we have never been modern" and leave the conundrums of modern philosophy behind us as we move into a networked future. What does a networked future hold in store for ethics and morality?

From ANT, we have learned that understanding all beings as informational in the sense of mediating mediators distributes agency and, therefore, moral responsibility among both humans and nonhumans instead of restricting agency and ethical concerns to autonomous rational subjects.[100] Luhmann, we recall, located the origins of morality not only in the adoption of an attitude of refusing to learn but, more importantly, in granting "respect" to the other as a potential partner in society. The act of social inclusion is the primary moral act since it is on this basis alone that conditions of praise and blame can be communicated as norms. For ANT, social inclusion is an issue of a very different kind than it is for traditional sociology or even for Luhmann. For ANT, everything is potentially included, both human and nonhuman, since everything can become a mediator and participate in networking. The informational, that is, relational nature of being makes the moral domain fundamentally inclusive. The meaning of ethical obligation is reconceived in ANT as an obligation to become that which an entity can be, much as if Aristotele's virtues were to be located in the potential of all beings to mediate and construct information. The fundamental difference to classical virtues as character traits of human beings is that for ANT, becoming virtuous is only accomplished through others, that is, by accepting and participating in the translating and enrolling activities of others as well as one's own.[101]

The hominin could never have become a hunter or a warrior, not even a "bad" one if he/she did not listen to what the stone had to say about becoming an ax. The relational ontology of ANT replaces traditional substance ontology with a notion of being as process, that is, a multitude of cooperative processes of translating and enrolling. Networks are not things, even ordered compositions of things; they are processes of networking. The network is the actor *in action*. Only the network can be virtuous since the actor is a construct of the network and exists only in processes of networking. No actor alone can be considered a moral agent, an addressee of moral imperatives, or be held accountable for moral transgression.[102] For Latour (2012, 455), this amounts to never-ending

---

100 ANT implies not only distributed agency but also distributed morality. Floridi (2013, 135) distinguishes between accountability and responsibility in order to allow moral attributes to be ascribed to nonhuman autonomous intelligent agents, that is, AIs, who are, according to Floridi, accountable but not responsible. We will discuss below why we find this option inadequate.

101 This marks a fundamental difference between our approach and that of Vallor (2016), who attempts to base an ethics for the digital age on "technomoral virtues." Vallor assumes a "basic moral psychology" (10) of the human species that fundamentally does not change and upon which classical virtues can be grounded. For ANT, it is the network that is the actor and any virtues that networks may be said to have are subject to the inherent flexibility and opacity of networks.

102 We will argue below that technical mediation, this is, networking, is a kind of agency that is best described by the concept of "design," which, as we will claim, could and should replace traditional ideas of moral agency dependent as they are upon free will, intentionality, and an ontological individualism.

"scruples" about the "good," "fair," or "optimal" distribution of means and ends. The actor is the network, and the moral quality of the network is related to the ongoing "responding" activities of all actors to each other. As we shall argue in Chapter 3, when discussing governance by design, networking is what the concept of "design" has come to mean. For a theory of governance as design, there is nothing that cannot be designed or redesigned in a "better" way. The stone ax can always be improved upon, and even a prehuman hominin can still become a better hunter or builder. What is good or bad is not merely the intentions or the actions of the hunter or builder, since intentions are programs of action constructed by all actors in the network and never by any single actor alone. What is good or bad is also not a matter of the consequences of actions, for these can never be calculated with any finality but only judged at certain times with regard to specific goals. Such relative assessments of good or bad consequences lead not to moral judgments, but issues of redesigning and improving. Moral judgments, to the extent that they are still possible, address the networking, which is the action of all participating actors, both human and nonhuman. The stone is not a mere object, while the hunter is the actor. The stone is not merely a means to an end, whereas the hunter alone chooses purposes and goals. One could argue that the ape is a perfect Kantian since, for it, the stone is only a means that has nothing to say on its own. The ape does not listen to what the stone can tell it about becoming an ax. For the ape, the stone is s "mere" tool, which can be used for good or evil, for whatever ends the ape chooses. For traditional ethics based on Kant, the stone is only a means and not an end. As Latour puts it, in the hand of an ape and, it could be added, in the hands of most moralists today, the stone has been made into an intermediary and is not respected as a mediator.

This situation changes the moment the stone is recognized and responded to as an actor that can teach the hominin something new. One could imagine, recalling Luhmann, that the hominin and the stone enter into a situation of double contingency. As soon as the stone is responded to as a participant in the construction of information, an actor-network can appear that creates a hunter or a builder. When it comes to information, there is no distinction between fact and value, just as there is no distinction between subject and object. Nonhumans are by their very being as mediators already values in themselves and subjects of agency. What does this mean for ethics? Although Latour did not propose an ethics of networks, it can be said that *moral responsibility is an issue concerning good or bad networking and not an attempt to justify acts against norms that are derived from something other than the activities themselves.* Furthermore, there is no one way in which networks can be better or worse. There are, therefore, no universal principles of right or wrong. Moral norms cannot be formulated in abstraction from concrete activities of networking. We will return to the implications of ANT for ethics when we argue for a theory of moral action as design in Chapter 3.

In conclusion, we recall that for Luhmann, morality under the conditions of modern functional differentiation of society has become obsolete and dysfunctional. This for at least two reasons. First, the fundamental moral issue is social inclusion or respect through which an entity enters into the social system. The articulation of the conditions under which respect is supposed to be granted or withdrawn, which takes the form of universal moral norms and is assumed to apply to society as a whole, has become afunctional, because society as a whole has no function, and thus also dysfunctional, because any attempt to normatively steer society as a whole runs up against the autonomous subsystems with their own cognitively oriented steering mechanisms, and therefore, morality should be avoided. Luhmann's diagnosis of the dysfunctional character of morality is based on an understanding of society as an autopoietic and operationally and informationally closed system. ANT, as we have seen, offers an alternative to general systems theory by proposing a theory of network order according to which networks are not closed, functional entities, but open, flexible, scalable forms of order that can be defined as information. This takes up, extends, and grounds Luhmann's notion of society as a system of meaning but interprets communication as processes of information construction by means of what we have called networking. What Luhmann describes as autopoietic and informationally and operationally closed systems can usefully refer to certain forms of functional networks within society or what ANT refers to as "black boxes." General systems theory, however, does not provide an adequate description of society as a whole and the construction of meaning that results in actor-networks. If society is not a closed system, could it be an open network? We are allowed to reopen the question of ethics and morality from the point of view of network order, an order in which morality is based on a completely different way of understanding social inclusion and social regulation.

The above discussion of systems theory and ANT may seem, at first glance, far away from the topic of digital ethics. We set out to hack digital ethics but have spent much time and effort discussing matters that seem entirely different. This detour, however, is necessary, because it provides us with the tools needed to hack into the current discourse of digital ethics and reveal its vulnerabilities, the bad code and sloppy programming that underlies and guides much of what calls itself digital ethics today. Systems theory and ANT have provided us with arguments, concepts, definitions, and questions that we can use to breach the legacy system upon which digital ethics is currently running. Let the hack begin!

Chapter Two

THE BREACH

2.1 The Philosophical Mythology of Humanism

2.1.1 The Philosophy of Information and Information Ethics

The network theory of order that ANT proposes opens new possibilities for understanding what ethics and morality can mean in today's world. The shift of perspective that we have been documenting began with the sociological interpretation of ethics that Durkheim, Luhmann, and Latour developed. These developments potentially place ethical discourse on a fundamentally different terrain than traditional philosophical anthropology with its assumptions of free will and fundamental distinctions between is and ought and subject and object. Furthermore, these developments raise the question of what kind of discourse is the proper home of ethics since neither traditional philosophy nor the social sciences have made it into the twenty-first century unscathed. Ethical discourse at the beginning of the twenty-first century finds itself on a terrain that could be called "posthuman," since the focus has been shifted away from human nature as an immediately knowable given from which ethical obligations and norms can be derived. Neither the bounded, unitary human individual nor a bounded, unitary social whole seems to still be credible. After Luhmann and Latour, ethics can no longer argue that because human nature is so, this or that ethical norm must be respected. Nevertheless, despite the theoretical advances that the past decades have witnessed, humanist individualism is still the usual form of moral discourse, for example, in discussions of human rights and the moral obligations derived from them. In a posthuman age, however, not only does human nature no longer offer a universal foundation for ethics—who knows what human beings are and what freedom and rationality mean—but also morality must be reconceived to include the agency of nonhumans.

The subject of moral discourse in the twenty-first century is no longer the autonomous rational individual, but complex socio-technical networks. For Luhmann, agency is the operation of an autopoietic and operationally and informationally closed system and not a matter concerning the free will of autonomous individuals. For ANT, the network is the actor, and the network is always made up of heterogeneous, hybrid actors, both human and nonhuman, physical, biological, and technical.[1] The theory of social systems, as well as actor-network theory (ANT), relativizes the human and ground ethical

---

1 To say the network is at once the actor and made up of actors points to the fractal nature of networks. Every actor within a network is itself a network.

discourse no longer on assumptions about human nature, rationality, and free will, but on concepts such as meaning, communication, and information. The shift toward new basic concepts for understanding society, reality, human existence, and also ethics is, of course, not limited to systems theory and ANT.[2] Although we consider these two theoretical programs to be the most ambitious and influential with regard to understanding the current state of ethical discourse, there are other important attempts to deal with the new horizons emerging from the advent of a global network society. One of these deserves special attention because it can be taken as the foundation of contemporary digital ethics. It not only acknowledges the novelty of the present situation but also epitomizes the legacy system upon which the discourse of digital ethics currently runs. This is the system we will hack into and which constitutes the target of our breach. It goes under the name of "information ethics."[3]

Among those who take the digital transformation and the advent of a global network society seriously is Oxford philosopher Luciano Floridi. Inspired by the "information revolution," Floridi (2011, 2013)[4] has devoted many groundbreaking studies to reformulating basic questions of being and ethics in terms of information. His program of a new foundational "philosophy of information" equals in scope and ambition to the theories of Luhmann and Latour. Floridi's philosophy of information proposes to "explain and guide the purposeful construction of our intellectual environment and provide the systematic treatment of the conceptual foundations of contemporary society" (2011, 25) and thus to represent "the *information turn*" in philosophy (emphasis in original). Floridi begins by emphasizing the unprecedented impact of digital technologies on society and human action. The invention and deployment of the computer as omnipresent and decisive technology of knowledge and communication has changed everything and is ushering in a new form of social order as well as a new understanding of human existence. This situation demands a new philosophical foundation that Floridi finds in the concept of "information." Floridi proposes to place the idea of information at the center of our understanding of reality, society, and human existence and also at the foundation of our ethical obligations.

> Today, philosophy faces the challenge of providing a foundational treatment of the phenomena and the ideas underlying the information revolution, in order to foster our understanding and

---

2 Neither Luhmann nor Latour, of course, are thinking in a vacuum. We focus on these thinkers because they can be said to exemplify contemporary responses to the theoretical exigencies of our historical situation.
3 See Froehlich (2004) for an early overview of information ethics. Floridi has become one of the leading proponents of information ethics. See Floridi (1999, 2013) for a critique of traditional ethical theories and a plaidoyer for a new metaethical, or "macroethical," theory based on the informational order of being.
4 It should be noted that the concept of "revolution" is typically modern and it may seem contradictory to employ a modern idea to explain the end of modernity. For modernity, revolution was a term associated with critique and emancipation, with the establishment of humanism and enlightenment. When speaking of an information revolution or a digital revolution, we do not wish to invoke these modern connotations.

guide both the responsible construction of our society and the sustainable management of our natural and synthetic environments. In short, we need to develop a *philosophy of information*. (Floridi 2013, xii; emphasis in original)

He goes on to say,

Information is something as fundamental and significant as knowledge, being, validity, truth, meaning, mind, or good and evil, and so equally worthy of autonomous, philosophical investigation. (ibid.)

It is undoubtedly correct to emphasize the revolutionary significance of information and communication technologies (ICTs) as well as the central role of the concept of information for understanding today's world. It is also correct to attempt to base ethics on the new realities of the global network society. We have seen that for both Luhmann and Latour, information has become a foundational concept pushing traditional conceptions of both the human individual and society out of the theoretical spotlight in the social sciences as well as philosophy. Within the theoretical framework that has emerged at the beginning of the twenty-first century, information appears as a foundational concept for theory construction regardless of the ontological domain, whether the focus is on knowledge, being, society, or ethics and morality. As Floridi points out, a decisive influence on this new philosophy of information is not only the development of ICTs but also "the ethical impact of Information and Communication Technologies (ICTs) on human life and society" (ibid.).

It should be noted that in Floridi's view, the information revolution did not begin millions of years ago and has been growing ever since, milestones of which have been the appearance of *Homo sapiens*, language, writing, complex societies, and so on but can be dated from the invention of the computer.[5] Although the advent of ICTs has undoubtedly raised information to a central category in describing what goes on in the world, digital information is not the only kind of information or even the best example of what information is. Digital information is a highly sophisticated form of information, embedded in extensive and complex socio-technical networks, depending on highly advanced and differentiated practices by many different actors. Digital information is the result of a very long history of socio-technical networking and mediation. It is therefore questionable when Floridi takes over much of the terminology and many of the assumptions found in computer science and informatics when defining what information is. We will

---

5   Floridi (2013) corrects this statement by supposing that information societies go back at least to the Bronze Age, that is, "the era that marks the invention of writing" (3) since information is historical and therefore must in some way be inscribed and transmitted. Recording and transmitting technologies may be considered as ICTs just as computers. Why then does the computer mark a decisive historical moment? Floridi goes on to speak of a "hyperhistorical era" in which "ICTs and their data *processing* capabilities are the necessary condition for the maintenance and any further development of societal welfare, personal well-being, as well as intellectual flourishing" (2012, 130; emphasis in original). This is the computer age. How people before the fourth millennium lived without information is an open question.

argue that Floridi's choice of digital information technologies as the point of departure for a theory of information, as well as an ethics of information, leads to an inadequate account of information, human existence, and society. One cannot escape the impression that all the right questions are being asked, but all the wrong answers are being given. After rightly pointing out that the digital transformation calls for new thinking on almost all crucial issues including ethics, Floridi seems unable to free himself, as we shall see, from a devotion to the philosophical mythology of humanism. ICTs, we must maintain, are not the key to understanding information; information is the key to understanding the digital revolution. Information is not to be understood from the perspective of the human, but instead, the human must be understood on the basis of information. This is what our hack will attempt to show. Let us begin our hack of the philosophy and ethics of information by looking more closely at Floridi's understanding of information.

2.1.2 *What Is Information?*

Floridi (2015)[6] begins with the so-called general definition of information (GDI), which arose within computer science and informatics circles. The GDI defines information as data plus meaning. Because meaning is involved, the GDI may be said to be concerned with "semantic" information, semantics being that branch of the science of language which accounts for the meaning of words. According to the GDI, information consists of data that is "well-formed" by some kind of syntactic rules. This is what makes the data meaningful. Luhmann defines meaning in terms of the guiding difference of "medium" and "form." For Luhmann, meaning arises when "loosely coupled" words (medium) are syntactically combined or "strictly coupled" to form meaningful sentences. Making sentences, or communicating, is the specific operation of the social system. Similarly, for Floridi, "data are the stuff of which information is made." This suggests a similar distinction to Luhmann in terms of matter and form. When data are "stuff," they are like formless matter that is well-formed by syntactical rules to become information. Well-formed, according to Floridi (2015), means "clustering together correctly, according to the rules (syntax) that govern the chosen system." The similarity to Luhmann's notion of form as "strict coupling" as opposed to the medium, which is "loose coupling," is apparent. Also, like Luhmann, for whom "form" is a "difference," Floridi defines information as "differences" or "a lack of uniformity within some context." An example is a black mark on white paper. The paper is the context, and the black mark is the break in the uniform whiteness of the paper. Information, it should be noted, is the perceived break and neither the mark nor the paper nor both together as simply coexisting. Just as Luhmann, Floridi defines difference as negation, that is, as a "lack" of uniformity. A lack is not something positive in itself. The whiteness of the paper is positive. The black mark is positive. But it is only when the black mark becomes a *lack of uniformity* on the white paper that there is a difference, that is, information. Otherwise, we wouldn't see anything

---

6 For a more detailed discussion, see Floridi (2011).

at all. In short, we don't know things, we know differences; we don't know data, we know information.

Although Floridi would deny the subjectivist implications of the GDI, the idea that information begins with something "given" that is not meaningful in itself but is somehow made meaningful by the activities of a cognitive agent is basically a Kantian epistemological approach. This is supported by a special method that Floridi proposes for the philosophy of information, which he calls "levels of abstraction" (LoA), or also "constructionism," as opposed to constructivism. Information is always a construction of meaning by an agent from a particular perspective, question, interface, purpose, frame, filter, aspect, and so on. All information is mediated through what Floridi calls a "level of abstraction." "Through an LoA, an information agent (the observer) accesses a physical or conceptual environment, the system. LoAs are, therefore, interfaces that mediate the epistemic relation between the observed and the observer" (Floridi 2011, 76). Floridi admits, "The method is Kantian in nature" and accordingly "is a transcendental approach, which considers the conditions of possibility of the analysis (experience) of a particular system." But he insists that this view "does not inherit from Kant any mental or subject-based feature" (60). To escape a subject-oriented epistemological approach to defining information, Floridi shifts ground to ontology.

Information for Floridi, as for Latour on our reading of ANT, is a form of being *sui generis*. Floridi proposes, therefore, an "information ontology" (2011, 339) according to which "the ultimate nature of reality is informational" (340). Information is that form of being that characterizes our world. Human beings are no exception. Human beings are "inforgs," that is, informational beings, and the world in which these beings exist is the "infosphere," that is, a world made up of information. What exists, the world and everything in it, is "cohering clusters of data," that is, "mind-independent, concrete, relational points of lack of uniformity" (340).[7] The shift to ontology occurs when Floridi insists that these cohering clusters of data that constitute the world are no longer to be understood in terms of the GDI. They are not mere data awaiting the well-forming activity of a knowing subject. They are "informational objects" or "informational entities" or, as Floridi also says, "structural objects."

> Structural objects work epistemologically like constraining affordances. they allow or invite certain epistemic constructs (they are affordances for inforgs like us, who elaborate them) and resist or impede some others (they are constraints for the inforgs), depending on the interaction with, and the nature of, the informational organisms that process them. (Floridi 2011, 340)

This account of how affordances are active in entities as a quality of their being and how these affordances, together with the cognitive abilities of certain organisms, create information leave the GDI behind. Information is no longer data + meaning since what is given is no longer "raw" data, but something that is already "clustered" or "structured."

---

7 Floridi seems unable to escape Kantian idealism regardless of his many disclaimers.

It is on the basis of the structural unity of the given that it is able to "constrain," that is, act upon the knowing subject, or have what Floridi calls "affordances." This account seems to fit quite well with what we described in Chapter 1 as "technical mediation." In Latour's terms, one could just as well say that all entities are endowed with abilities of translation and enrollment—based on the ontological principle of irreduction—which allows them to construct actor networks. In Floridi's terms, the stone is a structural object, that is, an informational entity that allows or invites certain epistemic constructs such as the ax, thus creating a hunter or a warrior. Despite these apparent similarities, it is unclear in Floridi's account how data can already "cohere," that is, how data are structured, related, and ordered and therefore qualify as information, but can still be considered as "given" and thus "mind-independent." Of course, a scientist could *infer* from the stone ax that the stone, in itself and independently of any network relations it may have, has certain *properties* such as weight, size, consistency, and so on that "constrain" or "afford" in such a way that it could become an ax. But these properties are the result of the scientist applying a certain level of abstraction. An archeologist would find properties in the stone that afford its place in certain rituals or social practices. The hunter himself would find still others that are different from the warrior or the builder or the museum curator, the antiquities dealer, the philosopher, and so on. All of these affordances and potentially infinitely more are what the stone *is*. The informational being of the stone is, therefore, principally unbounded and structured only by the networks in which it is involved. As soon as information constitutes the being of an entity, the entity is no longer a bounded individual, but a principally unbounded network. It can no longer be said to possess a "structure." Instead, one would have to say that it possesses the ability of "structuring" or that which we have called networking. We will return to this later.

Floridi's informational ontology, or as he also calls it "informational structural realism" (2011), claims that it is possible and reasonable to assume that informational objects or informational entities "are structural objects" (352). They are not "raw." They are not Kant's *noumena*. They have specific defining structures, and this is the basis of the constraints or affordances that they offer to cognition for processing. Informational entities are therefore not unformed clusters of data that can in principle extend in all directions infinitely, but "cohering clusters of data" (356), that is, *bounded unities*. These bounded unities are constituted by data in certain essential relations or, as Floridi also says, a "set of typed variables."[8] According to Floridi, being a set of typed variables is a

---

8 Floridi (2011, 359; emphasis in original) offers the example of a pawn in chess: "Its identity is not determined by its contingent properties as a physical body, including its shape and colour. Rather, a pawn is a well-defined cluster of specific *states* (properties like white or black, and its strategic position on the board) and determined *behavioural rules* (it can move forward only one square at a time, but with the option of two squares on the first move; it can capture other pieces only by a diagonal, forward move; and it can be promoted to any piece except a king when it reaches the opposite side of the board), which in turn are possible only in relation to other pieces and the logical space of the board. For a player, the actual pawn is only a placeholder, whereas the real pawn is an 'informational object.'" In terms of Luhmann's system theory, this would be a *function*. From the point of view of ANT, the pawn can be infinitely more, for example, a role in a political intrigue, an antiquity in a museum, a priceless work

transcendental condition of the possibility of knowing as well as of existence. What can be known are informational objects because only information can be known and because the world consists of informational entities. That these informational entities must be bounded individuals, however, does not follow from their informational nature. There is nothing in the nature of information that implies individual substances. As we saw in Chapter 1, information is a network phenomenon. Information knows no boundaries, such as those between system and environment, which are so crucial for Luhmann and, as we shall see, when discussing the informational self, for Floridi as well. Information, it must be emphasized, is not a thing, not even an informational thing. Information exists as networked, extended, and extending in principle endlessly in all directions, as essentially linked and related. Drawing a boundary around information, that is, distinguishing any particular set of typed variables as an individual entity, is arbitrary, situational, relative, and always subject to change. It would seem that either we must choose to preserve the substance ontology of Western metaphysics, even if we now speak of substances constituted by information, or we must accept a networked world that cannot be made up of bounded individuals. In short, if being is information, there are no "entities," not even "informational entities." There are only networks. And networks are not some kind of collective entity, but processes of networking. What Floridi calls "informational structural realism" amounts to nothing more than dressing up Western metaphysics and modern, above all Kantian, epistemology in the language of information.

Despite the theory of informational structural realism, Floridi's efforts to overcome Kantian subjectivism remain unconvincing as long as meaning is added to data by a cognitive agent. Either the affordances of structured, cohering clusters of data are the same as the "well-forming" activities of cognition and thus in themselves cognitive, or cognition is added to raw data by the knowing subject and we are back within the Kantian paradigm. For example, take the black mark on white paper. Is this data (being) or information (thinking)? According to the GDI, data are not meaningful until they are well-formed. Well-forming is either a process of being as in the case of "structural objects" or a process of thinking or both, in which case meaning is being and there is no need to construct meaning out of data, for data would not exist if they were not meaningful. It would seem that the idea of data plus meaning is itself meaningless since we couldn't even talk about data, let alone register, store, and query data if they had no meaning. The model upon which the GDI seems to be based is that whether by perception or by intuition, one opens one's (intellectual or sensory) "eyes" and something is there, something is "given." Either the given is meaningful in itself, or it is made meaningful by some kind of cognitive operations that "abstract" (see Floridi's idea of "levels of abstraction") only certain "relevant" features from the undifferentiated mass of data that are given in any situation. Simply constraining cognition as does Kant's sensory experience does not imply that sensory data are in any way meaningful in themselves. With regard to the GDI, one could say that this Kantian model is then taken up uncritically by computer

---

or art, and so on. For an empirical study of types and conditions of identity in contemporary society, see Young (2020).

scientists and applied to data processing. The computer accesses data from a database and through algorithmic operations gives the desired result, for example, the answer to a search query. Floridi seems unable to overcome the Kantian, that is, "idealist," version, which is implicit in the GDI. If information is data + meaning, then what is given is not already meaningful, but meaning is literally "added" on to data by some kind of syntactical or cognitive (abstracting) operation. The meaning constructing operation of well-forming, or applying syntactic rules, or what Floridi calls applying a level of abstraction is not itself data, not itself a given; otherwise, we would be involved in an infinite regress in which this new given would have to be well-formed, which would then be another given, and so on. Finally, the GDI demands that we ask: Where does well-forming come from? It must be constructed by the knowing subject even if the knowing subject is "constrained" in some way by the data.[9] If the data are already and necessarily "structured" by their very existence, then everything is in some way a cognitive agent, which is what ANT is proposing.

It does not help to define data "as mere *differentiae de re*, that is, mind-independent, concrete points of lack of uniformity in the fabric of Being" (Floridi 2011, 367; emphasis in original) that are "epistemically (still) virgin but (already) ontically distinctly-existing" so that they that are "*then* epistemically exploitable as resources, by agents like us, for their cognitive processes" (368). This returns to data + meaning. It is the model of data in a (structured!) database that await being given meaning by an algorithmic operation of a computer. For example, the number 27 is extracted from the database and well-formed by an operation that determines it to refer to the number of trucks available for transporting goods from a warehouse. The number 27, data, doesn't "mean" anything until it becomes information; that is, we know after the algorithmic operation that it refers to the number of trucks at the warehouse. This is how the GDI understands information. This data-processing model is misleading if used to interpret information in the philosophical sense. Floridi is taking a model of knowledge that was uncritically appropriated by computer science from modern epistemology. He then uses this already dubious model to go back and interpret the epistemology and even ontology from which it was derived in the first place. This is as if we try to interpret Kant by reading a manual for database engineering. It is the same mistake to attempt to understand what a hominin was doing three million years ago with a stone ax by consulting the *Critique of Pure Reason*. Let us be clear, if differences exist, whether in mind or matter, they do not need to be constructed by further differences to become information. Information and thus meaning is a difference and not a difference of a difference. Information need not wait until an existing difference that is somehow present in the world (Floridi's *differentiae de re*) is stumbled upon and distinguished by a knower from other things that are not differences.[10] In

---

9 Let us leave the question open at the moment of whether or not a computer or AI could produce information without this information being knowable or known by any human being.
10 For Luhmann following Spencer-Brown (1969), this is a "re-entry" of a difference into itself that allows an "unmarked space" to appear as background for distinctions, much as Floridi's white paper is background for the black mark. If I see a cat, I distinguish the cat from everything else that is not a cat. This is the unmarked space. But it is not really undifferentiated; it is

the world of information, there are only differences that make a difference or at least *can* make a difference. The very existence of differences *is* meaning and information and not merely the knowing of differences conceived of as the act of a conscious subject or even of an autopoietic system of communications. Consequently, on the level of a theory of meaning, it makes no sense to speak of anything being mind independent or mind dependent, since everything, including mind, is information and information is always already both mind and matter, both subject and object, both social and natural long before these distinctions were introduced to serve those purposes that modernity has given them. Consequently, it makes no sense to speak of data as somehow being merely given or even merely constraining and, therefore, meaningless until a conscious agent or a computer comes along and gives (adds) meaning through cognitive or algorithmic operations upon the data.

Norbert Wiener (1954, 17) attempted to settle many of these questions by declaring that "information is information, not matter or energy," which left the question open so that most have come to adopt the proposal of Gregory Bateson (1979, 428), that information "is a difference which makes a difference. Wiener's and Bateson's famous definitions of information are more fruitful and interesting than the GDI because there is no mention of data and no mention of meaning in the sense of what is known by a conscious subject or the result of syntactic combination. There is no attempt to define information epistemologically, but rather ontologically in the case of Wiener and "pragmatically" in the case of Bateson. We have only differences that either do something, that is, make a difference, or await an opportunity to make a difference. The stone waited perhaps hundreds of millions of years for the opportunity to become an ax. These differences are entities *sui generis*, that is, neither matter nor energy. If we add to this the definition of information in terms of Latour's principle of irreduction, which we have proposed above, we are left with a definition of information that seems to claim that information is an activity, a process, a change and not a thing that is either material, conceptual, or a mixture of both. In other words, and against Floridi's interpretation, there are no "informational entities" or "informational objects"; there is only networking. Information, therefore, is not something either inside or outside the knowing subject. It does not lie about in the world. In Bateson's definition, there is nothing simply "given" (*datum*); there is much rather a "giving" or, as Heidegger might say, an "event" (*Ereignis, es gibt*).[11] The question of whether or not this event or process is new and unexpected, or merely repeats what has already happened, which is a question that information theory has inherited from the mathematical theory of information (Shannon and Weaver 1949), together with the thermodynamic concept of "entropy," remains, as we shall see, important, "Making a difference" can be interpreted in terms of probability or expectations, quite apart from

---

    not yet differentiated; that is, the unmarked space, or phenomenologically speaking the "horizon," consists of all the differences waiting to make a difference. Nothing prevents me from going on to distinguish the cat from dogs, mice, trees, and so on. The point is that one cannot derive information from something that is not information.

11 Hubert Dreyfus (1995, 163) translates *Ereignis* as "things coming into themselves by belonging together."

binary code or any quantitative or mathematical considerations. The idea that information is improbable and, therefore, "negentropic" is, as we shall see when discussing Floridi's information ethics, of great consequence. With these preliminary remarks on the nature of information, let us turn to the implications of Floridi's philosophy of information for understanding ethics in the digital age.

2.1.3 Information Ethics

Floridi's philosophy of information serves as the basis for an "ethics of information."[12] What consequences does the above understanding of information have for ethics and morality? Floridi is right to claim that basing ethics on a philosophy of information has far-reaching consequences for moral discourse and for understanding the nature and purpose of digital ethics. Ethics can no longer be built upon traditional ontological distinctions between free human individuals who enter into social relations governed by normative expectations, on the one hand, and inanimate material objects making up the realm of nature, on the other hand. Instead of free human agents who use things as means for their ends, we now are faced with "information entities." From the point of view of Floridi's philosophy of information, all beings are essentially information. The world, at least if one thinks through the philosophy of information consequently, no longer consists of substances with attributes or knowing subjects naturally endowed with reason, free will, sensibility, and so on. Being is information. What consequences does this informational ontology have for digital ethics?

For Floridi, the ontological domain of information is the "infosphere." This is what Luhmann calls the social system and Latour calls the "collective." The infosphere consists of informational entities, that is, those beings that are information. Informational entities are all informational objects, but not all informational objects are informational agents. Informational agents are able to know and act upon informational objects. Human beings are informational agents, that is, "inforgs," or informational organisms.[13] The morally relevant actions of inforgs can be understood with regard to whether they increase, preserve, hinder, or destroy information. To explain what this means, Floridi adopts the concept of "entropy." Ever since Shannon and Weaver's (1949) *Mathematical Theory of Information*, the thermodynamic concept of entropy has been associated with information. Although Floridi (2013, 65) uses the concept "entropy" to describe information, he is careful to point out that his use of the term is different from Shannon and Weaver's concept of entropy, which describes information in terms of probability. To distinguish his "metaphysical" concept of entropy from that of Shannon and Weaver, Floridi states:

> Broadly speaking, entropy is a quantity specifying the amount of disorder, degradation, or randomness in a system bearing energy or information. […] In IE [Information Ethics], we

---

12 See Floridi (2013).
13 Of course, all organisms are informational not just human beings. What makes human beings special is self-consciousness or "identity." We will return to this below when discussing the ethical issue of privacy.

still treat the two concepts of information and entropy as being related, but we are concerned with the semantic and ontological nature of information. For example, as the infosphere becomes increasingly meaningful and rich in content, the amount of information increases and (what one may call, for the sake of clarity) metaphysical entropy decreases; or as entities wear out and finally disappear, metaphysical entropy increases and the amount of information decreases. Thus, in IE, entropy [...] indicates the decrease or decay of information leading to absence of form, pattern, differentiation, or content in the infosphere. [...] Metaphysical entropy refers to any kind of destruction or corruption of entities understood as informational objects [...], that is, any form of impoverishment of Being. (Floridi 2013, 66–67)

Floridi defines information as negentropy, that is, as the negation of entropy, which is nothing other than the introduction of order in chaos. Chaos, understood as the equal probability of all events, is the absence of information. According to Shannon and Weaver (1949), the more improbable a message is, the more information it contains. In other words, the more entropy there is, the less information, and the other way round, the more information, the less entropy. Based on these assumptions, Floridi (2013, 71) proposes four ethical principles:

0   entropy ought not to be caused in the infosphere (null law)
1   entropy ought to be prevented in the infosphere
2   entropy ought to be removed from the infosphere
3   the flourishing of informational entities as well as of the whole infosphere ought to be promoted by preserving, cultivating, and enriching their well-being.

These four ethical principles are to be understood as listed in the order of increasing moral value or importance. They define what information ethics says ought to be done. They are the norms of information ethics to which all are held accountable. What do they mean?

Entropy can be understood in two ways, either as the equal probability of all events or, in other words, as anything that can combine in any way with anything else, and therefore, anything is possible. Secondly, entropy can be understood as the impossibility of anything combining with anything else, or the absence of any combinations or relations whatever, in which case nothing is possible. Floridi opts for equating entropy with nothing being possible or, as he says, entropy "is comparable to the metaphysical concept of *nothingness*" (2013, 67; emphasis in original). In either case, since order of any kind is always a composite of elements that are selected and related in specific ways according to certain rules, it could be argued that data alone and by themselves are fundamentally entropic. Data are entropic because they must await being combined, or being well-formed, in order to be given meaning. Rule-based combinations of any kind may be defined as order as opposed to chaos. The moment elements are selected and related in specific ways and not others, not everything is possible. A stone is a stone, and not a stick, or an animal, or a hand. If the stone could turn into something else arbitrarily, this would be chaos. When elements are combined in specific ways and not others, order appears out of chaos, and entropy is negated. Well-formed data are information because they negate entropy. Well-forming data is a process or, as Luhmann would say, the operation of a system that is in itself highly improbable. The real question, Luhmann reminds us with regard to the social system, is why communication happens at all since it is highly improbable that only a very limited number of sounds that the human voice can produce are selected and combined in certain very specific ways in order to make words and sentences. Nonetheless, communication does happen, just as life happens based on inanimate chemical processes. What is decisive in the description of negentropy is not what is combined or said, but that something at all is combined or said. As Luhmann argues against Habermas, it does not matter whether we agree or disagree. Both agreement and disagreement are communication, and that is good for society. Since society exists as a system of communications, controversy can be good because it may lead to more communication than consensus does. As soon as we all agree, we stop talking. This makes it difficult, as Luhmann constantly reminded Habermas, to ground ethical values on consensus. Communication, as Luhmann points out, cannot itself be morally qualified. There is only communication or noncommunication. There is no good or bad communication unless, as Habermas claims, only some forms of communication are "rational," and rationality is always good. For Luhmann, there is only communication or noncommunication. Noncommunication would be the end of society. If society is assumed to be a value, then noncommunication is immoral. This a purely quantitative measure of moral value. The more, the merrier. Floridi appears to follow the same path. The more entropy is negated, the better off is the infosphere.

With regard to Floridi's ethical imperative of negentropy, it must be assumed that any information *qua* information is good since the infosphere exists as information and since Being or existence is in itself a value. It would seem, however, to follow from this that there is no information in particular that can be qualified as *either* good or bad, or rather, all information must be good since information is negentropy and negentropy is order instead of chaos. The goodness of information is, therefore, not a qualitative attribution, but an exclusively quantitative attribution. The more information the better, in the moral sense, regardless of what the information means, that is, independently of any qualitative or semantic judgment. If I say something bad about someone, this is information. If I say more bad things about this person, this is more information, and therefore, it must be good. This is the consequence that comes from declaring information to be good in itself and defining information as negentropy. Nonetheless, Floridi insists that an ethics of information must be able to qualify information as good or evil. This can only be done if some information leads to increasing entropy—this is evil—whereas other information leads to reducing or negating entropy, which is good. From the systems theory perspective, this amounts to claiming that certain kinds of communication do not lead to more communication, but to less. In fact, this is what Luhmann accuses moral discourse of doing. And this is why Luhmann asserts that the only thing for ethics to do is to warn society against morality. For Floridi, moral discourse has the opposite effect. It leads to more information and not less. Why is this so?

It is challenging, if not impossible, to make practical sense of imperatives to negate entropy. Imperatives like "Do unto others as you would have them do unto you" or "Do not lie" are hardly translatable into "Do no entropy," since entropy is a purely quantitative measure of the amount of information in any informational object and in the infosphere as a whole. This is a very different understanding of morality than what is usually understood as moral norms. If keeping promises is morally good, then it is so not because it increases the amount of information in the world. Lies are neither more nor less informative than the truth. Fake news, for example, has generated an enormous discussion on the responsibility of the media, the ethics of political communication, technical fixes, demands for regulation of the Internet, and of course, opportunities for political advantage and for rogue nation-states to conduct new forms of cyber warfare. If we were to measure all this in terms of data, it would amount to an enormous increase in the data available in the infosphere. We could argue quite plausibly that fake news has contributed substantially to increasing information and reducing entropy and is, therefore, morally good. Just because information may be demonstrably false does not imply it has no effects.[14] As Luhmann pointed out with regard to the supposedly moral value of consensus, if everyone agreed, this could actually harm society by leading to less communication instead of more. Does killing someone increase or decrease entropy? For example, if Hitler had been assassinated, would this have contributed to more or less information in the world, and according to what time limits are we to take the measure? If the atom bomb had not been developed and deployed, would this have led to more information or less? Who can say? What criteria can be applied? If we do not stop global warming, everyone agrees there will be catastrophic results. But this could also lead to breakthroughs in geoengineering, international cooperation, new forms of global governance, the overcoming of populism, and so on. This is true of all catastrophes, such as pandemics, which cause grave social and economic damage as well as loss of life but nonetheless inspire scientific research, political discussion, regulatory measures, and much more.

Floridi would certainly object that this is not what he means with the four principles. He points out that they are explicitly not formulated as imperatives directed to moral agents, but as indications of the responsibility of moral agents toward those informational entities that exist in the infosphere, that is, to patients of actions and not to the actors.[15] Every informational entity, on the basis of its negentropy, possesses inherent value and dignity. To act in such a way as to reduce the informational value and dignity of any entity, whether animate or inanimate, whether individual or collective, whether sentient or insentient, is morally condemnable. This is the hallmark, according to Floridi, of a non-anthropocentric, object-oriented, "ecological" ethics. It would probably not be opposed to Floridi's intentions were we to say that what he is proposing is an *ethics of responsibility* wherein the only imperative is "be responsible" to all beings. Recalling Luhmann's

---

14 See, for example, Klintman (2019) on the social and "adaptive" function of belief in fake news.
15 The object- or "patient"-oriented approach would also have to include respect and responsibility toward all those informational entities that *could exist* in the infosphere, which is not only infinite but also indeterminable and therefore impossible to calculate or foresee in any practical, that is, moral, way.

notion of "respect" as acceptance of the other into the moral domain, Floridi's emphasis on the moral patient as the primary addressee of ethical reflection suggests a significant extension of moral concerns to all informational beings. That said, we leave the dimension of morality, that is, of universal and absolute truths that no experience can challenge, call into question, or revise. As soon as the imperative to be responsible goes beyond merely acknowledging the other as moral patient and is filled with any practical content, we descend to the level of adaptive learning, wherein every level of abstraction, or, as Latour would say, every program of action, is subject to correction by learning. Are religiously motivated fanatics, who are responsible to God's word, but not to human suffering, worthy of moral praise or blame? Are political leaders who are responsible to national security, but not to justice and equality, worthy of praise or blame? Are business managers who are responsible to shareholders or even a wider circle of stakeholders, but not to social well-being, to be morally judged? Of course, we would say, but which is it, praise or blame? And who is to decide? And what consequences do their decisions have? Claiming that someone is irresponsible with regard to some information and, therefore, morally condemnable for some action that influences information is always disputable. From Luhmann's perspective, we may ask, what does morality or ethics contribute to the infosphere? What is its function? And if it does have a function, is the contribution of morality itself morally praiseworthy? If moral judgment is in any way intended to put a stop to bickering, uncertainty, compromises, trial and error, surprises, revolutions, fundamental transformations of society and human existence, and so on, then how can morality meet the requirement of negating entropy? All of these things can lead to more information rather than less. And if morality is intended to everywhere encourage discovery, innovation, transformation, differentiation, complexity, and so on, then what sense does it make to try to tell people what they should and should not do, thus limiting options and preventing the exploration of new paths with unforeseen consequences? Does Floridi's information ethics answer Luhmann's question of what function, what purpose morality fulfills in today's world?

2.1.4 The Informational Self

To attempt to answer these questions, let us take a closer look at an example to which Floridi has devoted much attention, and which has become a central issue in almost all discussions of digital ethics, namely, privacy. According to Floridi, the infosphere consists of informational entities and their interactions. These entities are either informational objects or informational subjects, that is, those entities that act upon or know informational objects. Some of these informational agents can be held morally responsible, that is, praised or blamed for their either entropic or negentropic actions. With this background, let us ask what this means in the concrete case of the much discussed issue of privacy. Practically no discussion of digital ethics fails to mention privacy as one of the most important ethical concerns of the digital age. Indeed, since privacy is nowadays primarily understood as informational privacy, digital ethics seems predestined to answer questions regarding what is morally acceptable with regard to gathering, storing, aggregating, sharing, and using personal information. This is, of course, not exclusively a moral issue. Privacy is, above all, a legal and regulatory issue. Since the Universal Declaration of Human Rights (1948), privacy is an official human right that is anchored in many international declarations, charters, and even national constitutions as well as in many laws and regulations. Legal privacy does not need morality or ethics, just as positive law does not need anything other than enactment and institution.[16]

With this legal, cultural, and political background, there would seem little need for ethics to get involved when discussing human rights. The issue would seem to actually not be an "issue" at all, since it is apparently already decided, enacted into law, and therefore beyond question. Human rights, after all, are "self-evident." Privacy is everywhere considered to be an indisputable value, an acknowledged right, and an integral part of human freedom and dignity. It is defined and protected by law and, therefore, does not need morality to ensure that it is respected and valued. Nonetheless, perhaps the fact that there is so much heated discussion of this seemingly obvious matter indicates that the value of privacy is not acknowledged by all. Indeed, it would seem that in the digital world, privacy has become an obstacle to economic development, advancement of medical research, effective public health, educational improvement, personalized products and services, and much more.[17] In a world in which value of all kinds is generated from data, it becomes questionable whether the strategy of withholding information and blocking data flows is not counterproductive and perhaps even, by Floridi's own standards, unethical. There is much that speaks against the right to privacy or any moral duty to ensure privacy in the digital world. In view of this controversial situation, it makes sense to ask whether Floridi's information ethics can show us a way out of this problematic situation.

Floridi is very clear; there is no middle ground. The right to privacy is a "fundamental and inalienable right" (2013, 243). This is based not only upon positive law or official pronouncements and declarations but upon a philosophical argument. The need for a philosophical argument arises from the fact that despite all the declarations, laws, and regulations in which a right to privacy is explicitly enshrined, no one seems to know what privacy is and what the right to privacy exactly means.[18] In addition to this, the philosophical foundations of a right to privacy appear to be uncertain, historically and culturally relative, and open to different interpretations. Floridi attempts to escape these difficulties by proposing a new "ontological interpretation" (228) of informational privacy in which personal information is constitutive of the very being of the human individual. Privacy as a fundamental and inalienable right is, therefore, to be based upon "considering a person as being constituted by his or her information" (ibid.). This implies that "a breach of one's informational privacy [is] a form of aggression towards one's personal identity" (ibid.). The consequence of this view is that the constitutive information of an

---

16 See Etinson (2018) on the two strands of human rights thinking, the ethical and the legal.
17 See, for example, the agenda of the digital single market strategy of the European Union, wherein the exploitation of data is acknowledged as the primary source of generating value in all areas of society (https://ec.europa.eu/digital-single-market/en).
18 For a discussion of the status of current privacy discourse, see Belliger and Krieger (2018a).

individual cannot in any case or for any reason be externalized, given away, sold, or otherwise allowed to flow beyond the bounds of the individual person. Personal information is, therefore, not something we "have," but what we "are." The boundaries preventing the flow of information and thus guaranteeing privacy are conceived of as "ontological friction" in the infosphere.[19] Not only is the individual person ontologically constituted by certain information, but there must exist real boundaries blocking the free flow of this information. An example of ontological friction is a wall that separates rooms in a house so that what is said or done on one side of the wall cannot be heard or seen on the other side. This is a physical boundary. Despite the common opinion that ICTs have eliminated such boundaries and made all walls transparent, Floridi is concerned to point out that ICTs also allow for virtual boundaries, for example, firewalls, encryption, or "privacy-enhancing technologies" (PETs) that "ontologically" conceal, hide, or protect digital information. The important point about the idea of "ontological friction" is that privacy resides in and depends upon the ability to, in some way, block flows of information. The right to privacy is, therefore, a right to keep information secret, to block the flow of information, to diminish or prevent the uses of information, and generally, to ensure that there is less information available than there would be without privacy.[20]

In order to understand Floridi's ontological theory of privacy, it is necessary to take a detour through his theory of the informational self. It is because the informational self is ontologically constituted by certain information that privacy is a fundamental right. Otherwise, as we shall see, privacy is only an instrumental right that serves to protect other more fundamental rights such as security, freedom, or property rights. Floridi feels compelled to offer an ontological interpretation of privacy in order to overcome the inadequacies of instrumental theories of privacy that are unable to explain why privacy is a fundamental and inalienable right. The theoretical basis of privacy as a fundamental right is, therefore, dependent on the theory of the informational self. It is necessary to understand what the individual person is as an informational entity. The guiding question becomes: What is the self from the informational point of view? Beyond renaming the human being as an "inforg," Floridi proposes an informational ontology of the self, which claims to answer the question of how the self can be a bounded individual constituted by information. We are dealing here with two questions. One question concerns the self as a bounded individual, and the other question concerns the nature of information such that it can constitute such a bounded individual. Only if human beings are essentially and primarily distinct individuals, and not, for example, primarily social beings, does anything like a fundamental right to privacy make sense over against other rights such as a right to freedom of speech and participation in society.

---

19 "*Informational privacy is a function of the ontological friction in the infosphere*" (Floridi 2013, 232).
20 "Privacy is the right of individuals […] to control the life-cycle […] of their information and determine for themselves when, how, and to what extent their information is processed by others" (Floridi 2013, 236). Floridi, as we will see below, defines the decrease of information within the infosphere as moral evil. This would appear to apply to privacy, which is here portrayed as a moral good.

Let us begin with the question of the informational self as a bounded, unique, unitary, and individual being. Before looking into the answer Floridi gives to this question, it should be noted that the question itself is not obvious or perhaps even necessary. Why must the self be a unity at all? Has not decades of postmodern criticism demonstrated the opposite, namely, that the unitary self of traditional Western subjectivism is a myth and what we are actually dealing with when dealing with ourselves is a fragmented, only loosely connected collection of various fragile and constantly changing identities.[21] Floridi (2014) himself often cites Freud's displacing of the unitary self from center stage as a "third revolution" and goes on to cite the digital revolution as a fourth revolution that displaces the human being as the unique bearer of "intelligence." It would seem that the unity of the self is something that must be argued for instead of simply assumed at the beginning of the twenty-first century. Floridi (2013, 215) attempts to avoid the entire postmodern critique of the idea of the autonomous rational subject, which lies at the basis of contemporary conceptions of privacy by distinguishing between *identity* and *individualization*. Individualization is what the self essentially is. In informational terms, the individual is certain information that *constitutes* the self to be what it is. According to Floridi, individualization is different from identity, which is the answer to the at-any-time-perspectival question of whether a certain entity is *the same entity* at time t1 as at time t2. It is, therefore, not the temporal dimension in which identity is at issue, which is decisive for the nature of the self. It is not the question of sameness through time or "diachronic" identity. Instead, it is the question of that individual that Floridi claims must logically be presupposed to even ask about identity. This individual being he calls "synchronic" individualization (2013, 215) as opposed to diachronic questions of personal identity, which admittedly can change over time. It is the individual being who *has* an identity, perhaps even many, changing through time. Along with postmodern critique, Floridi admits that this kind of identity is a question that can be answered in many ways, depending upon what is relevant for the purpose at hand. Is the butterfly the same as the caterpillar? It depends on what you are interested in when you ask the question. From one point of view, they are the same, but from another, they are different. When it comes to identity, in this sense of the word, Floridi admits there is no need for unity, clear boundaries, and indivisibility. Identity is the self as accessed or mediated through a particular question, interest, point of view, or that which Floridi calls a "level of abstraction."

It would seem to make good sense to suppose that whenever one speaks of the various identities "of" something or someone, one presupposes the unity and individuality of that something or someone "of" whom one is speaking. An actor, for example, may appear on stage in many different roles or wear many different masks, but it is still the one and the same actor behind all these roles and masks. Here one could recall Goffman's

---

21 For a summary of postmodern critique of the self, see Anderson (1997). Instead of schizophrenia, Anderson speaks of "multiphrenia" when describing the many identities that the self takes on. The self is described as "protean," that is, capable of changing to suit circumstances; "de-centered," that is, a creation of language and society; "hybrid," that is, composed of often conflicting heterogeneous elements; and finally, as Floridi himself remarks, dethroned by the four revolutions of Galileo, Darwin, Freud, and AI.

famous dramaturgical theory of social interaction. The social actor for Goffman moves from one social interaction to another by means of assuming appropriate roles as does an actor on a stage. One social mask is exchanged for another as the socially constructed "person" (*persona*, mask) moves through daily life. But who is the actor without any mask? Floridi points out that in order to even ask questions about identity, there must be something about which one is asking, that is, there must be some *individual* that acts as a kind of substrate—or substance!—that can somehow carry the various identities that are revealed by the many different questions that can be asked about it and the many social situations into which it can enter and leave. As Floridi (2015) puts it, "*Individualization* logically precedes *identification*" (emphasis in original). What is important here is Floridi's ungrounded assumption that whereas identity is relative to a perspective, a particular question, or as he says, a level of abstraction, individualization is not. Where then do we ever find an individual, even when looking into ourselves, without asking any question and without taking any perspective, and apart from any concrete social or historical situation? Floridi himself claims that there is no information that is not mediated by a level of abstraction. Concerning individualization, which is supposedly logically necessary in order to ask about identity at all, Floridi asks, "If the self is made of information (perceptions or narratives, or any other informational items one may privilege), then a serious challenge is to explain how that information is kept together as a whole, coherent, sufficiently permanent unity."[22] He immediately answers this question with reference to Kant's transcendental unity of apperception, which in his view solves the epistemological problem of the unity of experience but not the ontological problem of the being of this individual unitary conscious self. Quite apart from the issue of whether Kant's concept of the transcendental unity of apperception does not bequeath us more problems than solutions, there remains the issue of the relation between epistemology (knowing) and ontology (being) for a being whose being consists in its self-knowing.[23] "I think; therefore, I am," as Descartes succinctly put it. How do we keep the two questions of what I am (being) and who I am (identity) apart?

It should be noted at this point that the very question of how the self can be a unity, that is, what constitutes inforgs as bounded individuals, presupposes that human beings are bounded individuals in the first place and that this unity must be explained and also protected. As we shall see, this is where Floridi's information ethics leaves the newly conquered terrain of an informational ontology and falls back onto traditional Western notions of the individual, of substance, and of humanism. This for two reasons. First, the assumption that there must be some underlying substrate or substance, which is the self in order to even be able to ask about identity or work with identities in various life situations, is arbitrary and relative to the perspective one is taking just as much as any

---

22 Floridi cites Locke and Schechtman (1996) as answers to how information constitutes the self, that is, either as introspection of conscious contents or as narrative, the story a self tells about itself.

23 Kant's transcendental unity of apperception is rather like an empty trash bin marked only by "I" or "Me," and everything that is thrown into this bin becomes "mine," who we are, our identity.

question about identity also is. What distinguishes the question of individualization from the question of identity? Is not the individual once defined by certain constitutive information not also an identity, one among many others that may be constituted by other information? And if so, why is this one identity to be declared essential, constitutive, individualizing, and so on and the others not? If we were to bulge in upon Goffman's social actor "backstage" when he takes off one mask to put on another, we would still see someone and not an empty visage without any recognizable characteristics. Otherwise, we would not be able to ask them for their autograph. To distinguish identity from individualization by means of arguing that identity is always the answer to a particular question asked from a particular perspective for a particular purpose whereas in contrast individualization is free of any "level of abstraction" is not only inconceivable but also contradicts Floridi's own principle that all information whatsoever is always mediated by a level of abstraction.[24] Is not Kant's critical philosophy also a particular level of abstraction, a specific approach to questioning things, and one perspective among other possible views?

Secondly, it could be that the question of the "unity" of information is itself problematic. As we shall argue, it may well be precisely the nature of information to be unbounded, disunified, and relational. We have argued above in the discussion of ANT that *it is the nature of information to be connected to other information in principally unbounded networks*. The definition of information we have gained from ANT makes it clear that information is relational. Even for Luhmann's systems theory, information is meaningful only to the extent that it leads to other information, whether as cognitive contents or as communications. If there is reason to accept the networked understanding of what information is, then this would make it impossible for information to be constitutive of any such things as bounded, unitary individuals. Networks are constituted by information, but not individuals, who are constituted by networks for the sake of some program of action that may call for roles, identities, or functions. As we shall see, this is not only an important issue concerning understanding what information is and what an informational ontology must look like but also crucial with regard to understanding what kind of ethics can be derived from information. But let us not get ahead of the story and look now more closely at Floridi's interpretation of the informational self and the consequences he draws from this for the issue of privacy.

Interestingly, when it comes to describing the ontological unity of the informational self, Floridi does not rely upon the classical tradition coming from Locke, but uses conceptual models taken over from general systems theory, which rely upon the ideas of closure and exclusion.[25] For Luhmann, every system is constituted by the difference between system and environment. Every system must distinguish itself from its environment by selection of elements, relationing of the elements, and steering of the system operations. Without a clear difference between system and environment, the system cannot steer its

---

24 "Data are never accessed and elaborated (by an information agent) independently of a level of abstraction" (Floridi 2011, 87).
25 Floridi does not explicitly cite systems theory as the source for these ideas.

operations toward itself, that is, become self-referential and operationally closed. This is so for physical systems, for biological systems, for central nervous systems, and for consciousness as well as social systems. Floridi (2013, 218) does not speak of systems, but he explains the unity of the self as constituted by three boundaries, or as he calls them "membranes." These different membranes separate the system from the environment and are "encapsulated" within each other. The description of these boundaries is a description of the evolutionary development of the human being as a unitary conscious self, that is, what Luhmann would call a psychic system. The development of a cognitive system brings with it the progressive separation of mind from reality or, as Floridi says, "detachment from reality" (ibid.). First comes a physical or corporal boundary or "membrane," which, like matryoshka dolls, includes within itself a cognitive membrane, which in turn includes a conscious membrane. In other words, there is the organism, then the central nervous system within the organism, and finally, the cognitive or mental system within the brain. Each boundary or membrane constructs a system/environment difference. The corporeal membrane, such as the skin of an animal, separates the organism from the environment while at the same time allowing the organism to autopoietically— Floridi (2013) speaks of "auto-structuring," "auto-organizing," or "auto-assembling"— construct its own specific biological operations. The same mechanism of inclusion and exclusion constructs the cognitive and conscious systems within the organism.

> In the same way that organisms are initially formed and kept together by auto-structuring (i.e. auto-assembling and, within the assembled entity, auto-organizing) physical (henceforth corporeal) membranes, which encapsulate and hence detach [...] parts of the environment into biochemical structures that are then able to evolve into more complex organisms, selves too are the result of further encapsulations, although of informational rather than biochemical structures. The basic mechanism of encapsulation, detachment, and internal auto-organization, I suggest, is the same. (ibid.)

Let us note again, the "basic mechanisms" Floridi mentions from which individual selves are said to arise are those of systemic organization and not of information. Information appears as only one, indeed, the last "encapsulation." We are obviously not dealing here with a theory of the self derived from an informational ontology, but a theory of the self modeled as an autopoietic, operationally closed system "encapsulated" within an organic and a physical environment. After the organism has selected, relationed, and organized certain chemical elements into biological processes, the cognitive boundary that corresponds to the central nervous system does the same for nerve impulses, which allows for operational closure and, therefore, also informational closure of a cognitive system. Undifferentiated perturbations of the nervous system are received from the external or internal environment and autopoietically transformed into information by the operations of the central nervous system.[26] Within this cognitive system, there arises, according to Floridi, a further boundary that constructs the self as self-conscious.

---

26 This well-known description of cognition is not only the basis of traditional cognitive science, otherwise known as "Cartesian cognitive science" because of the implied distinction between

> Selves emerge as the last step in a process of detachment from reality that begins with a corporeal membrane encapsulating an organism, proceeds through a cognitive membrane encapsulating an intelligent animal, and concludes with a consciousness membrane encapsulating a mental self or simply a mind. (ibid.)

At this point, systems theory speaks of the emergence of meaning. What Floridi refers to as the "mental self" or "mind" corresponds to what Luhmann identifies as the psychological system. For both Luhmann and Floridi, this is self-consciousness. For Luhmann, there emerges a further system based on self-consciousness, namely, the social system that consists of communications. Floridi does not distinguish between the psychological system, that is, self-conscious individuals and the social system. Meaning is apparently a matter for conscious individuals alone. But these conscious individuals, or minds, are "detached from reality" in a way that Luhmann's systems theory does not accept. Floridi's model is decidedly Cartesian or, perhaps better, Kantian since meaning has receded to a virtual realm of its own far away from reality. How this is compatible with an informational ontology in which meaning and being are the same is an open question. For Luhmann, meaning is a higher level of emergent order than physical or biological systems and therefore includes physical as well as biological being within itself. For Floridi, on the contrary, it would seem that the infosphere is populated with conscious individuals, that is, inforgs, and what they know, namely, informational objects, which are virtual objects, models of reality, and thus "far away" from the real.

Furthermore, Floridi ignores the social dimension of meaning altogether, which for Luhmann is constituted by communication and not by cognition. In Floridi's infosphere, there is not only an unbridgeable gap between meaning and being, but there seem to be no social structures such as Luhmann's functional subsystems or even interaction systems such as Goffman described. Floridi would categorically reject Luhmann's assertion that society does not consist of human beings, but of communications. Indeed, it is difficult to understand what place society has at all in Floridi's philosophy of information. Floridi does not speak of society as a level of emergent order above that of conscious individuals. It would seem that Floridi's philosophy and ethics of information remain anchored in Western individualism and have missed the sociological and posthuman turn represented by the theory of social systems as well as ANT and, of course, by the entire critique of Western metaphysics and subjectivism that postmodernism has produced. From the hacker's perspective, this is just plain bad code. Although it would certainly be possible to understand the infosphere in terms of what Luhmann calls "society" or in the sense in which Latour speaks of the social as the sum of all actor-networks constituted by information, Floridi does not speak of society as an emergent level of order above that of conscious individuals. It is remarkable that after so much talk about the information revolution and a new information ontology and so much emphasis upon information and *communication* technologies, what we get is the same old story. Only the names have been

---

being and mind, but also the basis of epistemological constructivism, also known as "radical constructivism." See, for example, Maturana and Varella (1987) and von Glasersfeld (1995).

changed. The world still consists of things, living organisms, and self-conscious minds, just as it always did. Only now they are called informational entities. First, there are physical systems, then biological systems emerge from these, and finally, mind emerges within the big brains of certain biological organisms with a sufficiently complex central nervous system. Packing this well-known evolutionary scenario, which in itself has nothing to do with information and which is not derived from a philosophy of information, into a theory of the bounded individual inspired by systems theory and not an informational ontology, Floridi concludes:

> The three phases concern the evolution of organisms, then of intelligent animals and finally of self-conscious minds. Each phase contributes to the construction of the ultimate personal identity of the human organism in question. (2013, 219)[27]

If the self is defined at once as a bounded unity ("ultimate personal identity") and as an informational entity, then the question becomes how information can constitute a bounded, unitary self. As already mentioned, the very idea of a bounded self is problematic for many reasons. If we remain for a moment with the systems model, Luhmann described how a system of meaning achieves operational and informational closure by making "observations," that is, introducing distinctions, whether these are merely thought or communicated. The very close "structural coupling" or "interpenetration" of psychic systems and the social system makes it almost impossible to distinguish between individual experience and communication since whatever one experiences one can say and what one cannot say, in one way or another, one cannot think or even be aware of—as Wittgenstein remarked. In addition to this, there is the fact that people who do not communicate are not simply left alone to go about their private affairs somehow outside of society. Instead, they are diagnosed as "autistic" and accordingly subjected to various forms of "therapy" designed to bring them back into society. The social system does not recognize, respect, or accept the existence of human individuals who are somehow "outside" society.[28] It is hardly imaginable, despite Hobbesian stories of a "state of nature," that we could find an individual alone or isolated or as it were "in the wild." Finally, the fact that the social system does not limit itself to what actually is said, but includes what *can* be said—otherwise there would be no need for functional differentiation, generalized media, and so on to ensure that communication smoothly links up to further communication—implies that the boundaries of psychic systems and the social system are so porous as to be almost negligible. It may well be that I don't have to say everything

---

27 Apparently uneasy about bringing in theoretical models that have nothing to do with information, Floridi feels compelled to add: "There are still only informational structures. But some are things, some are organisms, and some are minds, intelligent and self-aware beings" (2013, 226).

28 The notions of "psychic pathology" or "abnormality," even when still subscribing to a Freudian individualism, which has been challenged by Winnicott as well as the systems therapy approach of Watzlawick, Jackson, Bateson, and others from the Palo Alto Group, are through and through social concepts.

I'm thinking, but what matters is that it *could* be said and perhaps someday *will be* said. All this implies that individual self-conscious minds are not "encapsulated" (Floridi 2013, 218) within brains, but "extended" into the social environment.[29]

This is not a problem for Luhmann since, for him, personal identity is through and through a social construction anyway. The "person" (*persona*, mask) is a construction of communication, that is, the sum of everything that has been said about someone, everything that is being said, and everything that will be said about this person by others as well as by the person himself. This is the well-known "narrative criterion of personal identity"[30] to which Floridi also subscribes. Personal identity, as well as individualization, are understood to be narratively constructed. We will return to narrative below when discussing how information can constitute a self. For the moment, it is important to note that Luhmann's description of the social system as based on communication, which is supported by Wittgenstein's argument against the possibility of a private language, shows that it is highly questionable to assume that the emergence of meaning results in bounded, unitary individuals and not in groups, communities, and societies. Who's to say which is more original, primordial, basic, individual I-consciousness, or collective we-consciousness? While the social nature of personal identity does not cause a problem for Luhmann, it does for Floridi, since a socially constructed person is not a bounded individual, a closed system, encapsulated in a brain, and constituted by certain information that belongs exclusively to it alone. Floridi's informational self, in distinction to Luhmann, must be constituted by information that is not linked up to other information and does not extend beyond the individual into society. Otherwise, privacy cannot be a fundamental right.

There is a further difficulty with Floridi's notion of the self, which should be mentioned in the context of the question of the bounded, unitary nature of the self. Quite apart from the problem of the social construction of the person, the idea that the mind is not individually bounded and enclosed, or as Floridi says "encapsulated," within an organism or a brain is supported by the "4E Cognition" thesis that has arisen within the new "non-Cartesian" cognitive science.[31] The 4E thesis argues that the mind is not bounded or closed within a mental or "virtual" domain far removed from physical reality. Instead, in a way reminiscent of ANT as well as Heidegger's notion of practical knowing, the mind is described as *embodied, extended, enacted,* and *embedded* throughout the body and the physical environment. According to the new non-Cartesian cognitive science, the mind is encapsulated neither within the brain nor within a "virtual" world generated by the brain but is integrally bound up with things in the environment and with practical interactions between organism and environment. Along these lines, still further support for the notion of an unbounded, non-unitary self comes from the theory of "distributed

---

29 This is also the conclusion of what is called "non-Cartesian cognitive science" (see Rowlands 2010) as well as the premise of many non-Cartesian forms of psychology and psychotherapy.
30 See the article on personal identity and ethics in the Stanford Encyclopedia of Philosophy (https://plato.stanford.edu/entries/identity-ethics/#NarCri).
31 For an overview, see Rowlands (2010).

cognition."[32] Proponents of distributed cognition claim that cognitive contents are not in the brain alone, but distributed among things, tools, artifacts, organizations, procedures, and ways of acting and interacting with others and with things. Mind, and therefore meaning, cannot be attributed to conscious individuals alone, but much rather mind must be understood as that which integrates individuals into socio-technical practices and is consequently distributed throughout these practices as well as the artifacts involved with them. In other words, there is no distinction between being and meaning, except in meaning itself, for whatever purposes the meaning system wishes to accomplish by this distinction. This is also the fundamental insight of ANT as well as the basis for understanding information not in terms of mental states, but as networking relations.

Finally, we close this detour through Floridi's theory of the informational self by mentioning that recent developments in neuroscience have added to the critique of traditional Western individualism by questioning the very existence of a unitary, conscious self. The "illusionism" thesis proposed by Frankish (2005, 2017), among others, claims that phenomenal consciousness is an illusion created by the brain to deal with the environment. It is neither logically necessary nor empirically justified to understand mind as a kind of thinking substance or individual being. To suppose, as Kant did, that there must be a unitary subject, a transcendental unity of apperception because I can call all my experiences "mine" does not necessarily imply that such a being exists, nor that it is a unity, that is, the same each time I make the claim, nor even that the claim is true. Consciousness may seem to exist because that is how the brain reduces the complexity of perception and neural processing. But there is no proof that it exists or any reason to justify assuming so.

Caruso (2012) and Caruso and Flanagan (2018) have gone on to develop the relevance of this thesis for notions of free will, moral responsibility, and retributive justice. For Caruso, neuroscience has initiated a "third wave of existentialism" in which the fundamental self-understanding of human existence is challenged by new assessments of cognition, consciousness, and free will. The embeddedness of cognition and action in the body and the physical, as well as social, environment makes it increasingly implausible to assume that social actors are autonomous, free, rational subjects. Despite the deep-rooted convictions about human freedom and autonomy in Western culture, the moral, legal, and penal institutions erected upon these apparently self-evident principles are questioned by findings of neuroscience. Caruso argues that upon the basis of neuroscience, traditional assumptions of responsibility and accountability for actions cannot be upheld and must be revised such that individuals alone are no longer bearers of moral praise or blame and legal sanctions. He demands a complete revision of the penal justice system and the ethical assumptions that support it. If one is suspicious of the physicalist assumptions of such hypotheses, similar arguments are being made from the point of view of "panpsychism." According to the theories of cognitive neuroscientist Donald Hoffman (2019), matter is essentially a form of consciousness. It may be, as Luhmann claimed, that consciousness is a necessary condition of communication, but

---

32 See Hutchins (1995).

consciousness could turn out to be fundamentally different from what Luhmann supposed when speaking of psychic systems. Even stones, after all, recalling our hominin and the stone ax, can contribute to the construction of meaning.

Summarizing what has been said, it would seem that Floridi's philosophy and ethics of information remain ontologically anchored in Western humanism and that he has missed the sociological, linguistic, and posthuman turn represented by the theory of social systems as well as ANT and, of course, by the entire critique of Western metaphysics and subjectivism that postmodernism, as well as certain trends in cognitive science and neuroscience, has produced. Were this the case, then our hack would have exposed serious bugs in the discourse of information ethics and revealed much bad code. But perhaps this judgment is too hasty. Floridi explicitly proposes an alternative to traditional metaphysics, namely, an ontology of information. Being is not substance, he tirelessly repeats, but information. The emergence of consciousness, which he describes in terms of evolutionary systems theory, must be understood from the point of view of information. Let us, therefore, turn to Floridi's explanation of how the informational self, the inforg, is constituted by information. Only if it can plausibly be shown that information can and does constitute an individual, bounded self does it make sense to ask how and why this information must be protected by a right to privacy and an ethical imperative to maintain privacy. How is the informational self constituted by information? What information constitutes the self?

2.1.5 Privacy

It is worthwhile repeating the two questions posed immediately above, namely, *how* is the informational self constituted by information and *what* information constitutes the self. These questions are important not only because they bear the entire weight of Floridi's theory of the informational self as an informational entity bearing an inherent right to privacy but also because he does not answer them. Instead, he simply assumes that the self is constituted by information and does not find it necessary to say exactly *what* information accomplishes this task and exactly *how* it does this. The assumption that the self is constituted by information is proposed as an "ontological" theory of privacy that is intended to avoid inadequacies of other privacy theories, specifically, instrumentalism, which Floridi calls "reductionism," and the "ownership" theory of privacy, in which information is something we *have*, but not what we *are*. Both the instrumental theory and the ownership theory of privacy fail to establish privacy as a fundamental and inalienable right. Only if the "inviolate personality" (Warren and Brandeis 1890)[33] is

---

33 Floridi (2013, 244) points out that for Warren and Brandeis in their famous grounding of a right to privacy, which stands at the beginning of American privacy law, it was not primarily property rights that were at issue, but the right to the "immunity of the person" or the "inviolate personality" (Warren and Brandeis 1890). What exactly this inviolate personality is, is controversial today, not only because this personality has always been violated by the physical and social conditions in which human beings live, but also because new technologies of brain–computer interface and brain-to-brain connectivity place autonomy, individuality, and

ontologically constituted by information can privacy be more than merely an instrument to avoid certain harms and a support for other more fundamental rights such as security, freedom, or property. In both cases, and this is why Floridi criticizes these approaches, we could get along quite well without privacy. In the case of harms that supposedly arise from the loss of privacy, other forms of legal protection could prevent harms that come from misuse of personal information. To prevent or mitigate the harm resulting from the misuse of information, privacy as a fundamental right or even as protected by law is not necessary. It is enough to describe misuse and effectively sanction it legally. If someone knows my credit card number but does not use this information to steal money, there is no harm and no crime. Identity theft, an example Floridi dwells upon at length, is a crime not because it violates privacy, but because it is theft. It misuses information to steal money or harm someone in other ways. In the case of privacy theories based on property rights, personal information is something we *have* and not something we *are*, and therefore, it can be alienated, traded, given away, or otherwise disclosed with due consent without there being any violation of a fundamental right. Freedom, for example, is entirely different. Freedom can be considered a fundamental right. One can argue that I cannot sell myself into slavery, because a valid contract presupposes free decision. But I can disclose all my personal information, and many people do exactly this without any hesitation in social media or many other ways. To suppose that these people are harming themselves or being harmed because disclosure of personal information somehow restricts their autonomy and freedom is unfounded and runs counter to the fact that the digital society is a media society in which almost everyone is interested in media presence and in showing off their uniqueness and difference to others. The so-called chilling effect of information disclosure may well have applied to the bourgeoise society of John Stuart Mill (*On Liberty*, published in 1859), but in today's exhibitionist culture, it is difficult to find.[34] Apparently, the to date 2.7 billion users of Facebook are not chilled by the fact that their personal information is exposed to many other people. The fact that it is increasingly difficult to identify any personal or social harms that demand the protection of privacy and equally difficult to deny people the right to disclose any information they wish leads Floridi to attempt to base the need for a fundamental right to privacy on an ontological interpretation of privacy in which people cannot do without privacy, that is, without barriers (ontological friction) blocking flows of information because, without such barriers, they would cease to exist.[35]

---

of course privacy into question. For a detailed discussion of privacy theory, see Belliger and Krieger (2018a).

34 There is no empirical correlation between creativity and secrecy. Performance art, artist cooperatives, theater, and so on all demonstrate that the public/private distinction is not coterminous to the distinction between conformism/innovation. For empirical evidence of how secrecy hinders creativity, see Goncalo et al. (2015).

35 "The information flow needs some friction in order to keep firm the distinction between the macro multi-agent system (the society) and the identity of the micro multi-agent systems (the individuals) constituting it. Any society (even a utopian one) in which no informational privacy is possible is one in which no personal identity can be maintained" (Floridi 2013, 243). This

Only if we *are* our information—and this is why it is important to ask which information this is—is privacy conceivable as a fundamental right. The question remains, what information constitutes the informational self? Since Floridi does not answer this question, we must ask *how* information can constitute the being of an individual person. One possibility is to examine how information is generally, and in most cases, gathered and ordered. Information is usually gathered and presented in two typical forms, either as a *list* or as a *narrative*. The list presents information according to some ordering principle, for example, alphabetical order, as in a dictionary or an encyclopedia, or numerically, or according to temporal succession, or priority with regard to some purpose, or even just randomly, as for example, a shopping list. Interestingly, the attributes of a substance in traditional Western ontology are presented as a list. If we describe something as a substance, a stone, for example, its attributes are a list of its weight, size, composition, shape, color, and so on. Floridi refers to such lists of attributes when defining the informational object as a set of "typed variables" (2011, 48) or as "cohering clusters of data" (356). In our reading, we do not see that Floridi clearly and definitively claims that the informational self is constituted by a list of attributes or as a set of typed variables. And if he does imply that this is so, we do not find this list anywhere explicitly put down.[36] The other way of ordering information is through narrative. A story puts information into a sequential order of events. First A happened, then B, then C, and so on. Narrative order is a well-known and much-discussed form of identity construction.[37] This is because a story includes not only events but also, and most importantly, actors who play certain roles (identities), pursue certain goals, and interact with other actors in the face of unexpected events.

Let us begin by looking at lists. Privacy regulations, for their part, do not appeal to narratives, but make lists of what is considered to be "personal" information such as name, address, telephone number, age, credit card number, driving license number, PIN, gender, ethnic or religious affiliation, medical records, and so on. Floridi (2013, 247) calls such information mere "labels" and seems to find them inadequate when it comes to defining privacy.[38] More adequate, but not infallible, in his opinion, are biometric markers

---

argument assumes identity must be unknown, which is difficult to imagine since others must be able to know who I am, if I am to be anyone at all.

36 Against the idea that one "owns" one's information, he does say that "'My' in 'my information' is not the same 'my' as in 'my car' but rather the same 'my' as in 'my body' or 'my feelings'" (2013, 244), but this does not say which information exactly is in question, which information about the body or emotions. He does mention DNA (247) as constitutive data, but this is a bad example since many people do share their genome and scientific research as well as medical treatment often demands this information. In addition to this, "my" DNA is shared with my family and interestingly with almost 99 percent with chimpanzees.

37 See for an overview the Wikipedia article on narrative identity (https://en.wikipedia.org/wiki/Narrative_identity) as well as the discussion of the narrative construction of order in Belliger and Krieger (2016).

38 "Each label in the list has no ontologically constative link with its bearer; it is merely associated with someone's identity and can easily be detached from it without affecting the individual" (Floridi 2013, 247).

of identity, such as fingerprints, iris patterns, facial characteristics, voice patterns, DNA, and so on. Floridi (2013, 248) considers biometric data to be "constitutive traits" of a person. It is interesting to note that biometric information is usually not included in lists of personal information relevant to privacy issues. Instead, biometric information is relevant in issues of authentication and authorization, where it is precisely the making public of this information that is required in order for it to have its authorizing or authenticating effect. Only if I share my biometric data do I gain access to certain services or products. Biometric information is useful only when it is made public. If I keep this information private, it has no use at all. Its purpose is to prove to others who I am by showing them information that could, presumably, only belong to me. Here we have an example of information that could, in some way, be considered constitutive of an informational self since biometric data can only belong to an individual person, but precisely this information is not private and cannot be kept private without losing its very purpose. It is information about myself that I *have* and can, therefore, externalize or make public when needed. Of course, this information can be misused if stolen. Theft, including identity theft, however, is not a privacy issue. It is a crime just as any kind of theft, to which one does not need to add a further offense called a violation of privacy.

It is questionable what the discussion of biometric information has to do with privacy at all and why Floridi even mentions it when what we are really interested in is what information constitutes a person so essentially and inalienably that it cannot be known by anyone without violating privacy.[39] Demanding that I show my fingerprint cannot be understood as aggression against my person when I need to use it to open my phone, access my office, withdraw money from my bank account, pass customs at the border, and so on. Passive biometric scanning, for example, registering how a user handles a device, which hand is used to hold the device, how the keyboard and mouse are used, and so on, has become a normal part of many Internet security applications. Furthermore, biometric behavior information of this kind has become a common part of commercial profiling with many applications beyond security concerns. Biometric information is admittedly personal information, but precisely for that reason, such information is not private. I can and must make such information public in many different contexts. Quite apart from the issue of whether such information constitutes the very being of a person, the question of ownership is also vague. Does the biometric information on my passport belong to me or to the government? What about my fingerprints in the police database or my company database? If biometric information is not owned by me and if it is constantly being registered and used in many social interactions, how can it constitute my being?

---

39 "If personal information is finally acknowledged to be a constitutive part of someone's personal identity and individuality, then one day it may become strictly illegal to trade in some kinds of personal information, exactly as it is illegal to trade in human organs (including one's own) or slaves" (Floridi 2013, 245). Quite apart from the fact that organs, for example, a kidney, is not at all like information that can be replicated at will, how are we to make sense of the suggestion to make the use of biometric data illegal?

Interestingly, this may also be said about the usual list of personal information, such as name, address, gender, age, income, and so on. None of this information is entirely private but must be disclosed in many different social interactions. What is striking about privacy regulations is not merely the vehemence with which they demand protection of personal information, but the many exceptions in which one cannot refuse to give this information to others. Of course, what is important for privacy issues is the question of consent to making certain information public, although in many cases, I have no choice, for example, paying taxes, entering a school, applying for a job, getting medical care, voting, joining military service, applying for a loan or bank account, and so on. It is hardly credible that I have a fundamental and inalienable right to keep this information private. Just try getting through the day with complete anonymity. More important than the issue of whether information is disclosed is the issue of whether information is misused, for example, identity theft, slander, stalking, and the like. As mentioned above, in cases of misuse of personal information, there are laws, or at least there should be, to sanction these as criminal acts, and it is, therefore, irrelevant to add to the already clearly identified crime a further offense against privacy. Most of the supposed harms that come from the loss of privacy could be more effectively ameliorated by clear identification and sanctioning of misuses of information than by attempting to establish laws and regulations protecting privacy when no harm or abuse of personal information results from disclosure.

In summary, we maintain that not only do lists of identifying attributes lack any constitutive value for the being of the self; they also cannot explain why the self is a bounded, unitary individual. Every limitation of how much information is to be included in a list is arbitrary. This problem is apparent when one considers how the General Data Protection Regulation (GDPR) of the European Union defines personal information, that is, that information which is protected by the right to privacy.

> "Personal data" means any information relating to an identified or identifiable natural person ("data subject"); an identifiable natural person is one who can be identified, directly or indirectly, in particular by reference to an identifier such as a name, an identification number, location data, an online identifier or to one or more factors specific to the physical, physiological, genetic, mental, economic, cultural or social identity of that natural person. (General Data Protection Regulation Art. 4)[40]

Important in this definition is that personal data extends to information that can be used to identify a person not only "directly," such as their name, but also "indirectly." The reference to indirect identification opens the door to endless amounts of information. Almost any information whatever can be aggregated with other information such that this information indirectly leads to the identification of an individual. There is virtually no limit on what could count as "personal data." This is not merely a practical problem that will have to be settled by the courts; it is a theoretical problem. Information is, by

---

40 https://gdpr-info.eu/art-4-gdpr/.

nature, connected to further information in ever-expanding networks. As data brokers have long known, it is easy and still entirely legal to gather extensive information about individuals for purposes of targeted communication, risk management, personalized advertising, and much more.[41] Whatever the GDPR is attempting to protect, it is not persons who are in any way ontologically constituted by information. If information ontologically constitutes anything, it is the entire infosphere and not individual persons who can exist, according to Floridi, only if their information is kept secret. By virtue of the network nature of information, informational selves cannot be bounded individuals. In terms derived from ANT, the network is the actor. As we shall see, this has consequences for how informational ethics must be conceived.

Having looked at the possibility of ordering personal information as a list, and finding it wanting, let us turn now to narrative. Although Floridi seems to favor the narrative ordering of information when it comes to explaining how the informational self is constituted by information (2013, 215), he offers no example of what information in what kind of story constitutes an informational self in a way that demands privacy. He does mention "intimate," "confidential," or "personal" information, which, in his opinion, should be kept private, but what this may be seems left to the discretion of the individual.[42] Individual discretion with regard to constitutive information, whether listed or packed into a story, implies that every informational self decides autonomously and independently what information constitutes its being and what does not. If everyone decides for themselves what information constitutes their being, not only can these decisions be revised, updated, reversed, and even completely denied; they also make it impossible to regulate privacy in any practical way. If whatever I declare to be private is private, then everyone has their own privacy rules, and no general regulation of privacy is possible. Furthermore, in this case, the self is not constituted by information, but instead by a sovereign autonomy of will, which contradicts Floridi's informational ontology. One cannot have both worlds. Either Nietzsche is right and the self is fundamentally constituted by freedom, will, and the power of sovereign decision, or the self is constituted by information. The moment everyone can decide for themselves what information constitutes their unique individuality, they can also choose to give that information away if they want. If Floridi is not to abandon his informational ontology of the self, then the answer must be that the self is constituted by information, which implies that it cannot lie at the discretion of each individual to decide what information constitutes it and what not. All the more reason to state clearly what information this is. It must be possible to answer this question if the individual is not to be allowed to arbitrarily decide which information constitutes itself and which does not.

We have argued that simply listing what counts as personal information, such as privacy regulations and laws do, may well indicate where you have to ask for consent to gather information, but, as we saw, no list can define which information constitutes the very being of an informational self, whether in terms of certain contents or in terms of

---

41 See the study by Christl (2017).
42 "Every day, a person may wish to build a different, possible better 'I'" (Floridi 2013, 246).

setting boundaries. What about narrative? Stories consist of actors and events. Neither certain events nor certain actors nor a certain amount of these can constitute an informational self as a bounded unity. No matter how complete or how personal and intimate a story is, every beginning and every end of a narrative is arbitrary and always subject to revision. As anyone who has watched a television series over many seasons or a Hollywood epic such as *Star Wars* knows, the story can go on indefinitely. The narrative form in itself cannot constitute a bounded unity no matter how hard one tries; the story could begin earlier or go on longer than it currently does. It could easily branch off in many unforeseen directions and include events and characters that previously were not included. Where exactly does "my" story begin? Does it start with my birth, that of my parents, of their parents? Does it begin at the founding of my country, the history of my culture, and so on? Where does it end? At my death? The death of my children? The end of my nation? We are left with the question: Which story consisting of what information constitutes me as a unique self? Apart from the reservations mentioned above, is it not so that narrative identity is also necessarily social identity? "My" story is a story told not by me alone, but by many other people in many situations for many different purposes. Indeed, my story is not "mine" in any exclusive or constitutive sense of the word at all but includes others and the entire world I live in, and perhaps goes on long after my death, as any biographer of historical personalities can attest. It would seem that neither can it be said which story constitutes an informational self to the exclusion of others nor can a list of such information do this job. What then is left of Floridi's informational ontology of the individual? And what does this somewhat dubious informational ontology contribute to an adequate formulation of ethics in the digital age?

Floridi's theory of the informational self rests upon two fundamental distinctions. First, there is the distinction between self and other with regard to knowing, that is, the difference between informational contents of consciousness that are exclusively and immediately "mine" and therefore constitute the unity of consciousness. Kant's transcendental unity of apperception is the basis for this view of the self. It should be obvious that this is not a bounded unity or, in any way, a private self. If Kant's transcendental ego demanded its privacy, there would be no knowledge, no science, no morality, and no civilization. Secondly, there is the distinction between the conscious self or "mind" that exists in a "virtual" domain distinguished as a system from the nonconscious, merely "cognitive" nervous system as well as from the living body, which itself is distinguished from the physical environment outside the body. According to Floridi, the conscious mind is literally "encapsulated" within the brain. This is the ontologically unitary and bounded self as opposed to the merely epistemologically unitary self derived from Kant. Non-Cartesian cognitive science has shown that there is little evidence that such an encapsulated mind exists. Furthermore, the notion of the mind encapsulated in a brain is derived from evolutionary systems theory and not from a philosophy of information. Indeed, neither of these arguments for the bounded, unitary individual is based upon information. The epistemological self is based on Kant's idealism, whereas the encapsulated self is based on the theory of evolution. Finally, we have seen that Floridi's claims that the self is ontologically constituted by information (how? which information?) are unconvincing. He cannot say which information constitutes a self, and he cannot show that this information is in any way bounded, unique, individual, and therefore ontologically "private." Where has this left us? What can be concluded from this discussion?

Either we have an informational ontology in which distinctions such as those between mind and matter, self and other, or introspection and external perception are more or less interesting and useful pieces of information along with everything else that exists, or we fall back upon a substance ontology where mind is a domain of reality independent of matter immediately known to itself such as Descartes's *res cogitans* or Kant's transcendental unity of apperception, and nature is a physical—and not virtual—world somehow outside of mind. It doesn't change anything to call all of these different substances information if they are still fundamentally distinct and still play their traditional roles in the well-known story of conscious individuals facing a world of things, of subjects and objects, of society and nature, of free will and determinism. If the mind is not immediately self-transparent but, as Floridi contends, mediated by information, that is, by information that constitutes the self as a bounded unity, then it must be possible to say what this information is. The fact that Floridi seems unable to do this is not accidental but depends upon the nature of information itself. Information is essentially not bounded. Information is inherently connected, related, and linked to other information. If we choose to begin not with traditional notions of the autonomous rational subject, and a physical world of inanimate matter out there beyond the subject, and if we do not attempt then to show how these traditional notions derived from a substance ontology can be interpreted in terms of information, but instead begin with information and ask what consequences this has for our traditional theories of the self, it becomes apparent that the self can no longer be understood as it has been in the Western humanist tradition and as Floridi attempts to do.

We have seen that for Luhmann, distinctions such as mind/matter and self/other have their proper home in the form of communication that he calls "theory" and which is meaningful within the functional subsystem of society called "science." In a court of law, the distinction between mind and matter would surely be out of place, and in politics, no one would understand what was being talked about. For ANT, traditional philosophical distinctions are links in a certain kind of network that associates certain actors, let us call them philosophers, universities, publishers, conferences, and so on, with each other and with certain socio-technical practices that could loosely be called "academic." Scientific and academic practices, as Latour has shown, are not isolated functional systems, as Luhmann supposes. They matter for society as a whole. They are linked to other networks and practices in law, media, and politics. We are not talking about "mere" theory or purely academic speculations. These distinctions are "real." They are differences that make differences. Theoretical discussions by philosophers and social scientists are information that affects what media communicate, what public opinions arise, what politicians decide, and what laws and regulations are enacted. This is why it is important to understand that information cannot exist only on one side of the distinction, namely, the mind, or why it is mistaken to assume that information is "virtual" while the rest of reality is physical or material. This is why it matters that there are no such things as bounded individual selves with exclusive claims upon certain inalienable information that supposedly constitutes their very being. If the informational self is to distinguish itself from some "other" in order to become a self, then it must distinguish itself within information and not from matter, not even from other minds. If it must draw a boundary around itself, then this must be an informational boundary. Informational boundaries are not really boundaries, but bridges, links, relations, associations that arise for practical purposes and are embedded in socio-technical networks.

We saw in the discussion of Luhmann's theory of social systems that informational boundaries are fundamentally different from physical or biological boundaries. Informational boundaries always include what is excluded. The outside is inside. The environment of the system of meaning is itself meaningful and, therefore, within the system. The environment of an organism, on the contrary, is not within the organism, but outside of it. This explains why the boundaries of the informational self cannot be modeled on the boundaries of physical or biological systems as Floridi attempts to do. The constitution of the informational self cannot be ontological, that is, a difference in being, but must exist as a difference that makes a difference, as information. Any boundary between self and other must be an informational boundary because being is relational. An informational ontology is a relational ontology. Everything exists as relation, as a difference that makes a difference. The point is that the distinction between self and other cannot be substantial but must be relational. From the perspective of an informational ontology, distinguishing self and other is actually a way of relating, a way of associating actors into networks. The act of distinguishing does not separate, it associates. It does not individualize as Floridi supposes, it "collectivizes," to use a term from Latour.

It makes no difference whether we are speaking of lists or narratives when it comes to describing information that is supposed to constitute a self. My story, no matter how personal or unique, is never uniquely mine but involves many others and is always at the same time their story too. We tell this story together. The story is not only collective but also unbounded. The beginning and end of a story are always arbitrary and subject to revision, extension, and integration into many other stories. Narrative does not allow for exclusion, sharp boundaries, and certainly for no such thing as ontological individualization. The narrative construction of identity does not block the flow of information. Consequently, it does not demand, require, or legitimate anything like Floridi's understanding of a fundamental right to privacy, which supposedly legitimates, even necessitates, ontological friction. Instead, narrative lays down the connections through which information flows into many channels and networks. It constructs actor-networks, such as the hunter or the warrior with his stone ax. The same is true for lists. No list of so-called personal information can constitute the ontological boundaries of the self. Any list of information that relates to a person cannot only be indefinitely extended but indefinitely shared and communicated. Informational being is connectivity and not individuality. Theorizing selves as individual informational entities, as Floridi attempts to do, has no place in an informational ontology. And if selves are not individual entities, boundaries are porous, flexible, situational, and practical arrangements always involving the cooperation of many heterogeneous and hybrid actors.

If there is anything like a right to privacy from the informational point of view, then it must be understood as the right to participate, not to withdraw and hide. If we are to acknowledge a right to privacy, then it should not be defined as a right to autonomously decide about flows of information, but to participate in negotiations about flows of information in differing contexts. Every actor has a voice—this is the "inviolate personality" that Warren and Brandeis (1890) referred to—but not a sovereign power of decision when it comes to regulating flows of information. Let us be clear, Floridi is right to argue that human beings *are* their information, but he is mistaken to assume that the information they are is exclusively their own or constitutive of what they are as individuals. The need to portray persons as bounded, unitary individuals who exist as certain inalienable information does not arise from the nature of information, nor the nature of the self, but the myths of Western humanism.[43] Floridi seems to be aware of this when he attempts to reinterpret individualism in terms of responsibility. "What goes under the label of 'Western individualism' is to be understood not so much in terms of the centrality of the single self, but rather in terms of the raising of a sense of personal responsibility" (2013, 252). Personal responsibility, however, does not depend upon privacy and secrecy, but much rather upon participation and engagement in society, the exercise of free speech, the creation and dissemination of information, and transparency and trust. It is through information that we have a voice, that we can be recognized as members of society, that we can demand to be taken seriously. Contrary to what Floridi assumes, it is by being known—and not by hiding behind a wall of ontological friction—that we can be identified as individual human beings with rights and duties. The information we are belongs to the many networks in which we participate, live our lives, identify ourselves, and contribute to the construction of meaning. Inforgs are indeed informational beings, and precisely for this reason, they do not have any such thing as a fundamental right to privacy. As informational beings they have a right to be a difference that makes a difference, that is, to be respected, to be able to participate, and to have a voice.

We have dealt at length with Floridi's discussion of privacy because it represents an example of how informational ethics are conceived in one of the most serious contemporary attempts to design a digital ethics. We have argued that despite fully acknowledging the significance of the digital transformation for ethical discourse in the twenty-first century, the philosophy of information and the ethics of information that Floridi proposes do not break new ground. Instead, what we are left with is a puzzling reaffirmation of the worldview of modern industrial society and Western humanism, and this on a theoretical basis that undermines the very myths of humanism Floridi attempts to uphold. Quite the opposite of presenting us with an ethics *for* the digital age, we are given an ethics *against* the digital age. The digital transformation that Floridi proclaims never took place. It is at once affirmed and denied. The denial comes from the fact that it threatens the traditional understanding of human existence and the values modernity has derived from this. We are left with the attempt to address the problems of the infosphere with norms and values that arose in a society that is passing and no longer represents the world in which we live. Lamentably, this is the current state of moral discourse at the beginning

---

43 It should be clear that myths are not simply false stories. On the contrary, myths are very important and exercise great influence. Myth is therefore not a pejorative term. It refers to a specific mode of knowledge.

of the twenty-first century. What Floridi as well as most other proponents of digital ethics represent is succinctly expressed in a recent Opinion of the Data Ethics Commission of the German government. Established in 2018 with the mission of providing the German government and parliament "with a framework on how to develop data policy and deal with algorithms, artificial intelligence and digital innovation" (Mission of the Data Ethics Commission),[44] general ethical principles that guide the commission's work on digital ethics are stated at the outset:

> Humans are morally responsible for their actions, and there is no escaping this moral dimension. Humans are responsible for the goals they pursue, the means by which they pursue them, and their reasons for doing so. Both this dimension and the societal conditionality of human action must always be taken into account when designing our technologically shaped future. At the same time, the notion that technology should serve humans rather than humans being subservient to technology can be taken as incontrovertible fact. Germany's constitutional system is founded on this understanding of human nature, and it adheres to the tradition of Europe's cultural and intellectual history. Digital technologies have not altered our ethical framework—in terms of the basic values, rights and freedoms enshrined in the German Constitution and in the Charter of Fundamental Rights of the European Union. Yet the new challenges we are facing mean that we need to reassert these values, rights and freedoms and perform new balancing exercises.[45]

The convictions and assumptions that inform this statement are typical of all current discussions of digital ethics in the Western world. On the one hand, humans are morally responsible, for they alone are moral subjects who chose goals and means based on their autonomy and rationality. On the other hand, humans are socially conditioned, and, although this is not explicitly stated, perhaps they are not as free and responsible as supposed by the myth of the autonomous rational subject. Regardless, it is an "incontrovertible fact" that in whatever way nonhumans, technologies, or societal constraints condition human freedom, humans must remain in absolute control of the situation. This is not only an incontrovertible fact; it is anchored in the Constitution of the German Republic, as well as many other European countries, and also in the Charter of Fundamental Rights of the European Union. This conviction is founded on a certain "understanding of human nature." This understanding of human nature is to be found in Europe's traditions. If we call these traditions humanist, then it is from humanism that "basic values, rights and freedoms" are derived. In the face of the digital transformation, we must therefore not reevaluate our traditions, reassess our understanding of human nature, and attempt to find new values. Instead, our traditional values must be "reasserted" in the face of challenges coming from digital technologies. This central position with regard to digital ethics has been affirmed in a recent programmatic statement

---

44 https://datenethikkommission.de/en/arbeitsauftrag-und-leitfragen/.
45 https://datenethikkommission.de/wp-content/uploads/191023_DEK_Kurzfassung_en_bf.pdf.

on the nature and scope of digital ethics from Floridi and others. Digital ethics is positioned as a bulwark against the erosion of human rights:

> The extensive use of increasingly more data—often personal, if not sensitive (Big data)—the growing reliance on algorithms to analyse them in order to shape choices and to make decisions (including machine learning, AI, and robotics), and the gradual reduction of human involvement or oversight over many automatic processes, pose pressing questions about fairness, responsibility, and respect of human rights. (Floridi et al. 2019, 9)

Of course, not everyone who cries "human" is a humanist in the sense of claiming privileged knowledge of an eternal and unchanging human nature and the ability to derive universal values and norms from this knowledge. After all that has been said above, however, the focus on privacy issues should make one suspicious. It would seem that wherever privacy takes center stage, which is almost everywhere in digital ethics, this can be taken as a good indication of humanist tendencies. It is, therefore, no accident that the above-cited Opinion of the German Data Ethics Commission, as well as the position paper by Floridi and his colleagues, locate privacy concerns at the center of digital ethics. When digital ethics are understood as an ethics primarily concerned with privacy, which is closely connected to freedom, autonomy, and dignity in one form or another, then there is reason to believe that the digital transformation has been overlooked. Despite all the talk about the opportunities and dangers of digital technologies and attempts to develop "digital ethics," the digital comes into view only as a challenge to traditional humanist values that must be "reasserted" at all costs. From this perspective, there has been no digital transformation of society; there is merely a digital challenge to the society we have known for at least two hundred years. When it comes to digital ethics, it appears that ethical discourse at the beginning of the twenty-first century is by and large an attempt to prolong the normative ethics of industrial society and the understanding of human nature typical of Western modernity. Floridi's answer to Luhmann's challenge to find a function for ethics in today's society is to say that information ethics functions to preserve modern Western values and social order in a world that is changing. What is at stake in discussions of privacy today is, therefore, not the exploitation of personal information by powerful state and corporate actors, threats to autonomy and dignity, but the demise of humanism and the world that it reflected. As Latour would say, privacy has become an "obligatory point of passage" into the digital age. Going through this narrow gate allows us to ask what the values and norms that arise in a global network society are. How does the digital transformation transform moral discourse as well? Where are new norms to be found, and how are they to be implemented if we no longer can rely upon the values and institutions of Western modernity? If it is true, as Latour claims, that *we have never been modern* and the modern parenthesis is coming to a close, what opportunities does this give us for renewing ethical discourse?

On the one hand, Floridi demands a radically new approach to understanding society and human existence based on information. This, we welcome and applaud. On the other hand, he joins almost all others today in retelling the same old story that has been told for hundreds of years. Only the names have been changed. This, we must reject.

We must resist the temptation to repeat our myths, as forcefully self-evident, intuitively true, and incontrovertible and undeniable as they might appear, and attempt to tell a new story. What if we take the digital transformation not as a threat to our traditions, but as an opportunity to culturally evolve into a different future? What if we suppose that we are not autonomous rational subjects, whose freedom, dignity, and autonomy depend on being bounded individuals with universal and inalienable rights, but instead, beings that are constituted by information, that exist in and as hybrid networks, that change with the networks we live in, that are constituted by relations and not be secrecy? What would this story look like? Who would be the actors? Where would the plot lead us? It could be claimed that the reason why privacy is so hotly debated today is not that digital technologies threaten privacy as never before, but that the right to privacy and the ethical and moral norms that support this right are derived from the philosophical mythology of humanism, which is being superseded by a new understanding of human existence, technology, and society that has its own values, norms, and forms of regulation that are waiting to be acknowledged and implemented.

2.2 Social Science Critique

The discourse of digital ethics is not restricted to the philosophical mythology of the autonomous rational subject and the universal norms and inalienable rights derived from it. There is another important and highly influential component of the legacy system upon which the discourse of digital ethics runs. This is *critique*. Critique is a specific form of discourse that arose in modernity and has characterized what it means to be modern for centuries. Critique stands behind "Enlightenment," which designates an entire period of modern thought. Furthermore, critique has become a form of knowledge closely associated with morality, political legitimacy, and social justice. Critique represents the autonomous rational subject in its struggle for freedom, justice, equality, and dignity. In order to understand the position and function of critique in the discourse of digital ethics, it is necessary to look more closely at what it means to be modern. We will describe modernity, following Latour, as a specific constellation of knowledge that can be called the "modern constitution." We will then briefly describe how critique arose within this modern constitution as a unique form of self-deception upon which modernity is based. Finally, under the titles of "platform society" and "surveillance capitalism," we will examine two representative examples of critique relevant to digital ethics.

2.2.1 The Modern Constitution

Many have proclaimed the end of modernity. At least since Heidegger, Western metaphysics, individualism, and humanism have been placed into question and, as the program of "postmodern critique" shows, even relegated to the past. It is not for nothing that the last decades have been dominated by many similar streams of thought grouped under the name of postmodernism or posthumanism. It is nothing new to declare the end of modernity. Furthermore, and more importantly, there is nothing anti-modern about it, since, as we shall see, such declarations stand within the modern tradition of critique itself. What is new and unheard of is the claim made by Bruno Latour (1993b), that we have never been modern in the first place. This is surprising and, at face value, difficult to believe. It may well be that modernity is passing, but that modernity never took place is startling and in need of justification. Of course, one could just put this claim aside as an exaggeration made to attract attention. Or one could simply write it off as nonsense. Although the temptation may be great to do this, perhaps it is worth taking a closer look to see what is behind this claim and whether it might lead us out of the many dead ends into which postmodernism seems to have led us. It is commonly known that postmodernism, or deconstruction, has left the world in fragments and pieces that no longer fit together into a coherent whole. The end of grand narratives, worldviews, unified interpretations of reality, and the ensuing "war of the worlds" (Latour 2002), which results from globalization and radical pluralism, are problems and not solutions. Where are we to go when no vision of the future is more than ideological self-indulgence? Perhaps, if we have never been modern in the first place, we don't need to be postmodern either. If this were somehow the case, we need no longer be ashamed of imagination and vision, and we can enter into the war of the worlds confident that there is something worth fighting for.

Let us recall Latour's ethnologist who discovers that science in action is not science, at least not in the sense in which modernity divides social reality into functional subsystems or ontological domains. What the ethnologist discovered was that the scientific laboratory is linked up to education, business, politics, law, and religion and this not by accident but in order to function as a laboratory. Instead of closed systems of communication coded by exclusive binary distinctions such as truth/falsity, legal/illegal, profit/loss, certification/noncertification of skills, and so on, what was discovered by carefully following the actors was a network of relations branching off in all directions and held together not only by human beings but also by microscopes, centrifuges, banks, courts, seminars, libraries, databases, business contracts, factories, logistics, computers, and much more. In contrast to this networking, which, as our ethnologist discovered, is what is really going on, for Luhmann, as well as for most modern social theory, modernity is characterized by functional differentiation of society and by the clear separation of the social realm from the realm of nature. What the ethnologist discovers is that the reality of modern society looks quite different from how modernity understands itself. Where modernity sees itself in terms of distinct systems and separate domains, society is actually made up of overlapping, intersecting, and scalable networks of human and nonhuman actors. Where the self-understanding of modernity sees free and autonomous rational subjects facing a world of natural facts governed by determinate causality, what is really there is a "collective" (Latour 2005, 14) of heterogeneous and hybrid actors, quasi-objects and quasi-subjects, all linked together in many different networks. Why this discrepancy? How is it possible that everything the moderns say about themselves is different from everything they are? Are we dealing with a kind of illusion that could simply be dispelled by pointing out that we were never modern in the first place?

To say that we have never been modern is to say that we need to neither spend great effort attempting to preserve modern values in a world supposedly hostile to them nor go out of our way to critique such values in order to throw off the yoke of modernity. The claim is that modernity simply never was what it appeared to be. In the case of humanist and Enlightenment ideals of the autonomous rational subject who is the addressee of universal, inalienable rights as well as moral praise and blame, we no longer need to go to the extreme of proposing an ontological theory of privacy in order to establish that this being actually exists and can still function as the basis of morality in the information age. We can just drop this entire discussion and move on. But where do we go? If we have never been modern, then what have we been? What are we if we can no longer call ourselves modern? If modernity has covered over or disguised what was and is really going on, how can we describe something that for centuries had no place in the world and now suddenly comes forward and claims center stage?

Let us begin by way of negation, that is, by attempting to describe what modernity is. This is a somewhat unusual *via negativa* because by describing modernity, we demarcate what we are not and thus, by way of negation, come to know what we are. If it is so that we have never been modern, then knowing what modernity is points to that which, because of the illusion of modernity, we have not seen. Latour (1993b, 13) describes modernity as a particular "constitution," which lays out a separation of powers much as a political constitution distinguishes the legislative, the executive, and the judiciary. The "modern constitution" distinguishes a realm of nature that is assigned to science as the domain of objective facts under the rule of determinate causality. Secondly, it describes a realm of human subjects who are at once capable of objective knowledge of scientific facts as well as being inescapably influenced by passions, prejudices, and mere opinions. Alongside "objective" scientific knowledge of the realm of nature, humans are deeply influenced by a knowledge that is merely "subjective." This subjective knowledge, as well as the passions and prejudices that rule human interaction and everything humans produce, makes up the realm of society, culture, and politics. This social and artificial realm is subjected to the contingencies of history and the vicissitudes of politics and power, and of course, the imperatives of morality. It is hierarchically organized with economic and political elites at the top. Beneath these elites are the informational elites, that is, those who control knowledge, access to information, and decisions about truth and falsity. Beneath them lie the military and police who ensure order. And at the bottom are the people, the autonomous rational subjects who are involved in a never-ending struggle for freedom, equality, justice, and dignity. Opposed to both society and nature, there is the realm of the transcendent, of God, who after the devastation of countless religious wars is no longer allowed to be involved in worldly matters. The moderns were those who successfully banned spirits from nature, religion from politics, and then withdrew into their own historical world where they heroically shouldered the burden of creating their destiny without the intervention of God or nature. Of course, this is not the whole story. As it turns out, nature did intervene in human affairs, but under exceptional and even "unnatural" circumstances. The moderns confined nature within the artificial boundaries and conditions of the laboratory and subjected it to challenges and tests through the scientific method and with the help of carefully constructed instruments. No longer did one first consult the Bible or the teachings of the ancients to discover the truth; one forced nature to speak through instruments and, in this way, make herself known to anyone who could see with an unprejudiced eye.

The moderns were those that unleashed the powers of technology, harnessed knowledge for practical purposes, and populated the world with artifacts and machines of all kinds. These things, however, were invisible. They had no voice in the modern polity. They were neither objective facts of nature, since they were constructed and thus artificial, nor were they mere products of reason, deduced from divine truths or indisputable logic. They were real things that depended as much on material attributes as on linguistic or pictorial descriptions. What were these strange beings that did so much to shape the world, but had so little to say about what it meant to be modern? Where does the laboratory belong in a world separated into society on the one side and nature on the other? What goes on in the laboratory is, at once, artificial and natural. The laboratory produces "hybrids," that is, things that are both artificial and natural, both social and determined by natural laws. In reality, society depends on these things, that is, technologies and knowledge of how things work, and nature depends on society, on laboratories, instruments, experiments, and technical expertise to speak for itself. Without all the artificial contraptions of the laboratory, we would know nothing of nature. Nature without society would be left in the hands of God, as would society without nature. The modern constitution separates society from nature, the realm of freedom from the realm of necessity, but in reality, the modern world depends upon their mediation, their cooperation, their symbiosis, their entanglement. Where does this cooperation take place? Where are all the hybrids to be found? They have no place in the modern constitution. They exist, multiply, condition everything in a space that does not exist. As Latour (1993b, 34, 37) puts it:

> The essential point of this modern Constitution is that it renders the work of mediation that assembles hybrids, invisible, unthinkable, unrepresentable. [...] Everything happens in the middle, everything passes between the two, everything happens by way of mediation, translation and networks, but this space does not exist, it has no place. It is the unthinkable, the unconscious of the moderns.

Let us recall our stone ax or Heidegger's hammer. The typically modern response to these would be: What are these things if they are not external entities whose attributes and behaviors can be perceived, measured, registered, compared, and cataloged? But as both our prehuman hunter and Heidegger's builder knew, they are not mere objects of disinterested knowledge. They are actors in networks of practical use and endeavor. It is they who make hunters and builders into what they are as well as that which is made by them. To make it clear that things are not primarily objects of disinterested knowledge, Latour speaks of "hybrids," that is, entities that are neither subjects nor objects. He also speaks of "quasi-objects" and "quasi-subjects" (1993b, 51). Latour's claim is that the modern constitution left these beings out of account; quite literally, it did not account for them. They were there. They prospered and attained great influence. They did more to make the modern world than did any objective facts or autonomous rational subjects. But they had nothing to say, were assigned no place in the modern constitution, were without representation and without any voice in modern affairs. Although the modern world was a world everywhere made up of these beings, that is, of actor-networks, official modernity knew nothing of them. The world of these beings was, therefore, never modern. It was nonetheless the real world and still is. This is why Latour can say that we have never been modern.

Insisting upon the unique way of being of hybrids and networks also explains why it is inviting to accuse Heidegger and also Latour of premodern, or anti-modern, sentiments. If the carpenter and not the scientist is the paradigm of human existence, if a hammer, a clay jug, a sculpture, or a painting of a pair of farmer's shoes are the paradigms of objects and not scientific facts, then what can this be if not a romanticizing premodernism? Instead of saying we have never been modern, Heidegger prefers to say we have forgotten Being. If we understand Being as "networking," then Heidegger and Latour are not as far away from each other as is often supposed. It is a mistake, however, to assume that the scientist is any different from the hunter or the carpenter or that a so-called objective fact is not just as subjective as an artifact such as a stone ax or a hammer. As our ethnologist who studied science in action discovered, the scientist is also involved in practices that are dependent upon and linked up with many different human and nonhuman actors. Scientific research is, in reality, a practical knowing in Heidegger's sense of dealing with a world of things bound up with other things in a referential context connected to many different programs of action. Even the data scientist who is dealing with "raw" data is only one actor in a network of computers, cables, bits and bytes, software, protocols, layers, databases, queries, and much more. Scientific practice is meaningful and constructs meaning in exactly the same way as Heidegger's carpenter building a house or as our prehuman hunter wielding a stone ax. All are *doing the same thing*.[46] What all these activities have in common is that they are constructing meaning through networking. The scientist in her laboratory and the informatic expert extracting data from a server, the prehistoric hunter, and the carpenter at his workbench, are all doing the same thing. What this is, is what modernity does not acknowledge or even suppose to exist, or at least, if the moderns admit that prehistorical hunters and humble carpenters do things, then such activities are those that distinguish modernity from past ages and so-called premodern practices. The historical caesura between the modern world and all that has come before it, and all that exists outside of it, is a construction of the modern constitution that prevents what is really going on in the modern world from coming into view. This is what it means to say that we have never been modern. But what does this mean for ethics and especially for digital ethics? If we have never been modern, then perhaps we don't need modern ethics and certainly do not need to prolong the moral discourse of modernity into the digital future.

The modern constitution assigns morality to the realm of freedom and society. The official ethics of modernity is derived from knowledge of human nature, which is either

---

46 Latour the empiricist has qualms about saying the same thing about everything, since this is exactly what metaphysics does. What all beings have in common, what is the same for all beings is Being. To say that everything is insofar as it is mediated in an actor-network is a metaphysical statement. When it comes to describing how things are different, we find Luhmann's systems theory approach more satisfying than Latour's (2012) attempt to describe modes of existence on the basis of a phenomenology of experience.

self-evident or discovered by the social sciences. Because humans are so, it is argued, there exist certain universal moral norms. The subjective, passionate, prejudiced, and often fallible side of human nature is to be corrected by the objective and normative knowledge of which humans are also capable. This knowledge is given to us either by philosophy or by the empirical sciences, above all the social sciences. It is because of this knowledge of what people ought to do that they can be praised and blamed for doing what they do. To understand the moral discourse of modernity, it is crucial to understand the connection between the typically modern form of thought that can be termed "critique" and "ethics." Critique is an integral part of the modern constitution. What is critique?

2.2.2 Critique

It can be said that critique began on a large scale with Descartes, whose method for attaining knowledge consisted of doubting everything that could not be ascertained with certainty:

> Several years have now elapsed since I first became aware that I had accepted, even from my youth, many false opinions for true, and that consequently what I afterward based on such principles was highly doubtful; and from that time I was convinced of the necessity of undertaking once in my life to rid myself of all the opinions I had adopted, and of commencing anew the work of building from the foundation. (Descartes, Meditation I, 1641)

The first survivor of methodological skepticism was the individual self, certain of its existence and freedom, *cogito ergo sum*. This is the birth of the autonomous rational subject, who was to become the hero of the humanist saga. The first victim of methodological doubt was tradition, including all the knowledge that had been handed down for centuries as the revealed truths of religion as well as the authoritative teachings of the ancients. Indeed, before the modern period, philosophy, theology, and knowledge of nature (natural philosophy as it was called) were all mixed up together. Descartes's methodological skepticism put an end to this and established not only the indubitable self-certainty of the *ego cogito* but at the same time also critique as the secular path to truth not only in matters of philosophy and science but also in questions of morality. Kant's "critiques" carried this tradition a step further in that morality and religion were to be accepted as legitimate only within the limits of pure reason. With the advent of the human sciences, pure reason was replaced, or at least rivaled, by empirical science, which translated moral indignation into claims to expose and debunk ideology, false consciousness, misuse of power, injustice, exploitation, and finally the destruction of nature as well.

The critical gesture consists of moving between the subject and the object without mediation and without even letting the one hand know what the other is doing. If it was proclaimed that human freedom was at liberty to make of the world what it wills, critique denounced human arrogance and the abuse of power by pointing out that the laws of psychology, economics, and sociology demonstrate that individual freedom is everywhere curtailed and libertarianism is a dangerous ideology. If it was proclaimed that science shows that humanity is governed by objective facts and causal determinism, critique appealed to pure reason, free will, and individual liberties, that is, to the myth of the autonomous rational subject. If it was proclaimed that law is based on eternal moral norms derived from direct knowledge of human nature, critique denounced this as blindness to the relativity of social and cultural norms, to the fact that laws are made by people or by sovereign rulers and not by God or pure reason. Against this proclamation, critique turned around and showed that human-made laws are always subject to judgment in terms of higher truths that are universally valid. Critique at once denounced both the subject and the object in the name of both the subject (society) and the object (nature), whereby the one hand pretended not to know what the other hand was doing.

One of the important consequences of critique was to hide, cover over, disguise, and pass over what was really going on, that is, the proliferation of hybrids and networks. As Latour puts it, "Everything happens by way of mediation, translation and networks, but this space does not exist" (Latour 1993b, 37). Another important consequence was to transform scientific discourse into a uniquely modern form of moralizing. Beyond the boundary of the functionally differentiated system of science, critique pursues a program of emancipation and political and social change.

Luhmann (2008, 107) noted that moral discourse in modern functionally differentiated societies was how the "actually practiced conditions of mutual respect and disrespect" were communicated. Luhmann suggests that moral discourse has become "moralizing" (*Moralisierung*). More important than specific norms or imperatives is the social function of moralizing communication, which consists of thematizing the conditions of respect or disrespect in any social situation whatever they may concretely be. Respect means acceptance, acknowledgment, access to opportunity, and equality. Without respect, there can be no social bond, no mutual recognition, no *alter ego*, and, therefore, no possibility of society emerging as a system of communication.

The connection between critique and moralizing arises from the typically modern conviction that the philosophical mythology of the autonomous rational subject must be accepted and acknowledged as the basis of society. This is so even when the social sciences demonstrate that this subject is conditioned, if not determined, by economics, psychological drives, political ideologies, and so on. The science that does the critique is somehow always free of the many factors conditioning the unfree subjectivity of the masses. No matter which hand is dealing the cards, the autonomous rational subject is the mythical hero of modernity. It is important to note that this hero plays a central role in a much greater mythological drama. It plays the role of constantly and courageously struggling for freedom, equality, justice, and dignity against religious, economic, and political elites who misuse power to oppress and exploit "the people." Despite the rule of law and democratic processes characteristic of modern Western societies, the hierarchical structure of social order has not fundamentally changed. The middle class, as well as the poor and marginalized, is inevitably on the short end of social power, opportunity, and privilege. The drama of emancipation and struggle for justice that unfolds on this stage determines the possible forms of moralizing today. This is not only to be found in the many critical gestures of the social sciences but also visible in the moral indignation or moral outrage that quickly comes into medial presence the moment the myth of humanism and the modern constitution is perceived to be challenged. The challenge to European humanism and the modern social order that the digital transformation and the global network society represent is countered by attempts to reassert the philosophical mythology of the autonomous rational subject as well as social scientific critique. As we will see below, both media scandalization and the activities of many civil society actors come to their aid. They together make up what we call the legacy system upon which digital ethics is currently running. The purpose of almost all forms of digital ethics today has nothing to do with assessing the values and norms appropriate to a global network society, but with reasserting the ethical framework of modern industrial society, its hierarchies, its elites, its forms of power and contestation of power against all challenges and by every means that modernity puts at its disposal. It makes no difference whether critique comes from left or right, or whether it aims to assert the rights of the middle class or the poor and marginalized. Both trajectories of critique are aimed at preserving, reasserting, and maintaining the modern constitution.

Modern moral discourse is inevitably entwined with critique, denunciation, and moralizing. This is how the two sides of human nature, fallibility, and perfectibility relate to each other within the mythological drama of modernity. Critique plays both sides of the constitutional divide, the subjective side and the objective side, while suppressing the middle, the place of mediation. If we have never been modern, then hidden behind or beneath the moral indignation of one half of human nature against the other half, behind the loud debunking of critique, either in the name of the subject or the object, or in the name of the autonomous rational subject as either an empowered entrepreneur or exploited laborer, there lies an entirely different social reality governed by a different morality. Latour (1993b, 45) remarks that there must have been an "unofficial morality" that guided the many decisions of all those involved with practical matters of networking:

> But underneath moral judgement by denunciation, another moral judgement has always functioned by triage and selection. It is called arrangement, combination, *combinazione*, combine, but also negotiation or compromise. [...] The same holds true for the unofficial morality that constantly selects and distributes the practical solutions of the moderns. It is scorned because it does not allow indignation, but it is active and generous because it follows the countless meanderings of situations and networks. It is scorned because it takes into account the objects that are no more the arbitrary stakes of our desire alone than they are the simple receptacle for our mental categories. Just as the modern Constitution scorns the hybrids that it shelters, official morality scorns practical arrangements and the objects that uphold it. Underneath the opposition between objects and subjects, there is the whirlwind of the mediators. Underneath moral grandeur there is the meticulous triage of circumstances and cases.

All the hunters, carpenters, engineers, scientists, and entrepreneurs responsible for producing hybrids; for constructing networks; for mixing up nature and culture, subjects and objects; and for disregarding the boundaries of the modern constitution, all of these people must have been and continue to be guided by another morality, by other norms and values than that which modernity officially proclaims. This unofficial morality was never part of modern critique. It was never acknowledged by the myths of humanism and the autonomous rational subject. Its norms and values were never appealed to by critique either from the left or from the right. The entire arsenal of modern critique has been mobilized to back up the ethical defense of humanism with social and political arguments and programs. Ethical discourse at the beginning of the twenty-first century can be seen as following a trajectory from philosophical arguments to government regulation. This trajectory, from morality to politics, however, is not a straight line. It takes detours through other forms of discourse. One of these is "critical social science" or "critical theory."[47]

Much discussion of digital ethics is carried on in the manner of critical theory and critical social science. Although critique does not always explicitly derive its goals from ethics, it is ethically motivated. It expresses itself in the form of moral indignation in the name of certain values that are usually assumed to be fundamental and inalienable rights as well as founded upon a specific form of social order. The modern critical gesture of denunciation of supposed violations of rights and norms can be called "critical moralizing," where "critique" designates the typically modern gesture of denunciation and the term "moralizing," following Luhmann, designates the attempt to assert the conditions of mutual recognition in any social context. We propose speaking of critical moralizing completely apart from any pejorative connotations as a technical term for how digital ethics is conducted in the nonethical discipline of social science critique. The ethically motivated critical moralizing that makes up this aspect of ethical discourse arises in fields such as sociology, psychology, media studies, cultural studies, and political science. There is no question that the digital transformation has called forth highly critical appraisals of contemporary society in this mode of discourse. This discourse is characterized by movement from ethical concerns to social and political concerns. Concerning the impact of ICTs on society, several areas have become focal points for the discourse of critical moralizing. In the following, we will look at two representative examples of critique. The goal is not to gain an overview of the many different forms of critique that currently contribute to the discourse of digital ethics. This would probably be impossible within the limits of a monograph. The goal is to get a feeling for critique as one of the components of the legacy system of ethical discourse that characterizes the moralizing efforts of what can be considered digital ethics today.

2.2.3 *Platform Society*

A good illustration of contemporary critical moralizing is offered by the Dutch media theorist van Dijck (2013, 2018). In a recent work, *The Platform Society. Public Values in a Connective World*, van Dijck, Poell, and Waal (2018) describe the challenge of the digital transformation in terms of the emergence of the "platform society." Platform society "refers to a society in which social and economic traffic is increasingly channeled by an (overwhelmingly corporate) global online platform ecosystem that is driven by algorithms and fueled by data" (4). According to van Dijck, the digital revolution can be

---

47 For an overview, see the Wikipedia article on critical theory (https://en.wikipedia.org/wiki/Critical_theory).

most clearly seen in the emergence of platforms, which are defined as "a programmable digital architecture designed to organize interactions between users—not just end-users but also corporate entities and public bodies" (ibid.). When speaking of the platform society, van Dijck does not mean only the so-called Big Five tech companies, Apple, Amazon, Alphabet, Microsoft, and Facebook, but those smaller companies that use in many ways the infrastructure offered by the larger companies. Also involved are "government, incumbent (small and large) business, individual entrepreneurs, nongovernment organizations, cooperatives, consumers, and citizens," who "all participate in shaping the platform society's economic and social practices" (4). The platform ecosystem is not limited to national boundaries but is "distinctly global" (ibid.). According to van Dijck and colleagues, the platform ecosystem operates utilizing three "platform mechanisms" that "shape social activity across economic sectors and spheres of life" (32). These platform mechanisms are "datafication," "commodification," and "selection" (ibid.). Van Dijck's critique consists of the claim that these platform mechanisms "upend established institutional arrangements and at times put traditional public values under pressure" (ibid.). Let us take a closer look at these mechanisms.

2.2.3.1 Datafication

There is a concentration of power in the hands of the Big Five platform corporations. Together, they "shape the core technological infrastructure, dominant economic models, and ideological orientation of the ecosystem as a whole." In addition to this, "they steer how sectoral platforms, society institutions, companies, and billions of users interact" (ibid.). Datafication plays a vital role in establishing and maintaining this dominance. Van Dick and colleagues follow Mayer-Schönberger and Cukier (2013) in defining "datafication" as "the ability of networked platforms to render into data many aspects of the world that have never been quantified before" (33). In principle, "every form of user interaction can be *captured* as data: rating, paying, enrolling, watching, dating, and searching but also friending, following, liking, posting, commenting, and retweeting" (ibid.; emphasis in original). The list can go on indefinitely when tracking of all kinds are added including user location data from cell phones and the data from body-tracking apps for fitness and health, surfing history, photos, videos, audio files, and much more. According to van Dijck and colleagues, datafication "endows platforms with the potential to develop techniques for predictive and real-time analytics, which are vital for delivering targeted advertising and services in a wide variety of economic sectors" (ibid.). This is not a one-way street. End users and consumers also can gain access to this data, "enabling them to trace the activities of friends and colleagues, keep track of public events, and participate in the online economy" (ibid.).

Van Dijck and colleagues emphasize that gathering information about consumers is not new. Both business and government have always been involved in collecting information about consumers and citizens. The digital transformation has simply intensified these practices and extended them to areas that before the rise of platforms were not accessible to quantification and analysis. As mentioned above, "every activity of every user can be captured, algorithmically processed, and added to that user's data profile"

(34). This allows platform corporations and business partners, as well as governments, to "profile demographic, behavioral, and relational characteristics of users" (ibid.). This radically transforms the traditional "public sphere" of democratic societies in which citizens and civil society organizations by means of investigative journalism, whistleblowers, and other forms of traditional information gathering monitor government activities and corporate abuses of power and participate in democratic practices of opinion building in order to control market failures. In the platform society, "the ability of citizens and societal organizations to monitor public activities and sentiments is fundamentally based on the systematic and automated collection and analysis of every form of user activity" (ibid.). This need not necessarily be a threat to democracy and traditional values. On the contrary, much much more information is now available to understand what is going on in society. Opinion building need no longer be based on gut feelings, ideological prejudices, or peer pressure but can be founded on data and evidence. In principle, datafication opens up possibilities of direct democracy that have yet to be explored and implemented. Nonetheless, van Dijck and colleagues emphasize that "platforms do not merely 'measure' certain sentiments, thoughts, and performances but also trigger and mold them, most visibly through their user interfaces" (ibid.). That powerful social actors including governments and businesses as well as the media themselves filter information and thus influence public opinion is also nothing new. Still, in the platform society, this seems to have become a more serious problem than ever before.[48]

2.2.3.2 Commodification

Commodification is the second mechanism of the platform ecosystem. It refers to the ways in which platforms turn datafication into profits. Since the business models of platforms determine the strategies, practices, and uses of datafication, and since datafication strongly influences the public sphere and, therefore, democratic society, it is important to understand commodification. Generally, commodification occurs via sales of data for the development and marketing of personalized products and services. Although the tenor of most social science critique is to condemn such business models as violations of privacy, van Dijck and colleagues offer a more nuanced view and point out that "commodification mechanisms are simultaneously empowering and disempowering to users" (37). Not only does comodification allow large corporations and their partners to profit from data, but small companies and individuals can participate as well. Strategies of commodification function by "enabling users to become entrepreneurs in their own right" and thus "potentially shift economic power from legacy institutions [...] to individual users" (ibid.). This positive view of commodification is, however, quickly corrected by reference to the usual critique of capitalism. The market tends toward "exploitation of cultural labor, the (immaterial) labor of users, and the further precarization of on

---

[48] See the discussions of "filter bubbles," "echo chambers," "targeted advertising," "manipulation," and "fake news," which have become omnipresent in popular as well as academic literature.

demand service workers" (ibid.). In addition to this, the concentration of power in the hands of a few big players is a danger in itself. Platform power is not to be understood in terms of the usual monopolies but as the result of "network effects." If everyone is on Facebook, then I have no choice but to join Facebook as well. If Facebook lets me use its services and data to drive my own business, then I have no choice but to use Facebook. Economies of scale, which are essential for effective datafication, can be attained only by a few large players. Once these have reached a critical mass, network effects guarantee their further success. What this means is that the business models and the influence of a few large players influence the entire economy. As van Dijck and colleagues put it, "Economic processes across sectors are increasingly being oriented toward and determined by platforms" (39), which leads to "new dependencies and hierarchies" (40). What is problematic about this situation is the "huge disparity in power relations" (ibid.). This brings us to the third platform mechanism, selection, moderation, or filtering.

2.2.3.3 Selection

Selection designates the fact that platforms do not merely pass all information available on without any moderation, filtering, or curation. Instead, they perform a "selection" of which information flows through their channels and to whom information flows. As David Weinberger argued in *Too Big to Know* (2012), there is simply too much information in the world to allow all this information to flow freely and without any kind of channeling or filtering. Some of us can remember when in the early days of the Internet, a search query would return millions of hits that were in no way ordered according to relevance or quality. Google's success is based on solving this problem. But Google's success was a filter, an algorithm that decided which information out of the almost infinite amount on the Web would be returned for any search query. The Google algorithm filters information, among other criteria, based on information users themselves produce. This same is true for platforms. Their algorithms also rely on information users themselves have put into the platform. As van Dijck (2018, 40–41) points out,

> Online platforms replace expert-based selection with user-driven and algorithm-driven selection. Users now filter content and services by "rating," "searching," "sharing," "following," and "friending." Hence, platform "selection" can be defined as the ability of platforms to trigger and filter user activity through interfaces and algorithms, while users, through their interaction with these coded environments, influence the online visibility and availability of particular content, services, and people.

Although it is admitted that user involvement in the filtering of information "appears more democratic than expert-based selection" (41), van Dijck and colleagues criticize the lack of transparency of algorithmic processes, which, after all, are driven by strategies of commodification and not of public welfare. She sees in this development a threat to the self-determination and autonomy of citizens and consumers, since "we now rely on algorithms just as we used to rely on credentialed experts, even though we know very little about the mechanisms defining those choices" (ibid.). The assumption seems to be that "credentialed" humans experts are transparent and always better informed and make better decisions than evidence-based AIs. Furthermore, the assumption is that the filtering of information in pre-algorithmic days was done by "experts." If this is what van Dijck is assuming, in our opinion, it is a very risky assumption. What would you do if your oncologist says you're fine, but an AI says you have cancer and need an operation immediately? Even if you don't understand how the algorithm works, wouldn't you at least ask your doctor to look at the laboratory results again or even consult another doctor?[49] Van Dijck and her colleagues would, apparently, trust the credentialed human expert and not the algorithm. Selection, therefore, represents a problem in itself, an issue that, according to van Dijck and colleagues, can be more closely described in terms of three types of selection. These are personalization, reputation and trends, and moderation.

Personalization is a type of selection. "Personalization depends on 'predictive analytics': the ability to predict future choices and trends on the basis of analyzing historical patterns of individual and aggregate data" (ibid.). According to van Dijck, the problem with this form of selection is again the lack of transparency of algorithmic decision making. As van Dijck puts it, "These automated choices are notoriously difficult to analyze or audit" (ibid.). The lack of transparency of algorithmic decisions is based not only on the fact that they are proprietary and thus not open to view but also on the fact that they change constantly with new business models and, finally, that they work together with continuously changing user data. In other words, we are faced with a complex sociotechnical system such that "it is impossible to determine how platform algorithms exactly work" (ibid.).[50] On the positive side, personalization appears to give everyone the information and access to services and products that they want. Despite this positive side to personalization, from the critical perspective, there are negative "societal consequences." For example, personalization "can lead to social fragmentation, enclosing users in 'filter bubbles' which bar them from being exposed to a wide variety of societal values and perspectives" (42). Van Dijck also mentions negative consequences in education where "a personalized algorithmic approach to learning may benefit individual students but may inadvertently diminish the emphasis on collective teaching and learning experience" (ibid.). Nonetheless, van Dijck admits that personalization is "precisely the reason so many people are attracted to platforms" (ibid.). Indeed, "customization and personalization also empower users as consumers and citizens, enabling them to quickly find the most attractive offer and the information they are interested in" (ibid.).

A further type of selection can be called "reputation and trends." Platforms not only filter information on the basis of personalization but also "identify trends among the larger user population and determine reputations of users" (ibid.). This goes hand in

---

49 A recent study showed that 64 percent trust a robot more than their boss (https://www.roboticsbusinessreview.com/ai/study-says-64-of-people-trust-a-robot-more-than-their-manager/).

50 The everywhere present call for transparency and explainability with regard to algorithms appears naïve when one considers how long it has been known that the operations of non-linear, complex systems of all kinds cannot be exhaustively explained and made predictable, especially when one also assumes that human decision making is transparent and explainable.

hand with the often-cited characteristic of Internet communication, and especially of social media, to allow certain information to "go viral" and be amplified way beyond any proportion to the validity or importance of the information. A further consequence of trending via ratings and user behavior as well as reputation evaluation is the replacement of "community-based modes of interpersonal trust" (43) by reputation ratings. Uber and Airbnb make it possible to get into a stranger's car or accept strangers into your home based on ratings. Not only does this open the field to all kinds of attempts to game the system and improve one's scores, but it is also again questionable whether such reputation ratings can effectively replace former "institutional guarantees" (ibid.).

The third type of selection is called "moderation." This means that platforms inevitably curate the information they mediate. Whatever criteria are used and whether the work is done by people or by algorithms, there is no agreement on how to do it rightly. Depending on who one asks, platforms, such as Facebook, moderate either too little or too much or they remove the wrong information instead of what really should be taken down, and so on. Platforms also involve users by allowing them to flag certain information as objectionable. Van Dijck confirms what many have said, that platforms do not have strong incentives to moderate against "objectionable" information because this reduces their clicks and their advertising revenues. Nonetheless, public pressure, media scandalization, and lobbying of interest groups have led to many platforms at least claiming to introduce publicly responsible moderation policies. Controversial issues with regard to moderation are threats to labor rights by canceling accounts of independent contractors such as Uber drivers, or limitations on free speech, or the balance between top-down moderation and peer-to-peer quality management or, finally, the question of whether AIs can moderate better than humans since both are biased.

All three types of selection, as well as the other platform mechanisms of datafication and commodification, represent new forms of economic and social practices that do not fit neatly within the ideological or regulatory framework of industrial society. Indeed, they are products of the digital transformation. They demand to be understood and evaluated in terms of values and norms derived from the global network society and not from the society they have left behind. Nonetheless, van Dijck and colleagues maintain a decidedly critical position concerning platforms. Platform society is not a positive development and must be judged accordingly. The critique operates by refusing even to consider the need for new evaluative criteria and interpretive frameworks and holds fast to the myths of modern industrial society. The possibility that the values and norms of modernity could be placed into question by the digital transformation remains entirely outside the scope of the perspective taken by van Dijck's critical project.

The mechanisms of the platform ecosystem of datafication, commodification, and selection are "geared toward the systematic collection, algorithmic processing, circulation, and monetization of user data" (ibid.). This is not a matter of one or two distinct innovative or disruptive technologies such as Facebook or Uber. Platforms link together and build a "platform ecosystem" that "shapes everyday practices" in almost all areas of life on a global scale. Platforms have "penetrated the heart of societies—affecting institutions, economic transactions, and social and cultural practices—hence forcing governments and states to adjust their legal and democratic structures" (2). Platforms are "gradually infiltrating in, and converging with, the (offline, legacy) institutions and practices through which democratic societies are organized" (2). In short, van Dijck and colleagues argue that platforms as representatives of what Floridi and others usually call ICTs "produce the social structures we live in" (ibid.). This is the digital transformation. But how is this transformation to be evaluated?

The challenge that platforms pose for ethics and social and political theory is framed by van Dijck and colleagues not explicitly as a challenge to humanism or human rights but as a conflict of public values versus private values. "Platforms are neither neutral nor value-free constructs; they come with specific norms and values inscribed in their architectures" (3). The values that van Dijck finds inscribed in the architectures of platforms are primarily values of "private benefit and corporate gain." These "private" values are portrayed as fundamentally opposed to traditional—above all European—values of "public interests and collective benefits" (2–3). From this perspective, the digital transformation "enables connectedness, while bypassing existing social institutions" (2). Van Dijck accordingly rejects the hype typical of many platforms, which claims that "connectivity automatically leads to collectivity" (ibid.). Opposing in this way connectivity to collectivity, van Dijck argues that "the connective qualities of online platforms […] do not automatically translate into public values" (3). Connectivity, or the affordances of ICTs, cannot be the guide for defining values and implementing norms. Where then are the values and norms of society coming from? Van Dijck appeals to tradition. According to van Dijck, "European societies are rooted in different ideological values from those introduced by many platforms" (3). This may be, but since the ideas of the free market, liberalism, and capitalism are European inventions as well as social welfare, it is difficult to accept the proposed opposition between European values and platform values. To assume that European societies have no stake in economic liberalism is somewhat one sided and seems to blind out much of European cultural and economic history. What would Adam Smith say were he to hear that he had no place in European tradition? Here it is apparent that van Dijck and colleagues take sides. They take sides within a long-standing and unquestioned tradition of critique of capitalism. Within this framework, there are only two options, either "right" or "left," and it is apparent that in keeping with most social science critique, van Dijck and her colleagues have chosen left. Despite internal differences, the left is united in condemning what is called "neo-liberalism" or "deregulation."

> To understand how datafication, commodification, and selection tie in with contemporary governance strategies, it is especially important to see how in neoliberal or advanced liberal democracies, calculative regimes of accounting, and financial management have been employed to enable […] a degovernmentalization of the state. […] It is in this framework of calculative regimes and deregulation that platform datafication takes shape. (2018, 46)

According to van Dijck and her colleagues, platform mechanisms of datafication, commodification, and selection "strongly correspond with the neoliberal reorganization of government and the penetration of market rationalities and principles in a wide variety of social activities" (ibid.). Neoliberalism is the real target of the critical enterprise. Even though the digital transformation in many ways, which van Dijck does not hesitate to mention, breaks with the framework of Western industrial society and its fundamental distinctions between entrepreneurs and workers, governments and citizens, individuals and society, none of these new avenues of development are explored. Instead, the critique falls back on the modern constitution and locates platforms either on the right or the left and condemns what is on the right and praises what is on the left. Although the world has changed, it's the same old story.

Furthermore, the critical enterprise of van Dijck and her colleagues seems to assume that Europe and the West should not change, even when societies everywhere, indeed globally, are changing. Van Dijck makes no convincing argument of why values should be aligned with traditional socialism and why they should not change in a changing world. Instead, she retells the well-known story of capitalist bad guys exploiting proletarian good guys where democratic government, because of majority rule, is automatically aligned with the exploited and disempowered masses. Of course, everybody wears hats in different shades of gray, but in effect, what we are being told is the story of industrial society from the socialist perspective. Western social theory has long accustomed itself to operating within the limits of what Latour calls the modern constitution. The modern constitution opposes individuals to collectives, subjects to objects, autonomy to heteronomy, and the public to the private spheres. Individual, autonomous rational subjects are pitted in a mythical struggle for freedom and dignity against powerful corporate and government actors who are out to exploit and oppress them. We do not deny that oppression is real and that the struggle against the abuse of power, exploitation, and inequality is one of the major contributions of European values to human history. Within the mythology of modernity, the private sphere is, in fact, often seen as the domain in which powerful actors abuse their power to enrich themselves and harm citizens. In contrast, the public sphere and government are often seen as defenders of the rights of individuals, of equality, and of justice. This is the story constitutive of modern Western society. But could this story not change? Could not another story envisage a different future? Or are we condemned to tell the same story over and over again as if it were made up of timeless truths and incontrovertible facts? Such timeless truths and incontrovertible facts are indistinguishable from the ethical values and moral norms that Luhmann felt society should be warned against. By reaffirming the mythology of modernity, van Dijck subscribes to a program of social science critique that aims at reasserting Western values and thus articulating what Luhmann called the conditions of social acceptance. But the society that is setting these conditions, that is, modern Western society, no longer exists. This is the form of moralizing typical of social science critique.

Although van Dijck explicitly acknowledges that "it is very difficult, if not impossible, these days to make a clear-cut distinction between the private and public spheres" (5), she does not take this fact as an opportunity to rethink traditional social theory. Instead, she falls back on "public values" that "are contested during the implementation of platforms" (ibid.). Even when the digital transformation has done away with the distinction between private and public, there are still "public values" that need to be defended and, as the German Commission on Data Ethics put it, "reasserted." What are these values? While acknowledging that values such as "innovation" and "economic progress," which drive the digital transformation, are considered by many to be public and not exclusively private values, van Dijck claims that "there are other public values at stake in the process to transfer social traffic and economic transactions to an online connective world" (ibid.). These are above all "privacy, accuracy, safety, and consumer protection" (ibid.). To complete the list of "other values that pertain to the common good and society as a whole," she adds "fairness, equality, solidarity, accountability, transparency, and democratic control" (ibid.). The distinction between private and public, which guides this critical program, locates the market on the other side of a clear moral line dividing right from wrong. What is public seems to be automatically morally praiseworthy, whereas everything private amounts to exploitation and is morally condemnable.

Van Dijck and her colleagues critically examine and find wanting platforms in the areas of news, transportation, healthcare, and education. Interestingly, in all these areas, the many positive public goods that come from gathering and using data in order to improve efficiency, create personalization, promote economic growth, ensure public health, and so on are put into question by the threats they pose to privacy and, closely associated with privacy, autonomy and freedom. These values are not portrayed as ethical issues but as social and political issues. The question is: "who is or should be responsible and accountable for anchoring public values in the platform society?" (5–6). She concludes that this question must be answered collectively by all actors involved, whereby the government must play the decisive role. She claims that "supranational, national, and local governments have a special responsibility in this regard" (6). "Particularly in the European context, governments are not just arbiters of market dynamics and level playing fields but can and should be proactive in negotiating public values on behalf of citizens and consumers" (ibid.). That citizens and consumers would automatically prefer to have their values proactively negotiated by the government instead of private enterprises is an assumption and not a fact. That platforms could and do play an important role in "negotiating public values" and this directly by the citizens and consumers concerned seems to lie outside the perspective van Dijck and colleagues takes on ICTs. Apparently, only the government can and should do the job of protecting citizens and consumers, who, for some reason, cannot defend themselves and apparently, after all that has been said, are in no way empowered by the digital transformation.

Despite an active and diversified civil society and many new and effective forms of governance involving nonhierarchical regulation, governments must act on behalf of citizens and consumers, who apparently have no voice of their own, at least, no voice that could be made heard without governmental force and regulation. Although, in theory, democratic processes should implement the voice of the people, today, one must ask which people are the ones being heard and whose voice is being followed. The rise of populism and the undermining of anything approaching what Habermas still idealized as a public sphere characterized by rational discussion has demonstrated the weaknesses of democracy. It is no longer any assurance of justice, equality, fairness, and so on to proclaim, as van Dijck does, that "governments need to adjust their instrumentation for regulation and control to protect a democratically agreed-upon set of public values" (6). There is no democratically agreed-upon set of values in any society today, and if one looks at populist successes in democracies everywhere, the values that seem to be agreed upon are certainly not those espoused by van Dijck and her colleagues. Even the assumption that "European public values are often at odds with the values inscribed in [the] architectures" (3) of platforms amounts to nothing more than a partisan opinion and hardly representative of what people in Europe, or anywhere else for that matter, really value, especially when one considers that about one half of the European population is actively using Facebook even after most authorities have called for boycotts. The assumption that any government today is truly "representative" of what people value is highly questionable even if the consequences of asking this question are so daunting that it is politically incorrect to ask at all. The values that many governments explicitly represent are not those the critical theorist supposes that the public subscribes to. The "special role" that van Dijck assigns to government in adjudicating value conflicts on behalf of the citizens is more myth than anything else and hardly a more effective solution to the challenges of the digital transformation than appealing to humanistic ethical norms and the inalienable rights of individuals on the purely moral level.

2.2.4 Surveillance Capitalism

A further instructive example of the shift from ethics to social and political concerns within the scope of modernity's attempt to deal with the digital transformation is Zuboff's work on "Surveillance Capitalism." Solidly within the modern critical tradition, Zuboff (2019) has little good to say about the digital transformation. Whereas van Dijck's notion of the platform society attempted a balanced description of both positive and negative—from the perspective of modernism!—aspects of the global network society, Zuboff assumes the typical posture of critical denunciation. This posture can be illustrated by the definition of surveillance capitalism at the beginning of the book. For Zuboff, surveillance capitalism is

> 1. A new economic order that claims human experience as free raw material for hidden commercial practices of extraction, prediction, and sales; 2. A parasitic economic logic in which the production of goods and services is subordinated to a new global architecture of behavioral modification; 3. A rogue mutation of capitalism marked by concentrations of wealth, knowledge, and power unprecedented in human history; 4. The foundational framework of a surveillance economy; 5. As significant a threat to human nature in the twentyfirst century as industrial capitalism was to the natural world in the nineteenth and twentieth; 6. The origin of a new instrumentarian power that asserts dominance over society and presents startling challenges to market democracy; 7. A movement that aims to impose a new collective order based on total certainty; 8. An expropriation of critical human rights that is best understood as a coup from above: an overthrow of the people's sovereignty. (Zuboff 2019, vii)

Apart from noting the unmistakable tone of critical denunciation that characterizes this contentious definition, what is instructive is the clarity with which humanist ethics and a certain mythology of society as a struggle of the oppressed and exploited against political and business elites draw the line between right and wrong. The moralizing intention is unmistakable. But it seems that this assessment of the impact of ICTs on society is more motivated by nostalgia for the industrial age and an accompanying inability to imagine a different form of social order than by an informed analysis of present-day socio-technical reality. Zuboff's portrayal of surveillance capitalism explicitly links privacy issues to economic exploitation as defined by the Marxist tradition and calls upon not only humanist values of freedom and autonomy but also values of justice, equality, and fairness as they are understood within the modern constitution. The book is exemplary for not leaving any stone unturned in the search for digital threats to the autonomous rational subject and traditional values. In general, Zuboff's work could be seen as the immune reaction of a deathly ill social and cultural body to the ICT disease that is slowly transforming it. Let us attempt to summarize her arguments by following the lead of the definition cited above.

We can roughly group the eight points of the definition cited above as follows: Surveillance capitalism is a new social and economic order:

1. A new economic order that claims human experience as free raw material for hidden commercial practices of extraction, prediction, and sales;
4. The foundational framework of a surveillance economy.

This new social and economic order is a threat to the traditional social and economic order:

5. As significant a threat to human nature in the twentyfirst century as industrial capitalism was to the natural world in the nineteenth and twentieth;
3. A rogue mutation of capitalism marked by concentrations of wealth, knowledge, and power unprecedented in human history.

The threat consists in violating privacy and manipulating behavior:

2. A parasitic economic logic in which the production of goods and services is subordinated to a new global architecture of behavioral modification;
6. The origin of a new instrumentarian power that asserts dominance over society and presents startling challenges to market democracy;
8. An expropriation of critical human rights that is best understood as a coup from above: an overthrow of the people's sovereignty.

And finally, this new social order is based on evidence, on data, on certainty instead of uncertainty:

7. A movement that aims to impose a new collective order based on total certainty

Let us begin with the last point, that the digital transformation is changing society by making it possible for the first time in human history to make decisions on the basis of evidence instead of intuition, gut feeling, cognitive bias, prejudice, personal experience, or group pressure. This development is nothing new. It is not something that Zuboff has discovered, exposed, and appropriately denounced as running against traditional ways of organizing cooperative action in society. It is well known under many names, among which are "data-driven society," "organizational intelligence," "datafication," "big data analytics," and similar concepts that have long been topics of discussion in all areas and on all levels. The "digital single market" strategy of the European Union is a case in point.[51] The digital single market strategy "aims to open up digital opportunities for people and businesses and enhance Europe's position as a world leader in the digital economy." The European Union, therefore, supports projects that aim at "ensuring that businesses, SMEs, and non-tech industries can benefit from digital innovations to create a higher value chain." Beyond concrete projects and programs, the European Union sees itself explicitly as a "data economy," that is, as an economy that "uses the potential of digital data to benefit the economy and society to its best," to which end it "addresses barriers that impede the free flow of data." At the base of this strategy lies the conviction that "Europe needs to foster the development and wide adoption of big data technologies" and that the "availability and access to data will be the foundation of any data-centric ecosystem" (Cavanillas et al. 2016, 8). This program can be realized only by acquiring data from many sources as well as "combining data from different sources and across sectors" (8). The data-driven society envisaged by the European Union is a "data ecosystem," which must "bring together data owners, data analytics companies, skilled data professionals, cloud service providers, companies from user industries, venture capitalists, entrepreneurs, research institutes, and universities."[52]

In a data-driven economy, it is data that generates value. The values that can be generated by gathering, aggregating, and analyzing data on a large scale accrue in all areas of society. In healthcare, for example, organizations are encouraged to "make use of comprehensive heterogeneous health datasets as well as advanced analytics of clinical operations" for purposes, among others, of "predictive modeling," "personalized medicine," and "analyzing disease patterns" (ibid., 6).[53] In the area of public services, it is imperative "to share data across government agencies and to inform citizens about the trade-offs between the privacy and security risks of sharing data and the benefits they can gain" (6). With regard to communication and media, it is apparent that the "domain of personal location data offers the potential for new value creation […] including location-based content delivery for individuals, smart personalized content routing" and "geo-targeted advertising" (6). In manufacture and production, new business models based on "individualized products" can be developed. Outlets and retailers can generate value by enabling new "interactions between retailers and consumers" grounded

---

51 See https://ec.europa.eu/digital-single-market/en, from which all citations come unless otherwise indicated.
52 A European strategy on the data value chain: DG Connect (https://ec.europa.eu/digital-single-market/en/news/elements-data-value-chain-strategy).
53 A detailed list of recommendations to the EU Commission for use of big data in healthcare can be found in the "Study on Big data in Public Health, Telemedicine and Healthcare—Final Report 2016" (https://ec.europa.eu/health/sites/health/files/ehealth/docs/bigdata_report_en.pdf). Today's experience with pandemics only underlines the importance of big data in healthcare.

in "location-based marketing, in-store behavior analysis, customer micro-segmentation, customer sentiment analysis" (6), and much more. In education, "learning analytics" makes personalized learning and evidence-based advising possible. The systematic monitoring of entire ecosystems elevates environmental protection to a new level. Smart homes, smart cities, smart buildings, smart energy, smart transportation, indeed, smart everything, as well as the Fourth Industrial Revolution is dependent upon the generation, aggregation, and analysis of data, that is, upon ubiquitous connectivity and free flows of information.

For Zuboff, all this amounts to an attempt "to impose a new collective order based on total certainty." And she's right. But what is this new order based on evidence? What are we talking about apart from imperatives to gather and exploit data and to make decisions in all areas based on evidence instead of gut feeling, intuition, bias, or group pressure? To understand what is at stake in Zuboff's critical program, we need to take a step back and look at the digital transformation from a different perspective than that which Zuboff herself takes. To this end, we propose to summarize the process of social change under the influence of ICTs by the concept of "datafication."[54] Datafication has to do with data. No matter how important data may be, what is done with the data, how value is generated from data is more important. This can be called analytics.

To describe the digital transformation in terms of data and analytics is admittedly an unwarranted simplification. Still, it can help to illustrate an important force behind many developments taking place in all sectors of society today, a force that is the target of Zuboff's critique. The idea behind datafication goes further and encompasses much more than big data analytics or business intelligence. Already in the early 1990s, David Gelernter (1993, 3) formulated the idea of "mirror worlds," which he defined as "software models of some chunk of reality, some piece of the real world," which are fed by "oceans of information" such that "the model can mimic the reality's every move, moment-by-moment." Today, one does not speak of "mirror" worlds, since a mirror image cannot predict outcomes and identify preventive interventions. But a "digital double" or "digital twin" can do this.[55] Not only can the model mimic reality, but because it is a "digital twin," it can show how any possible variable will influence the course of real events before they happen. This enables real-time interventions to prevent certain things from happening, for example, to prevent a machine from breaking down, or to influence outcomes of all kinds.

Datafication, as we are using the term, aims to create a digital model or a so-called digital twin of everything. It can be a machine, for example, an automobile, a heating system, a refrigerator, or a jet engine. With a digital model, one can do much more than with a physical model. As with the physical model, the digital model represents all states of the object system. This is the first step and can be considered as a particular kind

---

54 We are using the term "datafication" not in the same sense in which van Dijck defines it as a "mechanism" of the platform economy.
55 For an overview of "digital twin," see the Wikipedia article https://en.wikipedia.org/wiki/Digital_twin.

of analytics, namely, *descriptive analytics*. Because of sensors and wireless networks, it is possible to gather real-time data not only about the states of the system but also about everything that is going on in the environment of the system, which could influence the system. Via simulation, one can then change any internal or external variable and see what will happen. Contrary to the physical model, digital modeling of the system and its environment mean that we no longer need to wait until a problem occurs to start looking for a solution. We know in advance what problems will occur under what conditions. This is the second kind of analytics, namely, *predictive analytics*. Predictive analytics allow us to know, for example, when a machine needs to be serviced or when a part needs to be repaired or replaced before a machine breaks down.

In addition to descriptive and predictive analytics, there is a third form of analytics that can be called *preventive analytics*. When we know what problems could occur and what variables cause the issues, we can take preventive measures so that the problems do not occur. For example, if simulations show that above a specific temperature, a machine will develop problems, steps can be taken to ensure that the temperature remains below threatening levels. Preventive analytics goes beyond mere maintenance or problem solving and extends to process optimization, organizational optimization, and discovery. All this cannot be done when working only with a physical model. Preventive interventions and optimization cannot be done, at least not efficiently, within a physical environment. Preventive analytics are only possible based on datafication. Descriptive analytics tell us what is happening, predictive analytics tell us what will happen, and preventive analytics tell us what to do when we want to change the situation so that problems do not occur or certain outcomes do occur. Datafication, of course, is not limited to representing machines. Not only a particular machine but also the entire factory that produces the machine can become a digital twin and can be subjected to descriptive, predictive, and preventive analytics. This is what business analytics, to a certain extent, has long been doing and what the Fourth Industrial Revolution, as well as the Internet of Things (IoT), is all about. Smart homes, smart environments, smart cities, and much more are based upon datafication. Indeed, datafication makes evidence-based decision making in all areas possible, since it allows decisions to be informed by information about what will happen when this or that variable is realized. Datafication, however, takes evidence-based management to a higher level, since it allows not only problem-solving with regard to specific indicators but also scalable, real-time, ongoing monitoring and optimization of all processes and networks that in any way condition a system, a machine, a building, an organization, or even an entire city. Datafication can be applied not only to factories or businesses but also to whole cities, which then become "smart cities." Datafication does not stop with building digital twins of things, machines, or even cities. Living organisms, and even individual human beings, as well as entire societies, can become digital twins as well.

It is possible to produce a digital twin of a human being. The genome, the microbiome, epigenetic factors, all vital functions via wearable tracking devices, medical history, environmental influences, psychological profile, behavior, and so on, everything that is in any way related to a person's health or well-being can be datafied, aggregated, and subjected to a descriptive, predictive, and preventive analytics. This is called "personalized medicine," "connected health," or "smart healthcare."[56] Personalized medicine eliminates the difference between being healthy and being sick since one is always in some ways ill or in the process of becoming ill or in the process of becoming well. Medical care no longer comes into play only after one has developed symptoms. Instead, medical care becomes an ongoing activity that is involved in all aspects of life, including ongoing evidence-based interventions with regard to lifestyle, work, hobbies, eating habits and preferences, sport and fitness, and even how we arrange our houses and living spaces and what environmental influences we are subject to. All-encompassing monitoring and evidence-based decision making are, of course, not limited to healthcare. Datafication will transform education (see, e.g., learning analytics), ways of working, forms of organizing, production and distribution of knowledge, and many other activities. Datafication means that we will no longer make decisions about how we live, what we eat, what profession we learn, where we work, what partner we choose, and so on based on emotion, intuition, habit, or preference, but based on evidence.[57]

Evidence-based decision making can also be automated. This brings us to the fourth form of analytics, otherwise known as artificial intelligence and robotics. We can speak of *prescriptive analytics*. When my Tesla drives me home in autopilot mode, then it makes the decisions. These decisions are binding for me and, in this sense, prescriptive. They prescribe whether I turn left or right, whether I go fast or slow, and so on. What makes AI into AI is autonomous learning and decision making. AI is no longer a mere tool in the hands of humans. It no longer merely provides information or makes recommendations for humans to act upon or not as they see fit. It sets its own goals and acts upon its own ability to learn from "experience." AI makes its own decisions and is therefore much more a social partner, or even in Luhmann's sense of the word an *alter ego*, than a mere tool. A resolution of the European Parliament (2017) proposed to grant AIs a recognized and legally anchored "electronic personality." As AI becomes poised to take over many human activities and put people out of work, many propose to ensure a place for humans in the future economy by emphasizing creativity and emotional and leadership skills.[58] It is supposed that these are things that AIs can't do. Abandoning rational intelligence to the machines, humans retreat to emotional intelligence and the humanist-motivated claim that there should always be a human in the loop to make the final decisions; otherwise, human autonomy, self-determination, and freedom would be jeopardized.

Robotics can also be subsumed under prescriptive analytics. The hardware and software change, but the basic idea of datafication and analytics remains the same. Robots are mobile AIs. A robot is an intelligent, mobile, and autonomous system, IMAS for short. Hollywood has created an icon for robots, the Terminator. Although the Terminator was

---

56 For the digital transformation of healthcare, see Belliger and Krieger (2018b). For personalization in medicine and healthcare, see Prainsack (2017).
57 We take the liberty to remark as this point that for Zuboff this amounts to an attack on human freedom and autonomy, which under the conditions of datafication must be understood as the right to make mistakes, endanger one's own health as well that of others, and generally disregard the facts about almost all aspects of reality.
58 See, for example, the discussion about new work skills or twenty-first-century work skills.

at first negative, in subsequent episodes of the story, the Terminator became a hero instead of a villain. The Terminator changed from bad to good, from villain to hero, by being "reprogrammed." The digital transformation is currently "reprogramming" society as a whole to accept AIs as partners in all social endeavors. Much of contemporary digital ethics can be seen as a reaction to this transformation. There is no end to discussions, guidelines, calls for moratoria, and strict government regulation of AI. Even if much of this can be classified under "digital consumer protection" rather than serious ethical reflection, it does represent the extent to which AI is poised to reconfigure social order. Today's robots no longer look like the Terminator. They take on many different shapes and purposes depending on what kind of work they do, whether in industrial production or logistics, autonomous vehicles, medical diagnosis and therapy, informational assistants, military applications, and so on. When robots do look like humans, they are usually female, such as Sophia from Hanson Robotics, or Erica from Hiroshi Ishiguro, or Jia Jia from the University of Science and Technology of China. As an interesting aside, there seems to be a general tendency to feminize humanoid robots, and it is also apparent that humanoid robots are seen very differently in Asia than in the West. Sophia is obviously and intentionally a machine, whereas Erica and Jia Jia are intended to resemble humans as much as possible. Studies have shown that people trust and confide in robots as much as, if not more so than, in humans.[59] There is also little evidence to support preferences for the advantages of human decision making over that of AIs. Despite all the discussions about how AIs incorporate the biases, prejudices, and discriminatory practices of humans—which are caused by inadequate training data—AIs make their decisions based on much much more information than any human can comprehend or process.[60] Perhaps the meaning of digital transformation and datafication is not that humans must struggle to find their place in a world where decisions are increasingly evidence based by means of emphasizing differences and uniquely human characteristics, but by means of emphasizing similarities and cooperation in trusted networks of humans and nonhumans.[61]

After this detour through datafication and what it means for society and human self-understanding, let us return to Zuboff's critique of these developments under the name of surveillance capitalism. For Zuboff, what lies behind all this, and what is driving the digital transformation, is not the hope for a better future, the tangible results of evidence-based decision making in all areas, or obvious consumer interest in personalized products and services, but the evil intentions of business elites. These are the surveillance capitalists.

---

59 See, for example, the study sponsored be Oracle and Future, *Workplace from Fear to Enthusiasm. Artificial Intelligence Is Winning More Hearts and Minds in the Workplace*, 2019 (https://www.oracle.com/webfolder/s/assets/ebook/ai-work/index.html?source=:ow:ms:pt::RC_PDMK191009 P00032:LPD400002437&intcmp=:ow:ms:pt::RC_PDMK191009P00032:LPD400002437).

60 The critique of AI as biased and discriminatory is omnipresent in digital ethics. See, for example, the work of AINow (https://ainowinstitute.org/). The solution is more and more accurate data and not the proposed moratoriums.

61 Currently, much work is being done on human–robot interaction and trusted networks. See, for example, Abbass et al. (2018).

Although everyone in the data-driven economy is implicated, the ones who clearly wear black hats are Google, Facebook, and other tech giants who in conspiratorial consort with naïve and/or opportunistic government officials permit uninhibited data collection and exploitation. The focus on surveillance, which is a term burdened with a history of negative associations, is not new and not unfounded.[62] The European Union itself seems to have a bad conscience about the enthusiastic embrace of a digital economy since at the same time the digital single market strategy was launched, the European Union also launched the most restrictive privacy regulation the world has yet seen. The GDPR makes informed consent into the only legal basis for the collection and exploitation of personal data.[63] If one considers (1) the fact that informed consent is notoriously dysfunctional and ineffective, (2) that data analytics is effective only when many of the requirements of consent cannot be met, and (3) that the definition of what counts as "personal data" is any information that "directly or indirectly" (GDPR Art. 4) can identify a natural person—which implies any information whatsoever—then, in effect, the GDPR completely negates the idea of a data-driven society.[64] What this reveals is that Europe is a deeply divided society in which one side strives for digital transformation while the other attempts at all costs to prevent the emergence of a global network society. In the United States, many have joined in the chorus with EU privacy advocates even though privacy is not considered a fundamental right in the United States.[65] Privacy discourse in the United States is increasingly reflecting the hardened fronts already formed in Europe between those who support a data-driven society and those who are resisting the digital transformation with all means available. One of the major weapons of those resisting the digital transformation is privacy. In keeping with the program of modern critique, Zuboff takes her stand on the reactionary side of this controversy, namely, the side that rejects the digital transformation. She relies thereby upon the strategy of recasting privacy in terms of surveillance.

Let us return to Zuboff's definition. Surveillance capitalism is: "1. A new economic order that claims human experience as free raw material for hidden commercial practices of extraction, prediction, and sales; [and] 4. The foundational framework of a

---

62 For a summary of work in the area of "surveillance studies," see Lyon (2006) and Ball et al. (2012). The journal *Surveillance & Society* published by the University of North Carolina at Chapel Hill, NC, United States, represents the field of surveillance studies (https://ojs.library.queensu.ca/index.php/surveillance-and-society/).

63 Of course, the GDPR acknowledges other legitimations for gathering personal data. These are contractual obligations, legal obligations, emergency interventions, public interest, official obligations, and legitimate interest of data processors. See GDPR Art. 6 and Art. 7 (https://gdpr.eu/gdpr-consent-requirements/). Nonetheless, these are all referred back to and grounded in some form of informed consent.

64 The GDPR is an indication of how divided and uncertain Europe is with regard to the digital transformation. For a discussion, see Belliger and Krieger (2016).

65 Among them, interestingly, Google CEO Sundar Pichai (https://www.ft.com/content/3467659a-386d-11ea-ac3c-f68c10993b04). To a certain extent, this can be seen as the reaction of corporations to perceived dangers of government regulation arising from media scandalization and the lobbying of civil society actors, that is, as a calculated reaction to the "techlash."

surveillance economy" (2019). If the data-driven economy is to be understood as a "surveillance economy," it is necessary to define what is meant by surveillance. Interestingly, Zuboff herself does not define surveillance. She would, however, undoubtedly concur with Lyon's definition of surveillance as "a focused attention to personal details aimed at exerting an influence over or managing the objects of the data, or 'data subjects' as they are sometimes called" (Lyon 2002, 242).[66] What Lyon summarizes as "focused attention to personal details," Zuboff (2019, 99) describes in the Marxist tradition as "dispossession," whereby instead of real physical and material values, what is stolen is digital value. Unlike industrial capitalism, dispossession and exploitation do not lead to benefits of any kind for those whose data is taken. Industrial capitalism was directed at the production of goods from which workers also profited. Under the regime of surveillance capitalism, this is no longer the case. "Under this new regime, the precise moment at which our needs are met is also the precise moment at which our lives are plundered for behavioral data, and all for the sake of others' gain" (53). Citing Marx's comparison of capitalism with a vampire that feeds off human labor, Zuboff describes surveillance capitalism as a vampire that "feeds on every aspect of every human's experience" (9). The value that is usurped in capitalist fashion is personal data. This data is not the standard personal identifiers such as name, address, telephone number, email address, and so on. The usurped raw material of surveillance capitalism is obtained by surreptitious tracking, capturing, and aggregating of all possible digital traces that we leave in the Web, or in apps, or in the use of any digital device including smart home devices, body tracking apps, and so on. Let us note that although the process of datafication we have briefly described above covers all areas of society, Zuboff aims her critique only at the consumer market and business. Zuboff focuses on two fundamental points of critique: (1) surveillance is surreptitious; that is, we are not informed about what is going on, and (2) we do not benefit from this; only "others" benefit.

According to Zuboff, the practice of dispossession began when Google realized that it could monetize user data by enabling advertisers to address people based on their interests. Google invented *personalized advertising*, which, because of its apparent advantages to generalized advertising, or what could be called "spam," quickly became the standard of Internet advertising as well as the source of Google's wealth. Quite apart from the fact that there is no longer anything surreptitious about Google's personalized advertising practices, it is questionable why anyone would want the old impersonal advertising.[67] Spam is usually defined as unsolicited advertising, which is the typical mode of advertising in almost any form and any media. Think of any marketplace. Sellers and buyers gather for exchange. Sellers must somehow communicate to buyers what they offer. When a mass of people come together, the only way to communicate with everyone at once is to shout as loud as one can. This is the famous fishmonger, whose booming voice

---

[66] A more nuanced definition by Marx is to be found ni Ball et al. (2012, xxiv).
[67] Google is very open about personalized advertising and what it entails. See https://support.google.com/ads/answer/1634057?visit_id=637135683864881955-456313812&rd=1. A brief overview can be found at https://en.wikipedia.org/wiki/Personalized_marketing.

could be heard throughout the marketplace. Marketing is basically nothing other than shouting, that is, trying by whatever means available to tell as many people as possible what one is offering. Marketing communication consists of nothing other than trying to gain people's attention. Advertising is defined as a "non-personal message to promote or sell a product, service or idea."[68] Advertising, or what today is called marketing, is, by definition, nonpersonal, because until today there was no way that sellers could know who the buyers that might be interested in their product were. Despite all the sociologically and psychologically supported efforts to identify and persuade consumers, marketing has remained to this day on the level of a very expensive fishmongering.

With the advent of *digital marketing*, everything changes. It is now possible to know almost everything about potential buyers. Sellers can know who is interested in what, when, and how they want to be addressed. It is no longer necessary or useful to gain everybody's attention by shouting as loudly as one can. It is possible by means of datafication to know exactly who the customer is, what they are interested in, when they are ready to buy, and how they want to be informed about products and services. Digital marketing, or personalized advertising, is so different from traditional marketing that it has been suggested that this form of communication between sellers and buyers should no longer be called marketing at all. Indeed, some have proclaimed the end of marketing, because consumers are no longer seen as objects of persuasive communication, but as subjects involved in the development, optimization, and deployment of products and services.[69] Instead of consumers and consumption, one speaks of "prosumers," "crowdsourcing," "mass collaboration," "peer production," and "user generation." Whatever we chose to call it, it is an entirely new form of market communication. It should not be understood within the usual dynamics of an economy of attention, wherein those who shout the loudest reach the most and, therefore, supposedly make the most sales. If one considers that gathering and evaluating massive amounts of data about consumers is done by AIs and that the algorithms are designed to nudge in both ways, that is, to nudge not only consumers but also producers, then what we have is a form of "co-nudging," in which producers and consumers are so intimately involved with each other that they co-construct each other's identities and behavior.[70] If this is the case, Zuboff's story of manipulated and exploited consumers at the mercy of mighty marketers collapses and another tale of the empowered prosumer working together with "agile" producers in order to optimally meet everyone's needs takes its place.[71] Indeed, it is difficult to understand why anyone would rather have spam instead of being presented with products and services in which they are genuinely interested.

---

68 See the Wikipedia article on advertising (https://en.wikipedia.org/wiki/Advertising).
69 See, for example, Gill (2020).
70 Yueng (2017) speaks of "hyper-nudging" in order to designate the new quality of big data analytics in marketing.
71 For a short summary of the two stories, see Darmody and Zwick (2020). After describing both stories fairly, the authors seem to lack the courage to claim they have at least equal plausibility and portray the story of the end of marketing rather as fiction and Zuboff's opposing story as fact.

What Zuboff seems to take offense at is the fact that Google didn't first ask us if they could use "our" data for advertising purposes. Apart from the issue of whether tracking data is, in fact, "our" data, that is, owned by those being tracked and not those who enable the tracking, which Zuboff simply assumes, today we all know what is going on. Nonetheless, for those who have not yet realized this, it does seem objectionable that users were not completely informed about this new form of monetizing data and officially asked if they wanted personalized products and services. After all, informed consent is an established guideline for gathering and using personal information and also just plain common sense. In defense of Google and all the others who soon got into the new data economy, it could be said that (1) they themselves didn't know what they were discovering and where it would go; (2) they assumed that getting the services offered by Google, Facebook, and so on was enough in contractual exchange for user data; (3) they had no model of any business that actually entered into open, authentic, trusted, and interactive communication with consumers. As long as society was made up of producers and consumers within the framework of industrialism, asking people at every turn about what should be offered and how this should be done was neither a known nor an accepted form of producer/consumer relationship. In addition to this, it should not be forgotten that innovation and social change do not usually happen after everyone has been consulted and has agreed. It is interesting to recall what Henry Ford was reported to have said about innovation. Ford, who Zuboff usually cites with approval, was reported to have said that if he had asked people what they wanted, they would have said faster horses.[72] Zuboff's indignation and moral outrage about not being asked if her data could be used to design personalized products and services that are then offered via targeted advertising are understandable. Still, it also indicates a profound misunderstanding of the nature of innovation and social change and a deep mistrust of technology. Neither Steve Jobs, nor Bill Gates, nor Tim Berners Lee, nor Elon Musk first asked everyone before they changed the world. If she had been asked, Zuboff would presumably have said no, and we would not have the Internet, personal computers, smartphones, electric automobiles, and much more. One cannot escape the impression that a world without innovation is the one that Zuboff prefers. There is accordingly an unmistakable nostalgia in Zuboff's writing for the bygone days of industrial capitalism.

Industrial capitalism, despite all its faults, nonetheless, according to Zuboff, "depended upon its communities in ways that would eventually lead to a range of institutionalized reciprocities" (31). In industrial society, "the drama of access to affordable goods and services was bound by democratic measures and methods of oversight that asserted and protected the rights and safety of workers and consumers." Within companies, "durable employment systems, career ladders, and steady increases in wages and benefits" were institutionalized (ibid.). In distinction to industrial capitalism, surveillance capitalism is an economy based not upon the production of goods, but upon the production of

---

[72] There is no evidence that this quote comes from Ford himself. Nonetheless, it exemplifies the nature of innovation. For a discussion, see the article by Vlaskovits in *Harvard Business Review*, August 2011 (https://hbr.org/2011/08/henry-ford-never-said-the-fast).

"predictions" (93) about behavior that are sold on a "behavioral futures market" (8). Zuboff assumes that consumers receive no benefits in return from this form of capitalism. "Surveillance capitalism's products and services are not the objects of a value exchange. They do not establish constructive producer-consumer reciprocities" (10). Whereas industrial capitalism did offer consumers tangible goods, such as automobiles, refrigerators, television sets, and so on, surveillance capitalism steals users' data in order to produce predictions about behavior that are sold to "others," that is, advertisers who offer products and services that are assumed to be not related to the original contractual relationship between, for example, Google and its users, and also not to be of any benefit for consumers. Surveillance capitalists "predict our futures for the sake of others' gain, not ours" (11). Zuboff seems to forget that third parties who make use of user profiles do offer real products and services and not merely advertising. Sellers are not interested in expensive advertising for its own sake. They want to sell products and services. This is why they are advertising in the first place. It is precisely because digital marketing allows advertisers to know what users want that they are in the position to design and develop personalized products and market these products directly to those who are interested in them. Zuboff provides no evidence for the assumption that user data is not used to design and develop personalized products and services that do meet consumers' needs and correspond to consumers' interests.

If the first great moral transgression of surveillance capitalism is to take users' data without their consent, the second consists in not giving consumers anything in return. According to Zuboff, surveillance capitalists, just like industrial capitalists, own the means of production. These are no longer machines and factories, but digital technologies, above all machine learning technologies that are not used to produce goods, but instead, to generate predictions about people's behavior. Predictions, according to the trajectory of datafication from descriptive to predictive to preventive and even prescriptive analytics, can then be used to produce "behavior modification" (11). Following this line of reasoning, Zuboff proclaims that datafication is an entirely new and unprecedented form of power, which she calls "instrumentarian power" (8). Her condemnation is total. The economic imperatives of surveillance capitalism "disregard social norms and nullify the elemental rights associated with individual autonomy that are essential to the very possibility of a democratic society" (11). What is here coming to voice with unmistakable vehemence is the humanist myth of Western modernity. Zuboff is right in the assumption that the digital transformation does place traditional notions of human nature and the autonomous rational subject in question. Consequently, she asserts that "an information civilization shaped by surveillance capitalism and its new instrumentarian power will thrive at the expense of human nature" (11). Where she is wrong is in assuming that this is something that must be resisted at all cost and that human nature in its modern Western form can and should be preserved for all time.

Citing Yueng (2017) and Darmody and Zwick (2020, 9) argue that Zuboff "fails to grasp the ontological transformation ushered in by the age of networked, Big Data-driven, automated marketing" in which "individual autonomy and agency are severely limited." This can only then be seen as manipulation and loss of freedom if the autonomous rational subject is assumed to be unchanged and unaffected by the digital transformation and to be the standard upon which all things must be judged. Once integrated into a network in which data-driven automation influences, or nudges, both producer and consumer equally, human nature is no longer what it was in the age of industrial capitalism. As Darmody and Zwick (2020) put it, "The manipulation of consumer decision making at the pre-cognitive level now comes to be understood as an augmentation of consumer agency, autonomy, and power, rather than their loss." From this point of view, what Zuboff calls manipulation is actually empowerment.

Lyon's definition of surveillance cited above says not only that attention is focused on personal information but also that the purpose of this attention is to "influence or manage […] the data subjects." One cannot help but recall Foucault's famous discussion of Bentham's panopticon.[73] The panopticon was a prison in which all inmates were observed from a central tower, but themselves could not observe the observer. The knowledge that one was being observed, even if not actually true at any time, led to conformity to prison rules. This corresponds well to Zuboff's definition of surveillance capitalism as "2. A parasitic economic logic in which the production of goods and services is subordinated to a new global architecture of behavioral modification; 6. The origin of a new instrumentarian power that asserts dominance over society and presents startling challenges to market democracy; 8. An expropriation of critical human rights that is best understood as a coup from above: an overthrow of the people's sovereignty." Zuboff's notion of instrumentarian power locates the purpose of gathering and evaluating user data not merely for the purpose of optimizing advertising, that is, showing people ads that are relevant to their interests and thus improving the chances that advertising leads to sales. Surprisingly, surveillance capitalism, as opposed to industrial capitalism, is not primarily concerned with selling anything. The real goal of surveillance capitalism is behavior modification. What exactly does this mean?

It is commonplace and hardly worth mentioning that personalized advertising is more in tune with what people want and are interested in and, therefore, more likely to motivate someone to buy the products or services advertised than is spam. If sellers know what consumers' interests are, then they don't need to attract consumers' attention by shouting as loudly as possible. Personalized advertising does not require an economy of attention. If digital marketers do attract consumers' attention by targeted ads, they can assume there is a good chance their products will be purchased. Personalization means that sellers can predict that when a person is presented with certain information, they will act upon it, for example, when Amazon knows that someone is interested in science fiction novels. Amazon can predict that this person will be likely to buy at least one of the "relevant" books that they recommend.[74] The link between information and action, that is, between personalized advertising and consumer purchasing activity, is much tighter than with spam. This is why advertisers are willing to pay for what Zuboff calls "prediction products" (8). But is this "manipulation" of behavior?

---

73 For a good overview of the panopticon discussion with regard to workplace surveillance, see the Wikipedia article https://en.wikipedia.org/wiki/Panopticon. See also Foucault (1977).
74 Darmody and Zwick locate the central point of digital marketing in "relevance."

If this is what Zuboff means by "behavior modification," then the word is being used improperly, since the assumption seems to be that people are really not interested in what they evidently are interested in and really do not want to buy what they evidently do want to buy. People are supposedly being coerced into acting in ways that they would not act freely. Furthermore, the assumption is that personalized advertising does not take account of the interests of those to whom it is being offered. Both assumptions are unfounded. Interestingly, industrial capitalism and its specific form of market communication, known as spam, could, in fact, be accused of this kind of behavior modification. Since products were put onto the market without any certainty that anyone would buy them, this led to the well-known tricks of marketers, including psychographic profiling that was employed to persuade people to buy things they didn't want or need. The profit was made in the sale of the product and not in its use. To sell the product was enough. Beyond selling the product, producers had no interest in communication with consumers. In the age of datafication, on the contrary, value is generated by data that accrues only when devices are actually used. This forces producers to go to consumers and ask them what they want. The recent dominance of "agile" as the new standard in management as well as design, development, and production of goods and services in all areas is based upon finding out what people want and, in continuous, close cooperation with consumers, meeting consumers' needs.[75] In the new economy of data, it is use that generates value and not mere sales. Many companies have offered products and services for "free" because the value no longer lies in the product, but in the data generated by using the product. A data-driven economy is therefore no longer based on one-size-fits-all production, an economy of attention governed by spam, and a marketing strategy concerned only with persuading people to buy products they may well not use, but on personalized products and services, which themselves are based on finding out what consumers want and what they will use. The old adage "let the buyer beware" is now turned around in the opposite direction, "let the producer beware," since if consumers do not use the product, the investment has been for nothing. To suppose, as Zuboff does, that a data-driven economy bypasses users' desires, interests, and preferences represents a deep misunderstanding of what the digital transformation is all about and a complete misrepresentation of what producers and advertisers are actually doing. Again, we note that nowhere does Zuboff offer proof for the claim that personalized products and services do not serve the interests of consumers, but only the interests of "others." The "Big Other" that Zuboff (2015) puts in place of Orwell's Big Brother is equally fictitious as was Orwell's dystopian vision.

Concerning the thesis of instrumentarian power and the supposed goal of surveillance capitalism to modify behavior, it should be noted that there is little evidence that

---

75 Beginning as a new method for software development (see http://agilemanifesto.org/), "agile" soon became the standard for management in all areas. At the focus of agile management is "integrated customer engagement"; that is, care is taken "to embed customers within any delivery process to share accountability for product/service delivery" (https://en.wikipedia.org/wiki/Agile_software_development).

human behavior can be successfully manipulated in the ways Zuboff assumes.[76] Although manipulation is often cited as a threat endemic to the digital world, attempting to influence behavior is nothing new and not at all specifically digital. In general, human behavior must be modified. Another word for behavior modification is socialization, which points to the fact that individuals in society are not autonomous, self-determined, and completely free from external influences. Indeed, since the moment of birth, if not already earlier, everyone is trying to influence everyone else. Influence comes from family, friends, teachers, social institutions, employers, and much more. No human society has not attempted by all means possible to influence the behavior of its members. Traditional mass media have, in modern times, played an important and acknowledged role in information control and influence of the public. Of course, the humanist myth of the autonomous rational subject has never admitted this, or when it has been admitted, it has been done so as the target of critique, as if it could be otherwise. From the humanist perspective, humans are born free; that is, freedom is given, a fact, an incontestable reality, and all else that makes up the social realm is a restriction of liberty in one form or another. As Rousseau put, man is born free but is everywhere in chains. This view of human nature has no basis in reality. This is the myth of humanism.

Luhmann, among many others, pointed out that freedom is a social construct. People are not born free; they are born into a society of a certain kind at a specific time in history, which enables certain forms of freedom and prohibits others.[77] The autonomous rational subject is not a fact of nature, not even of human nature, but a social construction of Western modernity. What Zuboff assumes to be human nature is, in fact, a particular product of a particular society at a specific point in history, for the most part, a mythological construct and not a description of reality. The autonomous rational subject that Zuboff sees as the basis of democracy is a myth. She relies on this myth in portraying the dangers of surveillance capitalism. And we quickly admit that here again, she is right. The digital transformation does place the philosophical mythology of humanism into question. The digital transformation is a threat to human nature, as Western modernity has defined it. The digital transformation is disrupting traditional identities, traditional forms of social order, conventional business models, and traditional forms of information control. The problems arising from this disruption, however, are not adequately addressed by simply assuming that neither human self-understanding nor society can and should change and that history must be rolled back and fixed at the point of the Western industrial period and then this version of human existence and social order must somehow be forced upon the world by means of law and regulation. From this point of view, the attempt to "reassert" European values to block the emergence of a global network society resembles, in many respects, another singular achievement of Western modernity, namely, colonialism.

---

[76] For an overview on the topic of manipulation, see the article "Ethics of Manipulation" in the *Stanford Encyclopedia of Philosophy* (https://plato.stanford.edu/entries/ethics-manipulation/). For psychological manipulation, see https://en.wikipedia.org/wiki/Psychological_manipulation.
[77] For a recent discussion, see Willke (2019).

Throughout the book, Zuboff never asks if people do not actually want personalized advertising and personalized products and services. On the contrary, she assumes they do not, and this constitutes the very reason for the evil of surveillance capitalism. The entire critique of surveillance capitalism is based upon the assumption of a perfect crime. We have been robbed, and we don't know it. But even if we did know it and went so far as to consent to it, probably because we have been manipulated, we do not receive the promised benefits. Only "others" have profited from our loss. It is a double robbery. In the face of this accusation, how does Zuboff deal with the obvious success of the data-driven economy? If nobody wants it, if it violates people's rights, treads on human dignity, undermines democracy, and even threatens human nature, then why do people accept it so enthusiastically and why do governments initiate strategies and programs to enable a digital economy, spend enormous sums of money on research and development in digital technologies, and much more? At this point, Zuboff repeats a classical gesture of social science critique by claiming that people do not know what is going on. Even if they know that personal data is being gathered and used to design and offer personalized products and services, they are "psychologically numbed" (11) by the devious strategies and the ideology of surveillance capitalism. Altogether Zuboff (2015, 340) identifies 16 reasons why surveillance capitalism is successful and which constitute the dishonest cover-up of its crimes. These are:

1. Surveillance capitalism is "unprecedented." "The basic operational mechanisms and business practices were so new and strange, so utterly sui generis, that all we could see was a gaggle of 'innovative' horseless carriages. [...] This lack of precedence has left us disarmed and charmed."
2. Surveillance capitalism practices "invasion by declaration," that is, it asserts "its rights to bypass our awareness, to take our experience and transform it into data, to claim ownership of and decisions over the uses of those data."
3. Surveillance capitalism "found shelter in the neoliberal zeitgeist" and thus took advantage of the "historical context" of what Beck has called "second modernity."
4. Surveillance capitalism worked closely with government and did extensive lobbying in order to create "fortification" for its practices.
5. Surveillance capitalism developed the "dispossession cycle" which consists in "audacious incursions" into people's private sphere, followed by "a range of tactics" to suppress and/or divert resistance.
6. Surveillance capitalism created a "dependency" upon its services since the Internet has become essential in all areas of life.
7. Surveillance capitalism has created an economy in which the "self-interest" of all participants—except apparently the people—converge upon using personal data to develop and offer personalized products and services.
8. Surveillance capitalism is "inclusive" in that there is practically no alternative, no place outside its reach and therefore if one does not want to be an outsider and stand completely alone, one must participate.
9. Surveillance capitalism has managed to "identify" itself with innovation and entrepreneurship, both values held in high esteem by society.

10. Surveillance capitalism has taken on an air of "authority" as the locus of future developments and as experts about the future.
11. Surveillance capitalism skillfully employs "social persuasion" so that everyone does what it dictates.
12. Surveillance capitalism imposes a "dictatorship of no alternatives" in which "it is ever more difficult to identify avenues of escape."
13. Surveillance capitalism creates "new institutional facts" and "stabilize new practices" such that we fall into "inevitablism," that is, "we fall into resignation and a sense of helplessness."
14. Surveillance capitalism makes use of the "ideology of human frailty" in order to "legitimate their means of behavior modification: tuning, herding, and conditioning individuals and populations in ways that are designed to elude awareness."
15. Surveillance capitalism plays upon and fosters our "ignorance" of what they are really doing.
16. Surveillance capitalism moves fast, indeed so fast that "velocity is consciously deployed to paralyze awareness and freeze resistance while distracting us with immediate gratifications."

Characteristic of social science critique, Zuboff (2015, 343) concludes this list of immoral practices with an appeal for government regulation. Either critique has always appealed to the people to rise in revolt, or, if the people are unable or unwilling to do this because of police oppression or the power of ideology, there is left only the somewhat paradoxical appeal to government to act on behalf of the people. Although she often exposes government collusion with surveillance capitalism, and we are offered no reason to believe governments would suddenly be willing to change course, Zuboff nonetheless declares that

> we need laws that reject the fundamental legitimacy of surveillance declarations and interrupt its most basic operations, including the illegitimate renditions of human experience as behavioral data, the use of behavioral surplus as free raw material, extreme concentrations of the new means of production, the manufacture of prediction products, trading in behavior futures, the use of prediction products for third-order operations of modification, influence, and control, the operations of the means of behavioral modification, the accumulation of private exclusive concentrations of knowledge, […] and the power that such concentrations confer. (2015)

Behind Zuboff's portrait of surveillance capitalism, there lies not only what perhaps could be called twenty-first-century Ludditism, but the old story of a world in which mostly disempowered individuals attempt to pursue their interests pitted against powerful corporations and ambivalent government agencies. Behind this story stands the myth of workers and capitalists facing it off in a ring set up and refereed by a wavering, uncertain, and often partial state. Finally, to situate this story within the modern constitution, we are told of a world in which autonomous rational subjects can maintain their creativity and human dignity only through secrecy and disguise. In an earlier article, Zuboff (2015, 86) nostalgically bemoans the loss of "the historical relationship between markets and democracies," which was constituted by "traditional reciprocities in which populations and capitalists needed one another" (86). She acknowledges that the digital transformation has created a new world in which an "intelligent world-spanning organism" (85) replaces older social structures. The situation is new, but surprisingly nothing new is happening. Instead of acknowledging the many changes that networking on a global scale has brought about, she revives the old myth of almighty digital capitalists exploiting an unwitting and oppressed digital proletariat. Zuboff blinds out digitally empowered citizens, conversational markets, participatory culture, sharing economy, platform cooperatives, transparent and networked organizations, sociocracy, and digitally empowered social movements. Big Brother is replaced by Big Other. The names have changed, but it's the same old story. Neither this dystopian view is new, nor does it lead into the future. On the contrary, we see here again the attempt to reassert the lost values of modern Western society in the face of the digital transformation. We asked earlier why anybody would prefer spam to personalized advertising. One cannot escape the impression that Zuboff would rather put up with spam and all the now well-known harms created by an economy of attention than question the belief in a mythical autonomy that she never had anyway.

We need not spend more time on examples of how modern criticism attempts to deal with the digital transformation. The two examples discussed above illustrate both the tenor and the spectrum of such approaches. The one is moderate and finds some things in the affordances of ICTs that could be seen as positive. The other is much more denunciatory and sees practically nothing positive in the digital transformation. It places moral and critical thought solidly behind traditional values. The obvious inadequacies of this approach lead to the suspicion that the typically modernist agenda of critical social theory has lost its relevance in the digital age. The story tells of a hierarchical society in which autonomous rational subjects struggle against business and government elites to secure justice, equality, liberty, and dignity. Whether told from the right or the left, this story is perhaps no longer so convincing at it once was. Perhaps critique has seen its day, and those concerned to protect citizens' rights should look for new foundational stories and new ways in which this can be done.

Hacking digital ethics turns out to be much like analyzing and diagnosing the immune reaction of modern industrial society to the deeply rooted evolutionary changes the world is now going through. It seems that wherever people feel threatened in their autonomy, freedom, dignity, and even their supposed rational superiority by technological change, they feel compelled to do digital ethics. This compulsion often does not come from the "end users" themselves, who, as the well-known "privacy paradox" shows, go about their daily lives as if digital ethics did not exist, but from a tradition of critique of the sort we have illustrated by reference to van Dijck and Zuboff. Critique, however, is only one component of the legacy system upon which the discourse of digital ethics currently runs. Critique builds upon and presupposes the philosophical mythology of humanism. But critique and humanism themselves do not stand alone. A powerful ally aids them. This ally is *media scandalization*. The media play an important role in contemporary moral discourse. Without media scandalization, mobilizing moral outrage throughout the public sphere in the name of humanism and the struggle for freedom, dignity, justice, and equality would be mere academic self-indulgence and have little social impact. For this reason, we now turn to a discussion of the third component of the current discourse of digital ethics, media scandalization.

2.3 Media Scandalization

Scandal journalism is not usually understood as ethical discourse. Nonetheless, from a sociological perspective, scandals are a way in which society does "norm work" (Adut 2008, 4).[78] Public moral discussion and moral outrage are hardly ever associated with the treatises of professional philosophers or the publications of social scientists. Even the more popular forms of social science critique of the sort that Zuboff represents rarely attain broad public notoriety but remain within the sequestered domain of intellectual discussion. However, when supposed moral transgressions by persons or institutions of social significance are taken up by the mass media, everyone is called upon to make moral judgments, to praise or blame, to sanction or support the supposed transgressors. Scandals are the terrain upon which society, that is, "the public," is called upon to moralize. Public moralizing is an essential aspect of moral discourse and should not be excluded from any analysis of ethics. It also plays an important role in the discourse of digital ethics. Where would digital ethics be without the Cambridge Analytica Scandal, the Yahoo Data Breach Scandal, the many and ongoing Facebook scandals, to mention only a few? The call, the appeal that instigates public moralizing or social "norm work," as Ari Adut names public moralizing, comes inevitably from the mass media. Scandals in modern societies are always a product of the media (Luhmann 2000; Thompson 2000). The media, of course, are not the sole actors in scandals. There are transgressors and denouncers of transgressions. And finally, there is the public who must be scandalized, that is, who must react negatively to the accusation of transgression. If the public does not react, there is no scandal, no matter how much news media organizations may invest in publicizing a supposed transgression.

Luhmann noted that the mass media in modern functionally differentiated societies form a semi-autonomous subsystem organized by the binary code *news/non-news* difference. Mass media communication is the production of news as opposed to what is considered not to be newsworthy. News, as the name suggests, is what is "new," that is, what is surprising, unexpected, not already known. This definition of news coincides with Shannon and Weaver's famous definition of information as that which is improbable and unexpected. If I know something, then telling me about this again will not give me any information. What is known, expected, and unsurprising has

---

[78] Norm work is "a set of actions that encompass committing, publicizing, sanctioning, and responding to transgressions" (Adut 2008, 4). According to Andrews (2017, 97), "Norm work" for Adut "can involve pioneering and advancing new normative frameworks that challenge the prevailing normative order, to seeking the public enforcement of codified but under-enforced norms, and even the organization of reactionary resistance to burgeoning normative frameworks."

no informational value. This is why yesterday's newspaper is not worth much. What it contains is already known. It contains no news. Any media organization that attempted to publish what has previously been published by other media would quickly go out of business. According to Luhmann's functional definition of the media system, the media are that social system specialized in the production of communications that carry news.

Of course, anyone can say something new and unexpected. What makes the media into a social system specialized in this type of communication is the technology of mass media communications. The printing press, radio, and television are technologies with their own affordances. They are based on an informational economy of scarcity since printing, as well as broadcasting, can produce only a limited amount of information, and this through costly and complicated procedures. The mass media operate within an economy of scarcity of information, while on the other hand, they have a monopoly on information. Luhmann points out that in modern societies, the media have acquired an epistemological function. "Everything we know about our society, or indeed about the world in which we live, we know through the mass media" (Luhmann 2000, 1).[79] The media, and not what we see and experience with our own eyes and ears or learn in face-to-face interactions, are the source of almost everything we can claim to know. Even if we suspect that the media do not report the facts objectively, we have no alternative. According to Luhmann, this is a result of the functional differentiation of modern society. It is the "mechanical manufacture of a product as the bearer of communication" (2) that drives the differentiation of the media as an autonomous system. The technologies of mass media production, whether press, radio, or television, make interaction among copresent participants in communication negligible. Without direct and immediate feedback from copresent participants, which would set constraints on the media, they are faced with "high levels of freedom of communication" and a "surplus of possibilities for communication," which "can only be regulated within the system, by means of self-organization and the system's own constructions of reality" (ibid.). Two "selecting factors" play essential roles in how the media construct reality. These are assumptions about what should be communicated and about what audiences want to hear. The first assumption ascribes a "gate-keeper" function to the media. The media do not publish any and all information; they decide which information is to be disseminated and which not. Of course, within the advertising business model, this decision must be made with regard to what the mass media audience wants to hear. If the audience is not interested in the information the media disseminates, newspapers will not be bought, TV and radio programs will not have high quotas, and this will affect advertising revenues.

Thompson (2000) based his theory of scandal on the development of the mass media from an initially partisan representation of political programs relying on financial support from persons and organizations toward an advertising model that freed journalism from partisan obligations. This shift made the idea of watchdog journalism plausible. It revived the view of the press as a "fourth estate" responsible for watching over the actions

---

79 It is for this reason that Benkler et al. (2018) speak of an "epistemic crisis" in their analysis of the post-truth media system in America.

of the political and business elites in the name of the public.[80] Watchdog journalism, or what is now known as "investigative journalism," obliged the media to objective reporting of the facts, solid research, trustworthiness, and impartiality. It was assumed that the public was interested in the extent to which powerful social actors keep their promises to act in the public good. This is the basis for the assumption that what should be reported in the media is the truth and that the truth is what people want to hear. It is also the basis of the assumption that the media must not be partisan and should always portray all sides to a story or let all actors have a voice. These two assumptions lay the basis for media scandalization both as a possibility and as an institutionalized program. As we shall see, the development of media scandalization has moved increasingly away from truth claims and concerns about neutrality with their associated functions of reasserting moral norms more and more in the direction of entertainment and sensationalism with the effect of encouraging the scandalization of almost anything all the time.[81] There are many factors involved in this development. Among the most important are the digital transformation of the media. The Internet and social media have created a new order of knowledge that is no longer based upon scarcity of information. New media have done away with the gatekeeper function of traditional mass media as well as creating an intensified advertising business rooted in an "economy of attention." This affects not only the business models of the media but also the nature of public moralizing and, consequently, of moral discourse as a whole. Furthermore, these changes affecting mass media scandalization contribute to a situation in which traditional mass media become interested in the scandalization of digital media and digital technologies.[82] The strategy of media self-scandalization makes up an important component of contemporary digital ethics. One can read on a regular basis in the headlines of prominent international newspapers that new media have become a source of fake news, propaganda, and public disinformation. This stokes the fire of ethical criticism of digital media.

But let us not get ahead of the story. What is a scandal, and what does it do? For Thompson (2000, 13), a "scandal refers to actions or events involving certain kinds of transgressions which become known to others and are sufficiently serious to elicit a public response." There is a direct relation between scandal and morality since scandals necessarily involve "a transgression of norms or values" (27). Adut (2008, 23) confirms this internal relation between scandal and morality by defining scandals as "episodes of moral disturbance, marked by an interaction around an actual, apparent, or alleged transgression that draws sustained and negative attention from a public." For Luhmann

---

80 Going back at least to Edmund Burke in 1786, the idea of the press as a "fourth estate" along with nobility, clergy, and commoners had been long known in Europe, but was revived only when the media freed themselves from elite patronage and partisan affiliations and assumed the role of informing the public in advanced democracies.
81 See Kumlin and Esaiasson (2011) for empirical confirmation that scandals have increased.
82 Benkler et al. (2018) show that the high notoriety of the new media in accusations of corruption of the information ecosystem, for example, the creation of filter bubbles, echo chambers, Russian intervention, manipulation, fake news, and so on, in no way corresponds to the actual impact that the Internet and social media had before, during, and after the Trump campaign.

(2000), the system of the mass media selects information to the extent that it is in some way surprising, that is, to the extent that it is "news." This implies that in order to be disseminated in the media, some events "must break with existing expectations" (28). Norms and moral convictions constitute widespread and deeply rooted expectations of how people should behave. Violations of such deep-rooted expectations tend to elicit strong emotional responses such as moral outrage.[83] In comparison to other ways of attracting public attention, eliciting moral outrage makes scandalization appealing to the media. "By reporting such norm violations and scandals, the mass media are able to generate a greater feeling of common concern and outrage than in other ways" (29). For this reason, the media are acutely sensitive to possibilities of potential scandalization. Scandalization is the royal road to attracting attention. Indeed, "media representations of norm violations often take on the character of scandals" (ibid.). In keeping with Durkheim's theory of crime as a social phenomenon found in all societies that functions via public denunciation and sanctions to reaffirm or reestablish normative consent in a society, Luhmann claims that "the norm is actually only generated through the violation, whereas before it simply 'existed' in the mass of existing norms" (29). The scandal produces and strengthens "the sense of outrage and thus indirectly the norm itself" (30). The mass media thus are given "an important function in the maintenance and reproduction of morality" (31). Even when it is no longer assumed, as Durkheim did, that scandals function to reaffirm and reestablish moral consensus in society, they nonetheless activate moral discourse and moral outrage.[84]

We are concerned with media scandalization as an important component of the discourse of digital ethics. Of course, there are many scandals that on the face of it have nothing to do with the digital transformation. There are sports scandals, religious scandals, celebrity scandals, and, above all, political scandals. Indeed, there is no aspect of social life that cannot or is not scandalized. The content and the extent of scandalization seem to have nothing to do with the digital transformation. In addition to this, it is apparent that scandals directly related to digital technologies, such as the Cambridge Analytica Scandal, the many privacy scandals, the various data breaches and hacks that can become scandals, or scandals involving discrimination by artificial intelligence applications, make up only a small part of the daily dose of scandals contemporary media prescribe for the public. Nonetheless, the digital transformation has changed the media ecology drastically. It would be naïve to assume that the traditional mass media still dictate the agenda of scandalization and that moral discourse instigated by the media is unaffected by the digital transformation of the entire media ecosystem. The fact that scandalization takes place today in a contested field of media activity in which the old mass media are losing ground and being transformed by the new digital

---

83 See Goodenough (1997) for the classic sociological discussion of moral outrage.
84 Contemporary scandal scholars have moved away from Durkheim's view on the grounds that scandals do not necessarily reaffirm moral consensus in a society. They can just as well lead to conflict or transformation of norms. See Andrews (2017) for a discussion of the history of scandal studies.

media, that is, the Internet, social media platforms, Facebook, Twitter, the Blogsphere, and general media integration, cannot be ignored when describing contemporary media scandalization. Taking a step back from concrete scandals involving digital media as transgressors and looking at the transformation of the media themselves, it is crucial to recall Luhmann's assertion, that all we know about the world, we know through the media. This means that changes in the media are also changes in knowledge. ICTs are revolutionary not only in that they change how information is produced, distributed, consumed, and used but also because they change the order of knowledge itself. This is not the place to attempt a complete assessment of "new media," a topic that has attracted considerable attention in sociology, media studies, and communication science for decades.[85] For our purposes, it is of central importance to recall not only how ICTs are scandalized by traditional media leading to a moral discourse about digital information and communication technologies but also how this takes place within a contested field of media transformation affecting all aspects of society.

There is a consensus among media scholars that so-called new media are indeed new and do transform, if not completely replace, traditional mass media.[86] Mass media, as Luhmann rightly points out, arose within the functionally differentiated society of Western modernity. The mass media, as the name suggests, are characterized by mass distribution of information using the technologies of the press, radio, and television. The affordances of these technologies favored centralized information production and information filtering, which is also known as the gatekeeper function of the media. Centralized production concentrated informational power in the hands of a few. This is nothing new since the ownership and control over the means of the production and distribution of information and knowledge have always been in the hands of elites. The idea of the press as a "fourth estate," distinguished from ideological elites and in the service of the public, took hold only very late in the development of modern democracies.[87] The mass media could become a "watchdog" only if they did not thereby need to bite the hand that fed them. This became possible when media financing shifted from partisan elites to the broader public, who supported the media indirectly through advertising revenues. Although partisan influence of the mass media never completely disappeared, the appeal of investigative journalism to the public was sufficient to guarantee advertising revenue. Journalism became a "profession" with a code of ethics committed to objectivity, truthful reporting of facts, fairness, impartiality, and a concern for the public good. This corresponded well with the gatekeeping functions of a centralized media production and distribution, a function that went well beyond the press, radio, or television and included the realm of "experts" and "authorities" of all kinds—publishers, teachers, clergy, doctors, lawyers, and so on—who were in charge of granting access to knowledge

---

85 For a discussion of the new order of knowledge created by the digital transformation of the media, see Krieger and Belliger (2014).
86 For a review of literature and standpoints with regard to so-called new media, see Krieger and Belliger (2014).
87 See Thompson (2000).

and certifying its reliability. This modern regime of knowledge was inherently hierarchical, limited, exclusive, and reduced. It was based upon an economy of scarcity of information. The new media changed this order of knowledge completely and ushered in an order of knowledge that was essentially nonhierarchical, unlimited, connected, inclusive, complex, and open to everyone.[88]

According to Weinberger (2012), modern mass media, and the entire order of knowledge they created fundamentally constituted a hierarchical information regime that could be illustrated by a pyramid. At the bottom are the masses of information consumers. Above them are those who control the production and distribution of information. Above them are the business and political elites who own the means for production. And finally, at the top is money, which rules all. The new order of knowledge created by digital media is entirely different. It is nonhierarchical, inclusive, complex, and public. As Weinberger suggests, this new order of knowledge could perhaps best be illustrated by a cloud. No reference is intended to so-called cloud computing, but the cloud, nonetheless, is an interesting and useful symbol for the new order of knowledge that ICTs represent. In the cloud, there are no hierarchies because there is no scarcity. On the contrary, there is information overload. In the cloud, no one is higher up in the ladder, since every place, every position, every route of access or distribution is equal. Often-cited differences between old media and new media are: (1) whereas mass media consist of few channels, digital media offer many different channels. (2) Whereas mass media address a unified audience, digital media address many different audiences or publics. In the cloud there is no single, unified public, no silent majority. (3) Whereas few control the production and distribution of information under the regime of mass media, digital media give the means of information production and distribution to many. (4) Whereas mass media are one-way communication, digital media are many-to-many communication, interactive and conversational in nature. (5) Whereas mass media tended to have a gatekeeping function with regard to the evaluation, selection, and distribution of information, new media have no gatekeepers, everyone is an expert, and no one can filter information for others. Indeed, everyone is challenged to become media literate and be responsible for their own filters. The new order of knowledge that is being created by the affordances of digital media is nonhierarchical because there are no gates to keep. It is unlimited because there is no limit on the production, storage, or distribution of information. There is, therefore, no need for centralized senders or a unified receiver public. The new order of knowledge is inclusive and public because access to information is open to all. It is almost impossible to exclude anyone from information as the many leaks, hacks, and whistleblowers illustrate. The result is that there are now many publics, each with its own criteria of truth and relevance and no centralized, authoritative controls over the quality of information.[89] The cloud is complex and diversified. Paraphrasing Weinberger

---

88 See Weinberger (2012) for a comparison of old and new media and an analysis of the new order of knowledge that the digital transformation has created.
89 Benkler et al. (2018) document how this has led to the development of entirely separated media ecosystems, or echo-chambers in, for example, how the radical right in the United States could lock many people into a view of the world devoid of truth and critical constraints.

(2012, 40), who cites Newton's second law, for every fact on the Internet, there is an equal but opposite fact. In other words, everyone is obliged to either sink or swim in the flood of information on their own or with the help of their friends via social media.

In the early days of the Internet, this new order of knowledge raised many hopes in the democratization of knowledge, open access to information for all, bottom-up social activism, sharing economy, citizen empowerment, and much more. Today, these visions seem naïve and have everywhere been disappointed by phenomena such as the rise of monopolistic networks, the fragmentation of the public sphere into echo chambers and filter bubbles, the omnipresence of cyber criminality and hacking, corporate profiling, monetization of personal data, amplification of false or misleading information and accompanying fears of manipulation and the undermining of democracy, the unhampered activities of trolls and conspiracy groups, and the ever-increasing threats of cyberwarfare, foreign intervention in political processes, and so on.[90] The Internet has shown its dark side. This has led to a situation that leads traditional media, which have suffered financially as well as socially by loss of prestige and gatekeeper functions, to scandalize new media. The Cambridge Analytica Scandal, for example, was launched by the old media against the supposed transgressions of new media. The moral outrage mobilized by the revelations of the illegal use of Facebook data for political profiling and manipulative information that supposedly influenced the 2016 presidential election in the United States as well as the Brexit vote in the United Kingdom can only be explained by the social shock that these events created. Even though commercial and political profiling is nothing new, and even though no evidence has yet come forth showing that Cambridge Analytica, foreign disinformation campaigns, or similar tactics of political communication and information warfare actually do significantly influence voters, cries of violations of democratic values and fundamental rights and norms such as privacy continue to echo through the media, academia, and government as well.[91]

The ongoing scandalization of new media by old media takes place in a situation that has been fundamentally altered by the digital transformation. Scandalization can no longer operate with the assumption of a unified public, whose moral sensibilities can be mobilized against clearly identifiable transgressions. The new order of knowledge represented by the Internet, social media, platforms, and many kinds of news-related

---

90 See Belliger and Krieger (2018c) for a discussion of the disappointed hopes and reactions, above all, of the media to the dark side of the Internet and Benkler et al. (2018) for an empirically based analysis of the post-truth media ecosystem.

91 For the lack of evidence supporting the narrative of manipulation, see Gibney (2018), Kalla and Broockman (2018), and Benkler et al. (2018). For academic adherence to the manipulation narrative, despite lack of evidence, see the "Report of the Computation Propaganda Research Project Challenging Truth and Trust: A Global Inventory of Organized Social Media Manipulation" by Bradshaw, S., and Howard, P. N. 2017. Oxford Internet Institute. http://comprop.oii.ox.ac.uk/wp-content/uploads/sites/93/2018/07/ct2018.pdf. For government's belief in manipulation and the supposed threat to democracy, see "Privacy 2030. A New Vision for Europe" by Buttarelli, G. (2019). https://iapp.org/media/pdf/resource_center/giovanni_manifesto.pdf. And for a rare challenge to the strategy of old media to scandalize new media, see Ledwich and Zaitsev (2019).

websites is fragmented into many different publics, each of which constructs its own reality, its own criteria of truth, and therefore its own norms.[92] This permits almost any behavior at all to be scandalized since no matter what happens, there is a public somewhere in the Web that perceives this as an occasion for moral outrage. Moral outrage is, therefore, omnipresent. In addition to this, since the emergence of the Internet and the information flood, a new economic situation has arisen that can be termed the *economy of attention*. There is much more information available than people can consume because of limited spans of attention. When value is generated by the consumption of information, attention becomes a scarce resource for which media compete. Current media, both old and new, are locked into the economy of attention that has arisen out of the new order of knowledge. Information is consumed by attention, which is limited. The competition for attention drives business as well as politics in the digital age. Market presence or public presence is based not primarily on information, which has become secondary, but on the ability to attract attention. The playing field for media today is determined by the struggle to attract attention. Media production becomes directed toward the primary purpose of somehow mobilizing information consumers to look at some information or click on some link (clickbait). This leads inevitably to sensationalism, emotionally weighted content, as well as the blurring of boundaries between tabloid journalism and serious reporting. Since moral outrage is a relatively reliable way to attract attention and motivate information consumption, moral discourse is increasingly carried out in the media by scandalization, that is, the designing of information so that it shocks media consumers by uncovering alleged immorality, abuse of power, injustice, and so on.

The downside of the generalized scandalization of almost everything by the media is that scandal consumers become weary and saturated with appeals to moral indignation.[93] There arises a general apathy or cynicism concerning the normative foundations of society. Furthermore, the fragmentation of "the public" into many different and conflicting publics makes it all but impossible to speak of any norms as foundations of society as a whole. Not only does everyone have different moral norms, but these norms are everywhere continually being disrespected by politicians, business leaders, sports heroes, religious figures, institutions, and entire sectors, such as the media themselves. Already

---

92 The loss of "the public" as addressee of media communication disables as well as debunks the notion that the role of the media consists in keeping the public informed. In fact, there never was an informed or attentive public that could have been a politically effective recipient of watchdog journalism. See Schudson (1998), Delli et al. (1996), Zaller (1992), and Herbst (1998). Karpf (2019) argues that what the new media threaten is the shared belief in such a public, a belief that functioned to limit complete disregard of the truth by political elites. That this threat must be taken seriously is well illustrated by post-truth politics.

93 Scandal scholars have always warned against "scandal fatigue." See, for example, Thompson (2000), Adut (2008), and, more recently with regard to political scandals, Kumlin and Asaiasson (2011, 5): "Our characterization of the current state of affairs is *scandal fatigue*, denoting a situation where citizens are accustomed to scandal elections, where expectations of politicians may have dwindled, where views of an overly scandal-oriented media may have grown critical, and where—as a result—yet another scandal election does not make much difference" (emphasis in original).

Luhmann, long before the Internet age, pointed out the conflict-generating potential of morality. Furthermore, by systematically scandalizing the new media, the old media have set out upon the risky path of media self-scandalization. Traditional mass media have long been transformed into digital media providers. Every major and minor newspaper or television network has shifted most of their activities onto the Internet. They all maintain sites in major social media platforms such as Facebook, Twitter, YouTube, and so on. They all use the resources of the new order of knowledge to pick up stories from "citizen journalists" and distribute, amplify, and capitalize on the "clicks" that these channels generate. The scandalization of new media as distributors of misinformation, disinformation, or "fake news" comes back to haunt the traditional mass media since they pick up these stories and amplify them through their channels. Even traditional news media have succumbed to producing "clickbait" instead of objective, in-depth researched, and reliable information.[94] Against this background, calls for a return to the good old days of media gatekeeping and institutional filtering appear not only self-serving but also hypocritical and unrealistic.

Where does this leave moral discourse? What does media scandalization under the regime of the new order of knowledge mean for digital ethics? In general, it can be argued that media scandalization has effectively made moral discourse into an occasion for the reality construction of different groups. There is no moral discourse of society as a whole. There is no moral outrage that is not partisan, perspectival, and limited to only a specific sector of society, a particular group, or a certain public. There is no moral sentiment that does not arise and pursue a trajectory locked within its own filter bubble or echo chamber. The scandalization of almost everything that certain public figures say or do usually does not lead to a general public condemnation, but serves merely as a rallying point for supporters. The ongoing scandalization of Facebook, for example, has not led to a general public condemnation of Facebook, at least not if one considers what people do instead of what they say. The well-known "privacy paradox" shows that the media can influence what people may feel and how they may respond to questions posed by social scientists, but not what they do and how they actually use information. The consequence is that media scandalization has had the effect of transforming the discourse of digital ethics into the discourse of a particular public subscribing to a certain worldview and specific norms and values. As we have argued above in the discussion of the philosophical mythology of humanism, as well as of social science critique, it can be claimed that the particular public whose values and norms are activated by media scandalization of ICTs is the public motivated by nostalgia for the disappearing industrial society of Western modernity.

The conditions and effects of media scandalization of the digital transformation have made digital ethics into an echo chamber or a filter bubble. The current discourse of digital ethics is a world of information filtered through the lens of certain assumptions about the reality and values of Western industrial society. Through this filter, the digital

---

94 The rise of various "fact-checking" services only confirms that nothing the media presents is trustworthy.

transformation is perceived to question the heroic struggle of the autonomous rational subject for freedom, self-determination, equality, and justice against ensconced political and business elites determined to undermine morality and democracy through eliminating privacy, implementing AI-driven automation, and generally subordinating humans to machines, thus driving economic exploitation and manipulation of behavior. Despite all the commitments we may feel toward modern Western society and the moral outrage easily triggered by scandalization of supposed violations of modern values, the digital transformation may well mean the end of the modern myth. Industrial society is not the culmination of history, the fulfillment of human potential, or even an unshakeable foundation for moral norms and ethics. The digital transformation cannot be stopped by media scandalization. Still, it can be and is being used by the media to generate outrage and in this way to capture as much public attention as possible. If ethics is not to become dependent on emotional reactions of outrage, indignation, and practices of denunciation, it must be located within the conditions of the new order of knowledge and assessed for its ability to make sense of moral action under the conditions of the global network society. The status of ethical discourse at the beginning of the twenty-first century and within the context of the global network society leave ethics no other option than searching for new values and new forms of regulation based on the digital transformation. Of course, there is no going back to universalist claims. All norms must be articulated from a perspective, from a constructivist and partisan position. The many appeals coming from philosophers, social scientists, and political leaders in the West to reassert European values in the face of the challenges arising from the digital transformation openly acknowledge that claims to universal values and norms are only that, mere claims. Western nations may attempt to reinforce such claims with laws and regulations. Still, the legitimacy of such legal measures as well as their effectiveness not only within their national borders but internationally as well is open to question.

2.4 Civil Society Activism

The moral discourse of today's society can hardly be understood without taking account of the activism of many civil society organizations as well as semi-private and private counterparts who, on their own initiative, take on "watchdog" functions concerning the social dangers of ICTs. The public or publics who are appealed to by media scandalization find in these various actors their "representatives" vis-à-vis government and industry.[95] As the public dissolves and fragments, it is civil society activists that jump in to fill the gap. It is impossible to list all these actors, since there are so many and new ones are appearing almost daily. It is equally impossible to completely describe their various

---

95 The loss of "the public" brought about by new media in part accounts for the proliferation and hyperactivity of civil society actors, since as Zaller (1992) points out, politicians do not communicate directly with the public, but with public representatives or those who effectively claim to represent the public.

roles in contributing to contemporary digital ethics. A rough classification could be made as follows:[96]

1. Academic and semi-academic institutions: These are either within or associated with universities. They are usually funded with endowments from private partners, foundations, and donors. A short and very inadequate list of examples is
   - The *Alan Turing Institute*, which is the United Kingdom's "national institute for data science and artificial intelligence" supported to date by 13 universities with the goal, among others, "to train new generations of data science and AI leaders with the necessary breadth and depth of technical and ethical skills to match the UK's growing industrial and societal needs" as well as "through agenda-setting research, public engagement, and expert technical advice, drive new and innovative ideas which have a significant influence on industry, government, regulation, or societal views."[97]
   - The *Institute for Ethics in Artificial Intelligence* sponsored, among others, by Facebook at the Technical University of Munich, which "provides a platform for academics to conduct meaningful and interdisciplinary research with practical applications and in cooperation with industry and civil society."[98]
   - Stanford University's *Institute for Human-Centered Artificial Intelligence*, which "was established to advance AI research, education, policy, and practice to improve the human condition […] and aims to conduct research on fundamental and applied topics; convene stakeholders from academia, government, civil society, and industry to address critical technical and societal challenges; and educate student and leaders across all sectors."[99]
   - *The Royal Society*, whose goal since "its founding Charters of the 1660s, is to recognize, promote, and support excellence in science and to encourage the development and use of science for the benefit of humanity."[100]
   - The *Data Ethics Lab* at the University of Oxford, which is part of the Oxford Internet Institute and was launched in order "to tackle the ethical challenges posed by digital innovation."[101]
   - *AI4ALL*, a US nonprofit with the goal of making AI more diverse and inclusive.[102]

---

96 See Jobin et al. (2019, 391) for a worldwide list of institutions and organizations that contribute guidelines for AI as well as a somewhat different classification into private companies, governmental agencies, academic and research institutions, intergovernmental or supranational organizations, nonprofit organizations and professional associations, scientific societies, private sector alliances, research alliances, science foundations, federations of worker unions, and political parties.
97 https://www.turing.ac.uk/about-us.
98 https://ieai.mcts.tum.de/.
99 https://hai.stanford.edu/about/fundraising-policy.
100 https://royalsociety.org/about-us/mission-priorities/.
101 https://www.oii.ox.ac.uk/research/digital-ethics-lab/.
102 http://ai-4-all.org/.

2. Government or semi-governmental initiatives, projects, and organizations that are made up of partners from the scientific community as well as the private sector, but are affiliated with government programs, either on the national, international, or multinational levels. Again, with apologies to all who deserve to be mentioned but have been left out, a list of examples is
   - OECD, which in 2019 produced the OECD Council Recommendation on Artificial Intelligence.[103]
   - The G20-adopted 2019 Human Centered AI Principles.[104]
   - UK Center of Data Ethics and Innovation, which is "tasked by the Government to connect policymakers, industry, civil society, and the public to develop the right governance regime for data-driven technologies."[105]
   - The Data Ethics Commission of the German government. "The task of the Federal Government's Data Ethics Commission (Datenethikkommission) will be to build on scientific and technical expertise in developing ethical guidelines for the protection of the individual, the preservation of social cohesion, and the safeguarding and promotion of prosperity in the information age."[106]
   - The European Data Supervisor (EDPS), which is the European Union's independent data protection authority.[107] The "EDPS has been calling for a broad understanding of privacy and data protection as core values central to protecting human dignity, autonomy and the democratic functioning of our societies."[108]
   - The policy area of "Strengthening Trust and Security" of the digital single market strategy of the European Union, which "aims to open up digital opportunities for people and business and enhance Europe's position as a world leader in the digital economy,"[109] with the specific goal of "focusing on applications that combine digital policy, digital research and innovation, and deployment and provide for leadership in cyber security and digital privacy and digital trust policy, legislation and innovation."[110] Within this broad program is the "ONLIFE Initiative: Concept Reengineering for rethinking societal concerns in the digital transition," which will be discussed in detail below.[111]

---

103 https://www.oecd.org/going-digital/ai/principles/.
104 https://www.mofa.go.jp/files/000486596.pdf.
105 https://www.gov.uk/government/organisations/centre-for-data-ethics-and-innovation.
106 https://www.bmjv.de/DE/Themen/FokusThemen/Datenethikkommission/Datenethikkommission_EN_node.html.
107 https://edps.europa.eu/.
108 https://edps.europa.eu/data-protection/our-work/ethics_en.
109 https://ec.europa.eu/digital-single-market/en/policies/strengthening-trust-and-security.
110 https://ec.europa.eu/digital-single-market/en/content/digital-society-trust-and-cybersecurity-directorate-h.
111 https://ec.europa.eu/digital-single-market/en/news/onlife-initiative-concept-reengineering-rethinking-societal-concerns-digital-transition.

3. Professional organizations concerned not only with professional ethics but also with broader issues concerning ethical ICTs.[112] Examples are
   - The IEEE (Institute of Electrical and Electronics Engineers) has many projects in the areas of technology and ethics, for example, *TechEthics*, which is "seeking to ensure that ethical and societal implications of technology become an integral part of the development process by driving conversation and debate on these issues" and which "seeks to accelerate the generation of ideas, facilitate the vetting of those ideas, and, where applicable, drive consensus around those ideas" via "event production, content development, audience engagement and other activities."[113]
   - International Association of Privacy Professionals (IAPP), which claims to be the world's largest information privacy organization with the aim to "define, support and improve the privacy profession globally."[114]
   - AI professionals who are represented, for example, by the Neural Information Processing Systems Foundation (NeurIPS), "whose purpose is to foster the exchange of research on neural information processing systems in their biological, technological, mathematical, and theoretical aspects" and whose "primary focus […] is the presentation of a continuing series of professional meetings known as the Neural Information Processing Systems Conference."[115]
4. Private enterprises, such as large technology companies or consultants, who offer expertise with regard to implementing the technologies in question. Examples of this last type are
   - Gemserve,[116] whose Ivana Bartoletti is a prolific publicist and speaker at digital ethics conferences.[117]
   - Accenture[118]
   - Gartner[119]
   - And, of course, Microsoft, Google, Facebook, and other big and smaller players from the technology sector.
5. Classic nonprofit organizations such as
   - WEF (World Economic Forum)[120]

---

112 On the emerging profession of "digital strategist," see Hestres (2016).
113 https://techethics.ieee.org/about.
114 https://iapp.org/about/.
115 https://nips.cc/About.
116 https://www.gemserv.com/.
117 http://www.ivanabartoletti.co.uk/index.html.
118 https://www.accenture.com/_acnmedia/pdf-24/accenture-universal-principles-data-ethics.pdf.
119 https://www.gartner.com/en/newsroom/press-releases/2018-10-15-gartner-identifies-the-top-10-strategic-technology-trends-for-2019.
120 https://www.weforum.org/.

- Algorithm Watch "is a non-profit research and advocacy organization committed to evaluating and shedding light on algorithmic processes that have a social relevance, meaning they are used either to predict or prescribe human action or to make decisions automatically."[121]
- AI Now "is an interdisciplinary research center dedicated to understanding the social implications of artificial intelligence."[122]
- Electronic Frontier Foundation "is the leading nonprofit organization defending civil liberties in the digital world."[123]
- Privacy International "is a charity that challenges the governments and companies that want to know everything about individuals, groups, and whole societies."[124]
- American Civil Liberties Union has a section dealing with privacy and technology.[125]
- Electronic Privacy Information Center (epic) is a public interest research center established "to focus public attention on emerging privacy and civil liberties issues and to protect privacy, freedom of expression, and democratic values in the information age."[126]
- European Digital Rights (EDRi) "is an international not-for-profit association of 42 digital human rights organizations from across Europe and beyond. We defend and promote rights and freedoms in the digital environment, such as the right to privacy, personal data protection, freedom of expression, and access to information."[127]
- Center for Democracy & Technology (CDT) "is a champion of global online civil liberties and human rights, driving policy outcomes that keep the internet open, innovative, and free."[128]
- Center for Data Innovation "formulates and promotes pragmatic public policies designed to maximize the benefits of data-driven innovation in the public and private sectors. It educates policymakers and the public about the opportunities and challenges associated with data, as well as technology trends such as open data, artificial intelligence, and the Internet of Things."[129]
- Information Technology & Innovation Foundation (ITIF) "is an independent, nonprofit, nonpartisan research and educational institute—a think tank. Its mission is to formulate, evaluate, and promote policy solutions that accelerate innovation and boost productivity to spur growth, opportunity, and progress. ITIF's

---

121 https://algorithmwatch.org/en/what-we-do/.
122 https://ainowinstitute.org/.
123 https://www.eff.org/about.
124 https://privacyinternational.org/about.
125 https://www.aclu.org/issues/privacy-technology.
126 https://epic.org/epic/about.html.
127 https://edri.org/.
128 https://cdt.org/who-we-are/.
129 https://www.datainnovation.org/about/.

goal is to provide policymakers around the world with high-quality information, analysis, and recommendations they can trust.[130]
- Partnership on AI (PAI) "is a multistakeholder organization that brings together academics, researchers, civil society organizations, companies building and utilizing AI technology, and other groups working to better understand AI's impacts. The Partnership was established to study and formulate best practices on AI technologies, to advance the public's understanding of AI, and to serve as an open platform for discussion and engagement about AI and its influences on people and society."[131]
- The Open Data Institute founded by Sir Tim Berners Lee and its Data Ethics Canvas[132]
- The Omidyar Network has developed an Ethical Explorer Pack to help Silicon Valley develop ethical standards.[133]

6. Finally, there is a myriad of conferences and events usually organized and sponsored by the above mentioned and similar actors and in various combinations. Examples are
    - Symposium on Digital Ethics sponsored by the Center for Digital Ethics & Policy Loyola University Chicago.[134]
    - Digital Ethics Conference sponsored by Deutsche Telekom.[135]
    - Digital Ethics Summit sponsored by techUK.[136]
    - Conference on NeurIPS.[137]

We freely admit that subsuming so many different activities, organizations, and institutions under the rubric of "civil society activism" is careless and mostly unfounded. Nonetheless, no appraisal of moral discourse at the beginning of the twenty-first century would be complete without at least attempting to describe the contribution of such organizations, institutions, and actors. We acknowledge that this review is neither exhaustive nor perhaps even representative. The examples we look at may not be the most important or even the most influential, and they may not be representative of the entire sector. We hope, however, that the reader gains an impression of what these organizations do and of the importance of their contribution to the discourse of digital ethics. Although many civil society actors are "specialized" with regard to one technology, for example, AI, the range of topics addressed by these actors covers other technologies and problem areas as

---

130 https://www.itif.org/about.
131 https://www.partnershiponai.org/.
132 https://theodi.org/article/data-ethics-canvas/.
133 https://www.omidyar.com/blog/introducing-ethical-explorer-pack and https://ethicalexplorer.org/.
134 https://www.digitalethics.org/eighth-annual-symposium-digital-ethics.
135 https://www.telekom.com/en/company/details/digital-ethics-conference-558502.
136 https://www.techuk.org/digital-ethics-summit/about.
137 https://neurips.cc/.

well that are typical of digital ethics. There are, however, certain common features that describe roughly what the contribution of these actors to digital ethics is.

The tenor of the contributions of civil society, semi-private, semi-governmental, and private organizations lies not in developing new perspectives on ethics or new approaches to dealing with perceived problems. Rather it lies in achieving consensus on problem definitions and generating motivation for lobbying, publicizing, and pursuing programs for action. Furthermore, since many private players are involved, there is a more balanced and pragmatic approach to problems and solutions than is found in social science critique or media scandalization. It is much less clear who wears the white hats and who the black hats. Since it is often the explicit mission of many civil society actors to bring together stakeholders from government, business, science, as well as the public, the emphasis is placed on constructive debate, seeking common ground, and encouraging cooperation rather than distributing praise and blame or denouncing transgressions. Since participation is voluntary and civil society actors operate within communities of like-minded participants, and there are rarely grave differences of opinion on values. No one questions common interpretations of privacy, autonomy, the meaning of equality or justice, or the harms caused by loss of privacy or by discrimination.

No one challenges the modern social order, its myths, its normative assumptions, and its assumed universality. Instead, efforts are directed toward bringing accepted values and norms to bear on what is perceived as new or pressing problems with ethical implications. The "watchdog" function of civil society actors comes to the fore in directing attention to the social dangers of ICTs, for example, possible or actual discrimination of marginalized groups by AI applications in healthcare, policing, or social services; the always-present threat of privacy violations; the presumed dangers of profiling, tracking, and loss of freedom by automatic decision making; and the danger of uncontrolled social media and political manipulation. The list of "issues" is well-known and need not be rehearsed in detail here. Suffice it to say that the discourse of civil society organizations is designed to unite relatively like-minded actors around relatively consensual problem definitions and motivate them to cooperatively act both socially and politically to reassure the public, consumers, as well as government that problems are acknowledged and are being effectively addressed.

Significantly, this is the area of moral discourse where the many ethical guidelines, lists of principles, statements on ethical development and deployment of ICTs, and descriptions of ethical issues as well as appeals to implement digital ethics are to be located. It is civil society actors who are responsible for the many programmatic statements on the nature, scope, and topics of digital ethics. If one looks for ethical guidelines, norms, and imperatives, these are not primarily to be found in academic treatises on ethics, but in the pronouncements of many different civil society actors. What are these topics and issues? In a recent statement, Floridi (2019, 11) proposes that the domain of digital ethics be divided into three areas: "information and data (including generation, recording, curation, processing, dissemination, sharing, and use), algorithms (including AI, artificial agents, machine learning, and robots), and corresponding practices and infrastructures (including, responsible innovation, programming, hacking, professional codes, and standards)." Forms of digital ethics such as machine ethics, AI ethics, robo-ethics, IoT ethics, big data ethics, and so on are not, according to Floridi, to be considered independent areas of ethical endeavor, but "miss the point" because "we need a digital ethics that provides a holistic approach to the whole universe of moral issues caused by digital innovation" (ibid.). If we ask what this moral universe consists of, explicitly named critical ethical issues are "anonymity, privacy, responsibility, transparency, and trust" (ibid.). Most civil society actors, as well as academics, do not follow Floridi's proposal but concern themselves with proclaiming lists of values or guidelines for specific technologies, such as AI or robotics.[138]

The above-mentioned Opinion of the German Data Ethics Commission lists values such as "human dignity, self-determination, privacy, security, democracy, justice and solidarity, and sustainability." In the meantime, there are many lists of moral issues that make up the agenda of digital ethics. Interestingly, the many lists are surprisingly consistent. A recent survey of many publications on the topic (Floridi et al. 2018) finds that most lists of values for digital ethics can be reduced to beneficence, non-maleficence, autonomy, justice, and explicability. A recent self-proclaimed "global" survey (Jobin et al. 2019) of AI ethics guidelines, including 84 documents, reached a similar conclusion. The authors find that "eleven overarching ethical values and principles have emerged" (391). Judged by the number of documents in which these principles were mentioned, they are "transparency, justice and fairness, non-maleficence, responsibility, privacy, beneficence, freedom and autonomy, trust, dignity, sustainability, and solidarity" (ibid.). The authors note, however, that these principles are often interpreted differently. Interestingly, none of the source documents come from China, Russia, or Africa, and only one from India, which implies that the discourse of digital ethics is primarily a Western discourse and no at all "global," as the authors proclaim.[139]

These values serve as the basis for the many ethical guidelines that are produced and disseminated by civil society actors. A typical example is the Montreal Declaration for the Responsible Development of Artificial Intelligence (2017),[140] which consists of 10 principles: (1) well-being, (2) respect for autonomy, (3) protection of privacy and intimacy, (4) solidarity, (5) democratic participation, (6) equity, (7) diversity inclusion, (8) prudence, (9) responsibility, and (10) sustainable development.[141] The well-known OECD principles on AI include the following:

> "1) AI should benefit people and the planet by driving inclusive growth, sustainable development and well-being; 2) AI systems should be designed in a way that respects the rule of law, human rights, democratic values and diversity, and they should include appropriate safeguards—for example, enabling human intervention where necessary—to ensure a fair and just society;

---

138 See, for example, Bendel (2019), Coeckelbergh (2011, 2019), and Gunkel (2012, 2018a, 2018b).
139 This should not be surprising considering the commitments of ethical discourse in general and digital ethics in particular to the values, norms, and assumptions of Western modernity.
140 https://www.montrealdeclaration-responsibleai.com/.
141 https://www.montrealdeclaration-responsibleai.com/the-declaration.

3) There should be transparency and responsible disclosure around AI systems to ensure that people understand AI-based outcomes and can challenge them; 4) AI systems must function in a robust, secure and safe way throughout their life cycles and potential risks should be continually assessed and managed; and 5) Organizations and individuals developing, deploying or operating AI systems should be held accountable for their proper functioning in line with the above principles.[142]

A further example is the Universal Principles of Data Ethics by the private consulting firm Accenture, which consists of the following principles: (1) respect persons behind data; (2) attend to the downstream uses of datasets; (3) be aware that the provenance of data and the analytical tools shape the consequences of use; (4) match privacy and security safeguards with privacy and security expectations; (5) follow the law; (6) be wary of collecting data just for the sake of more data; (7) data can be a tool of inclusion and exclusion; (8) explain methods for analysis and marketing to data disclosers; (9) professionals should accurately represent their qualifications, expertise, and adhere to professional standards and strive for accountability; (10) aspire to design practices that incorporate transparency, configurability, accountability, and auditability; (11) products and research practices should be subject to internal and external ethical review; and (12) governance practices should be robust, known to all and reviewed regularly.[143] Finally, a last example of such guidelines and principles is the well-known Asilomar AI Principles, which include, among others: (1) safety, (2) failure transparency, (3) responsibility, (4) judicial transparency, (5) human values, (6) personal privacy, (7) shared benefit, (8) shared prosperity, and (9) human control.[144]

The above-mentioned values, guidelines, and principles are marshaled to combat threats perceived to arise from the digital transformation. These perceived threats are complex, interdependent, and overlapping such that it is difficult task to identify them clearly and thus target the specific "issues" to which they give rise. Who is the enemy? Where are they? How can they best be engaged? These questions must be answered before digital ethics can meaningfully be developed and deployed. What then are the problems that digital ethics addresses? Floridi, Cath, and Taddeo (2019), in the paper "Digital Ethics: Its Nature and Scope," propose, as we saw, grouping the issues with which digital ethics is confronted into three general areas: information and data, algorithms, and infrastructures. However, this is not the only way in which the domain of digital ethics can be mapped out. Many define ethical issues in terms of specific technologies, such as robotics, artificial intelligence, automation, social media, big data, IoT, human–computer interfaces, fake news, cyberwarfare, and so on. Regardless of which approach one takes, either areas or technologies, if one wishes to make a list of issues

---

142 https://www.oecd.org/going-digital/ai/principles/.
143 https://www.accenture.com/_acnmedia/pdf-24/accenture-universal-principles-data-ethics.pdf.
144 https://futureoflife.org/ai-principles/?cn-reloaded=1.

that must be dealt with by digital ethics, one is confronted with two major problems. First, areas, as well as technologies, are always changing. As soon as one has identified the issues, they shift ground, move to other areas or new technologies. Secondly, technologies and areas overlap and are difficult to distinguish clearly. Big data, for example, plays a role in artificial intelligence, which itself plays a decisive role in robotics and automation, which are all driven by algorithms and serve as the basis for infrastructure and so on. Furthermore, both technologies and areas are contextual in that they raise different issues depending on how, where, and why they are deployed, whether it be in healthcare, education, business, politics, research, industry, media, infrastructure, and so on. Depending on where technologies are deployed and for what purposes changes the conditions under which they are implemented and the accompanying issues that digital ethics may feel called upon to address.

It is almost impossible to describe all the relevant technologies and socio-technical processes that raise ethical issues today since almost all of the so-called disruptive technologies such as AI, big data, IoT, blockchain, and so on are linked together and with technologies and research in physics, biology, chemistry, computer science, data science, mathematics, and other disciplines. Is genetic engineering a digital technology? Biohacking, in any case, is one of the significant problem areas that arise within the broad scope of the digital transformation. What about nanotechnology, new materials research, neuroscience, quantum computing, the singularity, transhumanism, and many other disciplines, technologies, and programs that are contributing in unexpected ways to a radical reassessment of current conceptions of the world, society, and human existence?[145] All this makes the field of digital ethics challenging to define and delimit clearly. It would seem that digital ethics addresses the entire realm of what can be called the digital transformation of society and cannot, therefore, be considered a subdomain of general normative ethics.

The specific contribution of civil society actors to moral discourse today is important not only because it attempts to amend the failings found in both private and public sector deployments of ICTs and to reassure the public as well as government that action is being taken but also because it attempts to construct a normative social unity and value consensus in a highly diverse and pluralistic world. This can be said of neither philosophical humanism nor social science critique, and certainly not of media scandalization, which all tend to draw sharp boundaries and establish clear moral positions. Civil society actors generally engage morality on a more practical level employing educational programs, public action initiatives, dissemination of research, public–private cooperation, demonstrative self-regulation, setting up ethics commissions, and proclaiming ethical guidelines. For this reason, within the domain of civil society contributions to digital ethics, there is practically no discussion of value pluralism or value conflict. On the contrary, a fundamental value consensus, usually expressed in terms of human rights and democratic ideals, is assumed as given and beyond question. All are called upon to unite in the struggle against the moral

---

145 For an overview and assessment of these many factors, see the work of Roland Benedikter (https://de.wikipedia.org/wiki/Roland_Benedikter).

failings of those who are irresponsibly imposing technological changes upon society, while at the same time all are called upon to commit themselves to the established values of Western modernity. This need not be motivated by a nostalgia for bygone days or even by irrational fears of technology, but also by respect for the often devastating effects of public mistrust in technological innovation. Commonly cited examples are the disaster of the NHS care. data program,[146] or the case of Google Glas,[147] or the Cambridge Analytica Scandal.[148] Media scandalization, as well as social science critique, has been taken up by some of the more aggressive civil society actors and has substantially contributed to the current climate of "techlash," that is, a widespread reaction of public mistrust of technological innovation that greatly enhances the risks of investment in new projects, products, and services by both governments and business.[149] In this situation, any consensus is better than none and what other way offers itself to achieve stability both socially and politically than to rally around traditional values and norms and attempt—at least vis-à-vis the public—to assure everyone that technological innovation will not radically upset the apple cart. The world will remain, at least concerning its moral foundations, substantially the same.

In the face of the undeniable threat of radical transformation that ICTs bring, it is difficult to deny that many so-called disruptive technologies do question the normative order of Western society and humanism. Civil society actors roughly fall into two classes depending upon how they react to this threat. While some clearly join hands with social science critique and media scandalization in denouncing and condemning new technologies, many civil society actors are concerned to minimize the damage caused by social science critique, media scandalization, as well as the negative inputs of their more pessimistic colleagues in order to ensure that the obvious benefits of technological innovation will be accepted by the public. The bad guys in this scenario are almost always self-serving corporations and naïve government organizations duped by them into supporting or implementing immoral technologies and practices and thus failing to protect the public, a role that the civil society actors assume for themselves. The so-designated bad guys can only react to these accusations by attempting to reassure the public that they are at least trying to do the right thing and that they are not as naïve or opportunistic as they might seem. Private enterprises demonstrate this by participating in many civil society activities, by setting up ethics commissions, by proclaiming ethics guidelines, and lately, by publicly apologizing for perceived misdeeds and openly acknowledging the need for regulation.[150]

---

146 https://en.wikipedia.org/wiki/Care.data.
147 https://en.wikipedia.org/wiki/Google_Glass.
148 https://en.wikipedia.org/wiki/Facebook%E2%80%93Cambridge_Analytica_data_scandal.
149 https://itif.org/publications/2019/10/28/policymakers-guide-techlash. The term "techlash," derived from "backlash," was runner-up in Oxford Dictionary's 2018 word of the year selection. Oxford defines the term as the "strong and widespread negative reaction to the growing power and influence that large technology companies hold."
150 See, for example, the many public apologies of Mark Zuckerberg and a recent statement by Google CEO Sundar Pichai in the *Financial Times* (https://www.ft.com/content/3467659a-386d-11ea-ac3c-f68c10993b04).

Governments do the same. That the public can and will be protected not only by government regulation but also by ethical standards is an assumption that almost all share. However, the extent to which government regulation must enforce moral norms is contested. The private sector prefers self-regulation and is concerned to demonstrate that businesses are socially and ethically responsible. In contrast, those who generally oppose innovation and are closer to government prefer the implementation of laws and sanctionable regulations. A good example of the push for regulation is offered by AI Now, whose recommendations in the Annual Report 2019 include appeals to government to ban the use of affect recognition and facial recognition technologies; require public disclosure of AI industry's climate impact; give workers rights to contest AI uses and developments; enact biometric privacy laws; regulate the integration of public and private surveillance infrastructures; conduct algorithmic impact assessments with regard to climate, health, and geographical displacement; and require informed consent for use of personal data.[151] Despite a pervasive consensus on values, civil society moral discourse is divided into two camps. One camp sees government regulation as the solution, and the other appeals to self-regulation. Both camps, however, have pitched their tents on the field of modern Western society, its assumptions and values, and no vision of a different future is on the horizon.

The above remarks may seem too critical and even depreciative of the great efforts as well as the major investments made in this area. Let us be clear; we do not in any way disparage the work that many civil society actors do for achieving a more just society. We agree wholeheartedly with much of this work and applaud without reservation the motives and goals behind these efforts. What we place in question is whether attempts to maintain the norms and values of Western modernity are adequate responses to the digital transformation and the emergence of a global network society. That this question is legitimate can be illustrated by a recent programmatic statement arising from within the European Union's digital single market initiative. *The Onlife Manifesto. Being Human in a Hyperconnected Era* (hereafter simply *Manifesto*) can be seen as a typical expression of the moral discourse coming from civil society actors. The *Manifesto* is not only typical but also represents one of the most differentiated, thought-provoking, and instructive statements coming from this area of moral discourse. We, therefore, propose examining it more closely to characterize as well as illustrate the important contribution of civil society actors to digital ethics.

Surprisingly, we find that in the *Manifesto* modernity is not taken as an unshakeable foundation for ethical and social reflection but is questioned in almost all aspects. According to the *Manifesto*, which is intended to encourage debate in political circles on designing appropriate policy for the challenges of the global network society, modernity is questioned in several ways. Under the title "Game Over for Modernity?" the authors declare that "it is our view that the constraints and affordances of the computational era profoundly challenge some of modernity's assumptions" (Floridi et al. 2015, 3). Among

---

151 https://ainowinstitute.org/AI_Now_2019_Report.pdf.

the typically modern assumptions that must be questioned is the "alleged divide between technological artifacts and nature," which in the face of the realities of the digital transformation has become "illusory" and even "counterproductive" (4). Furthermore, the assumption that "ethics was a matter of rational and disembodied autonomous subjects, rather than a matter of social beings" must be challenged by "notions of distributed responsibility" (4). Third, whereas modernity privileged "hierarchical patterns [...] for social order," ICTs open up new "possibilities for direct democracy" and "call for rethinking the worldviews and metaphors underlying modern political structures" (4).

Despite the reservations that the authors of the *Manifesto* express regarding usually unquestioned modern assumptions and despite the uncertainties that the digital transformation creates for decision-makers and political leaders, the *Manifesto* admonishes that this situation must not "postpone difficult decisions." Instead of embarking upon an in-depth investigation into the potential effects of the digital transformation upon traditional assumptions and practices, in a rather startling turnaround the authors of the *Manifesto*, far from encouraging leaders to embark upon new forms of envisioning and enabling political as well as regulatory scenarios, rehearse the old fears and prejudices of industrial society. In this vein, the *Manifesto* repeats the standard claims that it is important for leaders to recognize that "experiencing freedom, equality and otherness in public spheres becomes problematic in a context of increasingly mediated identities and calculated interactions such as profiling, targeted advertising, or price discrimination" and that "public spheres are further undermined by increasing social control through mutual or lateral surveillance (*sousveillance*), which is not necessarily better than 'Big brother' surveillance" (5). As if the authors had suddenly forgotten what they found questionable and problematic with modernity, they do not even raise the issue of why public spheres are not instead enabled, empowered, educated, engaged, and otherwise optimized by ICTs. Furthermore, new forms of governance and regulation that replace ineffective top-down regulation are not even presented as a possibility to be systematically developed and implemented. The impression is unavoidable that despite lip service paid to the no longer ignorable critique of Western modernity, the authors can understand the unleashing of connected and open communication throughout society only as a horror scenario running in every way against traditional social theory and modern concepts of order. Nonetheless, but also in the form of rehearsing a well-known modern refrain, the authors of the *Manifesto* find themselves obliged to admonish that "the repartition of power and responsibility among public authorities, corporate agents, and citizens should be balanced more fairly" (5). How this can be done under the modern constitution is a question the *Manifesto* does not raise.

Finally, the *Manifesto* turns to the question of human self-understanding in the digital age and pleads for "dualities" instead of "dichotomies." According to the *Manifesto*, modernity understands the self in contradictory and opposing ways:

> On the one hand, in the political realm, the self is deemed to be free, and "free" is frequently understood as being autonomous, disembodied, rational, well-informed and disconnected: an individual and atomistic self. On the other hand, in scientific terms, the self is an object of enquiry among others and, in this respect, is deemed to be fully analysable and predictable.

By focusing on causes, incentives, or disincentives in an instrumental perspective, this form of knowledge often aims at influencing and controlling behaviours, on individual and collective levels. Hence, there is a constant oscillation between a political representation of the self, as rational, disembodied, autonomous and disconnected, on the one hand, and a scientific representation of the self, as heteronomous, and resulting from multifactorial contexts fully explainable by the range of scientific disciplines (social, natural and technological), on the other hand.

Although this description of modern self-understanding falls completely within what we have discussed above in terms of Latour's "modern constitution," it should be noted that the social sciences are here subsumed under the natural sciences such that the social, or relational, nature of the self falls out of political discourse and is relegated alone to science. Accordingly, the solution offered by the authors of the *Manifesto*, namely, that pollical discourse accepts the relational nature of the self, comes much short of where current social theory, as well as political initiatives, already stands. As we saw in the discussion of Luhmann and Latour above, social theory no longer starts from the problem of the one and the many, the individual and society, freedom and determination, and offers different solutions. When the authors of the *Manifesto* declare that political discourse must acknowledge that the self is both free and relational, they ignore the theoretical advances of sociology. They answer no question, solve no problem, and do not advance social or political theory one inch. Instead, they have simply restated the old dilemma of individuals and society. The modern constitution allows only three options: either the self is an autonomous rational subject; or the self is a heteronomously conditioned being determined by social, economic, psychological, or even genetic factors; or a third possibility, one must accept both and plead for a *both/and* solution. The human being is somehow at once both individual and social, both autonomous and externally conditioned, both free and subject to many determining and conditioning fluences. In short, society is both structure and agency. This is the theoretical framework that the authors of the *Manifesto* accept.

There is no question that modern social theory accepts the relational nature of the self, and only the most stubborn and uninformed liberalism or the most pessimistic determinism really believes in isolated individuals who somehow exist in Hobbes's state of nature or are mere pawns of social, economic, psychological, or genetic forces. Nonetheless, from the ethical and moral point of view of the *Manifesto*, human rights, privacy, and so on are entirely based on the autonomous rational subject. Whatever relations or conditions impact the individual subject, they must be measured, evaluated, and morally praised or blamed with regard to individualistically formulated human rights. From this point of view, the recommendation of the *Manifesto* that political discourse begins from a relational notion of the self does not represent an improvement or advancement over traditional ethical positions. Instead, the *Manifesto* merely reaffirms commitment to the mythology of humanism and the modern constitution.

Within this context, the *Manifesto* goes on to proclaim that the prospects of artificial intelligence based on big data and flows of information demand that "issues such as ownership, responsibility, privacy, and self-determination" be addressed by "new forms of thinking and doing at multiple levels" (5). Above all, this means we have to "rethink the notion of responsibility" within the context of "distributed socio-technical systems" (6). What this exactly means, however, is not spelled out in the *Manifesto*. Concerning questions of privacy, it should come as no surprise that the authors of the *Manifesto* declare that "we consider this distinction between private and public to be more relevant than ever" (6). While admitting that current views of privacy and the public sphere are problematic, the authors reaffirm that "we believe that everybody needs *both* shelter from the public gaze *and* exposure" (6; author's emphasis). This *both/and* solution should lead to an "empowering opacity of the self" in public and social interactions such that "the need for self-expression, the performance of identity, the chance to reinvent oneself, as well as the generosity of deliberate forgetfulness" (6) against all social or relational claims are guaranteed. As we already know from our discussion of Floridi's ontological theory of privacy, this means that the informational self must be surrounded by ontological friction such that certain information does not flow beyond its supposed borders. Behind all the proclamations of both/and notions of the self, there lies the ontological theory of privacy, which anchors the autonomous rational subject as principle addressee of both moral and political discourse. Once again, despite promising beginnings, we end up where we started, solidly within the myth of humanism and the modern constitution.

At this point, it may be helpful to take a step back and attempt to assess the contribution of the *Manifesto*, as well as of civil society actors in general, by describing the relation between morality and government regulation or law. Since it is the explicit or implicit intention of civil society players to influence government in the name of their perceived publics, the connection between morality and law is of great importance for understanding their contribution to moral discourse. The both/and strategy of the *Manifesto*, which we take as representative of most civil society actors, is not a new strategy. Modern ethics has always played a double game. This can be seen when the relation between morality on the one side and law or government regulation on the other is explicitly thematized. The relation of ethics to the law is usually understood as the opposition of natural law and positive law.[152]

In the theory of law, the division of powers typical of the modern constitution expresses itself by locating moral norms above the law. This is the natural law position. The ethical and moral norms of natural law are a guiding beacon, a foundation upon which law must be erected if it is to stand on sure moral ground. Furthermore, it is assumed that "the public" acknowledges and accepts the norms and values of natural law and therefore expects that their political representatives institute these norms and values in government regulations. This view has several problems. As we saw in our discussion of Luhmann's theory of morality, it is only where the law does not clearly regulate behavior that morality comes into play. Morality and law are two very different things. Morality appeals to the individual conscience. Moral norms are absolute truths

---

152 For an overview of the debate between natural law and positive law, see Murphy (2007) and Tebbit (2017).

that cannot be corrected by experience. Morality, therefore, is guided by the learning strategy of refusing to learn. No matter how much success one may experience by exploiting market distortions, stealing is morally wrong. Positive laws, on the contrary, are changed by experience. They are political realities based on the authority and sanctioning power of the state. Laws are social and historical constructions and not eternal, universal truths. The natural law theory attempts to base law on absolute, timeless, and universal norms derived from human nature. These norms are beyond the relativities of history and society. Positive law, on the contrary, is the law that is made by peoples and sovereigns. It is pragmatic and subject to change under the pressures of experience. For positive law, what works is more important than what is morally right or wrong according to inherently subjective and partisan moral positions. Positive law shields society against the dictatorship of moralism.

The modern constitution both distinguishes and unites the realms of law and morality, leaving a mysterious gap between values and laws, between moral responsibility and legal regulations. According to doctrines of positive law, the law is not given by any higher authority than the will of the legislating actors. According to natural law theory, the law must be grounded in fundamental moral norms beyond the relativities and vicissitudes of history. The official morality of modernity plays both sides of the fence. It plays one side when laws demand to be legitimated by what is right and good and not be expedience or mere pragmatic exigencies. It plays the other side by declaring upon the occasion that no higher authority could legitimately challenge the sovereignty of the people. On the one hand, rights and duties are indubitable and inalienable, whereas, on the other hand, laws are a reflection of historical and cultural situations. When society changes, laws change. Privacy, for example, is not and cannot be a fundamental right rooted in universal human nature. It is a historical and social convention depending on context and many other factors.[153] From the point of view of the modern constitution, on the one hand, pretenses to absolute truth can be criticized by reference to historical relativity. On the other hand, political pragmatism can be criticized with reference to absolute truths.

As we have argued above, the typical reaction of modernity to the perceived threat of the digital transformation is to attempt to reassert humanist values. Following the modern constitution, it tries to do this with both hands. One hand appeals to inalienable human rights, while the other hand appeals to legal regulation in the name of preserving modern democratic institutions as well as the sovereignty of the people. What comes out of this game is the both/and solutions we have seen in the examples discussed above. In the meantime, and unbeknown to these critical traditions, there was—and still continues to be—the invisible work of proliferating hybrids guided by the *unofficial morality of networking*. Thus, there arises a gap between what could be said about the law within the modern constitution and how human and nonhuman affairs are actually being regulated. The contribution of civil society actors to the discourse of digital ethics remains

---

[153] See, for example, the idea of contextual privacy proposed by Nissenbaum (2004) as well as American privacy law in general as opposed to European concepts of privacy as a fundamental human right.

entirely on one side of this gap. Lobbying efforts exhaust themselves in appealing to politicians to implement either inalienable human rights or pragmatic economic and social development in regulations and policies. Or better yet, somehow both the one and the other and all at the same time.

The global network society, based as it is on the unofficial or at least nonmodern morality guiding the deployment of hybrids, fills this gap with its unique form of regulation. This we propose calling *governance* instead of government. Governance is offered here not only as a term replacing government but also as a term replacing ethics and morality. Both ethics and government arose within the modern constitution and are defined in what they are as well as in how they are permitted to relate to each other by the modern constitution. If we have never been modern, we are not bound by these definitions and relations. We, therefore, feel free to propose *network governance* as the answer to the question of how the substance of modern values can be brought over into the digital age. The question of digital ethics thus becomes the question of network governance. Network governance is neither traditional ethics nor traditional governmental regulation. It is the form of regulation in which network norms influence practice in all areas and on all levels. The practice they guide, which is what ethical agency is, we will term *design*. If there is to be a digital ethics worthy of the name, it may be said to *consist of network norms as they enact network governance in practices of design*. Instead of telling actors what they should do, ethics and morality, after the "hack," which we are attempting in this book, will follow the actors and describe what they are doing and not what they ought to be doing. Digital ethics in its current form is a discourse crisscrossing many areas of society. The philosophical mythology of humanism, social science critique, media scandalization, and civil society lobbying form a complex legacy system of interdependencies, relations, and mutual reinforcements that together characterize what can be called the discourse of digital ethics. It is a daunting task indeed to attempt to redesign ethics on a new foundation or at least, in the spirit of an ethical hack, to change some parts of the code, the protocols, and the processes such that ethics might become relevant for guiding action in the global network society.

Chapter Three

THE REDESIGN

3.1 Network Norms

Luhmann based society on the mutual recognition of persons as equally capable of communication. Only then could the other be seen as alter ego. Without this recognition, why should anyone listen to what anyone else has to say? Once society emerged as a system of people listening to what other people say, that is, as a system of communications; the consequence was that not only human individuals but also things, artifacts, technologies, and indeed everything that was not communicating were banned from the social system into the environment. Nonetheless, as it turns out, all these banned entities returned through the back door of information. Communication needs information. As we learned from actor-network theory (ANT), information is constructed by humans and nonhumans symmetrically. The social system is not based upon exclusion, but inclusion of everything in the world. Indeed, society is not a closed system, but an open network. What is, is information. This is basically a posthumanist worldview. Society does not consist of human beings, but of communications, and communications are themselves based upon the translating and enrolling activities of both humans and nonhumans. Whatever human individuals might be, this is constructed by society and is situationally and historically relative. There is no such thing as human nature, given and eternal, and even if there were, historical societies would continuously interpret it differently.

Since the world consists of actor-networks, society, as well as nature and everything else within the world, is information in action, that is, information in the process of networking, associating, binding things together into collectives. Instead of systems, we have networks. Instead of communications, we have networking. Instead of closed systems, which are constituted by radical exclusion, we have open and flexible networks of both humans and nonhumans, all of whom are made up of information. This is where we stand at the beginning of the twenty-first century. What does this mean for ethics and, specifically, for digital ethics?

Equipped with this question, we hacked into the current discourse of digital ethics. Floridi, as we saw in the discussion of the philosophy of information, attempted to answer this question by declaring everyone and everything to be information, and nothing else. In the end, however, some information turned out to be more equal than other information. Some information was fundamentally private and asserted to constitute the unique, free—and thus morally responsible—individual. This is the reassertion of the autonomous rational subject as the locus of morality. It is an attempt to revive the myth of humanism in a posthuman world. Of course, these informational human beings are now called upon to respect all other beings, since all beings are made of the same substance, that is, information. Nonetheless, even an extended concept of agency does not dethrone the humanist ideal, whose individuality, freedom, autonomy, dignity, and above all, privacy, according to Floridi, must be maintained at all cost. Present-day moral discourse has become, as Luhmann pointed out, moralizing, moral indignation toward any perceived threats to the humanist myth, and the attempt to reassert the autonomous rational subject as the basis of ethics and society. What else can Floridi's ontological theory of privacy mean? Of course, what is at stake in digital ethics is not merely humanism; it is the entire modern constitution and the hierarchical structure of industrial society.

Digital ethics, in its present form, can be understood as the immune reaction of modern industrial society to the disease of digital technologies and the radical transformation of social order they initiate. Digital ethics today is moralizing in the sense of attempting to maintain the conditions of social acceptance, praise and blame, that characterize modern Western society. Moralizing, however, is not confined to the ethereal spheres of academic philosophy but has been deployed throughout society in various ways. The mythical hero of modernity, the autonomous rational subject, plays a vital role in a much higher drama, that of the struggle for freedom and justice against powerful economic and political elites. This struggle is carried on within limits imposed by the "modern constitution." The modern constitution distinguishes subject from object, individual from society, and society from nature and defines the terms of engagement as critique. Critique defends the subject against the object, the individual against society, society against nature—and vice versa for all the previously mentioned dualities—without providing any middle ground upon which networking, the proliferation of hybrids, as Latour calls informational beings, can be seen for what it is and accounted for within the modern worldview. Instead, critique is aided in its efforts to debunk ideology, expose abuse of power, and defend the individual by a mass media system that is driven by an inner necessity to generate and capture attention. The media turn to the production of moral outrage via scandalization. Media scandalization sets the "norm work" of society in motion and keeps it moving even when "the public" has long dissolved into a plurality of echo chambers and filter bubbles. In the gap created by the dissolution of "the" public, an increasing number of civil society watchdogs and advocates have stepped in pursuing aggressive lobbying aimed at reasserting the threatened values of Western industrial society in the name of their imagined publics. This is the rather sad state of moral discourse at the beginning of the twenty-first century. This is what digital ethics in its current form consists of. This is the legacy system upon which the discourse of digital ethics runs. This is the system that our ethical hacker has breached and must now attempt to redesign in subtle ways so that a truly digital ethics may appear for the first time.

It is important to emphasize that this analysis is not critique. It is a hack. Hacking is not interested in moralizing or denouncing. It is not interested in scandalizing anyone or anything. And it is not interested in lobbying or adding to the already long list of government regulations. We are not carrying on the modern tradition of critique in still another convolution of methodological skepticism. Instead, we follow Latour in proposing that we simply drop modern moralizing and ask what values are apparent in digital technologies. The question goes beyond asking what human beings are or may need to "flourish." It asks: What is the network in which humans and nonhumans build a world of meaning?

If there is to be a truly digital ethics, that is, an ethics for the digital age, then it must be founded neither on the basis of the autonomous rational subject nor on the basis of functionally differentiated social subsystems, but in a heretofore hidden area where mediation is happening, where networking is building the world of meaning. Neither the subject nor the object, neither the "is" nor the "ought," neither the individual nor society will help us, since these realms and beings owe their existence to the distinctions of the modern constitution that is no longer valid and no longer binding, even if the current legacy system of moral discourse, which we have examined at length above, cannot imagine anything else.

Latour never tires of saying that there is only one way to enter into this new realm and discover the unofficial morality that has always held sway there. "Follow the actors" has been written on the banner of science studies and ANT ever since its beginnings. What do we find when we follow the actors? The first thing we notice is that no matter whether we imagine a prehuman wielder of a stone ax, or Heidegger's carpenter, or describe what scientists in their laboratories everywhere in the world do, we are dealing with a network of humans and nonhumans "cooperating" by mutually translating and enrolling each other into networks. The contribution of things is difficult to describe after centuries of assuming that they actually didn't "do" anything but are passive objects under the determinate causality of natural laws. One of the most helpful attempts to describe what things do, that is, how they can be conceived of as possessing agency of some kind, has come from Gibson with the notion of affordances. Although Latour does not use this term, it expresses, in our opinion, very well how the agency of nonhumans in constructing actor-networks can be described. We have cited this passage before and will do it again here because it is helpful for attempting to discover the "unofficial" morality that has been guiding our collective decisions even when made invisible by the modern constitution. Gibson (1979, 129) writes:

> An affordance is neither an objective property nor a subjective property; or it is both if you like. An affordance cuts across the dichotomy of subjective objective and helps us to understand its inadequacy. It is equally a fact of the environment and a fact of behavior. It is both physical and psychical, yet neither. An affordance points both ways, to the environment and to the observer.

Recalling our example of the prehuman hunter with the stone ax, it could be said that the stone had specific affordances that suggested, urged, nudged, coaxed the hominin to behave in a certain way as both fashioning it and using it. The stone participated in constructing an actor-network that became the hunter or warrior wielding a stone ax. This is not technological determinism. Here nothing is "determined." Everything is mutual cooperation, negotiation, trial and error, learning, adjusting, compromising. Out of these processes, which can be subsumed under the terms of "translating" and "enrolling," there arises, or "emerges," an actor-network in which everything has been transformed. A mere hominin has become a "hunter" or a "warrior," and a mere stone has become an "ax." Neither of these beings existed before the work of translating and enrolling. After the work, they cannot go back to being what they were before, because something is holding on to them, even when they are not holding on to each other. This, we propose calling "meaning" or "information." Meaning or information is not to be equated with language, signs, syntactically formed data, or any kind of semiotic coding. Meaning and information emerged at least three million years before *Homo sapiens* arrived on the scene with their big brains, linguistic capabilities, and uniquely human subjectivity. Because there were meaning and information, big brains and language arose, not the other way around. What does this story, in case it is at all plausible, tell us about morality? When something holds on to us, this is a rule. If we suppose that after the actor-network arose, not everything was possible, then meaning is like a rule. It holds on to a particular constellation of actors such that they can do certain things, but not others. After the stone ax came into being, not just anything was possible. Other rules were added later on. For example, stone axes became ritual objects or status symbols, or many hundreds of thousands of years later, they became Heidegger's hammer or precursors of modern weapons or industrial sawmills. Whatever they became, and whatever other things participated in whatever other actor-networks, the rules that they embodied were not determinate natural laws, but normative rules governing not only who the actors were but also what they were supposed to do. In actor-networks, the "is" is the "ought."

The "unofficial" morality that guides our activities, and which could not be acknowledged, or even conceived of under the modern constitution, is derived from the things that modernity banned from society. It is a morality that takes into account the affordances of things. It is a morality that knows nothing of autonomous subjectivity, free will, individuality, or even progress. This morality consists of the rules emerging from the actor-networks that form themselves at the front of the construction of meaning. These rules are not anchored in the nature of things. They are neither eternal nor based on self-evident conceptions of the "good," nor even formulated as imperatives. Nonetheless, they are what any ethics or morality of the digital age consists of. Let us call them "network norms."[1] *Network norms are derived from the affordances of digital technologies.* If we admit that machines, technologies, and artifacts of all kinds are so influential in today's world that any attempt to ignore them is doomed to failure, we must also admit that these artifacts have become social partners in our world and, therefore, together with humans condition what this world is. Human existence, already 3 million years ago, but more obviously today, is through and through entangled with technology. Instead of speaking of society on the one side and technologies or things on the other side, as the modern constitution prescribes, let us speak of "socio-technical networks." Socio-technical networks are hybrid and heterogeneous actor-networks made up of both humans and nonhumans mutually conditioning and mutually creating each other. The world that humans and nonhumans create is the world of meaning, but what is actually doing the work of translating and enrolling actors into meaningful networks is information. Just as Luhmann described society as a system of meaning, in which communication

---

1   For a discussion of network norms in the context of a theory of the digital transformation of a global network society, see Krieger and Belliger (2014) and Belliger and Krieger (2016, 2018a).

autocatalytically and autopoietically generates itself, from the point of view of ANT, information creates information.

As Floridi pointed out, our world is dominated by what can be called information and communication technologies (ICTs). He goes so far, and we applaud him for this, as to speak of a "digital revolution." Of course, others have also proclaimed the advent of the digital age or have spoken of a global network society (Castells) that is emerging on the basis of ICTs. Floridi is significant because he takes the digital transformation as an opportunity to propose a radical reformulation ethics and morality. As we have shown at length in Chapter 2, Floridi's philosophy and ethics of information fall short of their ambitious goals and end by reformulating the myth of humanism. Even if we find his solutions problematic, we must acknowledge the questions he raises. Instead of attempting, as does Floridi, to reassert the challenged values of humanism on the terrain of information, let us ask what the challenge actually consists of. If we are not to understand digital technologies primarily as a threat to the autonomous rational subject, that is, as a threat to privacy, freedom, autonomy, and human dignity, but instead, as a new form of human existence, what does this mean? Who are we if we are not autonomous rational subjects and if modernity is indeed passing or even something we have never really been? What does the digital transformation tell us about ourselves and the world, once we acknowledge that it truly is revolutionary and has changed the conditions of ethical discourse? In short, what happens to digital ethics if we take the digital transformation seriously?

3.1.1 Connectivity

The affordances of ICTs tell us that being is being connected. *Connectivity* is perhaps the most important network norm. The very idea of networks is based on connectivity. Translation and enrollment of actors into actor-networks is done by digital technologies in terms of connectivity. This is what is different today than back at the time when the hominins were experimenting with stone axes or when Heidegger's carpenter was working at his bench. Today tools are equipped with sensors that register and generate data on how, where, and with what other devices they are being used. Every movement and every effect they produce is not only transformed into data, but this data is distributed throughout various networks, aggregated with data from other devices and users, and analyzed in multiple ways. This is not merely the Internet of Things; it is the Internet of Everything and Everyone. Connectivity is the foundation for what can be called "datafication," that is, the program of transforming everything and every event in the world into data, which is then analyzed in various ways to create a "data-driven society." The program of datafication relies on four forms of analytics. First, *descriptive analytics* uses aggregated data to construct a digital description of reality. Second, *predictive analytics* uses data to predict what will happen. Third, *preventive analytics* can use the predictions to intervene in reality so that undesirable outcomes do not occur. And finally, *prescriptive analytics* can automate interventions so that specific results occur without human decision and intervention. An example would be a self-driving automobile that not only prevents accidents from happening but prescribes how the car behaves without human intervention. This is datafication. Datafication is based on connectivity.

Connectivity is a network norm. There exists an almost irresistible normative value in connecting things; connecting people; connecting organizations and institutions; connecting producers with suppliers, with consumers, and even with competitors; and connecting government with citizens and governments with each other. There is practically nothing going on today that is not in some way or another based upon or influenced by connectivity. If we ask what the "unofficial" morality guiding decisions in the world of hybrids and networks look like, then it is a morality based on the norm of connectivity. There is no realistic "opt-out." There is no real possibility to "drop out" as the slogan once put it. There are more smartphones in the world today than people. Where can you go and what can you do if you don't want to be connected? This network norm alone makes it clear that privacy is a lost cause, and the humanist individual is no longer the dominant species populating the earth. Connectivity is not just nice to have; it is a norm; it influences how actors of all kinds are translated and enrolled into networks in the digital age. Connectivity is a normative force driving the digital transformation. It is almost impossible, or at least difficult, to circumvent or deny it. Connectivity can, therefore, be considered a "new value" as opposed to the "old values" of individuality, autonomy, and self-determination. For this reason, we propose connectivity be considered a "network norm," that is, one of the normative foundations of the global network society. A digital ethics that is appropriate for the digital age is an ethics based on the value and norm of connectivity and not on a supposed human nature and rights derived from it.[2] But what does this mean for human rights? What rights do connected beings have?

3.1.2 Flow

To be connected means that there are unforeseeable, uncontrolled, and ubiquitous flows of information, not only of data and information but also of people, of goods, of money, indeed, of everything. Connectivity implies the second network norm, *flow*. Everything flows in a connected world. Because of the nature of connectivity, flows can to some extent be regulated but not completely controlled by any central authority, any government, any CEO or CIO, or anyone at all. The network is global and ungoverned, at least if one also considers the "darknet," migration, global capital, hacking, and so on. Once reality has become connected, everything flows. Flow is not a consequence of networks that should be seen as problematic or even as a critical weakness of network infrastructure. Flow is much rather a normative value in networks. Networks are built with affordances that encourage, enable, promote, and permit flow. Floridi's attempt to

---

2   It is no accident that critique (see, for example, van Dijck and Zuboff, discussed in Chapter 2) has picked out connectivity as a prominent target. That connectivity does not equal collectivity (van Dijck) supposes not only that "collectivity" is normative and inherently of value but that values of community can only be realized in the forms that were possible in Western industrial society. Both of these assumptions, which van Dijck as well as Zuboff make, are actually uncritical.

guarantee privacy by introducing blockages, silos, walls, or what he calls "ontological friction" into the infosphere not only implicitly admits that such friction is not an essential part of networks, and must therefore with great effort somehow be built into them, but amounts to a futile attempt to break up connectivity and block flows. Ontological friction is not what the network wants. It is not what ICTs are telling us about who we are and what the world is. Floridi's plea for ontological friction and blocking information flows is an attempt to hold on to a world that is quickly vanishing, that recedes with each connected device, connected human, and connected organization. Defining human beings as inforgs, as Floridi does, turns out to be a radical move that undermines every notion of privacy and humanist individuality. Inforgs are those beings who are essentially defined by connectivity and flow. Connectivity and flow are holding on to us today in the same way the stone ax held on to the prehuman who found himself transformed into a hunter or a warrior. Even if the prehuman wanted to let go of the stone ax and return to being an ape, he couldn't. We do not control information. Information "controls" us. Indeed, it is what we are. Perhaps if anyone had asked the hominin if they want to become a hunter or a warrior, they would have followed Zuboff and said no. Technological innovation is risky. Today we are being transformed into inforgs whether we like it or not. No one is asking for our permission. Informed consent is simply not an option. If we are to understand what this means and begin to ask what the ethical implications of the digital transformation are, then we must drop the modern constitution and the myth of humanism and start listening to what things are telling us about ourselves. What the affordances of digital socio-technical networks are telling us is that we value connectivity and flows of information.[3] These are the new norms of genuinely digital ethics. They have nothing to do with humanism. They do not need privacy or individuals bent on self-determination at all costs. They represent a different form of order than Western industrial society with regard to knowledge, cooperative action, and human self-understanding.

This does not mean, as critical social science and media scandalization claim, that we no longer have any human rights, and we must abandon all the values we have held so dear and fought so hard to implement over hundreds of years. On the contrary, everyone and everything has rights. But these are not the old rights that we had in Western industrial society. Those who are attempting to "reassert" endangered European values are attempting to turn back history and deny socio-technological change. Current forms of digital ethics, as we have argued above, are not digital ethics at all, but the ethics of Western industrial society reformulated and repurposed as a bulwark against the digital transformation. The advent of a global network society brings a new order of knowledge, new forms of organization, a new self-understanding of human existence, and new

---

3 It is revealing that when Floridi does address the socio-technical ensemble of ICTs, for example, in the discussion of "distributed morality" (2013, 261) he simply assumes that ICT infrastructures contain values such as privacy. The "morality" of such "infraethics" is not derived from the ICTs, but from humanism. We will discuss distributed morality in detail later.

values. Among these new values are connectivity and flow. These two are, of course, not the only network norms.

3.1.3 Communication

Connectivity and flow make *communication* into a network norm. Of course, the right to free speech has long been recognized, if not everywhere implemented. The so-called free world is based on free speech. Perhaps Luhmann was right when he said that society consists of communications and not of human beings. We could support this assertion if everything and everybody were *allowed* to speak. If there is a moral imperative at the heart of Luhmann's conception of society as a system of communications, then it is that all have the right to speak and be heard. Indeed, this is what "respect" (*Achtung*) means as the moral basis of social inclusion. Communication as a network norm means that everyone and everything must be acknowledged as a potential actor, partner, mediator, cooperator, and co-constructor of networks. Luhmann is not the only one to found social being in communication. Habermas (1984, 1987) also based society on communicative action, but in a way typical for the modern constitution, he reserved the status of communicator to autonomous rational subjects alone and excluded the hybrids as well as the networks in which they exist. The modern constitution does not permit communication to be seen as what it is. When the stone, the hand, the wood, and certain animals translated and enrolled each other into an actor-network, which was the hunter or the builder, they were all communicating. Technical mediation is distributed and symmetrical agency. If it is networking that constitutes society and, indeed, the world, then the notion of "communicative action" must be extended to all things that construct actor-networks. Translating and enrolling must be conceived of as communicative action. What the stone contributed to the hunter wielding a stone ax was also communicative action. Communication is a network norm because it is irresponsible today to unnecessarily exclude anything from being able to have a voice, that is, to contribute in its own way to the construction of network order. Here is where Floridi's ethics of responsibility could be salvaged from the sinking ship of modern Western humanism and transferred to the global network society.

3.1.4 Participation

The discussion of the meaning and value of communication as a network norm brings us to the next network norm, *participation*. If communicative action is not limited to argumentative discourse among rational subjects, as Habermas supposed, but is extended to include every affordance and every effort to translate and enroll actors into networks, exclusion becomes problematic. Inclusion means participation. Participation is not only a right; it is a duty of all beings. Another word for participation, which has become a slogan of direct democracy, is empowerment. Participation is the value of empowerment. As Latour put it in his principle of "irreduction," no being is reducible to another or can reduce others to itself. Reduction is always in some way disempowerment in the sense that certain abilities of mediation are limited, circumscribed, channeled, and restricted. Mediators become intermediaries. Intermediaries are those actors that have become subordinated to functions. This is not evil; it is inevitable, since, as Luhmann has shown, networking can and does lead to the establishment of functional systems. Systems are nothing other than black boxes built on subordination and reduction among intermediaries such that a relatively fixed input/output operation comes into being. Systems arise almost naturally out of networks, the greater the networks become, and the more that depends on certain fixed operations. Systems constrain and channel the unbounded tendency of networks to generate complexity and change. Systems are indeed very useful. Even if systems are needed to reduce complexity, society would sink into an oppressive conformism without the normative force of participation.

A relational ontology is an ontology of participation. One cannot drop out, withdraw into secrecy, hide behind routine and conformism, and refuse to join in and participate in networks. One cannot completely relinquish one's right and duty to mediate. The principle of irreduction excludes nonparticipation. The network is the actor. Without the network, no one and nothing can do anything. There is no completely "autonomous" action. Under the old regime of humanism, individuals are autonomous. They can choose not to participate. They can drop out, walk away, hide behind walls of "ontological friction," withdraw into secrecy and privacy, and somehow—without the rest of us and the world around them—discover who they are. This is only possible if being is substance and not relation. The mythical image of the lone hero has many forms from ascetic monks to cowboys, existential loners, and unreachable superheroes. But it is just a myth, a myth that today is no longer morally legitimated by humanist individualism or existentialism. The affordances of socio-technical networks of all kinds make it not only impossible but also morally suspect to withdraw into secrecy and refuse to participate. There is no empowerment without participation. Participation means doing one's part in constructing information, effectively claiming the right to have a voice, making a difference that makes a difference. The network urges, enables, encourages, and even demands participation. This is why participation is a network norm. Participation, perhaps more than any of the other network norms, questions the legitimacy of individualism and undermines heroic humanism and absolutist claims to privacy as a fundamental and inalienable right.

3.1.5 Transparency

Connectivity, flow, communication, and participation all lead to the next network norm, *transparency*. Transparency is, in many respects, the opposite of privacy. Where privacy demands ontological friction in the infosphere, transparency demands that silos be dismantled, walls be torn down, distances be overcome, and data be aggregated, pooled, and made accessible to all. Transparency demands that it be made known where information comes from, what purpose it is intended to serve, and whether it is reliable, complete, and trustworthy. It is typical of current privacy discourse that reputable authorities openly propose a strategy of "obfuscation" (Brunton and Nissenbaum 2015), of intentionally creating and distributing false information, and willful corruption of information to preserve privacy. This strategy not only harms the individuals involved, who no longer receive the benefits of personalized products and services in areas such as healthcare and education, but also harms society that relies on trust and open communication to implement many public services. It is often noted that networks are based on trust, and that trust is based on transparency. If I don't know who is knocking at the door, I am hesitant to open it and let them in. If I don't know who is asking for a service or in need of assistance, I must first spend time and effort to find all this information out before I can do anything. Where it might be advantageous to hide your identity in situations characterized by totalitarian regimes, lack of the rule of law, and deep social conflicts, it has never been a solution to these problems not to come forward and fight for justice. If Martin Luther King and his followers had heeded the advice of privacy advocates, they would have stayed silently at the back of the bus and never come out into the open to demand their rights. There can be no effective democratic processes based on secrecy. There can be no social justice or equality based on obfuscation and willful corruption of information. Democracy lives from public presence, public discussion, and public action. Democracy is much more endangered by the irresponsible recommendations of privacy advocates than by openly acknowledging who one is and publicly claiming the rights that society supposedly guarantees. If there is a place for critique in today's world, then it would be in demanding that conditions favorable to participation be everywhere established and protected.

3.1.6 *Authenticity*

Transparency is closely related to the next network norm, *authenticity*. Authenticity is a network norm because it makes no sense to communicate, participate, and be transparent if one does not say who one is. The network erases the distinction between public and private. Social presentation of the self has long adjusted to the modern distinction between the social realm of role-playing and the private realm of internal subjectivity, the actor, so to speak, without a mask. This is the individual opposed to society, the individual outside of society before signing the social contract. Goffman famously divided the dramaturgical space of social interaction into a public "stage" upon which actors play their various social roles in the presence of others and wear the appropriate masks for these roles and a "backstage" area where actors are alone and exchange masks and rehearse their performances before entering the domain of public scrutiny. Embarrassment is the effect of being unable in certain circumstances to maintain this distinction between public and private, where audiences mistakenly see how actors fall out of roles, test behaviors, and change roles.[4] One consequence of today's digital world that consists of socio-technical networks is that the distinction between public and private disappears. Social media make public the details of persons' private lives and foster what has been called an "exhibitionist" culture of self-disclosure without embarrassment at the fact that one plays many roles and has many identities.[5] Popular TV formats such as Big

---

4   For a discussion of Goffman's dramaturgical theory of the social, see Belliger and Krieger (2016).
5   See, for example, Munar (2010).

Brother or Reality-TV are specialized in disclosing the backstage of social interaction. Public pressure to conform to role expectations has yielded to expectations of disclosure, "coming out" in all forms, and the celebration of difference and diversity.

The consequence has been to devaluate traditional efforts to maintain public appearances. Role-confirming behavior is no longer expected and praised, whereas behavior that disputes, denies, and contradicts role expectations is now considered a sign of honesty, integrity, and authenticity. Role-confirming behavior is often seen as inauthentic. Public figures who were once pressured to conform to role expectations are now seen as "liars" when they perform in public in ways that were traditionally expected of them, whereas blatantly lying in public, spreading misinformation, and disregarding standards of propriety are applauded and seen as "authentic." Under the conditions of the new order of knowledge in which everyone has their own truth, authenticity is valued more highly than truth and even more highly than traditional moral standards. In other words, lying is permissible as long as you are authentically lying, as long as you demonstrate by your public behavior that there is no difference between public and private. Authenticity, it must be emphasized, is not to be understood as a sort of correspondence between a private inner subjectivity and a public social subjectivity. Authenticity as a network norm is not about the typically modern struggle for self-realization. Authenticity is not a kind of personal truth according to the old correspondence definition of truth as *adaequatio intellectus ad rem*. When the human person has become an inforg, and when information is fundamentally relational, authenticity becomes the default condition of the informational self. The transparency of the network and uncontrolled flows of information make authenticity an imperative that cannot be ignored with impunity. No public mask can survive the leaks, the whistleblowers, the hacks, the exposures, and the general openness of the network that permits everyone to see through all the walls, enter all closed doors, break into all hiding places, and uncover all secrets. Not to acknowledge these affordances of the network, that is, not to be authentic, is a moral disgrace in the global network society and will be accordingly blamed and sanctioned.

A further important aspect of the network norm of authenticity has to do with responsibility. To say that authenticity is a network norm does not imply a new form of individualism or humanism. The network norm of authenticity does not contradict the network norm of connectivity. In the global network society, it is always the sociotechnical network of humans and nonhumans that is the actor. Even though none of the actors in a network are individuals in the humanist sense of the term, they are still called upon to be authentic. To say that the network is the actor does not mean renouncing responsibility and embracing anonymity. The collapse of the distinction between public and private and the transformation of the public sphere into an arena of ongoing trials, challenges, and proofs of authenticity have left no place to hide. Much has been said about the dangers of ICTs, artificial intelligence, automation, and networks, offering opportunities for shrugging off responsibility and claiming that "the system" is responsible for any problems that occur.[6] Authenticity stands in the way of this supposed danger.

---

6 This is known as the "responsibility gap" and refers to the fact that in situations of distributed agency, individuals seek to escape the burden of responsibility. Floridi (2013, 261; 2016b), for example, has taken up this topic and considers it an important challenge for digital ethics.

It does not, however, demand that some individuals bear the burden of systemic failures, whereas others go free. If a self-driving automobile causes an accident, who is to be held responsible? If an AI makes a mistake, who is responsible? Much of current digital ethics is concerned to make sure that someone is responsible and this someone, whether it be the user, the programmer, the company that makes the system, and so on, must be identifiable and held accountable.[7] There is always a need to find the person responsible who will be subject to moral blame and perhaps legal sanctions as well. This is a direct consequence of methodological individualism and the humanist tradition of ethics where free will and intentionality of an individual are assumed to be the foundation of morality. Traditional ethics asks: How can any group or collective be the subject of moral praise or blame? How can any actor incapable of conscious intentionality be held morally responsible? Why should anyone who neither intended harm nor directly participated in causing harm be blamed or sanctioned?[8]

To say the network is the actor does not mean that none of the human and nonhuman actors in the network are accountable. On the contrary, all the actors making up the network are responsible and accountable for what the network does. Networks are not systems. They are not wholes that are somehow greater than the sum of their parts. Actors in networks are not mere functions, even if many interactions in a network are black-boxed into routines or even automated. Networks cannot be analyzed in terms of parts and whole, individuals and group. This makes it difficult to apply traditional notions of "collective responsibility" to networks since these notions inevitably attempt to understand groups as if they were somehow superindividuals. Again, traditional ethical concepts cannot simply be carried over into the global network society. The premises of most discussions about collective responsibility all derive from modern assumptions about the difference between individuals and society and society and nature. Within the modern constitution, only autonomous rational subjects can be held morally accountable.[9] It is almost impossible to conceive of ethics not based upon free will and intentionality. Roles in networks, however, are neither functions within a system nor intentional free choices of individuals. Authenticity means that every actor in the network is a "mediator" and not a mere "intermediary."[10] Mediators are authentic in the sense in which Heidegger speaks of authentic *dasien*. They accept their role in the network and their responsibility for network actions because they know

---

7 Even current speculation about granting robots or AIs legal status as electronic persons (see Delvaux, http://www.europarl.europa.eu/sides/getDoc.do?pubRef=-//EP//NONSGML%2BCOMPARL%2BPE-582.443%2B01%2BDOC%2BPDF%2BV0//EN) is based on the conviction that only individuals are moral agents and can be held legally accountable. We will discuss these issues below under the title of distributed agency.

8 For a discussion of collective responsibility, see Smiley (2017).

9 This is not to say that notions of corporate responsibility are not possible within the modern constitution. Indeed, the legal system has long developed such notions. As Floridi (2013, 261; 2016) has argued, these notions can be useful for addressing issues arising from ICTs.

10 Latour distinguishes between mediators and intermediaries. Mediators are actors who are not subsumed to others, who maintain their ability to initiate translation and enrollment, that is, who continue to do networking, whereas intermediaries are reduced to functions.

that they exist as processes of mediation, of networking, Authenticity does not mean somehow being yourself opposed to the heteronomy of social constraints, but being as networking. Let us emphasize that network roles are not system functions. They are not comparable to traditional social roles or mechanical functions within a complex machine. As some have argued, a theory of distributed responsibility that moves beyond modern assumptions about free will and individual accountability requires rethinking moral imperatives as well as legal sanctions, which are usually addressed to individuals.[11] We will return to the question of a specific form of "network responsibility" in terms of "design" below. Here we are concerned to outline the new network norms guiding a truly digital ethics.

3.1.7 Flexibility

Connectivity, flow, communication, participation, transparency, and authenticity are network norms because the affordances of digital technologies influence socio-technical networks of which the world consists in specific ways and not in others. Digital networks are different from the stone ax, Heidegger's hammer, or a factory. They have their own affordances, which technologies of previous periods of history did not have. These affordances have led to the widespread recognition of a digital revolution or what is called "digital transformation." Contrary to how current digital ethics attempts to deal with this situation through reasserting the vanishing values of industrial society and Western humanism, these affordances lead to the network norms that we are attempting, at least in a provisional way, to outline. One important difference between the affordances of digital networks and previous networks is how digital networks relate to change. The functional subsystems of Luhmann's modern society value stability. Just as any system strives to maintain its organization through adapting to environmental changes such that its operations can be continued, so do the functional subsystems of society, including the organizations and institutions they consist of, strive to maintain sustainability. Sustainability is a value that today is ubiquitous. Many declarations and guidelines of digital ethics echo general normative ethics by naming sustainability among the most important values. Interestingly, sustainability is a concept based on the idea of functional stability derived from systems theory. Sustainability is a value because any system and any organism hate change. Once an organism is adapted to an environment, any changes in the environment or in the organism could be catastrophic. From a systems theory perspective, change is always a catastrophe. The idea and ideal of sustainability are deeply rooted in system imperatives of stability.

The concept of "sustainability" comes from forestry and refers primarily to resource management. The forest should be used in such a way that it can continue to be used for a long period of time. To cut down all the trees, something that has happened many

---

11 See for example Caruso (2012) and Caruso and Flanagan (2018). Floridi's (2013, 261) discussion of "distributed morality" relies on the idea of "infraethics," which is another word for what we term "socio-technical network."

times already in history with catastrophic consequences, would not be sustainable. In ecology, the concept of sustainability refers to the relations of human beings to their natural environment, that is, to the "ecosystem." What is essential in this context is the stability of the ecosystem, which should not be endangered by the reckless exploitation of resources. This definition of sustainability is based on systems theory. An organism is a closed system that should interact with its environment in such a way that it can remain viable and ensure its survival. The implication, much as in forestry, is that the resources in the environment that the organism needs in order to live are to be used in such a way that they are not depleted. The environment must remain stable and not change too much; otherwise, the viability of the organism that does not have unlimited possibilities of reacting to changes is threatened. If lions did hunt zebras to reduce their population, this would be unsustainable. Here again, the emphasis is on stability and preventing changes. Whether an organism intends to act in such a way that the environment remains stable, or does so by accident, or doesn't do it at all and eventually dies off is another matter. To say that sustainability is a value and a norm means that the environment should not change or that it is somehow "wrong" to change the environment or even to let the environment be changed by other factors. The value that sustainability signifies is stability. To act sustainably is, therefore, to do everything one can to ensure that the ecosystem remains stable and does not change.

The systems theoretical concept of sustainability overlooks that evolution itself is not sustainable or even based on sustainability. On the contrary, only when the environment changes does it become possible and necessary for organisms to "adapt" to these changes. In reality, the environment is constantly changing and has been doing so since time began. This is how natural selection works. The environment changes and this new environment "selects" those organisms that function within it. Those that don't die off. Natural selection depends upon variation and selection, and variation is another word for unsustainability. Evolution is possible only when things change and are not stable. Organisms come into being and disappear as environments change. No natural environment is sustainable, at least not from the perspective of those organisms that do not adapt to it. From the standpoint of those who do adapt and are temporarily viable, everything is fine, but only so long as everything stays as it is. Sustainability is only a value from the perspective of a particular organism that is successfully adapted to a specific environment. Sustainability is, therefore, an egoistic value. Sustainability is not a "natural" imperative. We may be interested in sustainable forestry, but other organisms are just waiting for more open pastures. Nature never wanted sustainability or was ever able to realize it. An ecosystem could be considered "balanced" only by forgetting that all those who couldn't walk the tight rope have already fallen off.

In the global network society, sustainability is a questionable value. This claim runs up against the fact that everywhere there are calls for sustainable living, sustainable building, sustainable production, sustainable agriculture, sustainable energy, and so on. Sustainability seems to be an undisputed and omnipresent value in our society and is regularly cited in digital ethics as well. Especially in a time when ecological problems have taken center stage on a worldwide scale, it would seem irresponsible, perhaps even madness, to call the value of sustainability into question. Nonetheless, we cannot turn the clock back to undo what has been done. We can only do more to ensure that whatever changes we make in the world's ecosystem do not needlessly restrict the viability of any form of being. This means that if we ask what is good for the whole world, then the answer is change and not stability. When it comes to change, there will be collateral damage, and basing ecology on systems theory is not helpful. Even to speak of an "ecosystem" is misleading and dangerous, since systems necessarily strive for stability. Systems don't like change. If we look around for a form of order that wants change and even thrives on it, then it would be networks and not systems. Perhaps we should stop speaking of ecosystems and start talking about "eco-networks." Networks are inherently flexible, scalable, unbounded, and open to many different participants and many different goals. Ecology is much more a network science than a system science. The values implied in networks are different from those implied in systems. For networks, change is a value and stability is not a value, but a problem, since it hinders the growth, proliferation, and transformation of networks. Sustainability, or stability, tends to fix actors into functions and demands that they become intermediaries subsumed to others. Sustainability is always a value in the service of oppression. If we are to move in the direction of geoengineering, as we must in order to deal with the climate problem, then we should start thinking about the world, Gaia, not as a system, but as a network. For this reason, *flexibility* is a network norm.

The list of network norms we have provided in all brevity is not asserted to be a complete list, nor perhaps even the most accurate list. Networks have always been with us, but the nonhuman participants have not all been the same, nor have they always led us to have the same values. The values and norms that the stone ax suggested to the hunter or warrior were surely different than those suggested to us today by ICTs. As we have been insisting throughout this book, the values of industrial society are different from those of the global network society. Whatever the affordances of our most significant nonhuman others have been, they have had a decisive say in what our values have been and what they are today. This is the "unofficial" morality that has guided Western society hidden beneath or blocked from view by the official morality of humanism. There is no such thing as human nature and no eternal and inalienable rights that could be derived from it. What these traditional values represent is the networks of industrial society with its need for individuals, systems, standardization, bureaucracies, and hierarchies. The global network society is very different. Individuals are no longer needed. Hierarchies are dysfunctional. Systems are everywhere being replaced by networks. This leaves morality in need of a fundamental reformulation. Attempts to date to describe a digital ethics have been little more than attempts to reassert the values of industrial society in the face of the demise of humanism. The discourse of digital ethics has been more reactionary than revolutionary. If we take the digital transformation seriously, then we must ask: What do the new network norms of the global network society based on ICTs permit us to say about morality? What forms of regulation can be derived from these new network norms? What would a truly digital ethics look like? These are the questions to which we now turn.

3.2 Network Governance

The network norms of connectivity, flow, communication, participation, transparency, authenticity, and flexibility are the new values. They are the new norms upon which any truly digital ethics must be founded. The philosophical mythology of humanism, social science critique with its own mythology of a society in which the struggle for emancipation is played out by autonomous rational subjects against political and economic elites, media scandalization of the digital, and civil society lobbying for government regulation all configure moral discourse according to the old norms and values of Western modernity. This is not digital ethics. As it turns out, what heretofore has called itself digital ethics has nothing to do with the digital, at least nothing beyond perceiving it as a threat against which the incontrovertible truths of humanism and Western industrial society must be reasserted. Since we have never been modern, and we now know this, we can drop all pretenses to the self-evident and inalienable rights of autonomous rational subjects and switch to the unofficial morality that has always guided the production and deployment of hybrids, that is, the construction of actor-networks. It is from this unofficial morality of networking that we will attempt to describe what digital ethics is as ethics for the global network society. We will formulate the new digital ethics not in familiar terms of moral imperatives that supposedly guide the decisions of free individuals, but in terms of what we shall call "governance by design." In the following, we will attempt to explain why it is at least plausible to reconceive moral as well as legal regulation in the global network society in terms of governance instead of traditional ethics on the one side and government regulation on the other. We will attempt to explain why a new form of governance should be understood from the point of view of design instead of traditional theories of action and agency together with their corresponding notions of responsibility and accountability.

Of course, we cannot simply deny that human rights exist or that values such as freedom, autonomy, dignity, democracy, and so on have any meaning or function. It is obvious and indeed incontrovertible that the values and norms of modernity have had great political and social significance. It cannot and should not be denied that in many areas of the world where there is no rule of law, where despotism tramples upon justice, where civil war is rampant, where free speech is impossible, and where inequality in many forms characterizes daily life, human rights and modern values represent the last hope of many people. We should not take this hope away. On the contrary, we must design a digital ethics that gives people new hope and new possibilities of realizing a just global society. If we have never been modern, this does not imply that we are excused from carrying the worthy goals of modernity forward into the digital future. But this must be done on a new basis. The modern constitution cannot fulfill the promises it has made. This is what the digital transformation means. The network norms we have derived from the affordances of ICTs must be able to take up the task where humanism and industrialism have failed. If there is to be a digital ethics worthy of the name, then it must show how the network norms can further the goals for which modernity was striving.

3.2.1 The Three Disruptions

The digital transformation has disrupted Western industrial society in at least three important ways. The first disruption is the posthumanist revision that no longer puts the autonomous rational subject at the center of history and society. The myth of humanism has become problematic in many ways, not the least of which is the fact that it seems to have taken its last stand on privacy. Privacy, as we have argued above, is an attempt to block connectivity and the free flow of information that is characteristic of the digital transformation and its new norms and values. Instead of privacy, the global network society values "publicy." Publicy is the default condition of the informational self.[12] Instead of privacy, actor-networks are essentially related, connected, unbounded, and open. As we argued above, Floridi's attempt to save the autonomous rational subject of humanism using an ontological theory of privacy fails to account for the relational nature of information. Inforgs, or what Floridi calls human individuals from the perspective of a philosophy of information, cannot be bounded individuals constituted by information that is in any way private. Instead of privacy, the informational self exists in the condition of publicy, that is, connected to many other actors, both human and nonhuman in many different actor-networks. This is the first disruption characterizing the digital transformation.

If the first disruption is the loss of the myth of humanism, the second is the loss of an age-old principle of social organization, namely, hierarchy. Since the earliest times, we have grown accustomed to organizing cooperative action among large groups through a hierarchy. Someone has to be the boss, the chief, the king, the leader, the president, and so on. Someone has to put an end to discussion and give orders that others carry out. The much discussed and not well-defined concept of "power" is always illustrated by hierarchies of one kind or another. Governmental bodies, businesses, educational institutions, religious communities, indeed, every form of cooperative endeavor among people is organized by means of power, which inevitably flows from the top down in the form of command and control communication. The pyramid could be seen as the best visualization of power. It is a structure that can be found in the organogram of almost every organization in society. Resistance to power or attempts to gain power are, therefore, always interpreted as bottom-up movements. This is the assumption that underlies all of social science critique under the modern constitution. From this point of view, it can be said that social communication has always been vertical; that is, orders come from the top, whereas compliance or resistance comes from below. The digital transformation disrupts traditional power by allowing effective communication and cooperation not only from one to many but from many to many. The affordances of digital technologies encourage lateral communication. Traditional bureaucratic organizations are becoming increasingly dysfunctional and uncompetitive in the global network society. Hierarchies are everywhere being replaced by network organizations based upon distributed decision making and self-organization.[13]

---

12 For a detailed discussion of publicy, see Belliger and Krieger (2018).
13 For a detailed discussion of the new networked forms of organization, see Belliger and Krieger (2016).

Finally, the third disruption is the transformation of the order of knowledge. Knowledge depends on media. Revolutions in media have always been accompanied by social and political revolutions. The invention of writing replaced oral tradition and changed society. The invention of the printing press and the electronic mass media changed society. The invention of digital media has also changed society. The new media, as we argued above when discussing media scandalization, have introduced a new order of knowledge that is nonhierarchical, unlimited, connected, inclusive, complex, and open to everyone. The new media are nonhierarchical because they give everyone the means of production and distribution of information. They are unlimited because the cost of producing and distributing information has drastically been reduced, thus eliminating the old economy of scarcity in information and knowledge. The new media are connected and, therefore, inclusive. Almost everybody has access to all the information in the Web. It is almost impossible to block or limit access to information, as all the leaks, whistleblowers, hacks, and disclosures demonstrate. The new order of knowledge is complex since there are no longer gatekeepers, authorities, institutions, or trusted sources of knowledge. Knowledge comes from anywhere, indeed, everywhere, as the acceptance of so-called citizen journalism by mainstream media shows. And finally, the new order of knowledge is public in a way in which knowledge heretofore has never been. The very idea of a public sphere arose in the modern period as a result of media proliferation and the increasing availability of information. But the public in the traditional sense of an arena in which citizens participate in democratic opinion-building has long become a global socio-sphere in which politics is only one of many forms of communication and participation.[14]

The three disruptions, posthumanism, nonhierarchical network organizations, and the new order of knowledge, create a global network society that can no longer be understood or regulated based on the values, norms, and forms of power typical of modern Western industrial society. Not only new norms but also new forms of organization and regulation are required if we are to move into the digital future.

3.2.2 Governance

The term "governance" has had a remarkable career in the past decades. By designating international development rules and practices of transnational organizations as well as corporate self-regulation with a view toward accountability and social responsibility, and public–private cooperation in the area of public services, governance has become a term for more or less informal, nonhierarchical, and networked forms of regulation in all areas of society.[15] Governance is not an extension of government. Whereas government is hierarchical, governance is self-organized, bottom-up, collaborative, and distributed

---

14 For a detailed discussion of the new order of knowledge, see Krieger and Belliger (2014).
15 "Governance is about the rules of collective decision-making in settings where there are a plurality of actors or organizations and where no formal control system can dictate the terms of the relationship between these actors and organizations" (Chhotray and Stoker 2009, 3). For similar definitions and an overview of governance theory, see Willke (2006), Sørensen and Triantafillou (2009), Sørensen and Torfing (2007), and Torfing et al. (2012).

regulation. It is the kind of regulation that is typical of and appropriate for networks.[16] Governance often rests upon shared responsibilities and commonly held ownership or use of resources. This brings governance into the vicinity of information-based networks, which, as we have argued above, are the foundation of network order. Actor-networks are essentially constituted by information that itself is necessarily distributed throughout the network and cannot be ascribed to any single actor either as constitutive characteristic (Floridi) or as private property. Because of the relational nature of information, networks constituted by information must be regulated in a similar way to the governance of common resources. Data or information is not a thing, a *res* in legal terminology, since data and information are non-rivalrous and non-excludable.[17] For something to be private property, it must be a thing, such as a chair that is rivalrous and excludable. The chair cannot be used by two people at once, and if one person owns it, others can be excluded from using it. I can sell my chair, and then it belongs to someone else, who can exclude me from using it.[18] Data and information are non-rivalrous and non-excludable. Many people can use the same information at the same time, and it is very difficult, if not impossible, as the futile attempts to achieve data security demonstrate, to exclude others from using it. Furthermore, information is the only resource whose use increases instead of subtracting from its quantity. This makes data and information into something much more like a common good or a public good instead of private property. Since it is such common or public goods that are usually regulated by governance instead of government, governance becomes a central concept for understanding how the global network society can be regulated.

Speaking of information as a public good is helpful as well as misleading. The term "public good" usually is, but need not be, defined in opposition to private property. The public/private binary difference, as we have argued above in the discussion of the nature of information as inherently relational, is not exhaustive of the possibilities for classifying resources. If something is not private, this does not imply that it is, therefore, automatically public in the sense of government-owned and administered. Beyond the dichotomy of private property versus government-owned and government-managed property, there is a third category that has been termed "common pool resources." Typical regulatory regimes for the administration of common pool resources are governance frameworks such as those investigated by Elenore Ostrom (1990, 2000, 2010) and Hess and Ostrom

---

16 Early on, governance was associated with network forms of order in distinction from either hierarchies or markets.
17 This is one of the reasons that the idea of a data commons or knowledge commons has become a major theme in the literature on the digital transformation. See, for example, Hess and Ostrom (2007) as well as the research reports by the D-CENT Project of the EU (https://dcentproject.eu/).
18 See Wikipedia articles on rivalry in economics (https://en.wikipedia.org/wiki/Rivalry_(economics) and on Excludability https://en.wikipedia.org/wiki/Excludability). Also helpful is the article on public goods in economics (https://en.wikipedia.org/wiki/Public_good).

2007).[19] After many years of empirical work, Ostrom showed the limitations of binary economic models of either private property regulated by a free market or government-owned property regulated by hierarchies when it comes to many forms of economic and social use of resources. Her contribution was to make it clear that "self-organized resource governance regimes" (Ostrom 2000, 138) have become of central importance in economic theory as well as practice. The dichotomy between public and private, regardless of whether we are talking about resources or actors, has become increasingly dysfunctional. This is, above all, the case when actors are seen as networks constituted by information.

As we have seen in Chapter 1, the relational ontology of information derived from ANT undermines the typically modern distinctions between individual and society, agency and structure, and subject and object. The regime of private property, as is privacy itself, is based upon the humanist assumption of bounded individuals and the Western ontology of substance. According to modern political and social theory, individuals can own property and enter into contracts to hold and administer resources collectively. This scheme may have made sense when dealing with material resources but does not apply to information. Information is not a thing, a *res*, and it cannot be so because it is fundamentally relational. There can be no sovereign decisions either to withhold or to externalize information. No boundary around information can successfully be established, which could be managed by an individual or a government. I can sell my automobile, but I cannot sell my information, even if I was allowed to, because information is not mine to own and to dispose of as I wish. This does not exclude monetizing information, but it hinders typically capitalist business models. Anybody can use information, but ownership is collective; that is, information belongs to the network. This implies furthermore that information cannot be said to constitute a bounded individual and thus ground a fundamental and inalienable right to privacy as Floridi's ontological theory of privacy would have us believe. Information cannot be isolated, locked up, contained within boundaries, externalized, or otherwise consumed in the same way as can things. Information constitutes not only what exists in the infosphere but also human existence itself as inherently relational. Floridi is right when he says that we *are* information, but the information we are is not *ours*. Information is a network phenomenon. Information arises in networks, and it constitutes networks and not individuals. Contrary to the myth of humanism, individuals are not the basis, the origin, of information, but a product of certain kinds of actor-networks. This implies that information can be "owned" and administered legitimately only by a network. Human beings, as Floridi says, are inforgs. However, this does not imply, as Floridi assumes, that humans are constituted by information as bounded individuals. Contrary to what the myth of humanism would have us believe, it is precisely because humans, as well as nonhumans, are constituted by information that they are relational beings existing in and as networks.

---

19 For Ostrom, common pool resources are seen as "subtractable"; that is, they are not nonrivalrous. The typical examples of fisheries, forests, and so on are material resources that can be depleted. This is not the case for information.

Human beings are informational beings and, as Luhmann pointed out, not material or biological beings. As long as humans were thought to be bounded individuals, Luhmann was right to ban them from society. Once human existence becomes meaning or information, it is through and through social and relational being. There can be no such thing as a fundamental right to privacy as well as a fundamental right to private property when it comes to information. Information, therefore, could be understood as a kind of common good, whereby one must insist that the meaning of the term "common good" or "common pool resource" cannot be defined in distinction to private or public goods and perhaps cannot even be considered a "good" at all.[20] If we do wish to think of information as a kind of resource, then it must be clear that it is a "resource" that is unique in nature. The binary distinction between public and private does not apply to the global network society. The collective of networks is not the society of which modern social theory speaks. As Luhmann argued, society does not consist of individuals. And as ANT has shown, society does not consist of systems that somehow steer individuals behind their backs. Neither individuals nor institutions nor governments are the major actors in what Latour calls the "collective" and what we refer to as the global network society. None of these can be owners of information at least insofar as information is understood to be mediation, translation, and enrollment or, simply, networking.

After what has been said, it should be clear why the term "common good" is misleading. The concept of common good has a well-established definition within modern social, legal, and political theory, which does not apply to the global network society.[21] The term is problematic not only because information is a unique kind of thing that cannot be owned by anyone, whether private or public, but more importantly because information cannot in the usual sense of the word be considered a resource, whether material or immaterial. Nonetheless, we find no better term to designate the nature of information when it comes to questions of regulation. We must acknowledge the fact that information cannot be adequately described within the modern constitution and accept the risk of misunderstanding when speaking of information as a common good or common pool resource. These terms, however, should be understood in the same way as Latour's concept of "collective." The collective is not merely another name for society. It is the name for a global socio-sphere constituted by networks.[22] From this point of view, regulating information amounts to constructing social order, which is a task that has traditionally been delegated to ethics, morality, politics, and law. In the following, we will speak of common good or common pool resource in order to describe information, but

---

20 A resource is usually understood to be "materials, energy, services, staff, knowledge, or other assets that are transformed to produce benefit and in the process may be consumed or made unavailable" (https://en.wikipedia.org/wiki/Resource). Since information cannot be consumed or made unavailable, it is questionable whether it can be considered a resource in the usual sense of the term.
21 The modern concept of common good is any resource that is rivalrous yet non-excludable; that is, the resource can be depleted, but it is difficult to exclude anyone from using it. Information does not correspond to this description.
22 For a discussion of the concept of the "socio-sphere," see Krieger and Belliger (2014).

we will always try to point out that the known and accepted definitions of these terms should not be trusted. With these terminological clarifications in mind, let us return to the discussion of governance.

Ostrom and her colleagues (Wilson, Ostrom, and Cox 2013, 22) describe what they call "core design principles," which appear in all successful self-organizing governance regimes that administer common pool resources. First, it is essential that such governance regimes clearly define the boundaries of the resource. In other words, the resource cannot be simply everything but must be delimited, circumscribed, and defined. People must know what it is whose use they are governing. Second, there must be a fair distribution of benefits and costs. What is fair and what is not is subject to negotiation among all stakeholders. Third, collaborative decision making must be implemented. Fourth, effective monitoring and conflict resolution must be in place. Fifth, there must be an acknowledged recognition of rights to self-organize. Sixth, there must be a coordination of the self-governing network with encompassing social structures, other networks, and broader society. These principles amount to a governance framework that characterizes successful collaborative administration and common pool resource governance. This framework is a sound basis upon which to address the issue of network governance in the digital age. Ostrom, however, did not base her analysis on a theory of networks. Apart from the fact that networks are based on information that resembles a common good, what do Ostrom's common pool resource governance principles have to do with a society made up of networks?

The digital transformation has brought the concept of "network" to the fore in social theory and poses new questions to the understanding of common pool resource governance. From the point of view of the network theory of order, the central question is: How do networks, in general, regulate themselves? In what ways do networks share governing principles with the common pool resource governance regimes Ostrom describes? Further, how do the network norms that we have derived from the affordances of digital technologies influence, condition, and shape both the governance principles that Ostrom describes and the general governance principles of networks? The new networks that have arisen on the basis of the affordances of digital technologies have generated their own norms and principles of regulation. How does governance look from the perspective of the new network norms that have been described above? After our hack has shown the vulnerabilities and "bad code" at the core of what currently calls itself digital ethics, answers to these questions lie at the basis of whatever digital ethics might become. Our hack is concerned with redesigning digital ethics as a theory of network governance.

Applied to networks, and especially to the digitally influenced networks constituted by the network norms of connectivity, flow, participation, transparency, authenticity, and flexibility, Ostrom's core design principles appear in a different light. Interpreted from the point of view of a network theory of order, Ostrom's principles can be understood in terms of

1. *taking account of*
2. *producing stakeholders*

3. *prioritizing*
4. *instituting and excluding*
5. *localizing and globalizing*
6. *separating powers*[23]

For Ostrom, self-organizing governance regimes must begin by defining what they are governing, its nature, extent, and uses. Translated into the exigencies of network governance, this means that the network must *take account of all actors*, both real and possible. Our (pre)human hunter or builder with his stone ax took account of specific stones, certain animals, certain pieces of wood, and so on, but left many other things out of account. The builder wielding a stone ax is an actor-network precisely because only certain actors are participating in the network and these actors are following a specific program of action. Although this network is very small, consisting of only a few actors in limited relations and with relatively simple purposes, this was not a closed system. Other actors could join in and change the network. For example, the network changed when the stone ax became metal or when a motor-driven chainsaw replaced the ax or when the builder became a worker for an industrial sawmill. As the history of the technology illustrates, many more actors joined in the network and transformed it in unforeseeable ways. As time went on, many more links were added. During this process, many activities were black-boxed into functional operations or closed systems. Generally, it can be said that the more extensive a network becomes, the more difficult it is to change the network, add actors, and redirect the program of action. This is because the more actors there are in a network, the more links and associations have been established and reinforced, and therefore the more effort must be expended to translate and enroll actors into other programs of action and change all these many links and associations. At every step in the development of a new technology, not only did actors join in and play new roles, but the programs of action also changed. The goal of the (pre)human builder may have been in some ways similar to that of the industrial sawmill, but much has changed, and much will change in the future. *Taking account of* actors is, therefore, an ongoing process and not on the same level as Ostrom's principle of defining the resource, which, of course, could also be revised, but is basically a founding event that is more or less fixed and stable. Once it has been decided that the common resource is a forest, then the forest usually remains a forest for a long time. This is what sustainability is all about. Successful common pool resource governance of the sort that Ostrom described is usually oriented toward sustainable use of a well-defined natural resource. This is not the case when the resource concerned is information. Furthermore, it is not the case when the object of governance is a network. Generally, it can be said of all the principles of network governance that

---

[23] These principles of network governance have been adapted from Latour's attempt at political theory (Latour 2004b). In order to signal that we are using these terms in the technical sense of network governance processes and not their usual meanings, we will write them in *italics* whenever so intended.

they designate processes and not structures. Networking is, in fact, processual and not to be understood as any kind of structure opposed to agency.

The second principle of network governance is called *producing stakeholders*. Here again, there are similarities but also important differences between Ostrom's core design principles of governance and the principles of network governance. For Ostrom, there must be a fair distribution of costs and benefits, which is a result of negotiations among stakeholders. What is fair is not objectively given by any external criteria and cannot be settled with reference to any external authority. Everything depends on negotiations between stakeholders. Circumscribing a network implies that it must be more or less clear who the actors, that is, the stakeholders in the network, are. What does the network consist of? Who has a say in how benefits and costs are distributed? What are considered benefits, and what are costs? The need to answer these questions is met by the second process of network governance, namely, *producing stakeholders*. It is important to note that stakeholders are not selected, elected, or otherwise found in the world. They are not in any way "given." Stakeholders are "produced." As we emphasized with regard to our prehuman hunter and the stone ax, neither the stone ax nor the hunter existed prior to their translation and enrollment into the network. The network is the actor, which means that networking constructs actors in specific roles for certain purposes or, as Latour puts it, "programs of action." Producing stakeholders is an ongoing process of identity construction on the basis of which roles, as well as privileges and responsibilities, are created and distributed. None of the actors, whether human or nonhuman, that have been constructed by networking, are fixed identities. Networking, as opposed to the selection, relationing, and steering of the elements and operations of a system, is fundamentally contentious and always open to revision. Actors are, as Latour puts it, "irreducible"; that is, they cannot be reduced to anything other nor can successfully reduce others to themselves. Actors are inherently relational and resist becoming substantialized. They are "mediators" and not "intermediaries" even when in many functional networks, or black boxes, they do take on relatively fixed identities, roles, and functions. Heidegger would say that actors exist as issues for themselves. As a guiding process of network governance, *producing stakeholders* keeps the question of who the stakeholders are alive and does not make the mistake of supposing order, and cooperative action can arise from hierarchical command and control communication, functional differentiation, or fixed identities.

Hierarchies, of course, are everywhere, even in networks. Ostrom noted that successful common pool resource governance must provide for forms of collaborative decision making that also allow for monitoring and conflict resolution. From the point of view of network governance, this may be understood in terms of what could be called *prioritizing*. Even though social space is flat, as Latour never tires of saying, not everything can happen at once, and not everyone is first in line when it comes to implementing any form of cooperative action. As a guiding process of network governance, *prioritizing* refers to what Luhmann would call reducing complexity and what in network terms amounts to narrative structuring.[24] Network organization is fundamentally narrative in that it is in

---

24 See Belliger and Krieger (2016) for a discussion of narrative as the basis of network order.

storytelling that actors are assigned roles in relation to one another and in relation to a general trajectory of events that are then related to each other temporally. The narrative construction of order is fundamental for all kinds of organizations, that is, cooperative action in society. Narratives do not necessarily have to have a beginning and an end, but they cannot tell everyone's story at the same time and in the same way. Sorting out which actors and activities and events are of importance and which are not is the task of *prioritizing*. Prioritizing, as all network governance principles, is less a principle than a process of ongoing negotiations in which all stakeholders participate. Nonetheless, at some point, certain roles and events are prioritized, and it is expected that the story serves as the basis for network activities and programs of action. The narrative agreed upon at any time serves as a criterion of compliance. There must, therefore, be some measures to monitor and encourage compliance. This leads to the next network governance principle of *instituting and excluding*.

When roles and programs of action have been narratively identified and ordered into expected trajectories, they are reinforced by many links and associations that tend to become *institutionalized*. Wielding a stone ax in a certain way could well have become relatively standardized and thus institutionalized, so it could be passed on to others and be recognized as a particular action of a specific actor. Institutionalization automatically excludes other ways of wielding the ax. Of course, one can do whatever one wants with a stone, but not everything one can do will be effective and also accepted as "hunting." Only those who have learned how to wield the ax "properly" in association with many other activities such as running, lying in wait, stalking, and so on will be considered "hunters." The more links and associations an actor and an activity have, the more institutionalized they become. In networks, as opposed to systems, these things are not fixed and integrated into a clearly bounded whole. Networks are always open and flexible with regard to the actors that make them up as well as the programs of action they pursue. Nonetheless, the more links and associations a network has, the more effort it takes to add new actors and change programs of action, since every link and every relation must be changed. When networks attain a certain size, they become stable and seem to exist on a level above the individual actors. Durkheim would speak of "social facts" or, as typical in sociology since Durkheim, "social structures" that determine the individual actors, as it were, behind their backs. Although ANT is notoriously opposed to any talk of social facts and rejects the distinction between agency and structure, it cannot be denied that certain networks, such as Luhmann's functional subsystems, have relatively strong inclusion/exclusion tendencies. As long as we are aware that what we are dealing with is a network and not a system, this need not cause problems. The network governance principles of *taking account of*, *producing stakeholders*, and *prioritizing* mitigate against excessive inclusion/exclusion processes. Another network governance principle that keeps networks open and flexible, while at the same time acknowledging the need for relative closure, is *localizing and globalizing*.

As a principle of network governance, *localizing and globalizing* acknowledges the fundamental openness of networks. Ostrom noted that successful common pool resource governance regimes are concerned to coordinate their activities with encompassing social structures and broader society. Since network order is a continuum and not constituted by bounded unities as is systemic order, networks must acknowledge their connectedness to actors, programs of action, and indeed, the entire world beyond their own at any time-effective trajectories. Let us recall the problematic idea of an "ecosystem," which we discussed above. The subject of ecology, as we argued, cannot be a system, since systems are necessarily constituted by an exclusive difference to an environment, whereby an ecosystem has no such constitutive difference. For this reason, we argued that one should probably not speak of an "ecosystem" at all, but much rather of an ecological network, which is principally unbounded. The task of acknowledging this openness while at the same time constructing manageable, efficient, and functional networks is expressed by the governance principle of *localizing and globalizing*. *Localizing* means that for particular trajectories and programs of action, many possible other actors and programs of action are not simply excluded, but *globalized*, while local relations, actors, and programs of action are prioritized. The well-known slogan "think globally, act locally" describes this governance process quite well. Thinking globally is not something that Luhmann's functional subsystems can do. They are universal, but only in the way in which operationally and informationally closed systems can be. They can only construct information that comes from beyond their borders according to their own criteria of relevance and meaning. They are indeed universal, and therefore in a certain sense global, only because they see everything exclusively from their own perspective. Thinking globally, in the sense proposed by the network governance principles of localizing and globalizing, is entirely different. It is the acknowledgment of and preparedness for possible informational intrusions from everywhere, at any time, and in any way.

When the political system regulates business activities, for example, imposing fines for environmental pollution, the economic system can only respond by constructing information in terms of profits and loss arising from such regulations. When businesses lay off workers, the political system can only react by constructing information in terms of winning or losing votes. If those incumbent in office perceive a chance of winning votes, the government takes action to alleviate the social problems caused by unemployment. In Luhmann's account, structural coupling of the political and the economic systems ensure that shocks generated by one system can be absorbed by the other system without destabilizing society all too much. Since networks are not operationally and informationally closed, *localizing and globalizing* work to keep networks open to information and not merely perturbations coming from beyond their "borders." This is what thinking globally and acting locally means. What is happening "outside" a network does not merely disturb but informs what the network is and does, which, of course, informs what is happening everywhere. Here again, this could easily be understood as a principle of ecology when ecology is not misunderstood as a systems science instead of network science. Localizing and globalizing could be seen as a kind of balancing act. Different and opposing forces must be held in balance. This is the explicit task of the last network governance principle, *separation of powers*.

Networks must maintain and withstand many divergent forces. Because of their openness and because even functionally subordinated intermediaries may at any time become independent mediators and change the network by introducing new and unforeseen translations and enrollments, networks must manage opposing forces. Whereas systems seem to be governed by a centripetal force of integration and functional subordination, networks must contend with the centrifugal force of expansion and change. For this reason, it is a fundamental principle of network governance to balance the processes of *taking account of, instituting and excluding,* and *localizing and globalizing*. As a governance process, separation of powers has the task of ensuring that the local cannot mistake itself for the global and the global cannot dictate conditions to the local, that *exclusion* is always open to inclusion, and that *prioritizing* remains an ongoing process. This balancing of the opposite or even antagonistic forces that at once make networks open and tend to draw boundaries could be called, with reference to modern democratic structures, *separating powers*. In democratic societies, the executive, legislative, and judicial functions of government are distinguished. This is intended to ensure that concentrations of power can be avoided and checks and balances are instituted. How exactly the process of separating powers is implemented in any specific network is an open question.

The network governance principles of *taking account of, producing stakeholders, prioritizing, instituting and excluding, localizing and globalizing,* and *separating powers* allow Ostrom's core principles of common pool resource governance to be translated into a theory of network order. It remains to show how these principles of network governance apply to those networks with which we are confronted today in the global network society. Although there is a difference between networks as they have been constructed before the digital transformation and the networks of today's global network society, the basic principles of network governance constitute the "unofficial morality" that Latour supposed lay behind the official morality of modernity. Governing networks that are guided by the new values and norms of connectivity, flow, communication, participation, transparency, authenticity, and flexibility are at once similar to and yet different from how networks have always been governed. If there is to be an ethics for the global network society, that is, a truly digital ethics, then it must consist in the governance of those networks that are above all conditioned by the affordances of ICTs. Hacking digital ethics is only then an ethical hack when a useful and reliable alternative to traditional digital ethics comes out of it. If the conventional discourse of digital ethics is full of weaknesses, bugs, and bad code and is motivated primarily by fear of losing heretofore comfortable legacy systems, what then is digital ethics as it should be?

3.3 Design

Legacy digital ethics, indeed, ethics in the modern world, establishes itself between morality and law and moves constantly from one pole to the other. What is universally true, for example, human rights, should be enacted into law. Government regulation, for its part, must be legitimated not only by democratic processes but above all by the universal truths and values derived from human nature. This typically modern constellation of morality and law, of individual freedom and government regulation, cannot perceive the digital transformation, which disrupts the myth of humanism and the social order of modernity founded upon it, as anything other than a threat. This perception is correct. The digital transformation does undermine the modern constitution. The global network society cannot be adequately regulated by either traditional humanistic ethics or the hierarchical regulatory regimes of modern industrial society. The reality of networks shows us, as Latour says, that we have never been modern and that humanist solutions will not work in a posthuman world. This has implications for digital ethics, which perhaps should not be called ethics at all, but instead, "digital governance."[25] *Digital ethics could be described as a governance framework and practice based on network norms.* It is to these norms that digital ethics appeals when faced with the task of saying how networks today and in the future should be regulated. Furthermore, the term "governance" designates the inseparable unity of morals and regulative action. The digital transformation presents us with a situation in which we no longer have morals on one side and government regulation on the other. Laws, just as morals and ethics, are actors in the network, along with many other actors such as technologies, humans, institutions, and much more. It is the network that is the subject and object of regulation as well as ethical reflection. To speak of network governance is to renounce any significant distinction between morals and law and, consequently, to reconstruct moral discourse on entirely different foundations as did Weston modernity.[26]

The unofficial morality that always guided the ways in which humans and nonhumans construct networks could be understood to imply a unique kind of agency. The agency in question we propose to call "design." The difference between morals up above in an ideal realm and law on the ground has collapsed. The hierarchies are gone. Social space is flat. We have only design to guide us. The prehuman who, together with certain stones and animals and sticks of wood, constructed an actor-network called a "hunter" or a "builder" was essentially involved in design. Translation and enrolling actors into a network is above all a question of design since it is always concerned with solving practical problems and bringing humans and nonhumans into cooperation with each other through constructing information. But what is design? Design is usually associated with handwork, production of consumer goods, industrial design, but as Herbert Simon recognized, design is a fundamental form of human existence and describes almost everything we do:

> Engineers are not the only professional designers. Everyone designs who devises courses of action aimed at changing existing situations into preferred ones. The intellectual activity that produces material artifacts is no different fundamentally from the one that prescribes remedies for a sick patient or the one that devises a new sales plan for a company or a social welfare policy for a state. Design, so construed, is the core of all professional training. […] Schools of

---

25 Unfortunately, the term "digital governance" or often "E-governance" is used to designate practices of management of digitally influenced processes in traditional organizations. "Digital governance is a framework for establishing accountability, roles, and decision-making authority for an organization's digital presence—which means its websites, mobile sites, social channels, and any other Internet and Web-enabled products and services" (https://digitalgovernance.com/dgblog/what-is-digital-governance/). This is not what we mean by the term and it may well be unadvised to use it at all.

26 Recently, the term "soft law" has come into vogue with many of the same connotations. See https://en.wikipedia.org/wiki/Soft_law.

engineering, as well as schools of architecture, business, education, law, and medicine, are all centrally concerned with the process of design. (Simon 1996, 111)

Just as the concept of governance, the idea of design has in recent years so extended its meaning and scope that it can take center stage in programs of action that had once been guided by concepts such as "modernization," or even "revolution" (Latour 2008, 5). The meaning of design "has been extended from the details of daily objects to cities, landscapes, nations, cultures, bodies, genes, and […] to nature itself." The scope of design includes, nowadays, almost everything, including humans, for even "humans have to be artificially made and remade." If all problem-solving activities—and action is fundamentally problem-solving—can be understood from the point of view of design, even the issue that human existence, as Heidegger put it, is for itself, then agency and action become concepts that must be interpreted in a very different manner than is usual in modern philosophy and social theory. Humanist-based theories of action and of government no longer seem to have the explanatory power present-day realities demand. What does it mean to "do" something? Must humanist notions of free will, intentionality, and moral action constitute the basis for understanding agency and, therefore, ethics and morality? Is cooperative action only to be organized by means of hierarchical government? If, as we have argued, moral agency is no longer to be conceived of on the basis of a philosophical anthropology, but on the basis of a theory of networking and an ontology of information, if we are no longer substances, and if agency is no longer exclusively human but nonhuman as well, then perhaps the concept of design can help.[27] This possibility becomes plausible the moment one considers that in all questions of design, the question of good or bad design is necessarily implied. As Latour puts it, "The decisive advantage of the concept of design is that it necessarily involves an ethical dimension which is tied into the obvious question of good versus bad design" (2008, 5).

As long as design was conceived of as an aesthetic add-on to purely functionally defined artifacts, the question of good or bad design was not a moral question. What makes design a moral issue is the transformation of the notion of agency to include not only the intentional actions of humans but the affordances of nonhumans as well. In addition to this, action is reconceived as a distributed agency that is characteristic of networks. Could it be that traditional theories of moral agency, of responsibility and accountability, and of what counts as morally good or evil can be replaced by a theory of design? Could it be that a theory of design addresses fundamental aspects of agency instead of merely aesthetic improvements on otherwise purely functional artifacts? Can design become a basic concept in a theory of governance, that is, a theory of how networks are regulated apart from traditional dichotomies of morals and law? Is it at all plausible that digital ethics is actually a theory of *governance by design*? Instead of "privacy by design" or "trust by design," which are often mentioned in contemporary discussions of digital ethics, we would have governance by design, which replaces everything that

---

27 For an interesting discussion of Latour's ideas on design that moves in this direction, see Stephan (2015).

heretofore has called itself digital ethics. To begin to answer these questions, let us return to the question of moral agency. Who is a moral agent, and what makes their actions morally relevant?

3.3.1 Attribution of Moral Agency and Responsibility

The core semantic of traditional moral discourse consists of concepts of moral agency and criteria for the attribution of moral responsibility and accountability. The digital transformation challenges these concepts by questioning humanist assumptions. Among those who have taken up these questions upon the basis of a philosophy of information and an information ethics, Floridi stands out as a significant witness to the importance of the issues involved. Floridi's foundational project of a philosophy and ethics of information proposes to extend the scope of morality beyond the actions of human individuals to include both the actions of nonhumans and the consequences of actions performed by collective actors, that is, networks of both humans and nonhumans. Floridi (2013, 137) argues that an information ethics must move beyond "limiting the ethical discourse to individual agents" to take account of two significant consequences of the information revolution. These are, first, the need for a concept of "distributed morality" that can deal with the global effects of "systemic interactions among several agents at a local level" (138) and, second, because "insisting on the *human-based nature* of the individual agents […] means undermining the possibility of understanding […] the appearance of artificial agents (AAs)" (ibid.; emphasis in original). What ethics must today deal with are "sufficiently informed, 'smart,' autonomous artifacts, able to perform morally relevant actions independently of the humans who engineered them" (ibid.). According to Floridi, these two problems can only be solved "by fully revising the concept of 'moral agent'" (ibid.).

Before we look more closely at how Floridi proposes to "fully revise" the concept of moral agency, let us recall that for Floridi "good" and "evil" refer not to traditional morally qualified actions such as stealing, lying, killing, caring for the needy, honesty, and so on but to increasing or decreasing the amount of information in the infosphere. This shift from the traditional ethics of deeds carried out by free and accountable agents to an ethics of informational acts has major consequences. To begin with, the informational ontology that lies at the basis of this view implies that no matter what happens, it is information of one kind or another that is doing the acing and that has effects on other information. This recalls Luhmann's definition of society as a system of communications that consists no longer of human beings performing communicative actions, but of communication operating upon communication. For Floridi, as for Luhmann, the measure of the "good" is no longer qualitative but quantitative. From Luhmann's point of view, the more communications, the better for society. For Floridi, the more information, the better for the infosphere.[28] This implies that all events whatsoever are morally relevant,

---

28 Luhmann, it should be noted, does not understand increasing the quantity of communication as a moral norm as does Floridi the quantity of information.

since whatever contributes to negentropy (increase of information) in the infosphere is morally good, whereas whatever increases entropy, thus decreasing the amount of information, is morally bad. Of course, one could claim that there are morally neutral events that neither increase nor decrease the amount of information in the infosphere. Should it turn out that most of what we do all day long is negligible for the infosphere, this becomes a problem for a moral theory claiming to regulate human behavior. We will return to this problem below when discussing Floridi's theory of "distributed morality." For the moment, let us note that the consequence of Floridi's theory of informational good and evil is that the entire world and everything in it is morally relevant and falls within the purview of moral evaluation. There is nothing that cannot or should not be morally evaluated, subject to praise and blame and to ascriptions of responsibility and accountability. This is the first consequence of Floridi's attempt to "fully revise" the concept of moral agency and radically reconceptualize ethics on the basis of a philosophy of information.

Second, there is a special problem with the idea of agency when moral actions are informational in nature. Since all beings in the infosphere *are* information and do not merely make information on the basis of certain cognitive abilities they might by nature be endowed with, and since information is dynamic, a difference that *makes* a difference, the moral agent is inseparable from the moral patient, or in other words, there is no ontological distinction between subject and object. We can no longer assume that certain agents, who are endowed with special cognitive abilities, which could be called mind, as well as a unique ability to make decisions that can be called free will, choose to increase or decrease the amount of information in the infosphere and thus make themselves subject to moral praise or blame. Instead, we have a world in which *information acts upon itself*. Inforgs, that is, human beings, let us recall, *are* information. Indeed, everything that is, is because it is information. Since, as we have argued on the basis of ANT, information is relational as well as dynamic and processual, every information in some way mutually affects every other information. This makes it very difficult, if not impossible, to distinguish agents from patients and is from ought. To assess the moral consequences of any informational event, one would, in principle, have to "count" all the information in the infosphere before and after the event. Only then could one say whether more or less information has resulted from the event. Even if this were possible, it would still not be able to ground any moral judgment since it takes time for the informational consequences of an event to unfold and become knowable. In principle, one would need an infinite time span to judge whether any event "in the end" led to more or less information. Consider the butterfly effect. And finally, even if the temporal unfolding of informational consequences was no obstacle, how could one inventory of information in the infosphere be compared contrafactually—what would the world be like if this had happened instead of that—with any other? What would the world be like if Hitler had been assassinated? How do we know? When would we be able to make a judgment? What are all the relevant factors that would need to be taken into account?

Floridi does not face these problems or attempt to answer the questions they raise directly. Instead, he appears to pursue a strategy of what could be called "incremental extension" of the moral domain. The first such extension is the enlargement of the class of moral agents to include not only autonomous rational subjects but certain entities that can be classified as "artificial agents," otherwise known as artificial intelligence or robots. The second extension of the moral realm concerns not agents but actions, that is, the consequences of actions that can be morally qualified. The expansion of morally qualifiable agents and activities, Floridi discusses under the title of "distributed morality" and "infraethics." We will first take a look at his extension of moral agency and then turn to distributed morality and infraethics. After reviewing Floridi's attempt to address these questions, we will look at recent contributions that go beyond the solutions that Floridi proposes.

Floridi proposes to extend moral agency beyond human beings by introducing the distinction between responsibility and accountability. Human beings, who are capable of conscious intentions and free decisions, are not only accountable for what they do but also responsible. Certain nonhumans, that is, what Floridi calls artificial agents (AAs), can now also do morally significant things independently of their human creators and should be held accountable. But since such AAs are not conscious and do not have free will, they cannot be held responsible. Let us note at the beginning that it is questionable whether accountability can conceptually be divorced from responsibility.[29] Merriam-Webster defines accountability as "an obligation or willingness to accept responsibility or to account for one's actions." Accountability presupposes a free choice for which reasons must be given upon request. Accountability does not imply that the reasons given must be accepted or agreed upon as sufficient to justify the act after the fact by everyone concerned. In most disputed cases, the courts will decide. But the fact that the courts can decide implies, that is, at least in cases where laws have been broken, that legal and perhaps even moral judgments can be made. In the case of AAs, it could be argued that there are certain degrees of freedom as well as the ability to give reasons for a decision even if there is no consciousness, intentionality, or what Floridi calls "mind." He, therefore, argues for a "mindless morality" (148) in all cases where AAs can be held accountable but not responsible, since such agents lack consciousness and intentionality. What does accountability mean when applied to nonhumans?

It would seem that at least two criteria must be fulfilled for the actions of a nonhuman to be morally qualified. First, the nonhuman must be the "source" of an event. Second, the event must be morally "qualifiable." As already noted, any action that either increases or decreases the amount of information in the infosphere is morally qualifiable. Since this can apply to anything at all, it would seem that there is nothing that does not fall under the category of moral relevance. Even purely natural events such as earthquakes or storms have consequences for the infosphere since they "happen" only if they are in some way transformed into information, for example, measured by the damage they do, registered on some instrument, interpreted as signs of God's wrath, mobilizing humanitarian organizations and international aid efforts, and so on. Any information ethics worth the name must be based on the value of information, and this implies the moral

---

29 See the article on accountability in Wikipedia: "accountability is the acknowledgment and assumption of responsibility for actions" (https://en.wikipedia.org/wiki/Accountability).

relevance of all information and informational events. There is no activity with informational consequences that is not morally qualifiable. As Floridi (2013, 147) puts it: "*An action is said to be morally qualifiable if and only if it can cause moral good or evil, that is, if it decreases or increases the degree of metaphysical entropy in the infosphere*" (author's emphasis). Of the two criteria that must be fulfilled for the actions of a nonhuman to be morally relevant, the criterion of moral qualifiability is given with any informational impact whatsoever. This leads to the other criterion of accountability and the question of what can be considered a "source" or morally qualifiable actions.

The moral accountability of nonhumans arises not only from the effects actions of a nonhuman may have on the infosphere but from the fact that the nonhuman must be a "source" of an event. But what makes something into a source of an action? A source is not a cause. Smoke is caused by fire, but fire cannot be held morally accountable for the smoke. Or can it? It can be asked why the fire broke out. Even if no human action, whether intentional or not, can be found as the source of the fire, there are many open questions about adequate safety precautions, building regulations, risk assessments, inadequate warning systems, unprepared or ill-equipped fire departments, and much more. Natural catastrophes such as earthquakes, tsunamis, mudslides, pandemics, and so on always raise questions about early warning systems, response preparedness, rescue protocols, crisis management, negligent authorities, irresponsible loss of life and property, among other things. Every supposedly natural event has moral repercussions and an ethical dimension since nature has long ago become culture in one way or another. If we have learned anything from the present-day ecological crisis, it is that humans and nonhumans are inseparably bound together in so many ways that the division between nature and culture, subjects and objects can no longer be maintained. We have learned from ANT that there is no such thing as purely natural causes or objective facts. Therefore, it would seem that a source of any informational change whatsoever must be considered a moral agent. Does this imply that any nonhuman at all can be held morally accountable and not merely those AAs that seem in many ways to be like us? Floridi does not go this far. He is very restrictive in attributing accountability to nonhumans. In his view, a "source" in the morally relevant sense of a cause of morally qualifiable action can only be an entity that (1) acts with a certain degree of freedom, that is, autonomy; and (2) interacts with the environment, that is, outputs become inputs to the system; and (3) is capable of changing its rules of internal information construction and of action; that is, it is capable of learning or of adaptation.[30] Although this definition would apply to many animals, Floridi intends this to be a typical description of a sophisticated AI or robot, since robots may be considered intelligent, autonomous, interactive systems.

Interestingly, when it comes to illustrating what AAs are, Floridi does not choose one of the well-known humanoid robots, such as Sophia, from Hansen Robots, as an example but gives the example of an email spam-detection software whose "actions" effect valued information by algorithmic filtering.[31] If the software should not function properly, and

---

30 See Floridi (2013, 140).
31 More relevant and much discussed are examples of AIs that "discriminate" against minorities in one way or another, self-driving automobiles that cause accidents, autonomous weapons

valuable information is lost, the software can be considered a moral agent that must be held accountable. Although it is questionable that a spam-filtering software fulfills the requirements of autonomy, interactivity, and adaptability, which, according to Floridi, a nonhuman must meet to be considered a moral agent, let us nevertheless assume the software is an AA, as Floridi defines it. We cannot hold the software "responsible" for its failures since it does not have the psychological component of conscious intention, as does a human. But, according to Floridi, we can hold the AA morally, and not merely technically, accountable. What does accountability mean in this case?

> Since AAs lack a psychological component, we do not blame AAs, for example, but, given the appropriate circumstances, we can rightly consider them sources of evil, and legitimately re-engineer them to make sure they no longer cause evil. (2013)

Accountability, we may assume from the above statement, means that certain nonhumans are subject to a moral imperative of "re-engineering." The moral judgment that the AA has done evil results in "legitimate re-engineering." That engineering and re-engineering must be "legitimate" implies that the functionality of technical artifacts is not a merely technical goal, but a moral goal as well. The addition of the moral dimension to technical considerations means that the design of an AA includes the involvement of human users, social consequences, questions of damage to information, and the general status of the infosphere. Of course, this applies to all artifacts and not merely the AAs that Floridi wishes to include in the domain of morality. No artifact stands alone and can be judged merely on the basis of functional criteria, whatever they may be, but must be judged as a complex, social-technical network in which the state of the infosphere, and not merely technical or esthetic issues, is at stake. Technology, no matter how autonomous, intelligent, adaptive, and so on it may or may not be, is never neutral. As Latour might put it, technical mediation is always a moral issue. The question of whether a technology functions well or not is the same question of whether it is morally good or evil, but only, of course, if the big picture is in view and not merely a small area of the infosphere. Floridi's thesis of the moral accountability of nonhumans, if we extend it beyond the narrow and unfounded restrictions he imposes with regard to which nonhumans can qualify as moral agents, collapses the distinction between humans and nonhumans with regard to agency and transforms questions of good or bad design into questions of moral good and evil. This becomes apparent when Floridi speaks of re-engineering as a kind of moral reprobation or "punishment" with regard to nonhumans.

> We are not punishing them, anymore than one punishes a river when building higher banks to prevent a flood. But the fact that we do not "re-engineer" people does not say anything about the possibility of people acting in the same way as AAs, and it would not mean that for people "re-engineering" could be a rather nasty way of being punished. (2013)

---

systems, medical diagnosis systems, automatic trading systems on stock exchanges, social robots of all kinds, and so on.

In whatever way we interpret this surprising statement, it could be read as an invitation to consider human re-engineering instead of the present retributive justice system as an appropriate way of dealing with criminality or moral failings.[32] Floridi clearly denies "that we should reduce all prescriptive discourse to the analysis of responsibility" (151), where it is assumed that only consciously intentional humans can be considered morally responsible. Prescriptive discourse should also be applicable to AAs, which are morally accountable but not morally responsible. To assume that AA could also be held morally responsible would imply that AAs can be subject to "punishment." But what does punishment mean? Even if AAs are only accountable, but not responsible, this does not free them from the consequences of praise or blame. On the contrary, they can be punished in the form of re-engineering. The interesting point here is that the imperative to "re-engineer" morally accountable AAs is similar to the imperative to punish morally responsible humans. Both imperatives are moral since AAs must be considered moral agents and not humans alone. Both are directed toward changing the situation, that is, doing something to ensure that the morally blamable actions do not recur. These considerations bring the ideas of punishment and re-engineering into proximity. This nearness allows us to build a bridge between intentional free agents who are punished for wrongdoings and unconscious AAs, or socio-technical networks, that are re-engineered for their wrongdoings. Perhaps the extension of moral agency beyond free, intentional human subjects opens the door to shifting attention away from the apparently questionable need for attribution of responsibility and accountability, the search for who did it, and allows ethics to focus on socio-technical networks, which then become the subjects of moral judgment. Floridi's strategy of extending the moral domain beyond traditional anthropocentrism makes it possible to turn the tables and consider re-engineering as a form of sanction for the moral transgressions of humans as well as machines, at least to the extent that humans are not understood as bounded individuals completely independent of the technical systems in which they are embedded.

The prospect of re-engineering or still better design applied to human existence is not science fiction or even a dystopian vision of a cyborg future. In a way, socialization, education, training of all kinds, as well as the various regimes of "governmentality," "bio-politics," or "power-knowledge" that Foucault has described, can be considered forms of moral engineering. Foucault (1991) defines governmentality as "the ensemble formed by the institutions, procedures, analyses and reflections, the calculations and tactics that allow the exercise of this very specific albeit complex form of power, which

---

32 Retributive justice is "that form of justice committed to the following three principles: (1) that those who commit certain kinds of wrongful acts [...] morally deserve to suffer a proportionate punishment; (2) that it is intrinsically morally good [...] if some legitimate punisher gives them the punishment they deserve; and (3) that it is morally impermissible intentionally to punish the innocent or to inflict disproportionately large punishments on wrongdoers" (Stanford Encyclopedia of Philosophy "Retributive Justice," https://plato.stanford.edu/entries/justice-retributive/). See Caruso (2012) for a critique of retributive justice on the basis that neuroscience has shown that human free will is largely a myth and notions of retributive justice are no longer tenable.

has as its target: population, as its principal form of knowledge: political economy, and as its essential technical means: apparatuses of security." From the point of view of ANT, governmentality must be conceived of as a socio-technical network involving both humans and nonhumans and viewed as an ongoing process subject to the constraints of network governance and not Foucauldian power. Furthermore, and more important for the task of reconceptualizing ethics, the socio-technical network, or the power-knowledge regime, must be conceived of as a product and process of design. Finally, to do justice to Foucault's critical intentions, this implies that regimes of power-knowledge must be subject to moral judgments about good or bad design.

Before turning to the second move Floridi makes in order to extend the domain of morality to coincide with the infosphere, it should be noted that for ANT, agency is not only always distributed but also always *symmetrical*. Humans and nonhumans do not do anything differently from each other on the level of technical mediation. From an ANT perspective, it cannot be argued that whereas humans are responsible, nonhumans (but only some!) are merely accountable. For ANT, both humans and nonhumans (all of them and not merely Floridi's AAs) are symmetrically responsible and "accountable." Agency, for ANT, is symmetrical in that both humans and nonhumans *do the same thing*. All actors, both human and nonhuman, translate and enroll actors into a network, or in other words, they construct information. In short, Floridi seems at least to partially agree with ANT when he argues that moral agency does not require free will, consciousness, intentionality, mental states, or cognitive and linguistic abilities, even if some form of "consciousness," as theories of panpsychism suppose, may be considered a requirement for the emergence of meaning and information.[33] The agreement, however, is only partial as Floridi's discussion of distributed morality shows. Understanding distributed agency and distributed morality from the perspective of ANT shows that ethics and morality need no humanist presuppositions. We can very well have ethics and morality without intentional, free agents. But this is a consequence that Floridi decidedly does not intend.

Let us now look at the second move Floridi makes. This move consists of two parts, which he calls "distributed morality" and "infraethics." For Floridi, distributed morality is to be understood not from the point of view of agents, as it usually is, but from the point of view of the consequences of actions. Usually, distributed responsibility refers to the collective responsibility of groups of actors. This is also called distributed agency. After long being considered a secondary form of agency somehow added on to the primary agency of individual intentional actors, today distributed agency has come into its own right as perhaps the original and primary form of doing anything.[34] From the point of view of ANT, for example, agency is always distributed among all actors in a network.

---

33 See Hoffman (2019).

34 See Enfield and Kockelman (2017) and Oppermann (2014, 3), who writes: "Agency assumes many forms, all of which are characterized by an important feature: they are material, and the meanings they produce influence in various ways the existence of both human and non-human natures. Agency, therefore, is not to be necessarily and exclusively associated with human beings and with human intentionality, but is a pervasive and inbuilt property of matter, as part and parcel of its generative dynamism."

Distributed agency in the case of actor-networks means that no single actor in the network is alone responsible for the actions of the network. Indeed, the network is the actor. The hominin, the stone, the animals, or wood, all do something in order for the actor-network, which can be called a hunter or builder wielding a stone ax, to come into being. The hominin alone, or 3 million years later a human, is not the actor. Even today, from an ANT perspective, agency is always distributed. This is what the myth of humanism and the modern constitution attempt to conceal, and it is also what modern ethics systematically overlooks. An indication of the importance of this general tendency toward reconceptualizing agency as distributed can be seen in Floridi's shift from agency to consequences when developing a theory of distributed morality. It would seem that to protect humanist assumptions, Floridi steers away from questions of agency when it comes to discussing the moral implications of networks.

When discussing distributed morality, Floridi shifts attention away from problems of agency to problems of consequences. Agency, let us recall, can be "mindless"; that is, AAs and multi-agent systems (MAS), including hybrids of humans and nonhumans, cannot be held responsible but at most accountable. This means that problems of moral attribution must arise from considering the effects of actions and not be preoccupied with searching for "who" does the action. "The consequence of a mindless approach is that we need to evaluate actions not from a sender but from a receiver perspective: actions (included MAS', artificial and supra-agents') are assessed on the basis of their impact on the environment and its inhabitants" (Floridi 2013, 266). Recalling that, in principle, every informational event could be said to either increase or decrease the amount of information in the infosphere and thus become morally qualifiable as either good or bad, the question arises of how to morally qualify those informational events that have apparently no effect. Indeed, most things that happen and most of what we do all day, that is, supposing we are normal people and not rulers of nations or captains of industry, appear to be insignificant, unimportant, and without any serious consequences for the infosphere. Such actions, like making a cup of coffee in the morning or walking the dog in the evening, are morally neutral and fall outside the scope of moral evaluation. Since they neither increase nor decrease the amount of information in the world, they would seem to be morally neutral. Considering that historically significant events happen rarely, this implies that most of what happens and what we do is morally irrelevant, which reduces the scope of moral relevance and moral evaluation drastically. What are informational moralists to do in the face of massive and ubiquitous insignificance? Floridi's answer to this problem is to declare that many activities do acquire moral significance when they are aggregated and scaled up to a global level by means of systems or networks of humans and nonhumans, or in other words, platforms.[35] Recalling van Dijck's critique of the "platform society," which we discussed in Chapter 2, assemblages of many users

---

35 "I intend to use 'distributed morality' (DM) to refer only to cases of moral actions that are the result of otherwise morally neutral or at least morally negligible [on this distinction, see below] interactions among agents constituting a multi-agent system, which might be human, artificial or hybrid" (Floridi 2013, 262).

through digital aggregators can transform otherwise small and apparently insignificant actions into large-scale effects. Many seemingly insignificant acts of many hardly identifiable agents once they are aggregated through platforms do seem to make a substantial difference either for good or for evil.

Floridi uses the concept of distributed morality to explain how such apparently morally neutral actions can lead to effects that must be morally judged. Unlike van Dijck, Floridi does not focus on the well-known global platforms such as Uber, Airbnb, Facebook, and so on. Examples he mentions—all from the United Kingdom, and all examples of the "good"—are "the shopping Samaritan (RED); plastic fidelity: the Co-operative Bank; the power of giving: JustGiving; socially oriented capitalism; P2P lending" (267). In all of these examples, the underlying mechanism is the same. In the RED platform, each time someone buys a product, the company that offers this product gives up to 50 percent of its profit to supporting AIDS help in Africa. The Co-operative Bank provides credit cards that are linked to specific charities such that the use of the cards results in contributions to these charities. Of course, we could cite Airbnb as an example of a platform that although it enables optimal use of living space, allows home or apartment owners to earn extra money, and gives many people opportunities for cheap accommodation while traveling, it also leads to abuses such as speculators buying up inner-city housing, driving up prices, and excluding those who need affordable living space in cities. The point is that small-scale activities once aggregated and scaled up by platforms can lead to significant differences in society, which must be morally evaluated. This is the task that van Dijck undertakes in the discussion of critique of platform society (see Chapter 2). For van Dijck, as we saw, the moral conflict arising from such forms of distributed morality is the conflict between what she sees as "public values" of an explicitly socialist sort as opposed to the "private values" of liberalism. Van Dijck rehearses the typically modern story of markets in opposition to governments, whereby government, contrafactually, is assumed to defend the rights of the "people" instead of the interests of influential elites. Government in this story is assigned the role of containing the immoral egoism of private marketers within morally, that is, socially acceptable bounds. Although Floridi would most probably accept this story, his primary concern is quite different. He is interested in ethics and moral theory and not social science critique. For him, what is important is that the global scale at which platforms operate transforms what would otherwise be morally neutral or insignificant actions into large-scale effects that are no longer ethically neutral. Distributed morality, therefore, makes it possible to morally qualify many activities and their consequences that would otherwise not be subject to moral judgment. It extends the moral domain into areas that formerly were not within the purview of moral assessment.

Floridi's extension of the scope of moral evaluation to include many seemingly small and insignificant actions that once they become aggregated and thus "distributed" have serious consequences raises the question of how these consequences are to be evaluated. For van Dijck this question was already answered by the modern mythology of the struggle of autonomous rational subjects for freedom, equality, and dignity against the abuses of power and exploitive actions of business and government elites. What van Dijck calls "public values" represent in Floridi's information ethics a specific form or dimension of the ethical, which he calls "infraethics." Infraethics is derived from the concept of "infrastructure." Infrastructure refers to how a society deals with the problems of efficient, effective, and fair implementation and distribution of energy, transportation, communication, food, and water and what is often called "utilities." Infrastructure is a foundation of social order, a kind of condition of the possibility of community life. Floridi assumes that there is such a thing as an *ethical infrastructure* consisting of shared values, worldviews, institutions, and so on, which allows society as a whole to make moral judgments, assign praise and blame, and sanction wrongdoers. This ethical infrastructure or "infraethics" could be equated with what sociologists and anthropologists call "culture" since it includes "a first-order framework of implicit expectations, attitudes, and practices that *can* facilitate and promote morally good decisions and actions" (272). Floridi cites a list of values such as "trust, respect, reliability, privacy, transparency, freedom of expression, openness, fair competition, and so forth" (ibid.), a list that obviously reflects the worldview of modern Western society.

Although the concept of infraethics is itself subject to ethical judgment, for example, which society has a "good" or "bad" infraethics, Floridi clearly assumes, as does van Dijck and most others who address society from a moral point of view, that the institutions of Western modernity embody and exemplify a good infraethics, that is, an infraethics that can be relied upon to judge issues of distributed morality rightly. These are the "public values" that van Dijck simply assumes everyone agrees to and which therefore offer incontrovertible criteria for judging the moral failings of platforms. Floridi goes much further when he emphasizes that infraethics "does not seek to uncover the morally good and evil," but "addresses a different problem, namely what sort of facilitating framework makes the morally good more likely to occur, and then become more stable and permanent" (273). Infraethics from this perspective is not concerned with values, but with "moral enablers." Interestingly, Floridi argues that the processes and institutions of infraethics should be seen as "agents in themselves" (274), that "when properly designed and regulated, can act as promoters and facilitators of the morally good" (ibid.). The ethical infrastructure that facilitates and supports the implementation of values is itself not a value, but, according to Floridi, "[is] better understood as intra-components of the moral system, metaphorically comparable to the lubricant of the moral machinery" (ibid.). This idea points in a similar direction to what we have discussed above as governance and design. Traditional ethical discourse, which is primarily concerned with identifying, praising and blaming, and sanctioning wrongdoers on the basis of humanist values, finds itself in today's world of complex hybrid networks forced back upon notions such as distributed morality and ethical infrastructure. These notions must be addressed on a different level and with different semantics than that which traditional ethics offers. The idea of infraethics is useful when attempting to describe how digital ethics can be redesigned as network governance.

The upshot of this discussion of Floridi's attempt to extend ethics beyond its traditional range of application limited to human beings alone and to include nonhumans, almost all activities and events, indeed, society as a whole, within the moral sphere is that a consequent ethics of information dethrones humans from their unique moral position, elevates nonhumans into the moral sphere, and extends the moral domain to include the entire world as well as the processes and institutions of governance required to bring order into the infosphere. This means that moral discourse can no longer be primarily concerned with questions of agency, accountability, and responsibility but should be concerned with complex networks of humans as well as nonhumans and with questions of how these networks can facilitate the good. Accountability means that social-technical networks can be praised and blamed from the point of view of their design, that is, good design or bad design. Responsibility implies that praise and blame fall upon the designer, who, in the case of bad design, is morally responsible for a redesign. And since the human and nonhuman agents distributively, inseparably, and co-constructively are agents and thus designers, they are the addressees of moral praise and blame in the form of imperatives to design and redesign. These imperatives, however, cannot be formulated on the basis of traditional values, but on the basis of regulative processes of network governance. For ANT, everything is accountable and responsible. In contrast, for Floridi, despite his forward-looking vision of an infraethics, only humans are responsible because only humans have conscious intentions to do either good or bad. *Our proposal to speak of agency as governance and of responsibility as well as accountability as issues of design explicitly leaves behind traditional notions of morality and ethics.* Moral blame is no longer a personal condemnation referring to a bad character, an evil will, or irresponsible actions. Instead, it is a question of good or bad design and the imperatives or redesign. Instead of Floridi's imperative to do no evil in the sense of decreasing the amount of information in the infosphere, or to do good by increasing information, what we have from the point of view of ANT is the imperative to design well and redesign when necessary. But what is design? Before we take up this question, we will look at other important contributions to reconceptualizing moral discourse in today's world that illustrate the problems of the traditional language of agency, responsibility, and accountability and shed a critical light on Floridi's attempt to "fully revise" the concept of moral agent (2103, 238).

Among those scholars who have made important contributions to addressing the moral issues of the digital transformation are Verbeek (2011, 2014), Hanson (2009), and Coeckelbergh (2019). For Verbeek, who is influenced by ANT, moral agency can never be ascribed to human individuals alone for the simple reason that humans relate to the world through technologies. Human action is always technologically "mediated," and therefore, moral decisions are produced not by autonomous agents with free will alone, but also always through the technical artifacts that enable human perception, judgment, and action. For Verbeek, "technologies are intrinsically involved in moral decision making" (2014, 77). Verbeek does not, as does Floridi, ascribe moral agency to technical artifacts themselves. Instead, he argues that "moral agency needs to be understood as a fundamentally hybrid affair" (ibid.). Floridi's solution is still based on the assumption that actions are performed by individual agents, be they human or nonhuman. This assumption prevents one from understanding that agency cannot be ascribed to any individual. Verbeek speaks of "composite moral agency" (78), which means that technological artifacts "should be located in the realm of moral agency" (ibid.), but only under the condition that one understands morality as a "coproduction of humans and nonhumans" (ibid.). This understanding of the contribution of nonhumans to agency should not be equated to Latour's technical mediation. It is not symmetrical. For Verbeek, things do not have agency, but rather things "help to organize people's moral behavior and perceptions" (80). Technologies "help to shape human interpretations of the world on the basis of which human beings make decisions" (81). It is still the human beings that make the decisions. But these human beings are no longer the autonomous rational subjects of modernity. Without the mediation of technologies, the particular actions of which people are capable would not be possible. Without automobiles, guns, medical diagnostic technologies, and so on, certain kinds of actions and moral decisions would not be possible. To sum up, for Verbeek, "morality is a hybrid affair; it cannot be located exclusively in things, but not in humans either" (ibid.). It is interesting that for Verbeek, this understanding of agency has a direct relation to design. "Conceptualizing the moral significance of things does not undermine human responsibility by blaming cars for accidents, but rather expands the ways in which we can design, implement, and use technologies in responsible ways" (80).

Hanson (2009, 2014) opposes "methodological individualism" to what he calls "composite agency theory." Methodological individualism proceeds from the assumption that only human individuals possess consciousness, free will, and the ability to calculate the effects of their actions and that, therefore, only humans can be considered moral agents and accordingly be held morally responsible. In this "individualist" view, things, artifacts, and technologies may serve as instruments or tools that humans use to do things but themselves can in no way be considered moral agents or attributed moral responsibility. Hanson argues that methodological individualism and its corresponding ethical individualism cannot do justice to present-day reality. In much the same way as Verbeek, Hanson argues that composite agency implies "joint responsibility." Joint responsibility means that the "composite" of humans and nonhumans, which is necessary for a specific action, is "jointly" responsible for the act. It is not the human individual alone who can accomplish many activities in today's world. Almost always action is possible and is performed by a composite of humans and nonhumans. Without this composite, an action is not possible. This implies that intentionality, which is usually considered an attribute exclusively ascribed to conscious individuals, must be attributed to the composite of humans and nonhumans. Hanson argues that only an act that is possible can be the object of an intention. If there are no cars or people did not drive cars, then it would be impossible for anyone to "intend" to run someone over with a car. A medieval knight could not have intended to shoot someone with a revolver. Running someone over with an automobile or shooting someone with a gun is only possible because people drive cars and have certain kinds of weapons at their disposal. It is, therefore, not acceptable to attribute the responsibility for running someone over only to the human being without also including the car. If the composite of humans and nonhumans alone can do the action, or even have the intention to do the act, then it is the composite that must be attributed agency and moral responsibility.

Hanson's view is quite different from Floridi's extension of moral agency by distinguishing between responsibility and accountability. For Floridi, only certain AAs under specific conditions can be included in the realm of moral agency. But these AAs cannot be held responsible. For Hanson, it is always the composite of humans and nonhumans that bear moral responsibility as well as accountability and never just humans or certain special nonhumans independent of the networks in which they are involved. In fact, in many cases, we do hold composites responsible for what they do. Of course, we do not punish the car that ran someone over. Still, we do dismantle and reconfigure, perhaps even re-engineer as Floridi proposes, the composite of driver, car, and maybe also alcohol when it contributed to the deed, and so on. We take away the person's driver's license, we impound the vehicle, we order that it be repaired if mechanical failures were responsible for the accident, we impose a cure for alcoholism, and so on. For Hanson, in a vein similar to Floridi's distributed morality, it is the deed that defines the doer and not the other way around.

Coeckelbergh (2019)[36] pleads for a "relational approach" to the question of the attribution of moral responsibility to artificial intelligence. Although he explicitly maintains the traditional conviction that only conscious, free, and intentional agents, that is, human beings, can be held morally responsible, he admits that traditional ethics comes up against serious problems when attempting to deal with AI and other complex socio-technical networks.[37] For understanding what responsibility means, Coeckelbergh follows Aristotle, who named two conditions for attributing moral responsibility for an action. First, "an action must have its origin in the agent" (4), which means that only if someone freely decides to do something and also is capable of doing it can they be held responsible. Second, "one must not be ignorant of what one is doing" (ibid.), or in other words, the agent must know what they are doing. This is usually called intention. Only an agent with free will, the ability to act upon decisions, and knowledge of different options to choose from can be a subject of moral attribution.[38] Only such an agent can be held morally responsible. For Coeckelbergh, it is clear that "an AI cannot really act 'freely' (as in: 'having free will') or 'know' (as in: 'being aware of') what it is doing" (ibid.). Nonetheless, it has become obvious that many technical systems, including AIs, pose problems concerning agency as well as knowledge that cannot be adequately dealt with on the basis of traditional notions of agency and responsibility.

With regard to questions of agency, Coeckelbergh points out that there are many deployments of AI in which humans "do not have sufficient control of the use of AI" (2019, 5) to allow attribution of responsibility. When one attempts to attribute responsibility, no one is to be found. This is known as the "responsibility gap" (Matthias 2004) that opens up when no one has control over the operations of a complex system. A responsibility gap can occur for various reasons. First, it can be that the AI operates

---

36 We follow the pagination of the online version in all citations of Coeckelbergh's text.
37 "It is assumed that, even if AI technologies gain more agency, humans remain responsible since only the latter can be responsible: artificial intelligence technologies can have agency but do not meet traditional criteria for moral agency and moral responsibility. Nevertheless, there are many challenges with regard to responsibility attribution and distribution, not only due to the problem of 'many hands' but also due to what I call 'many things'" (Coeckelbergh 2019, 2). What Coeckelbergh is referring to is the inherent anonymity and opacity of complex systems that undermines classical conceptions of freedom.
38 This is also the standard definition of freedom that can be found in Lock (*An Essay Concerning Human Understanding*, Book 22, Cap. 21, Paragraph 27). Willke (2019) convincingly argues that the traditional understanding of freedom is inadequate to the complexity of today's society.

independently of human intervention, for example, high-frequency trading algorithms for financial transactions or an autonomous automobile that "makes decisions" independent of human intervention. These systems operate either too quickly for human intervention or entirely independently of human decisions. Another reason for a responsibility gap can be that there are so many people involved in the development, deployment, and operation of a system that it is impossible to find a single person who can be held accountable. This is known as the "many hands" problem (van de Poel et al. 2012). In the case of an autonomous automobile causing an accident, who is to be held responsible? Is it the software developers, the manufacturer, the company that deploys the car, the "driver," other drivers involved, or the regulators who should have foreseen such eventualities, or is it finally a tragic accident for which no one can be held responsible? In such cases, Coeckelbergh admits, it makes sense to speak of "distributed responsibility."

When speaking of distributed responsibility, there are difficulties in understanding just how the "distribution" is made. It may be that among the many hands (people) involved, some could or should be held more responsible than others. Is the project leader of the developer team more responsible than team members? Is the CEO of the manufacturer more responsible than the quality control supervisor? Among the many engineers and other professionals and workers involved in the production of an autonomous vehicle, who are more responsible than others? Or should everyone be held equally accountable? And what about the users of AI? What responsibility do they share? There are many different kinds of users. For example, a hospital may decide to implement AI diagnostic technology. When something goes wrong, who is responsible: the board of directors, the CEO, the doctor in charge of the department, the consulting physician, the patient who does not demand a second opinion, among others? In addition to the problem of identifying relative levels of responsibility, there is the problem that many actors may intentionally misrepresent their contribution or in other ways attempt to evade taking responsibility. To mitigate against this possibility, all contributions from all actors to a complex network would have to be identified, tracked, registered, and made accessible when needed, which is most likely an impossible task. For these reasons, the many hands problem opens up a responsibility gap that makes the traditional attribution of responsible agency difficult if not impossible.

Along with the problems of AI actions without human intervention and the many hands problem, there is the problem of the temporal dimension in which the agency of complex socio-technical networks takes place. The various contributions of the many hands at work in a complex project occur along an indefinite and perhaps continuous and ongoing temporal trajectory that is difficult to identify, monitor, and determine. As Coeckelbergh remarks, "In the case of technology use and development, there is often a long causal chain of human agency. In the case of AI this is especially so since complex software often has a long history with many developers involved at various stages for various parts of the software" (2019, 7). How far back in the development of software does one need to go to identify where and when a decisive piece of code was written, by whom, for what purpose and follow what changes it went through over a period of time that perhaps extends months or even years? This question can be asked not only of code or software but also of hardware and many other things, artifacts, and technologies that are involved in a complex socio-technical network. This means that we are not dealing only with a problem of many hands, but as Coeckelbergh (2019) remarks, with a problem of "many things."

> In AI process and history, various software is involved but also more literally various things, material technological artifacts: things that are relevant since they causally contribute to the technological action, and that may have some degree of agency. There are many interconnected elements. For example, a malfunctioning sensor interacting with the software of an airplane may causally contribute to its crash; it is then important to find out how the technological system as a whole is structured and who is responsible for the development, use, and maintenance of its parts (for example a sensor) and the interaction between the parts.

The "many things" problem can also be formulated as the "black box" problem, namely, that the operations of a complex network are not transparent, knowable, explainable, or in every detail identifiable. In fact, this is what complexity means. Complex systems are notoriously anonymous and opaque. The reality of complex systems, quite apart from whether we are talking about AI, is that "there are many interconnected elements." In order to attempt to attribute responsibility for the actions of complex networks, it, therefore, becomes necessary "to clarify all these structural and temporal relations and interactions: not only the social interactions and roles of humans but also their interactions with things and the relations and interactions between things. In this sense, responsibility for technology is not only a matter of faces but also of interfaces" (8). Since interfaces and interactions between technologies go beyond any specific machine or system, it is difficult to determine what the addressee of responsibility attribution is. As Coeckelbergh remarks, "It is not clear where AI ends and the other technology begins" (ibid.) or even what one is talking about when speaking of AI. Since systems, in general, are defined by clear boundaries, a finite set of elements, and specific goals for their operations, the problem of many things suggests that we should speak not of complex systems but complex networks.

Networks, as opposed to systems, do not have clear boundaries, are composed of indefinite elements, and pursue multiple and changing purposes. The network has no easily definable inside or outside. If one cannot determine what causes of action are internal to a system, or better network, or are external to it, then it is difficult to know if the agent is acting "freely" or not. Freedom, as Aristotle, and Kant as well, pointed out, requires that actions not be caused by external forces but originate within the agent system. This leaves the question open of how the Aristotelean criterion of free decision can be at all applicable to complex socio-technical networks. For Coeckelbergh, these problems and open questions do not mean that attribution of responsibility in the case of complex socio-technical networks is impossible. On the contrary, "for responsibility attribution, it is important to clarify precisely what technical components are involved in a technological system, how they interact and interface, and how they contribute(d) to a problem and relate to human actors" (ibid.). This demand comes directly from the assumption that traditional criteria for attribution of responsibility can and should be maintained in today's world. The very nature of complex socio-technical networks would seem to place this assumption in question. But even if it were possible to identify who did it, the ability to identify a free and capable agent is only one of the criteria necessary for the attribution of moral responsibility. There is also the second of Aristotle's criteria, namely, the criterion that the agent, once identified as such, *knows* what it is doing.

With regard to Aristotle's criterion of knowledge, Coeckelbergh asks, "In what sense do people involved in the use and development of AI know or not know what they are doing?" (9). Even if one admits that programmers usually know what an AI system is meant to do, it is evident that there are many unintended and unforeseen consequences of AI implementations. Much of contemporary digital ethics discourse is concerned with the problems of bias and discrimination in AI systems. Minorities and marginalized groups often are not treated fairly by automatic decision making, whether it be with regard to credit risk, job screening, prison sentencing, suspicion of criminal activity, or even correct identification. It is no secret that AIs are dependent on the reliability of the data they are trained on and that most existing data sets are the results of biased and discriminatory activities, classifications, and judgments of humans acting in societies rampant with structural prejudices, racism, misogyny, xenophobia, homophobia, and so on. This being known, some (see, for example, Kleinberg et al. 2019) have argued that AI implementations need not be stopped, as organizations such as AINow[39] demand, but can be used to expose discrimination. Apart from the many issues of bias and discrimination that dominate contemporary digital ethics with regard to AI, there are legitimate concerns about the unforeseen uses and consequences of many AI systems such as the effects of automatic decision making on food or real estate prices, the functioning of communication and transportation systems, the social effects of the Internet of Things, Industry 4.0, smart homes and smart cities, or also the much-discussed effects of surveillance technologies (see the discussion of Zuboff's "surveillance capitalism" in Chapter 2) on behavior and attitudes. For Coeckelbergh (2019), all this raises the question: "To what extent developers should be aware of the potential alternative uses and misuses of their creations?" (9). This problem is magnified by the fact that even the experts often do not understand how AI works. There is an issue of a fundamental lack of transparency or unexplainability in certain AI technologies, notably machine learning and neural networks. If responsibility can only be attributed if the agent knows what it is doing and how it is doing it, it would seem that AI and many complex networks, including the people involved in these networks, cannot be held morally responsible. Coeckelbergh admits that "for advanced automation systems, machine learning AI or not: non-transparency and the absence of a sufficient degree of explainability creates a huge problem for the responsible use of AI and other automation technologies" (11). How can this problem be solved?

In the face of the fact that agency, at least with regard to complex socio-technical networks, has become *anonymous*, since we cannot identify the agent, and *opaque*, since the agent, as well as the patient, cannot understand fully what is being done and the consequences of actions, Coeckelbergh still does not give up traditional assumptions

---

39 https://ainowinstitute.org/.

about attribution of moral responsibility. Instead, he proposes a "relational approach to responsibility problems" (ibid.). The "relation" that is here decisive is that between moral agents and moral patients, that is, between those doing morally significant acts and those affected by such actions. Coeckelbergh points out that this relationship implies that moral agents have a responsibility to be accountable, that is, to respond, to communicate, or to be able to explain what they are doing and why they are doing it. The patient "demands" that the agent act responsibly "in the sense that she is expected and asked to (be able to) give reasons for her actions" (ibid.). The concept of relational responsibility emphasizes that responsibility means not only being responsible "for" some act but being responsible "to whom," that is, "answerability" (ibid.). The patient has, therefore, the right to an explanation. "The responsible patient demands an explanation from the responsible agent," which implies that "the agent needs to be able to explain to the patient why she does or did a particular action" (12).

Quite apart from the problem that is posed by attempting to strictly distinguish between agents and patients when dealing with complex socio-technical networks in which users, as well as producers, are inextricably involved, Coeckelbergh's demand amounts to maintaining the criterion of explainability despite the admitted anonymity and opacity of complex networks. Coeckelbergh demands that admittedly anonymous and opaque "agents" still be required to explain what they are doing and why. He concludes:

> Ethics of AI, then, should foster the development of AI that supports responsibility on the part of the agents of AI (users, developers) in both of these senses: they should be able to take responsibility for what they do with the AI and should be responsible in the sense of answerable to those affected (or their representatives). (Coeckelbergh 2019)

This "ethical requirement of explainability and answerability [...] needs a sufficiently transparent system as the basis for the (potential) answers" (ibid.) that must be offered. How can this requirement be met? Coeckelbergh mentions technical measures that are capable of opening the black box of AI systems as well as legal measures that "give people a right of explanation" (ibid.). Coeckelbergh is not alone is making these demands. As noted above, almost all guidelines for ethical AI and technologies generally emphasize the need for transparency and explainability.[40]

For digital ethics, accountability seems to mean explainability. A moral agent is accountable when he/she/it can explain how and why certain things happen to those affected by what he/she/it is doing. Accountability, in this sense, means that those affected by a technology can be told how the technology works, who has done what, why, or what exactly went wrong in cases of technological failure. Accountability, however, is an ambiguous norm. On the one hand, it means explainability, and on the other hand, it means responsibility. In terms of explainability, the accountability gap is not a gap between anonymous and opaque socio-technical networks and the ethical norms to which they should comply, but a gap between what the network can say about itself

---

[40] See, for example, the "Global Landscape of AI Ethics Guidelines" by Jobin et al. (2019).

and what those affected by it can understand about how it works. Explainability is a vague and uncertain standard to meet since it is difficult, if not impossible, to know what constitutes "understanding."[41] Despite what ethicists and regulators might suppose, understanding is what moral patients say it is and not something that can be objectively described. If someone understands an explanation, then fine, and if they don't, one can try to explain again. If they still don't understand, one can say it's their fault, or one can say that the system cannot be explained. How many people can understand Einstein's theory of relativity or quantum mechanics? Many experts have said that one should not try to understand quantum mechanics, but simply do the math and leave what it might mean an open question. Explainability can, therefore, not be an ethical norm, since it may well be that an action or a process cannot be understood by those affected by it. Ought implies can. If something cannot be understood, there can be no normative expectation of explainability. On the other hand, accountability means responsibility in the sense of being subject to moral praise or blame. Merely understanding why something happened has nothing to do with whether what happened is morally right or wrong, or that someone or some organization can be held responsible and morally praised or blamed. One may be able to explain the repressive actions of the police by referring to the authoritarian policies of the government. But whether or not these policies are just, legitimate, and morally acceptable or not is a different question. One may be able to make supposedly discriminatory outcomes of an AI system understandable by reference to biased training data, but the question of what exactly is to be considered discrimination and who or what is to blame is an entirely different issue that has nothing to do with understanding how the AI works. Despite these difficulties, accountability has become a central issue in digital ethics and is inseparably bound up with such fundamental ethical concepts as agency, responsibility, and moral praise and blame.

It may be that the digital transformation has created a world in which it is not possible to find responsible agents and adequately explain what complex networks do and how they do it. If this is the case, and it remains to be shown that it is not, we must conclude that traditional notions of agency and of the attribution of moral responsibility, as well as demands that agents identify and explain themselves, are not helpful. It is not an adequate response to the digital transformation to stubbornly repeat unrealistic demands that we be given explanations allowing us to find those responsible for network failures and hold them accountable. Perhaps such agents no longer exist. Perhaps, if it is so that we have never been modern, they never did exist. Perhaps traditional notions of agency, responsibility, accountability, praise, and blame based as they are upon the autonomous

---

41 Under the pressure of an asserted, but controversial "right to explanation" (see https://en.wikipedia.org/wiki/Right_to_explanation for an overview), derived from consumer protection and privacy regulations (see, for example, GDPR (Art. 13, 14, and Recital 71), regulators are offering legal definitions of explainability. See, for example, the United Kingdom's Information Commissioner's Office document "Explaining Decisions Made with AI" (https://ico.org.uk/for-organisations/guide-to-data-protection/key-data-protection-themes/explaining-decisions-made-with-artificial-intelligence/). It would seem that in the future it will be the courts and not the engineers and scientists who will decide what an explanation is.

rational subject are not adequate to today's world. It may be necessary to drop the entire semantics of moral agency. It would seem that what the above discussion of moral agency and the problems of attribution of moral responsibility in a world characterized by complex socio-technical networks shows is that the entire humanist discourse of moral agency collapses. The consequence would be that the semantics of moral agency, free will, responsibility, accountability, and praise and blame can no longer be used to develop an ethics for today's social and technical reality. What alternative semantics, what other ethics, do we have?

3.3.2 Case Study: Google's Framework for Internal Algorithmic Auditing

One recent attempt to solve the two problems of many hands and many things from the perspective of accountability comes from Google with the participation of the Partnership on AI.[42] Under the title *Closing the AI Accountability Gap: Defining an End-to-End Framework for Internal Algorithmic Auditing*, the authors propose a six-step process for the purpose of "defining and monitoring potentially adverse outcomes, and anticipating harmful feedback loops and system-level risks" (Raji et al. 2020, 33). With regard to AI systems, but with potential application to all socio-technical networks, the proposed auditing process intends "to anticipate potential negative consequences before they occur, in addition to providing decision support to design mitigations" (ibid.). Unlike Coeckelbergh and many others, accountability for the authors of the auditing framework is not primarily an explanation of how things work but is broader in scope. Accountability is "the state of being responsible or answerable for a system, its behavior and its potential impacts" (34), which potentially includes users as well as producers, and nonhumans as well. Responsibility means compliance to ethical norms. In line with traditional assumptions, the authors do not think that algorithms can be held responsible since they "are not moral or legal agents," but "the organizations designing and deploying algorithms can through *governance* structures" (ibid.).[43] The move from moral admonitions to governance is important. The governance structures that guarantee accountability and responsibility do not aim to ensure merely technical or functional compliance but also ethical compliance.

> A separate governance structure is necessary for the evaluation of these systems for ethical compliance. This evaluation can be embedded in the established quality assurance workflow

---

42 See Raji et al. (2020).

43 This marks an important difference between Google's Auditing Framework and the typical moral admonitions illustrated by Floridi et al. (2020), wherein the authors describe "the essential factors that support and underwrite the design and deployment of successful AI4SG [AI for Social Good]." These factors are: (1) falsifiability and incremental deployment; (2) safeguards against the manipulation of predictors; (3) receiver-contextualized intervention; (4) receiver-contextualized explanation and transparent purposes; (5) privacy protection and data subject consent; (6) situational fairness; and (7) human-friendly semanticization. These demands are not governance structures or processes, but moral admonitions.

but serves a different purpose, evaluating and optimizing for a different goal centered on social benefits and values rather than typical performance metrics such as accuracy or profit. (ibid.)

For Google, auditing is related to ethics as compliance is related to regulation. This means that the work of establishing rules and standards, whether technical or moral, goes *before* auditing and is not part of the audit, which is concerned only with ensuring compliance with existing regulations. The ethical work of establishing norms and values that should guide AI, or for that matter, any socio-technical network, must be done outside of and before the audit. The audit process itself is not ethics. The proposed framework for closing the accountability gap in AI is, therefore, a matter of "auditing" in the classical sense of "tools for interrogating complex processes, often to determine whether they comply with company policy, industry standards or regulations" (34). What is new about Google's proposal is that the standards to which compliance are to be evaluated are ethical norms and values and not merely technical standards. Also new, as we shall see, is the proposal that the audit be *internal* and not external to the design and development of an AI system. Google's governance framework can be understood as the response of the industry to the demands critics make that AI be ethically accountable. Digital ethics has been especially critical of AI and especially active with regard to proclaiming guidelines for AI, but there have been few answers to the question of how ethical demands are to be implemented. This is where Google's proposal fills a gap. It does not attempt to describe or ground any moral norms or values. But it does offer a concrete and practical answer to the question of how compliance to given norms can be demonstrated. Furthermore, and more relevant to our concerns, it could be understood as a stepping stone to new approaches to digital ethics.

Citing well-defined and long-implemented methods for safety audits, risk assessment, and responsible innovation in industries such as aerospace, pharmaceuticals, medical technology, or the financial sector, the authors propose to adapt and extend these principles and practices to create a framework for the "internal" auditing of AI systems. Internal audits are carried out by the organization developing an AI system and not, as is usual for most auditing, by external experts or specially designated auditors. An internal audit accompanies the development of an AI system from its inception, instead of coming only after development and deployment. In addition to this, an internal audit has access to information and persons who are usually not easily accessible to outsiders. This makes the auditing process, at least in principle, a part of the design and development process. Indeed, it could be asked how the proposed framework differs from what could be called "good design" and why it needs to be described as a separate process called "auditing" at all. Of course, the answer to this question is ready to hand. An audit is usually not concerned with ethics, with establishing norms or values to which socio-technical systems should comply, but with the evaluation of compliance to already established standards. Ethical norms are not embedded in or derived from the auditing process itself. What determines whether a design is "good" or "bad" is not a quality of the design process itself, as we propose below that it should be, but an external criterion. The proposed framework for closing the accountability gap, therefore, is not itself digital ethics, but a method for judging whether or not designers and developers comply with specific ethical guidelines that are given at the outset. We will argue below that this need not be so. It could be that the accountability gap can only be closed when there is no gap between the auditing process and the design and development process. With this question in mind, a question to which we will return when discussing the nature of design below, let us take a closer look at how the authors propose to "close the accountability gap" for AI. The framework is called SMACTR, which stands for the six phases of scoping, mapping, artifact collection, testing, reflection, and finally, a post-audit.

Scoping, as the name suggests, refers to the activities involved in determining the scope of the audit. Where does the project come from? What exactly is the product or system that is to be designed and developed? What are the goals? Apart from functional specifications, what ethical values and norms are guiding the project? The scoping phase must answer these questions. As the authors put it, "The goal of the scoping stage is to clarify the objective of the audit by reviewing the motivations and intended impact of the investigated system, and confirming the principles and values meant to guide product development" (39). The authors emphasize the ethical aspect of this phase. There are two "artifacts" that are produced at this stage: the "ethical review of system use case" and a "social impact assessment." "When a potential AI system is in the development pipeline, it should be reviewed with a series of questions that first and foremost check to see, at a high level, whether the technology aligns with a set of ethical values or principles" (ibid.). What the principles are and whether the proposed system complies with them is documented in an ethical review. In addition to ethical review, the scoping phase must produce a social impact analysis that explicitly requires the inclusion of diverse perspectives and reflection on possible bias. The social impact assessment aims to "describe how the use of an artificial intelligence system might change people's ways of life, their culture, their community, their political systems, their environment, their health and well-being, their personal property rights, and their experiences (positive or negative)" (ibid.). This is a very demanding requirement that can hardly be completed within the scope of any kind of audit. Indeed, if we take this demand seriously, the scope of the project seems to extend in all directions indefinitely. How can this challenge be met? We will offer an answer in the discussion of governance by design below. At the moment, let us return to Google's proposed solution.

What is required in this first phase of the audit goes way beyond what can be ascertained by interviewing a few representatives of user groups that might be affected by the system. In many ways, scoping is similar to what we have described above as the network governance principle of *taking account of*, which itself is related to Ostrom's common pool resource governance principle of determining the nature of the resource to be administered and its intended uses. Governance must always begin with answering the question of what is to be governed. The important issue here is guaranteeing that the nature and scope of the network or, in the case of Google's audit framework, the AI project, is determined in such a way that no potential voices are left out of account. Furthermore, from the point of view of network governance, this means that we are talking about an ongoing process and not a stage or phase in an audit. This problem highlights the crucial difference between governance and auditing. An audit is an evaluation of a process and not the process itself. Governance, on the contrary, regulates the process. Of course, good governance can include audits, but the audit is then part of an ongoing and encompassing governance framework and not an independent instance that has a clear beginning and an end and a clearly defined domain of application.

The second stage of Google's end-to-end framework for algorithmic auditing is called "mapping." The purpose of this stage is "to map internal stakeholders, identify key collaborators for the execution of the audit, and orchestrate the appropriate stakeholder buy-in required for execution" (ibid.). The question to be answered at this stage is who is involved in the project, with regard to both those designing and implementing the project and those who audit the project. At this stage, the authors propose that all documented and known issues with the technology be collected and made available for review as well as that interviews with key stakeholders and collaborators be undertaken using ethnographic methods to gain a deeper understanding of the design and development processes to be used in the project. As this methodology suggests, the auditors are external observers, much like an ethnologist working in the field. There is an interesting methodological debate in ethnology about whether external observation is less reliable than participatory observation and the extent to which the ethnologist can become a participant in the culture being studied and still retain scientific objectivity. "Going native" is automatically associated with losing the distance and objectivity necessary for scientific description, while on the other hand, it is asserted to be the only way a foreign culture can be understood. One can only understand what a particular custom or ritual means when one can participate and experience it from the inside. Otherwise, one is only talking about what informants say, but not what it means as experienced. Here again, the distinction between governance and auditing becomes essential. Since the audit framework that Google proposes, despite emphasizing that it is a matter of an "internal" audit, maintains the distance between auditors and designers and developers, it would seem that the "internal" perspective is not internal in the ethnological sense at all. The auditors are concerned with compliance and not with themselves contributing or being able to contribute to the design and development of the system. They are not participant observers, but external observers. This is reflected in the fact that the results of the stakeholder interviews that are supposedly undertaken following ethnological methods are documented in a "stakeholder map" and an "ethnographic field study" (40).

Here again, there is a striking resemblance to what we have described above as the network governance principle of "producing stakeholders." One of the core design principles of Ostrom's common pool resource governance regimes demands that the distribution of costs and benefits be determined by negotiations among stakeholders. Good governance, for Ostrom, requires not only that the resource to be collectively administered be clearly circumscribed but also that those involved be clearly identified. Similarly, in network governance, it is necessary to produce stakeholders, whereby the idea that stakeholders are not merely given but "produced" is essential. What the authors of Google's auditing framework describe as "mapping" should be seen as an act of construction, of producing those who are to play important roles in the design and development of the AI system in question. This phase of the audit implies, again, that what we are dealing with is much closer to governance than to auditing. As Latour would put it, the network is the actor, which means that stakeholders are produced by the network and not merely given. As with all network governance principles, producing stakeholders is much more a process than a principle or a stage that is done and then finished. Just as scoping, mapping must be understood to be an ongoing process of identity construction on the basis of which roles, as well as privileges and responsibilities, are created and distributed. From the point of view of governance instead of auditing, the implication is that going native is the only way for the auditors to gain access to the stakeholders and thus enabling what the Google framework demands, but this is only possible at the expense of becoming a stakeholder oneself.

The third stage of the SMACTR framework is called the "artifact collection stage." From this point on, it is clear that we are dealing with auditing and not governance. From the point of view of auditing, documentation is necessary to ensure transparency and accountability. The auditors must have access to documentation of all aspects of the design and development process, the stakeholders involved, and known issues with the technology. This extensive documentation is what closes the accountability gap since it now becomes possible to fulfill Coeckelbergh's demands that AI developers be responsible to those affected by AI systems by being able to explain how systems were designed and developed. Every step of the design and development process is documented. Examples of documents that are to be collected at this stage are "a record of data and model dynamics through application-based systems" and "other product development artifacts such as design documents and reviews, in addition to systems architecture diagrams and other implementation planning documents and retrospectives" (ibid.). Artifacts produced during this phase are a "design checklist" or "inventory" of all documentation that is expected to be generated by the design and development process. Also, anticipated risks or harms caused by the system and clear declarations of intended use cases and purposes of the system are documented in "datasheets and model cards" (ibid.). However, it remains questionable what use such documentation is to users affected by the system. Can their demands for an explanation really be met by extensive technical documentation? Would Coeckelbergh's demand for relational responsibility truly be met by handing over a thick bundle of documents? If not, what other kinds of explanation could they be given? And finally, as we saw above when discussing accountability as an explanation, who is to decide what counts as an explanation?

The fourth stage is the actual testing of the system. Until this stage, the auditors have only collected documentation. Now they do hands-on testing of whether or not the system complies with the ethical norms that were designated in the scoping phase. The testing process results in two artifacts: a report on the "adversarial testing" aimed to find bugs or risks in the system and an "ethical risk analysis chart" that assesses the likelihood of a failure and its severity. After thorough testing, the "reflection stage" compares test results with ethical demands and determines what ethical concerns are raised by the system. It is at this fifth stage in the auditing process that an "algorithmic use-related risk analysis," a "remediation and risk mitigation plan," an "algorithmic design history file," and finally an "algorithmic audit summary report" are produced. These documents enable the sixth stage, namely, the "post-audit" decision-making process about whether to implement the system as planned, to redesign certain system functions, not to deploy, or to deploy in a different manner than initially proposed, and so on.

This short description does not do justice to the differentiated and carefully worked-out auditing framework the authors propose to close the accountability gap in AI. Nonetheless, it does allow us to point out both the strengths and the possible shortcomings of Google's proposed solution. The authors themselves conclude with a reminder that the very idea of an internal audit is open to the objection of partiality. On the one hand, an audit demands objective, impartial, and non-biased evaluation. This demand is usually met by seeing to it that the audit is carried out by experts external to the processes and the organization that is being audited. How can an internal audit be objective and impartial? For this reason, the authors admit the limitations of the idea of an internal audit. "To avoid audits becoming simply acts of reputation management for an organization, the auditors should be mindful of their own and the organizations' biases and viewpoints" (42). There must be an awareness "that internal audits are only one important aspect of a broader system of required quality checks and balances" (ibid.). To be a credible audit, the internal audit must, in the end, be reexamined and checked by an external audit. A purely internal audit is no audit at all. On the practical level, however, the Google framework is an ingenious solution to the accountability gap that will undoubtedly foster trust in AI and reassure AI's critics. The theoretical problem here is that the very concept of an audit requires that the evaluation process be separated from the design and development processes that are being evaluated. Ethical judgments are not part of the design process, but external to them.

A second difficulty is that the auditing process is non-iterative and comes only at certain well-defined and segmented phases or stages. The moral judgment about whether a system complies with specific ethical standards comes only at the end of the process. Google's innovative proposal of an "internal" audit does not change the basic concept of what an audit is and how it works. At this point the difference between auditing and governance becomes crucial. Even though the audit may be internal and thus accompany the design and development process, it does so only by documenting the various stages, decisions, and activities, but not by intervening, correcting, participating, and thus becoming a part of design and development process itself. Governance, however, is exactly this. It is the self-regulatory intervening, correcting, and participating in the design and development process. The audit paradigm is concerned with compliance to standards that are established by external authorities, fixed at the outset, and themselves never part of the design and development process. Ethics are not being designed, only technical artifacts. Even when the designers follow the demands of agile project management and design thinking and involve the end users of a product in the conception, planning, prototyping, producing, and implementing of the product and through iterative processes often change the specifications, use cases, expectations, and so on of the product, the auditors do not. The auditors are not flexible and agile when it comes to assessing the ethical standards to which the product ought to comply. They do not ask the stakeholders, the designers, and users what values they want to see embedded in the product. They simply assume that the demands of those proclaiming ethical guidelines are valid and must be accepted as standards to which the product must comply. These considerations lead to the question of what it is that we are talking about when speaking of design? What is the process that is finally responsible for complex socio-technical networks?

3.3.3 What Is Design?

If the world consists of information that is embodied in complex socio-technical networks, which because they are anonymous and opaque do not lend themselves to traditional moral and ethical evaluation, moral agency, as Floridi rightly remarked, must be fundamentally reconceived. In order to understand what agency can mean when we no longer presuppose the autonomous rational subject of Western modernity, let us turn to a form of agency that in recent years has gained enormously in significance and scope. This is design. Latour finds at least five "advantages" that the concept of design offers, which indicate "a sea change in our collective definition of action" (4). These five characteristics of design show how networking, mediation, the construction of meaning, and, therefore, the regulation of social order in today's world can be understood as design. First, design is "humble" as opposed to the *hubris* of revolution, modernization, progress, and sovereign decision. Prometheus is often cited as the hero who stole fire from the Gods and gave it to humans. His path was direct and unwavering. He took what he wanted and, as we know, suffered the consequences. The idea of the humble designer is much closer to the story of Daedalus than of Prometheus. Daedalus was the craftsman who never took a straight path toward his goal, but always took clever detours and enlisted the help of many things along the way. He was a designer and not a hero. His attitude was humble, and he respected what things had to offer in constructing solutions. Latour sees in the growing significance of the concept of design a "post Promethean theory of action" (ibid.).

The second advantage of a theory of action based on design is "an attentiveness to *details* that is completely lacking in the heroic, Promethean, hubristic dream of action" (ibid.; emphasis in original) that typifies modernity. The ideal of progress, of enlightenment, of critique, and of humans building their own destiny, which defines the modern spirit, has never been part of what it meant to design something well. On the contrary, "a mad attention to the details has always been attached to the very definition of design skills" (ibid.). This does not necessarily imply that design cannot be in any sense "revolutionary," but if it is, then in a way that does not trample over everything that came before it and neglect many aspects of the present simply pushing them aside in order to swiftly march into the supposedly better future. Latour points out that today when we are forced to consider redesigning the earth's climate, "what it means to 'make' something is also being deeply modified" (ibid.). Making is no longer a heroic act, but an act that takes account of many things, many details, and many voices. To be well made, that is, well designed, today means that planning and development are "agile," that is, always in close and open communication with all participants, stakeholders, interested parties, and users and able to change and adjust quickly and flexibly to changing needs and preferences.[44]

---

44 See for a short summary of "design thinking" the Wikipedia article https://en.wikipedia.org/wiki/Design_thinking. For "agile," see Wikipedia https://en.wikipedia.org/wiki/Agile_software_development.

The third advantage of the concept of design comes from its inseparable connection with meaning. Design, as is the case with any artistic endeavor, aims at meaning. Artifacts, solutions, programs, processes, organizations, indeed, whatever is designed demands interpretation. "Design lends itself to interpretation, it is made to be interpreted in the language of things" (ibid.). "Whenever you think of something as being designed, you bring all of the tools, skills and crafts of interpretation to the analysis of that thing" (ibid.). What following the actors reveals is that things are not mere matters of fact, not objects that are simply given, but hubs in networks of relations that are often extensive, complex, contradictory, open-ended, and undetermined. As Latour (2004a) puts it, matters of fact become *matters of concern*.[45] Just as Floridi and many others, Latour also recognizes the significance of the digital transformation in bringing to awareness the informational nature of reality. "When almost every feature of digitized artifacts is 'written down' in codes and software, it is no wonder that hermeneutics have seeped deeper and deeper into the very definition of materiality" (ibid.). Despite his acknowledgment of the close association between design and hermeneutics as well as of the significance of the digital transformation, Latour himself does not go so far as to develop his notion of technical mediation and his relational ontology of irreduction into an explicit theory of meaning and information in which design could then come to designate the fundamental character of agency.[46] Design, as Latour points out, is the construction of meaning. It is that activity that distinguishes the hunter wielding a stone ax from the stone picked up and used by an ape. The ape is not a designer. Design is *meaning in action* instead of action without meaning. Interestingly, design is the only action that, according to Floridi's imperative to increase the amount of information in the infosphere, could be qualified as morally good.

The fourth advantage that the idea of design, according to Latour, brings to understanding the nature of action is that design "never begins from scratch: to design is always to *redesign*" (5; emphasis in original). This aspect of design is what Floridi appealed to under the title of re-engineering as an appropriate moral response to systemic failures. We do not punish machines or complex networks when they are found to cause morally qualifiable harm. What we can do and *ought to do* is to re-engineer or "redesign" them. Latour traces the roots of this possibility directly to design. Design stands in opposition to creation, revolution, and autonomy. Design can, therefore, never be critique in the modern sense of Descartes's methodological skepticism or Kant's appeal to radical self-determination. The tradition of critical sociology is not a tradition of design. "Designing is the antidote to founding, colonizing, establishing, or breaking with the past. It is an antidote to hubris and to the search for absolute certainty, absolute beginnings, and radical departures" (ibid.). This aspect of design is similar to what Heidegger says about human existence being "thrown" into the world (*Geworfenheit*) and being necessarily conditioned by the given historical situation. What for Heidegger constitutes *dasein*'s facticity,

---

45 See Stephan (2015) for a discussion of Latour's notion of matters of concern from the point of view of design theory.
46 For the development of ANT into a theory of meaning and information, see Krieger and Belliger (2014).

historicity, and finitude is what makes action understood as design fundamentally different from usual conceptions of moral agency based as they are upon free will, sovereign decision, self-determination, and autonomy. The autonomous rational subject may be able to become a revolutionary, but he cannot be a good designer. The reason for this is that the designer must be humble enough to take account of many things, many details, all their possible meanings, and where they have come from. This implies that it is never merely something, some object, a single artifact, an individual entity that is designed, but a network with relations branching out in all directions, into the future as well as the past. Design means taking something up into a network and thereby constructing not only a particular thing but re-engineering an entire network. Indeed, design is networking.

Finally, the fifth advantage offered by design is "that it necessarily involves an ethical dimension which is tied into the obvious question of *good versus bad design*" (ibid.; emphasis in original). As Latour puts it, "The spread of design to the inner definitions of things carries with it not only meaning and hermeneutics, but also morality" as if "materiality and morality were finally coalescing" (ibid.). Once it is clear that objects are also subjects, that matters of fact are matters of concern, that substance has become information and meaning, and that action is design, the ought can no longer an ideal to which reality must aspire, but instead it becomes a quality of the real. This is the consequence of an informational ontology and informational ethics. Whenever information constructs itself, design is at issue. Technical mediation, networking, and the construction of information are preeminently ethical issues. But we are no longer talking about ethics and morality as a kind of add-on to the functional activities of modern life. Recalling Luhmann's functional subsystems, "good" business, "good" research, "good" education need not be morally good, but merely functionally successful. From the functional perspective, this is the only good there is. This is why modern society everywhere attempts to add on to every profession, every social action, an applied ethics. From the point of view of a global network society, function is subordinated to design and not the other way around. Good design is not a mere aesthetic add-on to functionality, just as a network is not a system. Heidegger may well have been right when he designated technology as *Gestell*, that is, the subordination of all activity to functionality and systemic closure. But *Gestell* is not networking. Heidegger's critique of technology was not talking about the unofficial morality guiding the production and deployment of hybrids. He was referring to the dominance of the systemic paradigm of order in the modern world. The digital transformation has brought forth another world mapped out by points of reference different from the primacy of functionality, autonomous rational subjects, the strict distinction between society and nature, the unbridgeable gap between subjects and objects, and the constitutive distinction between what is and what ought to be. If there is to be an ethics for this world, and if this world is fundamentally conditioned by the digital transformation, then design is perhaps how moral action must be understood.[47]

---

[47] The broader social and moral implications of design have long been discussed under the title of "social design." See, for example, Papanek (1984) and Margolin (2002). For the association of ethics with design, see Dignum et al. (2018).

3.4 Digital Ethics

We have argued that digital ethics in its contemporary form is not digital ethics at all but instead the attempt to reassert the values, norms, and regulatory regimes of Western industrial society in the face of the digital transformation. Contemporary ethical discourse runs on legacy systems composed of the philosophical mythology of humanism, the tradition of modern social science critique, media scandalization, and the efforts of a multitude of what can be designated civil society actors lobbying for either more or less regulation. What appears everywhere today as morality and ethics comprises these four forms of moralizing and has little to do with the digital transformation apart from perceiving it as a threat to traditional values and institutions. Moralizing, following Luhmann's definition of the word, is the attempt to articulate the "actually practiced conditions of mutual respect and disrespect" that establish any community or society. Moralizing functions socially to construct a specific form of the social bond, a horizon of mutual recognition, and the very possibility of participating in society. Indeed, what is at stake in morality and ethics is a world, that is, convictions about reality, truth, human nature, and, last but not least, the good. The rightness of this world, its reliability, and the assumption that this is the only world we've got and that therefore it must be the best of all possible worlds is what our hack has called into question. The pride of the hacker lies not only in revealing the bugs in established systems but also in at least attempting to suggest how things could be done better. If the discourse of digital ethics currently leaves the task of an ethics for the digital world undone, then what can our hack contribute to changing this unfortunate situation?

The first requirement of a digital ethics is to orient itself on the values and norms inherent in the affordances of digital networks. The orientation toward the affordances of nonhuman actors is what Latour has called the "unofficial morality," which, although it effectively guided the construction and deployment of hybrids throughout history, was hidden by the modern preoccupation of humans with themselves and the anthropocentric ethics that expresses this preoccupation. Latour insists that we have never been modern, and therefore, the path to ground digital ethics on the unofficial morality that modernity covered over is open to explore. What are the values and norms inherent in digital networks? We have proposed to name these "network norms" *connectivity, flow, communication, participation, transparency, authenticity,* and *flexibility*. These are the new values of the global network society. These are the values that replace what has heretofore been understood as human nature, pure reason, the will of God, or the unsurpassable achievements of European cultural evolution. These are not norms or values in the traditional sense of imperatives stating what human beings "ought" to do and become, as opposed to what they sadly are. The network norms that make up the unofficial morality of networking are beyond the distinction between "is" and "ought." They are not intended to guide the behavior of autonomous rational subjects understood to be those beings with free will and intentionality and, therefore, capable of being attributed moral responsibility. Network norms apply to nonhumans as well as humans. They govern actions that are *at once distributed and symmetrical*, that is, the actions of networks. Networks are neither individual nor social nor purely technical. The norms and values that govern networks are neither the product of free will nor any higher power, whether cultural, political, social, or moral. Perhaps one should not speak of "norms" or "values" at all but leave these terms to traditional ethics. Instead of norms and values, digital ethics would be concerned with networking, governance of networking, and design.

The network norms are not typical ethical imperatives, but instead, descriptions of how successful networks under the conditions of digital affordances, *provided they are designed well*, work. The network norms are indeed rules. They do influence, nudge, and perhaps often compel compliance. They are a form of regulation that most closely resembles what has come to be called governance instead of government. This comes from the fact that networks are constituted by information. As we saw, Floridi's philosophy of information recognizes the ontological priority of information, but not its relational nature. This becomes apparent in the attempt of his ethics of information to preserve the autonomy and individuality of the humanist individual by means of privacy. ANT showed us that information is relational, and therefore, no bounded individuals can be constituted by information. What is real is networks and not substances. Networks are constructed by information. In networks, agency is at once distributed and symmetrical because all actors involved co-construct information. No single actor is either responsible or accountable but always the network. Indeed, the network is the actor, and every actor is always a network. We no longer have autonomous rational subjects acting on the basis of free will and bearing, therefore, moral responsibility for their actions. Instead, we have a world in which information acts upon information. Already Luhmann envisioned society as a system of communications wherein communications act upon communications, and human beings are consequently banned into the environment of the social system and are allowed to remain in society only as artifacts of communication. For Luhmann, only communication communicates, and therefore, society does not consist of human beings. Similarly, for ANT, information acts upon information, and therefore, human beings do not create information. Instead, under certain historic circumstances, information constructs some actors as human beings and can, therefore, construct them otherwise whenever this should be required.

This "posthuman" view of social order is a world in which both humans and nonhumans participate symmetrically in the construction of information. To be philosophically correct, one would probably have to put this fundamental statement the other way around; information uses humans and nonhumans to construct itself. Information constitutes the networks of which our world consists. Floridi's philosophy of information arrives at a similar conclusion in that being is information, and human beings are inforgs that exist in an infosphere. Despite his attachment to Western humanism, Floridi does follow the lead of new technologies far enough to propose extending moral agency beyond human beings to include some machines as well as envisioning an ethical infrastructure that could be understood as a governance framework providing forms of regulation that go beyond traditional values and norms. We have seen that others as well, such as Verbeek, Hanson, and Coeckelbergh, acknowledge the need to depart from traditional moral discourse in order to address the unique moral issues posed by the digital transformation. In the end, as we have tried to show, the conventional moral semantics of agency, praise and blame, responsibility, accountability, and punishment or retribution seems no longer able to constitute a consistent and viable moral discourse. What then is left? Perhaps nothing is left, and we must start over, start anew in a new situation. This is the proper task of digital ethics.

Because of the relational nature of information and its unique ontological status, information cannot be regulated by either public or private forms of ownership or administration. The unofficial morality of networking that Latour speaks of is better understood as a governance framework than trying to describe it in terms of the traditional regulatory and moral semantics of agency, decision, responsibility, accountability, and things that can be owned and administered. Governance, as we saw above, is reducible neither to law nor to morality. Recalling Luhmann's distinction between morality and law, whereby law is characterized by adaptive learning and morality by the refusal to learn, governance is something different from both. Principles of governance are much more like practical rules of thumb derived from experience but not easily revisable the more complex networks become. Since they are processes and not principles in the usual sense of fixed criteria to which procedures must comply, they do not fit neatly into either the statutes of positive law or the universal truths of morality. The traditional options of either adaptive learning or refusal to learn are no longer exclusive. There is a new possibility, namely, constructing networks, mediating, developing and deploying hybrids, or simply networking. To say that moral agency is no longer a helpful idea is to assume one can talk about agency in other ways. We propose speaking of *design*. Design in this sense of the term we are proposing is not something that only certain people who are known as "designers" do. It designates the fundamental nature of action, agency, responsibility, and knowledge apart from humanist assumptions about autonomous rational subjects. Digital ethics, therefore, is not an ethics about moral agents, about the values they should hold, about the responsibilities they bear, and about the accountability to which they are called. Digital ethics does not consist of lists of guidelines about what makes computer programming, deployment of autonomous socio-technical networks, business, or political decisions good or evil—digital ethics concerns itself with a governance framework defining and thus regulating "good" design.

Digital ethics is a design process instituted in a governance framework that is influenced by the network norms of connectivity, flow, communication, participation, transparency, authenticity, and flexibility. Much of what Latour has found as promising and significant in the concept of design already anticipates, or formulates in its own way, what could be understood as digital ethics. What is the governance framework of digital ethics, and what are the principles of good design that constitute it?

As mentioned above, the general principles of network governance, those principles that make up the unofficial morality that has always guided the assembly of hybrids, can be said to be

1. *Taking account of*
2. *Producing stakeholders*
3. *Prioritizing*
4. *Instituted and excluding*
5. *Localizing and globalizing*
6. *Separating powers*

These governance principles, or much rather processes, apply to all networks or even more correctly to the activity of networking as such and not exclusively to digital networks. For these governance processes to become the basis of digital ethics, they must be interpreted in terms of the affordances of digital technologies. The affordances of digital technologies have created new values that we have termed "network norms." What do the above-listed general network governance principles look like when they are understood from the point of view of network norms?

The problems that traditional accounts of moral agency and responsibility face in today's world of complex socio-technical networks show that nonhumans have become significant "agents," "voices," and "stakeholders" in society. They demand to be *taken account of*. The network governance process of *taking account of* manifests itself after the digital transformation in practices of design that implement the network norms of *connectivity* and *flow*. Good design of socio-technical networks looks to see that all relevant voices are connected and that the flow of information is secured. This notion of good design is completely opposed to Floridi's claim that privacy demands disconnecting sources of information and blocking information flows. But it is completely in accord with his moral imperative to increase the amount of information in the infosphere. Only by connectivity and flow can all relevant voices be heard and taken account of. Coeckelbergh, as we saw above, pleads for the design of complex networks that allow maximum transparency and accountability. This can only be approached by a design that implements connectivity and flow. From this point of view, design stands in service of responsibility and accountability. Designing for connectivity and flow, furthermore, amounts to what Floridi calls ethical infrastructure since it aims to engineer and re-engineer socio-technical networks in such a way that all relevant voices can be heard, can contribute to the collective, and can be answerable to each other. Only within a governance framework that operates by implementing connectivity and flow through good design is a relational notion of responsibility, such as Coeckelbergh suggests, realizable. Responsibility means putting all actors in the network into relations that allow information to flow, be exchanged, and be utilized. This could be called "responsibility by design" and could also serve as an excellent example of what Hanson terms "composite agency." Only when actors are connected and when information is allowed to flow can actors contribute to the collective. The importance of such contributions to democracy has been expressed in notions of free speech.[48] That all actors are allowed to participate is one of the core governance principles that Ostrom already identified for successful common pool resource governance regimes. When dealing with information, which is more like a common good than private property, it makes no sense to unnecessarily exclude anyone or anything or to limit in any way the construction of information; indeed, it is morally questionable and would amount to bad design. Good design is design for *connectivity* and *flow*, for this is how all relevant voices can be taken account of.

---

48 See Balkin (2004, 2008, 2016) for a theory of democratic culture based on the right to free information construction. For a discussion, see Belliger and Krieger (2016).

As Coeckelbergh noted, complex socio-technical networks are composed of many parts, elements, technologies, people, organizations, and involve inseparable and mutual relations between agents and patients. This means that socio-technical networks are characterized by the problem of many hands as well as the problem of many things. For this reason, they are notoriously anonymous when it comes to attribution of responsibility as well as opaque when it comes to accountability. Good design addresses this problem by implementing the network governance principle of *producing stakeholders*. Stakeholders are produced by following the network norms of *communication* and *participation*. Not all components or elements of a complex network are stakeholders. Many are not mediators, but, as ANT puts it, mere intermediaries, that is, functional elements in systemic black boxes. Insignificant components could still at any time become significant and make decisive contributions to the network, its identity, trajectory, or program of action. Indeed, any actor in a network can become a mediator and change the network in significant ways. The fact that actors in a network cannot be reduced to functional elements is an essential characteristic of networks as opposed to systems. It is also something that good design must take account of. Nonetheless, since every network has a trajectory, a program of action, and specific goals that it pursues, not all components are at any time involved in the mediation of the network and in the construction of information. Those who are can be considered stakeholders. Producing stakeholders means identifying and enabling *communication* and *participation*. *Communication* and *participation* are what stakeholders do. Good design produces stakeholders who are those actors in the network that *participate* and *communicate*.

There is no doubt that the digital transformation has made the production of stakeholders more distributed, complex, varied, and much greater in number than in traditional hierarchical forms of order. The above-cited problems of many hands and many things are a result of the disruptive dynamics of networking in today's world. This accounts for the apparent anonymity and opacity of complex socio-technical networks as well as for the fact that almost everyone and everything can appear as participants and sources of information. Anonymity and opacity mean that there are no longer authorities, experts, gatekeepers, instances, institutions, or organizations that can easily be identified and held accountable or responsible or who could by means of top-down, command, and control communication limit the *communication* and *participation* of stakeholders. Consumers have become prosumers, patients in the healthcare system have become experts on their own illnesses, citizen journalists have transformed the news media, whereas media content of all kinds is being produced and distributed by anyone and everyone who has access to a computer, a smartphone, and the Internet. One speaks of "participatory culture" or a "democratic culture" to describe how communication and participation have become norms in the digital age. Good design must see to it that these norms are rightly implemented, for example, by shedding light in the darknet, by clearing the Internet of trolls and those who spread misinformation, and by efficiently sanctioning the various forms of cyber criminality and cyber warfare that are currently disrupting and discrediting the digital order of knowledge. Much of digital ethics revolves around attempting to deal with these problems. Traditional humanist ethics demands adherence to values of privacy or strict government regulation. A digital ethics worthy of the name would focus on good design as the key to network governance and the form in which digital ethics can adequately address the problems of the global network society.

It must be emphasized that when speaking of "good design," we are not talking about specific individuals who can be called "designers" and who are to be held responsible for entire networks, but about all actors in a network, both human and nonhuman. As we have argued, all actors in a network exercise distributed and symmetrical agency and are therefore collectively responsible. Contrary to what might be feared, distributed agency does not imply anonymity. The many-hands problem does not force us to renounce attribution of responsibility. But it does urge us to renounce the temptation to describe the moral universe in terms of perpetrators on the one side and victims on the other. The reality of complex socio-technical networks is such that dichotomies such as that between produces and so-called users or what in the General Data Protection Regulation (GDPR) are called "data subjects" as opposed to "data controllers" are no longer useful. The digital transformation has created a society in which it makes little sense to speak of moral agents and moral patients. Everyone is involved, everyone is collectively responsible. If the network is the actor, the network becomes responsible. Traditional concepts of moral agency, as we argued above, no longer describe personal or social reality. Design is what the network does. And design can be either good or bad.

Ostrom had already discovered that successful governance of common-pool resources demands self-organization and distributed decision making. This is all the more a demand when the resource that is being governed is information, which, as we noted, can be understood as neither private nor public property but is "owned," if one can speak of ownership at all, by the network that constructs it. Quite apart from whether issues of ownership can helpfully be raised with regard to information, which ontologically is not a thing of any kind but a process, it is important to understand that the governance of information by design is a matter concerning the network and not any particular actors within a network. When speaking of good design, we are not talking about whether this or that particular actor in a network does the "right" thing, is morally to be praised or blamed, or is even to be held accountable. Demands such as these, to the extent they make sense at all when dealing with complex socio-technical networks, are to be addressed to the entire network. This makes it particularly important for a network to design itself with a view toward the governance principles of *prioritizing, instituting,* and *excluding*. These principles guide processes that organize the network by determining who does what for what purpose when and how. With regard to networks influenced by the affordances of ICTs, these general principles of network governance can be implemented by following the network norms of *transparency* and *authenticity*.

Much has been said in digital ethics about the value of transparency. Usually, transparency is associated with accountability and means that the operations of a socio-technical network, for example, an AI, can be known, causally described, and understandably explained to those affected by the network. Explainability, in this sense, is a requirement of some legislation, such as the European GDPR,[49] and it is almost universally listed in guidelines for ethical AI.[50] The model of accountability here is that of producers or data controllers providing sufficient information about what they are doing so that users or data subjects can consent to or reject the processes they are subjected to. The only significant act that a data subject or user can perform is to say yes or no. Beyond this, they do not participate in the network. They are not responsible for the network. Indeed, they are not part of the network at all, but part of the external effects the network produces. Explainability in this traditional sense of the word, however, is not what the network norm of transparency means. As a network norm, transparency presupposes that all participate in the network and that the contributions of all actors in a network are openly communicated or at least able to be communicated.

Good design is transparent when one knows where information comes from, what it is intended for, what uses can be made of it, and under what conditions it can be transformed and used for other purposes. This is not explainability as it is usually understood and prescribed as an ethical requirement of good AI and other automated systems. Explainability in the sense in which traditional digital ethics uses the term is derived from legal rights of persons to be given reasons for decisions that affect them adversely, for example, credit ratings, loan rejections, and so on. What in these circumstances counts as a "reason" or as an "explanation" is open to judicial interpretation. In general, it can be said the intention of the network norm of transparency in all its forms is to enable, empower, and promote participation in network processes. Transparency is not merely the basis of informed consent. It does not mean that the operations of complex sociotechnical networks can be exhaustively described in language anyone could understand so that they can decide themselves if they want to participate or not. If you ask your doctor why she recommends a certain therapy, you cannot expect to be given an answer that details the entire biochemical, molecular, and metabolic processes, among others, and conditions, causal chains, relations, and interactions a certain molecule instigates or influences in the human body. This would not help you decide to accept the therapy or perhaps even ask for a second opinion unless, of course, you happened to be a medical doctor or biologist yourself. As a network norm, transparency does demand that you have access to all your medical data and are allowed to post this information, for example, in an online patient community and obtain the opinions of others with similar diagnoses or therapies. Transparency means that you, as a patient, are an important participant in the healthcare process and not merely a consumer of healthcare services. This applies to other areas as well, such as education. Transparency enables participation and not merely the largely fictive legitimation for a supposedly sovereign decision called informed consent.

Transparency demands that good design also follows the network norm of *authenticity*. Good design for *authenticity* means that the network does not make it easy to hide, to dissemble, to create false or misleading information, to keep secrets, or to misrepresent

---

49 See Recital 71 as well as Article 15 of the GDPR.
50 See Jobin et al. (2019).

oneself, or otherwise disguise who and what one is, and what role one plays in the network. Secrecy and disguise were long held to be essential values in a hierarchical society where lack of the rule of law put many at risk of abuses of power. Exposure to abuse of power is one of the reasons most often cited for the value of privacy. *Transparency* and *authenticity* mitigate against privacy, since they tackle issues of discrimination or abuse of power openly and publicly. Open challenges to discrimination are more in keeping with democratic procedure than are strategies of secrecy and disguise associated with privacy. The often-cited importance of trust in cooperative action of all kinds, and most notably in networks, is not furthered by secrecy and disguise. In general, it can be said that one trusts only those one knows. If I know who is knocking at the door, I am more likely to open it. Privacy advocates attempt to further trust by exactly the opposite strategy, namely, secrecy and disguise, which inevitably foster mistrust. This places in question the utility and even the moral rightness of organizational, political, and business, secrets, among others, and the social value of entire intellectual property regimes. The present economic order, which attempts to make information into property, may, in fact, be detrimental to social good. The digital transformation has created a new order of knowledge in which it is increasingly dysfunctional to attempt to make information of any kind proprietary and to lock information up behind copyright laws and privacy regulations. Information, as we have argued above, is not a thing that can be owned, and it does not serve the collective to restrict its creation, distribution, and use. The many "open source" or "creative commons" initiatives bear witness to this new order of knowledge.[51] Designing for *transparency* and *authenticity* does not imply chaos, lack of regulation, and complete disregard of the conditions of creation and use of information. On the contrary, implementing the network norms of transparency and authenticity allows for the general network governance principles of *prioritizing*, *instituting*, and *excluding* to be applied to the construction of cooperative action. Why is this so?

Cooperative action, which is another word for society, or what Latour calls the "collective" is no longer necessarily gathered around any central authority, no matter how this authority might be legitimated. The global network society is characterized by network organizations, which are distinguished from traditional hierarchical organizations in many ways. For example, top-down, command, and control communication is replaced by bottom-up, self-organizing, lateral communication. Information is not filtered through various gatekeepers and does not flow along fixed and foreseeable channels but flows in many directions in unforeseeable ways. Closed and stable systems become open and flexible networks. How can order be established and socio-technical networks become goal-directed, limited, functioning organizations under conditions in which information is nonhierarchical, unlimited, connected, inclusive, complex, and public and in which hierarchies of all kinds are breaking down and becoming dysfunctional? Studies in the area of organization theory have long emphasized the structuring role of narrative

---

51 On the significance of the knowledge commons, see Hess and Ostrom (2007) and the work of the D-CENT-Project of the European Union (https://dcentproject.eu/ and https://www.nesta.org.uk/project/d-cent/).

in bringing people, technologies, and resources of all kinds into a shared and efficient program of action.[52] The narrative construction of identities, roles, functions, events, and goals brings loosely coupled elements, what Luhmann would call a "medium," into a "form," that is, into a delimited, functional whole. This is an organization. Within an organization, not all actors are doing the same thing. Certain actors are *prioritized*. They are like hubs in that they channel and configure more information than others. As social network analysis has shown, this need not be the official managers. Every good story has its central figures, its "protagonists," even if these are not single individuals, such as the CEO, but technologies, teams, departments, and so on, and even if they are continually changing as the story progresses. *Prioritization* is expressed and becomes effective in the narrative construction of cooperative action.

Another characteristic of narrative order is that every story follows a specific trajectory. Any single event leads only to a certain number of "possible" following events and originates from only a certain number of previous events. The temporal distribution of narrative events not only makes only certain events possible or even probable but also necessitates a trajectory of events toward specific goals. No organization does everything. A factory produces furniture, but not at the same time automobiles or pharmaceuticals. A school produces certified skills and competencies, but not legal judgments or political success. Both Luhmann and Latour have documented the major trajectories of organizations in society.[53] Those actors, processes, and events that have become prioritized with a view toward a certain goal can be said to be *institutionalized*. *Prioritization* and *institutionalization* lead to and are based upon the network governance principle of *exclusion*. Already Ostrom noted that successful common pool resource governance regimes must begin by defining the resource that is to be administered. In the same way, every socio-technical network, despite the fact that networks are not constituted by exclusion in the way that systems are, must be directed to only certain goals and not all possible goals at once. A story that pursued every possible ending would not be a story that makes any sense. No actor would know who or what it was, what role it plays, why it plays this role, and if it does not play many other roles at the same time. For cooperative action to be efficient, only some stories can be told and others are put on the shelf, left in the wings, or placed in a drawer to be used later on. Network governance, therefore, relies on prioritizing specific stakeholders; instituting certain roles, processes, and events; and excluding others that would prevent the network from following a goal-directed trajectory. With regard to the affordances of digital technologies and the network norms derived from them, prioritization, institutionalization, and exclusion are achieved not by means of top-down, command, and control communication, but through *connectivity*, *flow*, *communication*, *participation*, and *transparency* and *authenticity*. As mentioned above, transparency and authenticity foster open communication and thus allow a narrative ordering to emerge from the mediating work of the actors and not from executive decisions of any central authority,

---

52 See Czarniawska (1998) and Belliger and Krieger (2016) for a discussion of the role of narrative in the communicative construction of organizations.
53 See, for example, Luhmann (1989, 1995), and Latour (2012).

hidden agendas, or strategies of power maintenance. This is not only an assumption of organization theory, but it is also becoming standard praxis in such forms of organizing as holocracy, sociocracy, network organizations, and similar new types of management emerging in all areas of society.[54]

Traditional digital ethics is based upon top-down, hierarchical forms of cooperative action and exhausts itself in recommendations, prescriptions, normative demands, and so on in the modus of moral directives. Without exception, all kinds of contemporary digital ethics, be it philosophical humanism, social science critique, media scandalization, or the lobbying of civil society actors, do not entertain the possibility of good design through network governance as the proper form of moral discourse in the twenty-first century. If it is at all plausible that moral agency can be understood as design and that "good" design is that which follows the network norms derived from the affordances of digital technologies via network governance, it should be apparent that what has heretofore called itself digital ethics must renounce any pretension to being able to address the needs of the global network society. This becomes all the more apparent when we consider the other network governance principles, *localizing* and *globalizing* and *separating of powers* from the point of view of design and the network norms that good design implements.

Although every narrative construction of order, of cooperative action, and organization prioritizes, institutionalizes, and excludes, no story has an end or even a beginning for that matter. Narrative order is unbounded, as anyone who has followed a TV soap or one of the many Hollywood epics over the years can testify. New characters can enter the story, and unforeseen events happen continuously. Old characters, who were once protagonists, disappear and new ones appear. Indeed, there seems to be no end. In addition to this, new beginnings are to be reckoned with. The story can be pushed indefinitely into the past; forgotten origins come to light, historical settings are recreated, and so on. This implies that no set of goals or exclusion of other possibilities or of other actors in any organization is definitive or in any way "constitutive" of the network. Networks, as opposed to systems, are not *constituted* by exclusion, but only *regulated* by it. Networks are therefore governed through regulating their relations to other networks that lie beyond the local, delimited, and prioritized actors and goals that at any one time and place define the network. Networks link up in many ways to other networks beyond the at-any-time operative trajectories and cast of actors. This linking up is referred to as *localizing* and *globalizing*. *Localizing* and *globalizing* are regulatory responses to the realities of the global network society in which connectivity and flow, communication and participation, as well as transparency and authenticity create a global socio-sphere in which everyone and everything is connected to everyone and everything.[55]

We do not need to wait for the Internet of Things or the Fourth Industrial Revolution; the digital transformation has already created a global socio-sphere: Latour would speak

---

54 See Belliger and Krieger (2016) for a discussion of new forms of management and organization emerging in the global network society.
55 For a discussion of the concept of "socio-sphere," see Krieger and Belliger (2014).

of "collective" and Luhmann of "world society." It is because of the global socio-sphere that the Internet of Things and Industry 4.0 become possible and not the other way around. This reality has long been known and popularized under the slogan "think globally, act locally." It is therefore surprising that contemporary digital ethics takes no notice of this situation and has not only assumed the universal validity of Western values and traditions but explicitly set out upon a course of attempting to enforce these values, norms, and assumptions upon the world. It is interesting to note that the "global landscape" of AI ethics guidelines described by Jobin et al. (2019) includes no contributions from China, Russia, or Africa and only one from India. The authors admit that this is remarkable but find no other explanation than the typical gesture of critique by citing the imbalance of power between the first and the third worlds. Why, we may ask, is digital ethics an exclusively Western discourse? Could not an adequate explanation of this fact lie in the exclusively Western values, norms, and worldviews that are assumed as the basis of this discourse? The explanation for the fact that digital ethics is local (Western) but not global could simply be that no one is allowed to participate that does not from the very beginning subscribe to Western modernity as the measure of all things. Judged by the network governance principles of localizing and globalizing, here is where good design applies the network norm of *flexibility*.

Design for flexibility is good design because it admits from the outset that things can change. There are no universal, eternal, incontrovertible values, norms, or truths of human nature or of society. The achievements of European cultural evolution, which are often cited in digital ethics discourse as fundamental and unquestionable values, are admittedly great achievements but are historical realities nonetheless, historical realities that can and will change. Current efforts of digital ethics in all its forms to counter the threat of change that the digital transformation brings by enshrining these values in the constitutions of nations, international treaties, global governance institutions, and legal regulations represent precisely the opposite of good design. Indeed, this is not design at all, but a new version of heroic, Promethean modernism. The many civil society actors who are busy developing ethical guidelines for all kinds of technology are far away from moral agency understood as design. Regardless of whether one pleads for more or less government regulation, this misses the point and misunderstands the consequences of the digital transformation entirely. Governance and not government is the demand of the hour. And governance, we propose, means design and not merely nongovernmental regulation.

Good design is that which follows the network norms within the general framework of network governance. This implies designing for the possibility of change. As noted above, networks are constantly changing, scaling up and scaling down as they globalize and localize, integrating new actors via connectivity and flow, and enabling these actors to communicate and participate in the narratives that organize the network. All this can only be successfully implemented when networks remain flexible. *Flexibility* means that stories, no matter how convincing and apparently self-evident they might be, can always be told differently. *Flexibility* means that narrative construction of order is an ongoing process that must at all times be respected, fostered, allowed, and channeled in productive ways. Today one has become accustomed to acknowledging and even praising innovation. Organizations of all kinds and in all sectors are reorganizing so that innovation becomes the decisive product and not any already established products or services. Only that organization that fosters innovation has a competitive advantage by ensuring sufficient internal complexity to be able to viably react to unforeseeable changes in the environment. This is what "agility" is all about. Agility, which has become standard in good business and management, is the result of the network norm of flexibility. It is not for nothing that flexibility is often discussed under the title of "design thinking." Good design is the implementation of the network norm of flexibility via the network governance principles of localizing and globalizing, as well as what Latour calls *separation of powers*.

The network governance principle of *separation of powers* is borrowed from democratic political theories, which emphasize the need to keep the executive, judiciary, and legislative functions of government distinct from one another. Networks are admittedly not modeled on the governments of nation-states and do not necessarily have these three types of powers or functions. As Luhmann and many others have pointed out, functional differentiation brings with it a separation of social "powers" into closed systems that constitutively exclude each other. Although many social functions can be black-boxed in the terminology of ANT, this does not imply that this is the best solution or even that functional differentiation is the best way to organize society. Network differentiation could be an alternative to functional differentiation since networks are constitutively open, flexible, and multipurposed. Paul Baron's distributed network model,[56] which became the model of the Internet, was originally a security concept that was designed to replace the age-old idea of centralism to ensure connectivity and communication in the event of a nuclear attack. The point of Baran's distributed network is that every hub in the network is principally on equal footing with all others and that at any time any hub whatever could take over the task of channeling information should other hubs become inoperative. The idea is not checks and balances, which was the goal of the political theory of the separation of powers, but instead distributed responsibility and the enabling of participation by all actors in the network. This is the design principle that ensures that networks implement checks and balances. The distribution of decision making as well as provisions for compliance monitoring and sanctioning are core design principles that Ostrom found in successful common pool resource governance regimes. These are also constitutive features of network organizations.[57] Good design implements the network governance principle of separation of powers by ensuring flexibility via decentralization and distribution of decision-making responsibilities. This, of course, can be effectively implemented only when connectivity, flow, communication, participation, transparency, and authenticity

---

56 See https://www.rand.org/about/history/baran.html. See also Belliger and Krieger (2018c) for a discussion of the network norms from the point of view of security.

57 See, for example, sociocracy (https://en.wikipedia.org/wiki/Sociocracy). The more or less explicit demand is that networks implement both internal and external auditing within themselves.

are the norms guiding design. If design is guided by these network norms, it could be considered "good" design.

Good design is what digital ethics, as we wish to define it, is all about. Good design is the digital ethics that our hack attempts to introduce into society and thereby replace the current form of digital ethics that, as we have argued throughout this book, has no right to the name. Hacking digital ethics can be considered an ethical hack if it does not stop at merely revealing the bugs of the legacy system of ethics currently running in our society, but if it suggests how things could be done better. This is what we intend when reconceptualizing moral agency as design and by redefining design as network governance, thus repurposing network governance for the digital age by orienting it on the network norms derived from the affordances of digital technologies. The digital transformation offers an opportunity, indeed, the necessity, of revising moral discourse and ethics for the global network society. Our hack has attempted to take up this challenge. No matter how ethical a hacker may be, or claim to be, one hack alone does not change the world. No hacker can earn respect by claiming to have single-handedly fixed all the bugs or altered the course of history. Indeed, such an unwarranted claim is far from our intention. We have attempted to show how the current discourse of digital ethics depends on an outdated, legacy system composed of the philosophical mythology of humanism, social science critique, media scandalization, and the activities of many private and semi-private organizations lobbying for regulations of one kind or another. We have developed an "exploit" to hack into this system based upon the theory of social systems and ANT. With the concepts, definitions, and questions these contemporary theories offer, we have shown that current digital ethics is not digital at all, but the attempt to reassert the values of Western industrial society and modernism in the face of the digital transformation. We hope that at least this part of the hack will cause some of the players in this game to rethink their strategies, fix the bugs, and patch their false promises.

The pride of the hacker, however, does not end with exposing the bugs and bad code of legacy systems, but in attempting to fix the bugs and change code for the better. We have shown how social systems theory, ANT, and an adequate philosophy of information can serve as the basis for embarking upon new forms of ethical reflection. We have at least hinted at the direction this reflection on morals and ethics adequate to the global network society could go by emphasizing the importance of governance instead of government and of design as an appropriate way to understand moral agency. We have finally suggested that by attending to the affordances of digital technologies, we may be able to discern new network norms that, in practice, guide the construction of networks in today's world and enable founding digital ethics upon solid programing. This is what hacking digital ethics is about. We remarked in the introduction to this book that although the goals may be noble, the work is dirty, and the hacker risks making enemies on all sides. No one with vested interests in maintaining the modern Western world and fending off the future will appreciate this hack. At the most, we can hope that other hackers will support our efforts to make things better.

One final word. The reader, who has followed the argument until the end, will surely not be satisfied. They might say: You have shown that ethics and morality must be reconceived as governance by design, but what about government, what about law and regulation? How can we imagine a world ordered by self-governing networks that themselves must answer to no higher authority, are subject to no oversight and, in the case of failures, to effective sanctions? It is not for nothing that the discourse of digital ethics, as you portray it, is closely linked to appeals for government regulation. The world you would have us believe in remains nothing more than a utopia without consideration of the place of government in your scheme. Governance alone will bring not order into the global network society, but chaos.

Of course, we could answer these questions and objections with reference to the fact that we are concerned in this book only with ethics and morality and not with law and politics. This would contradict, however, our fundamental suspicion of the modern constitution, wherein the distinction between morality and law plays an important role. If we reject the modern constitution, we must address the question of the role of government in a world ordered by governance. We, therefore, propose that government play the role of the auditor, which evaluates, certifies, and even establishes the broad framework within which network governance regimes are allowed to operate. Every network must design its own governance regime but must submit this framework for governmental approval as well as governmental auditing. Clear and effective auditing processes and sanctions must guarantee that network governance regimes fulfill their promises and follow the network norms and governance principles they are based upon. We admit, however, that this solution may not free us from the accusation of being utopian since our current political order can only imagine government on the level of nation-states, whereas networks are global and therefore evade the jurisdiction of any government. Perhaps we must admit that we are describing a utopia, that the vision of a global government goes beyond present-day constraints and realities. If so, then we stand guilty not only of being hackers but of being utopian hackers. Ethical hacking could indeed be inextricably bound up with utopian motivations. In defense of our position, we can only offer the claim that if there is anything our current world needs more, it is a viable vision of a better world.

BIBLIOGRAPHY

Abbass, H. A., Scholz, J., and Reid, D. J., eds. 2018. *Foundations of Trusted Autonomy*. Springer Open. https://link.springer.com/content/pdf/10.1007%2F978-3-319-64816-3.pdf.
Abbott, O. 2020. *The Self, Relational Sociology, and Morality in Practice*. Cham: Palgrave Macmillan.
Adut, A. 2008. *On Scandal*. New York: Cambridge University Press.
Aggleton, D. 2016. "The Disunity of Factical Life: An Ethical Development in Heidegger's Early Work." *Gatherings: The Heidegger Circle Annual*, vol. 6: 25–50.
Anderson, W. T. 1997. *The Future of the Self: Inventing the Postmodern Person*. New York: Putnam.
Anderson, M., and Anderson, S. L. 2011. *Machine Ethics*. Cambridge, MA: Cambridge University Press.
Andrews, D. J. 2017. "On the Theory and Study of Scandals." PhD dissertation, School of Humanities and Social Sciences, UNSW Canberra. http://unsworks.unsw.edu.au/fapi/datastream/unsworks:48248/SOURCE02?view=true.
Arbib, M. A. 2012. *How the Brain Got Language: The Mirror System Hypothesis*. New York: Oxford University Press.
Ashby, W. R. 1958. "Requisite Variety and Its Implications for the Control of Complex Systems." *Cybernetica (Namur)*, vol. 1, no. 2.
Balkin, J. M. 2004. "Digital Speech and Democratic Culture: A Theory of Freedom of Expression for the Information Society." *New York University Law Review*, vol. 79, no. 1. https://papers.ssrn.com/sol3/papers.cfm?abstract_id=470842.
———. 2008. "The Future of Free Expression in a Digital Age." *Pepperdine Law Review*, vol. 36: 101–18.
———. 2016. "Cultural Democracy and the First Amendment." *Northwestern University Law Review*, vol. 109. https://ssrn.com/abstract=2676027.
Ball, K., Haggerty, K. E., and Lyon, D., eds. 2012. *Routledge Handbook of Surveillance Studies*. London: Routledge.
Bateson, G. 1979. *Mind and Nature: A Necessary Unity*. New York: E. P. Dutton.
Belliger, A., and Krieger, D. J. 2016. *Organizing Networks. An Actor-Network Theory of Organizations*. Bielefeld: Transcript.
———. 2018a. *Network Publicy Governance. On Privacy and the Informational Self*. Bielefeld: Transcript.
———. 2018b. "The Digital Transformation of Healthcare." In *Knowledge Management in Digital Change*, edited by K. North, R., and Maier, O. Haas, 311–27. Cham: Springer International.
———. 2018c. "You Have Zero Privacy Anyway—Get over It: Von Personal Privacy Management zu Network Publicy Governance." In *Informatik Sprektrum*, edited by Peter Pagel and Thomas Ludwig, vol. 41, 328–47. Berlin, Heidelberg: Springer.
Bendel, O., ed. 2019. *Handbuch Maschinenethik*. Wiesbaden: Springer VS.
Benkler, Y., Faris R., and Roberts, H. 2018. *Network Propaganda: Manipulation, Disinformation, and Radicalization in American Politics*. Oxford: Oxford University Press.
Bijker, W. E., Hughes, Th. P., and Pinch, T., eds. 1987. *The Social Construction of Technological Systems: New Directions in the Sociology and History of Technology*. Cambridge, MA: MIT Press.
Breazeal, C. L. 2004. *Designing Sociable Robots*. Cambridge, MA: MIT Press.
Brunton, F., and Nissenbaum, H. 2015. *Obfuscation. A User's Guide for Privacy and Protest*. Cambridge, MA: MIT Press.

Callon, M. 1991. "Techno-Economic Networks and Irreversibility." In *A Sociology of Monsters: Essay on Power, Technology and Domination*, edited by J. Law, 132–64. London: Routledge.
Caruso, G. D. 2012. *Free Will and Consciousness. A Determinist Account of the Illusion of Free Will.* London: Lexington Books.
Caruso, G. D., and Flanagan, O., eds. 2018. *Neuroexistentialism. Meaning, Morals, and Purpose in the Age of Neuroscience.* Oxford: Oxford University Press.
Cavanillas, J. M., Curry, E., and Wahlster, W., eds. 2016. *New Horizons for a Data-Driven Economy. A Roadmap for Usage and Exploitation of Big Data in Europe.* Cham: Springer.
Chhotray, V., and Stoker, G. 2009. *Governance Theory and Practice. A Cross-Disciplinary Approach.* UK, London: Palgrave Macmillan.
Christl, W. 2017. *Corporate Surveillance in Everyday Life.* https://crackedlabs.org/en/corporate-surveillance.
Coeckelbergh, M. 2011. "Is Ethics of Robotics about Robots? Philosophy of Robotics Beyond Realism and Individualism." *Law, Innovation and Technology*, vol. , no. 2, 241–50. doi: 10.5235/175799611798204950.
———. 2019. "Artificial Intelligence, Responsibility Attribution, and a Relational Justification of Explainability." *Science and Engineering Ethics*, vol. 26: 2051–68. doi: 10.1007/s11948-019-00146-8.
Corballis, M. 2003. *From Hand to Mouth: The Origins of Language.* Princeton, NJ: Princeton University Press.
———. 2017. *The Truth about Language: What It Is and Where It Came From.* Chicago, IL: University of Chicago Press.
Czarniawska-Joerges, B. 1998. *Narrative Approach in Organization Studies.* Thousand Oaks, CA: Sage.
Darmody, A., and Zwick, D. 2020. "Manipulate to Empower: Hyper-Relevance and the Contradiction of Marketing in the Age of Surveillance Capitalism." *Data and Society*, vol. 7, no. 1: 1–12.
Delli Carpini, M. X., and Keeter, S. 1996. *What Americans Know about Politics and Why It Matters.* New Haven, CT: Yale University Press.
Dignum, V., Baldoni, M., Baroglio, C., Caon, M., Chatila, R., Dennis, L., Génova, G., et al. 2018. "Ethics by Design: Necessity or Curse?" *Association for the Advancement of Artificial Intelligence.* http://www.aies-conference.com/2018/contents/papers/main/AIES_2018_paper_68.pdf. Accessed January 21, 2019.
van Dijck, J., Poell, T., and de Waal, M. 2018. *The Platform Society. Public Values in a Connective World.* New York: Oxford University Press.
van Dijck, J. 2013. *The Culture of Connectivity: A Critical History of Social Media.* New York: Oxford University Press.
Donald, M. 1991. *Origins of the Modern Mind: Three Stages in the Evolution of Culture and Cognition.* Cambridge, MA: Harvard University Press.
Dreyfus, H. 1995. *Being-in-the-World.* Cambridge: MIT Pres.
Enfield, N. J., and Kockelman, P. 2017. *Distributed Agency.* Oxford: Oxford University Press.
Entman, R. M. 2012. *Scandal and Silence: Media Responses to Presidential Misconduct.* Cambridge, UK: Polity.
Etinson, A. ed. 2018. *Human Rights: Moral or Political?* Oxford: Oxford University Press.
Floridi, L. 1999. "Information Ethics: On the Philosophical Foundation of Computer Ethics." *Ethics and Information Technology*, vol. 1: 37–56.
———. 2006. "Four Challenges for a Theory of Informational Privacy." *Ethics and Information Technology*, vol. 8, no. 3: 109–19.
———. 2010. *Information: A Very Short Introduction.* Oxford: Oxford University Press,
———. 2011. *The Philosophy of Information.* Oxford: Oxford University Press.
———. 2012. "Hyperhistory and the Philosophy of Information Policies." *Philosophy & Technology*, vol. 25, no. 2: 129–31.
———. 2013. *The Ethics of Information.* Oxford: Oxford University Press.

———. 2014. *The Fourth Revolution: How the Infosphere Is Reshaping Human Reality*. Oxford: Oxford University Press.

———. 2015. "Semantic Concept of Information." In *Stanford Encyclopedia of Philosophy*. https://plato.stanford.edu/entries/information-semantic/#1.2.

———. 2016a. "On Human Dignity as a Foundation for the Right to Privacy." *Philosophy and Technology*, vol. 29: 307–12.

———. 2016. "Faultless Responsibility: On the Nature and Allocation of Moral Responsibility for Distributed Moral Actions." *Philosophical Transactions of the Royal Society*, vol. A374. doi: 10.1098/rsta.2016.0112.

Floridi, L., Cath, C., and Taddeo, M. 2019. "Digital Ethics: Its Nature and Scope." In *The 2018 Yearbook of the Digital Ethics Lab*, edited by C. Öhman and D. Watson. doi: 10.1007/978-3-030-17152-0_2.

Floridi, L., Cowls, J., Beltrametti, M., Chatila, R., Chazerand, P., Dignum, V., Luetge, C., et al. 2018. "AI4People—An Ethical Framework for Good AI Society: Opportunities, Risks, Principles, and Recommendations." *Minds & Machines*, vol. 28, no. 4: 689–707. doi: 10.1007/s11023-018-9482-5.

Floridi, L., Cowls, J., King, T. C., and Taddeo, M. 2020. "How to Design AI for Social Good: Seven Essential Factors." *Science and Engineering Ethics*, vol. 26. doi: 10.1007/s11948-020-00213-5.

Foucault, M. 1977. *Discipline and Punishment: The Birth of the Prison*. New York: Vintage Books.

———. 1991. "Governmentality." In *The Foucault Effect: Studies in Governmentality*, edited by Graham Burchell, Colin Gordon, and Peter Miller, translated by Rosi Braidotti and revised by Colin Gordon, 87–104. Chicago, IL: University of Chicago Press.

Frankish, K. 2005. *Consciousness*. Milton Keynes, UK: Open University/Open University Worldwide.

Frankish, K., ed. 2017. *Illusionism as a Theory of Consciousness*. Exeter, UK: Imprint Academic.

Froehlich, T. 2004. "A Brief History of Information Ethics." Barcelona, Spain: bid.ub.edu. http://bid.ub.edu/13froel2.htm.

Fuchs, P. 1992. *Die Erreichbarkeit der Gesellschaft: Zur Konstruktion und Imagination gesellschaftlicher Einheit*. Frankfurt a.M.: Suhrkamp.

Gelernter, D. 1993. *Mirror Worlds: Or the Day Software Puts the Universe in a Shoebox ... How It Will Happen and What It Will Mean*. Oxford: Oxford University Press.

Gibney, E. 2018. "The Scant Science behind Cambridge Analytica's Controversial Marketing Techniques. Nature Peers into the Evidence for 'Psychographic Targeting.'" *Nature*, March 29. https://www.nature.com/articles/d41586-018-03880-4.

Gibson, J. 1979. *The Ecological Approach to Visual Perception*. Boston, MA: Houghton Mifflin.

Gill, C. 2020. *The End of Marketing. Humanizing Your Brand in the Age of Social Media and AI*. London: Kogen Page.

von Glasersfeld, E. 1995. *Radical Constructivism: A Way of Knowing and Learning*. London: Falmer.

Goncalo, J. A., Vincent, L. C., and Krause, V. 2015. "The Liberating Consequences of Creative Work: How a Creative Outlet Lifts the Physical Burden of Secrecy." *Journal of Experimental Social Psychology*, vol. 59: 32–39.

Goodenough, W. H. 1997. "Moral Outrage: Territoriality in Human Guise." *Zygon*, vol. 32, no. 1: 5–27.

Gunkel, D. J. 2012. *The Machine Question: Critical Perspectives on AI, Robots and Ethics*. Cambridge, MA: MIT Press.

———. 2018a. "Mind the Gap: Responsible Robotics and the Problem of Responsibility." *Ethics and Information Technology*, vol. 22. doi: 10.1007/s10676-017-9428-2.

———. 2018b. "The Other Question: Can and Should Robots Have Rights?" *Ethics and Information Technology*, vol. 20, no. 2: 87–99.

Habermas, J. 1984. *Theory of Communicative Action. Vol. 1: Reasons and the Rationalization of Society*, translated by T. McCarthy. Cambridge, MA: Polity.

———. 1987. *Theory of Communicative Action. Vol. 2: Lifeworld and System: A Critique of Functionalist Reason*, translated by T. McCarthy. Cambridge, MA: Polity.

———. 1996. *Between Facts and Norms: Contributions to a Discourse Theory of Law and Democracy*. Cambridge, MA: MIT Press.

Hanson, F. A. 2009. "Beyond the Skin Bag: On the Moral Responsibility of Extended Agencies." *Ethics and Information Technology*, vol. 11, no. 1: 91–99.

———. 2014. "Which Came First, the Doer or the Deed?" In *The Moral Status of Technical Artefacts. Philosophy of Engineering and Technology*, edited by P. Kroes and P. P. Verbeek, vol. 17. Dordrecht: Springer.

Heidegger, M. 1996. *Being and Time*, translated by J. Stambaugh. Albany, NY: State University of New York.

Herbst, S. 1998. *Reading Public Opinion: How Political Actos View the Democratic Process*. Chicago, University of Chicago Press.

Hess, C., and Ostrom, E., eds. 2007. *Understanding Knowledge as a Commons. From Theory to Practice*. Cambridge, MA: MIT Press.

Hestres, L. E. 2016. "The Emerging Ethics of Digital Political Strategists." In *Controversies in Digital Ethics*, edited by A. Davisson and P. Booth. New York/London: Bloomsbury.

Hoffman, D. 2019. *The Case Against Reality. Why Evolution Hid the Truth from Our Eyes*. New York: W. W. Norton.

Hutchins, E. 1995. *Cognition in the Wild*. Cambridge, MA: MIT Press.

Iovino, S., and Oppermann, S. 2014. *Material Ecocriticism*. Indiana: Indiana University Press.

Jäggi, C., and Kreiger, D. J. 1991. *Fundamentalismus. Ein Phänomen der Gegenwart*. Zürich: Orell Füssli.

Jobin, A., Ienca, M., and Vayena, E. 2019. "The Global Landscape of AI Ethics Guidelines." *Nature Machine Intelligence*, vol. 1, September: 389–99.

Kalla, J. L., and Broockman, D. E. 2018. "The Minimal Persuasive Effects of Campaign Contact." *General Elections: Evidence from 49 Field Experiments. American Political Science Review*, vol. 112, no. 1: 148–1666. doi: 10.1017/S0003055417000363.

Kane, R., ed. 2002. *Free Will*. Malden, MA: Blackwell.

Karpf, D. 2019. *On Digital Disinformation and Democratic Myths*. Mediawell. https://mediawell.ssrc.org/expert-reflections/on-digital-disinformation-and-democratic-myths/.

Karsenti, B. 2012. "Durkheim and the Moral Fact." In *A Companion to Moral Anthropology*, edited by D. Fassin, 21–36. Hoboken, NJ: Wiley-Blackwell.

Kleinberg, J., Ludwig, J., Mullainathany, S., and Sunstein, C. R. 2019. "Discrimination in the Age of Algorithms." *Journal of Legal Analysis*, no. 10: 1–62.

Klintman, M. 2019. *Knowledge Resistance. How We Avoid Insight from Others*. Manchester, UK: Manchester University Press.

Kohn, M., and Mithen, S. 1999. "Handaxes: Products of Sexual Selection?" *Antiquity*, vol. 73: 518–26.

Krieger, D. J. 1996. *Einführung in die allgemeine Systemtheorie*. Stuttgart: UTB.

Krieger, D. J., and Belliger, A. 2014. *Interpreting Networks: Hermeneutics, Actor-Network Theory, and New Media*. Bielefeld: Transcript.

Kroess, P., and Verbeek, P-P., eds. 2014. *The Moral Status of Technical Artefacts*. Cham: Springer. doi: 10.1007/978-94-007-7914-3.

Kumlin, S., and Esaiasson, P. 2011. "Scandal Fatigue? Scandal Elections and Satisfaction with Democracy in Western Europe, 1977-2007." *British Journal of Political Science*, vol. 42, no. 2: 263–82.

Lagerkvist, A., ed. 2019. "Digital Existence: Ontology, Ethics and Transcendence." In *Digital Culture*. London: Routledge.

Latour, B. 1987. *Science in Action: How to Follow Scientists and Engineers through Society*. Cambridge, MA: Harvard University Press.

———. 1992. "Where Are the Missing Masses? The Sociology of a Few Mundane Artifacts." In *Shaping Technology/Building Society: Studies in Sociotechnical Change*, edited by W. E. Bijker and J. Law. Cambridge, MA: MIT Press.
———. 1993a. *Pasteurization of France*. Cambridge, MA: Harvard University Press.
———. 1993b. *We Have Never Been Modern*. Cambridge, MA: Harvard University Press.
———. 1994. "On Technical Mediation." *Common Knowledge*, vol. 3, no. 2: 29–64.
———. 1996a. "On Interobjectivity." *Mind, Culture, and Activity*, vol. 3, no. 4: 228–45.
———. 1996b. "Review of Ed Hutchins' Cognition in the Wild." *Mind, Culture, and Activity*, vol. 3, no. 1: 54–63.
———. 1999. *Pandora's Hope: Essays on the Reality of Science Studies*. Cambridge, MA: Harvard University Press.
———. 2002. *War of the Worlds: What about Pace?* Chicago: Prickly Paradigm.
———. 2004a. "Why Has Critique Run Out of Steam? From Matters of Fact to Matters of Concern." *Critical Inquiry*, vol. 30 (Winter): 225–48.
———. 2004b. *Politics of Nature. How to Bring the Sciences into Democracy*. Cambridge, MA: Harvard University Press.
———. 2005. *Reassembling the Social: An introduction to Actor-Network Theory*. Oxford: Oxford University Press.
———. 2008. "A Cautious Prometheus? A Few Steps Toward a Philosophy of Design (with Special Attention to Peter Sloterdijk)." In *Proceedings of the 2008 Annual International Conference of the Design History Society*, edited by F. Hackne, J. Glynne, and V. Minto, 2–10. Falmouth, England: Universal.
———. 2010. *On the Modern Cult of the Factish Gods*. Durham, NC: Duke University Press.
———. 2012. "The Whole Is Always Smaller Than Its Parts. A Digital Test of Gabriel Tarde's Monads." *British Journal of Sociology*, vol. 63, no. 4: 591–615.
———. 2013a. "What's the Story? Organizing as a Mode of Existence." In *Organization and Organizing: Materiality, Agency, and Discourse*, edited by D. Robichaud and F. Cooren. New York: Routledge.
———. 2013b. *An Enquiry into Modes of Existence. An Anthropology of the Moderns*. Cambridge, MA: Harvard University Press.
———. 2017. *Facing Gaia. Eight Lectures on the New Climatic Regime*. Cambridge, MA: Polity.
Latour, B., and Woolgar, S. 1979. *Laboratory Life. The Construction of Scientific Facts*. Beverly Hills, CA: Sage.
Law, J. 2019. *Material Semiotics*. www.heterogeneities.net/publications/Law2019MaterialSemiotics.pdf.
Ledwich, M., and Zaitsev, A. 2019. "Algorithmic Extremism: Examining YouTube's Rabbit Hole of Radicalization." *arXiv*, December 24. https://arxiv.org/pdf/1912.11211.pdf.
Levy, S. 1984. *Hackers: Heroes of the Computer Revolution*. Garden City, NY: Anchor Press/Doubleday.
Luhmann, N. 1977. «Interpenetration—Zum Verhältnis personal und sozialer und sozialer Systeme." *Zeitschrift für Soziologie*, Jg. 6. Heft 1. January: 62–76.
———. 1982. "The World Society as a Social System." *International Journal of General Systems*, vol. 8, no. 3: 131–38.
———. 1989. *Ecological Communication*. Chicago: University of Chicago Press.
———. 1990. *Essays on Self-Reference*. New York: Colombia University Press.
———. 1991: "Paradigm Lost." *Thesis Eleven*, vol. 29, no. 2. doi: 10.1177/072551369102900107.
———. 1992. "What Is Communication?" *Communication Theory*, vol. 2, no. 3: 251–59.
———. 1995. *Social Systems*. Stanford, CA: Stanford University Press.
———. 2000. *The Reality of the Mass Media*. Stanford: Stanford University Press.
———. 2008. *Die Moral der Gesellschaft*. Frankfurt: Suhrkamp.
———. 2012. *Theory of Society*, vol. 1. Stanford: Stanford University Press.
———. 2013. *Theory of Society*, vol. 2. Stanford: Stanford University Press.

Lyon, D. 2002. "Everyday Surveillance. Personal Data and Social Classifications." *Information, Communication & Society*, vol. 5, no. 2: 242–57.

———, ed. 2006. *Theorizing Surveillance. The Panopticon and Beyond*. London, UK: Willan.

Malafouris, L. 2013. *How Things Shape the Mind: A Theory of Material Engagement*. Cambridge, MA: MIT Press.

Margolin, V. 2002. *The Politics of the Artificial: Essays on Design and Design Studies*. Chicago: University of Chicago Press.

Matthias, A. 2004. "The Responsibility Gap: Ascribing Responsibility for the Actions of Learning Automata." *Ethics and Information Technology*, vol. 6, no. 3: 175–83.

Maturana, H., and Varela, F. 1973. "Autopoiesis and Cognition: The Realization of the Living." In *Boston Studies in the Philosophy of Science 42*, edited by R. S. Cohen and M. W. Wartofsky. Dordrecht: D. Reidel.

———. 1987. *The Tree of Knowledge. Biological Roots of Human Understanding*. Boston: Shambhala.

Mayer-Schönberger, V., and Cukier, K. 2013. *Big Data: A Revolution That Will Transform How We Live, Work, and Think*. Boston: Houghton Mifflin Harcourt.

McKenzie, W. 2004. *A Hacker Manifesto*. Cambridge, MA: Harvard University Press.

Meillassoux, Q. 2008. *After Finitude: An Essay on the Necessity of Contingency*, translated by Ray Brassier. London: Continuum.

Merton, R. K. 1973. "The Normative Structure of Science." In *The Sociology of Science. Theoretical and Empirical Investigations*, edited by N. W. Storer. Chicago: University of Chicago Press.

Mittelstadt, B., Allo, P., Taddeo, M., Wachter, S., and Floridi, L. 2016. "The Ethics of Algorithms: Mapping the Debate." *Big Data and Society*, vol. 3: 1–21.

Mizzoni, J. 2017. *Evolution and the Foundations of Ethics. Evolutionary Perspectives on Contemporary Normative and Metaethical Theories*. London, UK: Lexington Books.

Munar, A. M. 2010. "Digital Exhibitionism: The Age of Exposure." *Culture Unbound: Journal of Current Cultural Research*, vol. 2, no. 23: 401–22.

Murphy, M. C. 2007. *Philosophy of Law*. Oxford: Blackwell.

Nelson, E. S. 2008. "Heidegger and the Questionability of the Ethical." *Studia Phaenomenologica*, vol. VIII: 411–535.

Nissenbaum, H. 1996. "Accountability in a Computerized Society." *Science and Engineering Ethics*, vol. 2, no. 1: 25–42.

———. 2004. "Privacy as Contextual Integrity." *Washington Law Review*, vol. 79: 101–39.

Ostrom, E. 1990. *Governing the Commons: The Evolution of Institutions for Collective Action*. Cambridge, UK: Cambridge University Press.

———. 2000. "Collective Action and the Evolution of Social Norms." *Journal of Economic Perspectives*, vol. 14, no. 3: 137–58.

———. 2010. "Beyond Markets and States: Polycentric Governance of Complex Economic Systems." *American Economic Review*, vol. 100: 1–33.

Papanek, V. 1984. *Design for the Real World: Human Ecology and Social Change*, 2nd ed. London: Thames & Hudson.

Parsons, T. 1951. *The Social System*. Glencoe, IL: Free Press.

Parsons, T., Shils, E. A., Allport, G. W., Kluckhohn, C., Murray, H. A., Sears, P. R., Sheldon, R. C., et al. 1951. "Some Fundamental Categories of the Theory of Action: A General Statement." In *Toward a General Theory of Action*, edited by T. Parsons and E. Shils, 3–29. Cambridge, MA: Harvard University Press.

Prainsack, B. 2017. *Personalized Medicine. Empowered Patients in the 21st Century?* New York: NYU Press.

Railton, P. 2019. "Moral Metaphysics, Moral Psychology, and the Cognitive Sciences." In *Metaphysics and Cognitive Science*, edited by A. Goldman and B. P. McLaughlin, 73–98. Oxford: Oxford University Press.

Raji, I. D., Smart, A., White, R. N., Mitchell, M., Gebru, T., Hutchinson, B., Smith-Loud, J., et al. 2020. "Closing the AI Accountability Gap: Defining an End-to-End Framework for Internal

Algorithmic Auditing." In *Conference on Fairness, Accountability, and Transparency (FAT* '20)*, 33–44. Barcelona, Spain. ACM Digital Library, New York. doi: 10.1145/3351095.3372873.

Reid, J. D. 2019. *Heidegger's Moral Ontology*. Cambridge, UK: Cambridge University Press.

Rosenthal-von der Pütten, A. M., Krämer, N. C., Hoffmann, L., Sobieraj, S., and Eimler, S. C. 2013. "An Experimental Study on Emotional Reactions towards a Robot." *International Journal of Social Robotics*, vol. 5, no. 1: 17–34.

Rowlands, M. 2010. *The New Science of the Mind: From Extended Mind to Embodied Phenomenology*. Boston, MA: MIT Press.

Schudson, M. 1998. *The Good Citizen: A History of American Civil Life*. New York: Simon & Schuster.

Shannon, C. E., and Weaver, W., 1949. *The Mathematical Theory of Communication*. Urbana, IL: University of Illinois Press.

Simon, H. 1996. *The Sciences of the Artificial*. Cambridge, MA: MIT Press.

Smiley, M. 2017. "Collective Responsibility." In *The Stanford Encyclopedia of Philosophy*, edited by Edward N. Zalta, summer 2017 ed. https://plato.stanford.edu/archives/sum2017/entries/collective-responsibility.

Sørensen, E., and Torfing, J., eds. 2007. *Theories of Democratic Network Governance*. London: Palgrave/Macmillan.

Sørensen, E., and Triantafillou, P., eds. 2009. *The Politics of Self-Governance: An Introduction*. Farnham, UK: Ashgate.

Spencer-Brown, G. 1969. *Laws of Form*. London: Allen & Unwin.

Stahl, B. C. 2006. "Responsible Computers? A Case for Ascribing Quasi-Responsibility to Computers Independent of Personhood or Agency." *Ethics and Information Technology*, vol. 8, no. 4: 205–13.

Stephan, P. F. 2015. "Designing 'Matters of Concern' (Latour)—a Future Design Challenge?" In *Transformation Design. Perspective on a New Design Attitude*, edited by W. I. Jonas, S. Zerwas, and K. von Anshelm, 202–26. Basel, Switzerland: Birkhäuser.

Tebbit, M. 2017. *Philosophy of Law. An Introduction*, 3rd ed. London: Routledge.

Thompson, J. B. 1995. *The Media and Modernity: A Social Theory of the Media*. Stanford, CA: Stanford University Press.

———. 2000. *Political Scandal*. Cambridge, UK: Polity.

Torfing, J., Peters, B. G., Pierrre, J., and Sørensen, E. 2012. *Interactive Governance: Advancing the Paradigm*. Oxford: Oxford University Press.

Vallor, S. 2106. *Technology and the Virtues*. Oxford: Oxford University Press.

Van de Poel, I., Nihlén Fahlquist, J., Doorn, N., Zwart, S., and Royakkers, L. 2012. "The Problem of Many Hands: Climate Change as an Example." *Science and Engineering Ethics*, vol. 18, no. 1: 49–67.

Vanderstraeten, R. 2002. "Parson, Luhmann and the Theorem of Double Contingency." *Journal of Classical Sociology*, vol. 2, no. 1: 77–92.

Verbeek, P-P. 2011. *Moralizing Technology: Understanding and Designing the Morality of Things*. Chicago, IL: University of Chicago Press.

———. 2014. "Some Misunderstandings about the Moral Significance of Technology." In *The Moral Status of Technical Artefacts*, edited by P. Kroes and P-P. Verbeek, 75–88. Dordrecht, Netherlands: Springer.

Wallach, W. 2015. *A Dangerous Master: How to Keep Technology from Slipping beyond Our Control*. New York: Basic Books.

Wallach, W., and Allen, C. 2009. *Moral Machines: Teaching Robots Right from Wrong*. Oxford: Oxford University Press.

Warren, S., and Brandeis, L. D. 1890. "The Right to Privacy." *Harvard Law Review*, vol. 4, no. 5: 193–220.

Watzlawick, P., Beavin-Bavelas, J., and Jackson, D. 1967. "Some Tentative Axioms of Communication." In *Pragmatics of Human Communication: A Study of Interactional Patterns, Pathologies and Paradoxes*. New York: W. W. Norton.
Webb, D. 2009. *Heidegger, Ethics and the Practice of Ontology*. New York: Continuum.
Weinberger, D. 2012. *Too Big to Know. Rethinking Knowledge Now That the Facts Aren't the Facts, Experts Are Everywhere, and the Smart4est Person in the Room Is the Room*. New York: Basic Books.
Wiener, N. 1948. *Cybernetics: Or Control and Communication in the Animal and the Machine*. Paris: Hermann & Cie.
———. 1954. *The Human Use of Human Beings: Cybernetics and Society*. Boston: Houghton Mifflin.
———. 1961. *Cybernetics or Control and Communication in the Animal and the Machine*, 2nd ed. Cambridge, MA: MIT Pres.
Wieser, M. 2012. *Das Netzwerk von Bruno Latour. Die Akteur-Netzwerk -Theorie zwischen Science & Technologs Studies und poststrukturalistischer Soziologie*. Bielefeld: Transcript.
Willke, H. 2006. *Global Governance*. Bielefeld: Transcript.
———. 2009. *Governance in a Disenchanted World. The End of Moral Society*. Cheltenham, UK: Edward Elgar.
Willke, H. 2016. *Dezentrierte Demokratie Prolegomena zur Revision politiascher Steuerung*. Frankfurt a.M.: Suhrkamp.
———. 2019. *Komplexe Freiheit. Konfigurationsprobleme eines Menschenrechts in der globalisierten Moderne*. Bielefeld: Transcript.
Wilson, D. S., Ostram, E., and Cox, M. E. 2013. "Generalizing the Core Design Principles for the Efficacy of Groups." *Journal of Economic Behavior & Organization*, vol. 90: 21–32.
Young, K. 2020. *The Domains of Identity: A Framework for Understanding Identity Systems in Contemporary Society*. London: Anthem.
Yueng, K. 2017. "'Hypernudge': Big Data as a Mode of Regulation by Design." *Information, Communication & Society*, vol. 20, no. 1: 118–36.
Zaller, J. R. 1992. *The Nature and Origins of Mass Opinion*. Cambridge, MA: Cambridge University Press.
Zuboff, S. 2015. "Big Other: Surveillance Capitalism and the Prospects of an Information Civilization." *Journal of Information Technology*, vol. 30: 75–89. doi: 10.1057/jit.2015.5. https://ssrn.com/abstract=2594754.
———. 2019. *The Age of Surveillance Capitalism. The Fight for a Human Future at the New Frontier of Power*. London: Profile Books.

INDEX

abstraction, levels of 93, 95, 102, 105, 107
actor-network theory 6, 14, 65, 73, 187
Accenture 172, 177
accountability, moral 112, 216–34, 246–49
actor-network 70, 75–77, 78–87, 187–223
actors, in actor-network theory, follow the actors 67–68, 70–87, 89, 189–90, 196, 209, 244
Adam Smith 139
adaptation 19, 42n37, 53–69
adaptive learning 28–29, 34, 38, 41, 61, 65–66, 245
advertising, personalized, marketing communication 118, 134, 144, 150–62
aesthetic, aesthetics 3n2, 215
affordances 7, 69, 79n92, 93–95, 139, 161, 164–65, 180, 189–90, 199, 208, 243, 246
agency, moral, social 3, 5, 7, 25, 69, 73, 79, 85, 215, 216–34
AI, artificial intelligence, guidelines for ethical AI, good AI 12, 18n14, 83, 23, 83, 123, 147, 163, 170–73, 176, 216–18, 228
AI4ALL 170
AINow 148n60, 173, 180
Alan Turing Institute 170
algorithm 96–97, 123–24, 133–34, 136–38, 151, 173, 175, 177–78, 180, 219, 229, 234, 237–38
Algorithm Watch 173
Amazon 134, 154
American Civil Liberties Union 173
analytics, of data, descriptive, predictive, preventive, prescriptive 134, 137, 144–49, 153, 191
anonymous, anonymity, of complex socio-technical networks 230–32
apperception, transcendental unity of 106, 112, 119–20
Aristotle 10, 12, 20, 83, 228, 230–31
art, social subsystem, and morality 3, 26–27, 33–34, 38

attention, economy of 5, 151, 154–56, 162, 164
authenticity, in relation to *dasein*, as network norm 2, 7, 10, 196–99, 202, 243, 250
autonomy 3, 34–36, 49, 61, 112, 118, 123–25, 140–43, 153–54, 171, 175–76, 192, 219, 241
autonomous rational subject 2, 6–7, 34–36, 49, 75, 85, 89, 105, 120, 125, 127, 130–32, 143, 153, 156, 158, 182, 187–89, 198, 202, 224, 240, 243
autopoiesis, autopoietic systems 17–34, 39, 44, 52, 59, 66, 83, 89, 108, 191

Being, beings 2, 10n2, 12, 19, 31n29, 45–46, 59n61, 61, 64, 68n73, 75–76, 78, 82, 84, 91, 95–96, 98–102, 109, 106, 109, 113, 129, 191
Benedikter, Roland 178n145
big data, analytics of, 4, 13, 124, 144, 176–78
black box, actor-network theory 67, 80n95, 87, 209–10, 212, 247
body tracking 134, 150
bureaucracy 201
business, social subsystem, economic system 26–27, 33–42, 58, 72, 126, 134, 203, 242

Cambridge Analytica, scandal of 160, 163, 166, 179
capitalism, surveillance, industrial 3, 43, 125, 135, 139, 142–58, 224, 231
Castells, Manuel 191
catastrophe, natural, social 101, 199, 219
categorical imperative 2, 10, 15, 35, 38
Center for Data Innovation 173
Center for Democracy and Technology 121
Center of Data Ethics and Innovation 121
civil society 5–6, 132, 135, 141, 169–85, 202, 243, 252
click bait 138, 167–68
closure, operational, informational 50, 52, 55, 58–59, 63, 107–8, 211, 242

INDEX

cloud 144, 163, 165
code, system code, binary code, bad code 1, 2, 4–5, 8, 13, 18–21, 34, 36–40, 45, 51, 53, 55, 62–64, 87, 98, 109, 113, 136, 160, 208, 213, 229, 241, 255
Coeckelbergh, Mark 176n138, 226–32, 234, 238, 244, 246–47
cogito ergo sum 11, 55, 130
cognition, distributed 12, 20–21, 24, 28, 45, 55n56, 56, 67–68, 78, 81, 94–95, 108n26, 109, 111–12, 131, 133, 180, 187, 199, 208, 243
cognitive, cognitive expectations 27–29, 40n35, 48, 51, 54–55, 59n61, 68, 69n74, 76, 77, 80, 81, 83, 93, 95–97, 107–10, 111–13, 119, 143, 154, 217, 222
cognitive science, non-Cartesian, 4Es 12, 18n14, 108n26, 111, 111n29, 113, 119
communication, as system operation, as three-fold selection, as network norm, top-down, many-to-many, as rational action, technologies of 7, 18, 20, 21–27, 30, 36, 40, 42, 48, 50n50, 53–54, 60, 66, 72, 81, 83, 91, 100, 111, 131, 160–61, 194, 203, 218, 225, 243
complexity, in systems theory, in socio-technical networks, 18–20, 26, 26n23, 31, 62, 102, 112, 195, 228n38, 230, 254
connectivity, as network norm 7, 121, 139, 145, 191–92, 192n2, 203, 208, 213, 243, 246, 251, 254
contingency, double 19, 22, 26, 27, 30–34, 31nn28, 29, 34, 36, 38, 61–62, 66, 74n83, 86
correlationalism 68n73, 78n91
critique, social science, modern constitution 5–6, 8, 49, 90n4, 105, 125–60, 185, 188, 192n2, 196, 202, 203, 240, 241, 243, 252
cybernetics 16n11, 20

Daedalus 240
Darwin, Charles 12, 105n21
das Man 2
data 81, 81n5, 92–97, 99–103, 103n17, 107n24, 115–17, 115n35, 118, 123, 129, 133, 134, 137, 143, 150, 177, 190, 191, 205, 231, 238
data analytics, descriptive, predictive, preventive, prescriptive, as datafication 3, 134–35, 136, 138, 139, 144–49, 150, 151, 153, 155, 191, 192

data commons 205n17
data contollers 248–49
data-driven economy, society 4, 133, 149, 150, 152, 155, 157
data ethics 176, 177
Data Ethics Commission, *Datenethikkommission* 123–24, 140, 171, 176
Data Ethics Lab Oxford 170
data subject 150, 154, 234n43, 248–49
D-CENT Project EU 250n51
democracy 1, 14n7, 39n48, 135, 141, 142, 143, 154, 156, 157, 166, 166n91, 169, 176, 181, 194, 196, 202, 246
Descartes, René, Cartesian 2, 11, 12, 43, 55, 78n90, 83, 84, 106, 108, 109, 111, 111n29, 119, 120, 130, 131
design, definition of, governance by, redesign 7–8, 14, 50, 65, 85n102, 86, 122, 185, 187–88, 199, 202, 208, 213–16, 240–43
difference, as information 68, 77–77, 92–98
differentiation, functional, stratified, segmental 15n9, 27, 49, 64
Digital Ethics Conference 174
Digital Ethics Summit 174
digital ethics, discourse of, as applied ethics 4, 6–8, 12–13, 49, 63, 87, 90, 98, 102, 122–25, 132, 133, 148, 159, 160, 163, 168, 174, 175–79, 185, 188, 192, 193, 199, 202, 208, 213–16, 225, 231, 232, 235, 243–56
Digital Single Market Agenda 103n17, 144, 149, 171, 180
digital transformation, as revolution 3, 3n3, 4, 6–8, 13–14, 90, 92, 122–25, 132, 133, 138–42, 145, 148–49, 155–56, 159, 162–63, 168, 169, 178, 181, 189n1, 191, 199, 202, 203, 205n17, 208, 213, 216, 226, 233, 21, 243, 246, 247, 250, 252, 253, 255
digital twin 143, 145, 145n55, 146
disruptions, of knowledge, of social organization, of human self-understanding 3n2, 5, 158, 203–4
distinctions, binary, guiding 6, 37, 47, 51, 80, 81, 83, 89, 96n10, 110, 120, 126, 189, 206
double contingency 26, 27, 30–31, 31n28, 32–36, 38, 61, 66, 74n83, 86
Durkheim, Emil 14–17, 20, 22, 27, 30, 31, 32n30, 36, 41, 44–45, 48, 57, 61, 62, 64, 68, 83, 84, 89, 163, 211

echo chambers 13n48, 162n82, 166, 185n89, 188, 167

economy of attention 5, 151, 154, 155, 159, 162
ecosystem 28n25, 44, 57, 58–60, 63, 145, 200–201, 212
Eigentlichkeit 2
Electronic Frontier Foundation 173
Electronic Privacy Information Center 173
electronic person 62n65, 147, 198n7
elements, of system, of network 17–19, 52, 54, 55n55, 57, 58, 60, 67, 76, 79, 80, 84, 99, 105n21, 107, 108, 210, 230, 247, 251
emergence, levels of emergent order, definition of 6, 20–21, 31, 44–45, 66, 68, 77n89, 81–82, 109, 111, 113, 156, 180, 222
Enlightenment 11, 36, 90n4, 125, 127, 240
enrollment, as process of network construction 21, 71, 73, 76–78, 80, 94, 191, 198n10, 207, 210, 212
Entschlossenheit 2
entropy, negentropy 97–102, 217, 219
European Data Supervisor 171
European Digital Rights 173
European Union 103n17, 117, 123, 144, 149, 171, 180
evolution 21, 41n37, 46, 62, 78, 108, 110, 113, 119, 200, 243, 253
explanation, explainability, as accountability, as moral demand 137n50, 231–33, 234n43, 238, 248–49

Facebook 114, 134, 136, 138, 142, 149, 152, 160, 164, 166, 168, 170, 172, 224
filter bubbles 135, 237, 262n82, 166, 168, 188
flexibility, as network norm 199, 253
Floridi, Luciano 6, 12, 79, 81, 98–125
flow, network norm 192–94
form, laws of, 147
Fourth Industrial Revolution 145, 146, 252
Foucault, Michel 154, 221, 222
function, of morality 39–43
functional, functionalism 16–19, 20, 32, 57, 64, 79, 215, 220, 234, 236, 242, 251
functional differentiation, of society 26, 26n23, 27, 30, 31, 32n28, 33–39, 49, 57, 62–63, 86, 110, 126, 161, 164, 254
functional networks 67
functional ontology 19, 20, 43
functional subsystems, of society 26, 34–39, 51, 62–63, 72, 120, 126, 189, 199, 212

Galileo 12, 105n21
Gemserve 172
Gartner 172
Gelassenheit 2
General Data Protection Regulation GDPR 117–18, 149, 149n63, 248
Geworfenheit 241
Gibson, James J. 69, 79n92, 189
global network society 3–8, 13, 14, 43, 49n48, 50, 62, 63n66, 65, 90–91, 124, 132, 138, 142, 149, 156, 169, 180, 185, 190n1, 191–207, 213, 242, 243, 250, 255
globalizing, as network governance principle 209, 211–13, 245, 252–54
Goffman, Erving 26, 105–7, 109, 196
Google, Google Glas, audit framework for AI 136, 149, 150–53, 172, 179, 234–39
governance, common pool resource
governance, network governance, by design 7, 86, 101, 139, 141, 177, 181, 185, 202–13, 214–15, 222, 225, 226, 234, 239, 244–56
guidelines, ethical, for artificial intelligence 4, 13, 36, 42n42, 148, 170n96, 171, 175–79, 199, 232, 235, 236, 239, 245, 249, 253
Gunkel, David J. 24n20, n22, 176n138

Habermas, Jürgen 20, 35, 45n32, 36, 38n34, 42, 100, 141, 194
hacking, ethical, hackers, method of 1–8, 14, 35, 46, 50n50, 61, 87, 90, 92, 109, 113, 159, 163, 185, 188, 208, 213, 243, 255–56
Hegel, George Wilhelm Friedrich 46–47, 83
Heidegger, Martin 2–3, 10, 10n2, 21n15, 45, 59, 61, 64, 67n70, 74–76, 78, 81, 97, 111, 125, 128, 129, 189, 191, 198, 199, 210, 215, 241–42
Hobbes, Thomas 2, 28, 30, 31, 34–35, 110, 182
holocracy 252
human nature 6–7, 9n1, 10–12, 14–17, 20, 33, 36, 38, 49, 61, 65, 79n92, 89, 90, 123–24, 129–32, 142, 143, 153–54, 156–57, 184, 187, 192, 201, 213, 222n34, 243, 253
human rights 36, 38, 61, 89, 103, 103n16, 124, 139, 142, 143, 164, 173, 176, 178, 182, 184, 192, 193, 202, 213
humanism 4–7, 10n2, 24, 29n27, 62, 65, 78n91, 89–125, 132, 133, 139, 156, 159, 168, 178, 179, 182–85, 187, 191, 193, 195, 199, 201–6, 213, 223, 243, 244, 252, 255

INDEX

Hutchins, Edwin 112n32
hybrids 128–32, 184, 185, 188, 192, 194, 202, 223, 242, 243, 245

ICT, information and communication technologies 7, 83, 91, 104, 133, 139, 141, 142, 145, 159, 164, 165, 168i, 169, 172, 175, 178, 181, 191, 193, 193n3, 197, 201, 202, 213, 248
Identity, and agency, construction of, postmodern critique of, fragmentation of 3, 12, 36, 37, 49, 70, 80, 94n8, 98n13, 103, 105–7, 110–11, 114n35, 115–17, 119, 121, 183, 196, 210, 238, 247
IEEE 172
inclusion, social 18, 22–25, 27, 44, 46, 52, 61, 80, 85–87, 108, 176–77, 187, 194, 211, 213
individual, as autonomous rational subject, ontological, as social construct, as psychic system 2, 5–7, 11–16, 20–25, 27–28, 30–31, 34–36, 38, 41, 45–49, 53–57, 62, 65–66, 68, 75, 78, 83, 85n102, 89, 91, 94–95, 98, 103–22, 125, 130–31, 140, 142, 144, 153, 156, 158, 171, 181–83, 187–89, 192–93, 195–99, 201–3, 206–7, 211, 213, 216, 221–22, 226–27, 242–44, 248, 251
Information Technology & Innovation Foundation 173
information, definition of, ontology of, as relational, philosophy of, ethics of, as common good, as property 1, 3, 5–7, 17–22, 23n19, 25, 27–28, 32–33, 34n31, 40–41, 46n44, 48, 50–53, 56, 58, 58n60, 65, 57n70, 69, 77–87, 89–127, 135–38, 145–49, 152, 154, 156, 160–68, 175, 177, 182–83, 187–88, 190–97, 203–9, 212, 214–20, 222–26, 240–51, 254–55
Institute for Ethics in Artificial Intelligence 170
Institute for Human-Centered Artificial Intelligence 170
instituting and excluding, network governance principle 209, 211, 213, 248, 250, 251
integration, of individuals into society, of functional subsystems into society 21n16, 25–26, 26n23, 35–36, 41, 41n37, 213
intermediaries, as opposed to mediators 67, 194–95, 198n10, 201, 210, 212, 247
Internet of Things 13, 146, 173, 176, 191, 231, 252, 253
International Association of Privacy Professionals 172

irreduction, principle of 80n95, 82, 94, 97, 194, 195, 241

justice, as ethical value 3, 14n7, 102, 112, 125, 127, 131, 140, 141, 143, 159, 160, 169, 175, 176, 188, 196, 221n32

Kant, Imanuel 2, 10, 10n3, 11, 15, 34–36, 38, 56, 60, 68n73, 78n90, 86, 93–96, 106–9, 112, 119–20, 130, 230, 241

Latour, Bruno 6, 7, 62n65, 63, 66–76, 78n90, 80, 82–86, 89–94, 97–98, 102, 109, 120–21, 124–29, 131–32, 140, 182, 188–89, 194, 207, 209n23, 210, 213–15, 220, 226, 237, 240–43, 245, 250–52, 254
law, as social subsystem, positive, natural, of reason 11, 14, 16, 26, 32n30, 34, 37–40, 49, 57, 66, 68, 68n72, 83, 103, 114, 117, 120, 126, 128, 131, 156, 169, 176, 177, 180, 183–84, 189, 190, 196, 202, 207, 213–15, 218, 245, 250, 255–56
liberalism, neo liberalism 81n96, 139, 182, 224
localizing, as network governance principle 209, 211–13, 252–54
Luhmann, Niklas 6, 16, 17, 19–65, 66–68, 70–72, 74n83, 76, 78, 80–87, 89–92, 94n8, 96n10, 98, 100–102, 107–13, 120–21, 124, 126, 129, 131, 133, 140, 147, 156, 160–64, 168, 182–83, 187–88, 190, 194–95, 199, 207, 210–12, 216, 242, 243–45, 251, 253, 254
Lyon, David 149n62, 150, 154

Malafouris, Lambros 69n75, 74n83
manipulation, of behavior 135n48, 153–54, 156n76, 162n82, 166, 166n91, 175
many hands problem 228n37, 229–30, 234, 247–48
many things problem 228n37, 230, 234, 240, 242, 247
Marx, Karl 1–3, 57, 83, 143, 150
Maturana, Humberto & Varela, Francisco 16n11, 17n13, 54, 58n60, 108n26
meaning, theory of, as a system, definition of, and information 1–3, 10n2, 12, 13, 17, 18n14, 20–21, 21n16, 29n27, 31n29, 44–48, 50n50, 50–53, 55n55, 56–57, 59–71, 59n61, 64n67, 67n70, 75–76, 78, 80–81, 82n98, 83–84, 87, 90–93, 95–97, 107, 109–13, 121–22, 129, 148, 188–90, 202, 207, 222, 240–41, 241n46, 242

media, mass media, new media, and scandalization, and the economy of attention, symbolically generalized, social 5–7, 31–34, 37, 38, 101, 110, 114, 132, 135, 138, 150, 156, 159, 160–69, 175, 177, 179, 185, 188, 193, 196, 202, 204, 243, 252, 255

mediator, mediation, technical, intermediaries 67, 70, 72, 74–78, 80–86, 85n102, 91, 93–94, 105, 128, 129n46, 130, 132, 131, 189, 194–95, 198–99, 201, 207, 210, 212, 220, 222, 226–27, 240–42, 245, 247, 251

Meillassoux, Quentin 68n73

Microsoft 134, 172

mind 12, 20, 91, 93–94, 96–97, 108–12, 119–21, 217–18, 223

mirror system hypothesis 74n83

mirror world 145

modern, modernity, modern constitution 2, 3–8, 11–12, 14, 17, 20, 21n16, 24, 26–27, 29, 29n27, 31, 31n28, 34–44, 49, 63, 64–65, 68n73, 73, 74, 78n90, 83, 84, 86, 90n4, 95–97, 122, 124, 125–33, 138, 140, 142, 143, 149, 153, 156, 158–61, 164, 168–69, 175, 179–85, 188–90, 193–94, 196–99, 202, 204, 206–7, 213–15, 223–25, 227, 233, 240–43, 253, 255, 256

morality, function of, distributed, unofficial 5–7, 12, 14–17, 20, 22, 23–25, 27, 28n24, 29, 29n26, 31, 32, 32n30, 34–36, 38–44, 48, 53, 57, 61, 64–66, 68, 85, 85n100, 86–87, 89, 91, 98, 100–103, 119, 125, 127, 129–30, 132–33, 162–64, 168, 169, 178, 183–85, 187, 189–92, 193n3, 198, 199n11, 201–2, 207, 213–18, 220, 222–27, 242–46

myth, mythology, definition of, of humanism 4–7, 35n32, 49, 49n49, 74n83, 89, 92, 105, 122, 122n43, 123, 125, 131–32, 138, 140, 142, 153, 156, 158–59, 168–69, 175, 182–85, 187–88, 191, 193, 195, 202–3, 206, 213, 221n32, 223–24, 243, 255

nation state 37, 53, 62, 63n66, 101–3, 119, 134, 141, 169, 204, 215, 223, 254, 256

nature, as opposed to society, state of nature, as ontological domain, as essence, as object of science 16, 19, 28, 31, 33, 45–46, 50, 52–53, 59, 62, 71, 83–84, 93, 98, 110, 120, 126–28, 130–32, 181, 187–88, 198, 200, 215, 219, 242

negation, as logical operator, as source of distinctions 47–48, 59, 60, 78, 81, 92, 99

network governance 7–8, 185, 202–13, 214, 222, 225–26, 236–38, 245–48, 250–56

network norms, 7–8, 185, 187–202, 208, 214, 243–48, 250–53, 254n56, 255–56

networking 7–8, 48, 67n71, 68, 75–76, 76n86, 81, 81n96, 83–87, 91, 94–95, 97, 112, 126, 129, 132, 159, 184, 187–89, 194–205, 199, 202, 207, 210, 215, 240, 242–47

NeurIPS 172, 174

neuroscience 12, 112–13, 178, 221n32

NHS care.data 179

Nissenbaum, Helen 184n153, 195

Nietzsche, Friedrich 2, 12, 34, 118

nonhumans 4–5, 7–8, 23–25, 61, 62n6, 66, 69n76, 70, 73, 75–76, 81n96, 82, 84–86, 89, 123, 148, 187–90, 197, 206, 214–16, 218–20, 222–23, 225–27, 234, 243–44, 246, 248

normative expectations 3, 27–30, 44, 61, 98

Obfuscation 195, 196

OECD 171, 176

Omidyar Network 174

ontology, functional, relational, of information, of substance 6, 19, 20, 29n27, 43, 85, 93, 94, 95, 96, 98, 104, 106–10, 113, 115, 118–21, 195, 206, 215–16, 241–42

Open Data Institute 174

Ostrom, Elinor 205–6, 208–11, 213, 236–37, 246, 248, 250n51, 251, 254

Parsons, Talcott 16n11, 20, 30, 31–32, 32n30, 33, 74n83

participation, as network norm 7, 122, 194–95, 199, 202, 204, 208

Partnership on AI 174, 234

personal identity, personality 105, 110–11, 111n30, 113, 113n33, 114n35, 122, 177

personal information 102, 104, 114–16, 116n39, 117–19, 121, 124, 149, 149n63, 150, 154, 157, 166, 173, 180, 196

personalization, of advertising, of medicine, of products and services 103, 135, 137, 141, 144–47, 147n56, 148, 150, 150n67, 151–55, 157, 159, 196

persons, as social constructions 15, 15n9, 16, 23–24, 27, 36, 39, 42, 47, 49, 52–55, 66, 68, 103–4, 106, 111, 187, 197

platform, as characteristic of society, mechanisms of 125, 133–42, 145n54, 159, 164, 166, 168, 223–25

Plato 12, 29

politics, as opportunism, as functional subsystem 5, 26, 34–35, 38, 40, 40n35, 42n42, 52, 63, 68n72, 120, 126–27, 133, 167, 167n92, 178, 204, 207, 221, 256

posthuman 3, 24–25, 27, 56n57, 62n65, 65, 69, 78n91, 89, 109, 113, 125, 187, 203–4, 214, 244

postmodern, as critique 24n20, 49, 64n67, 67n70, 105, 109, 113, 125–26, 131

Prainsack, Barbara 147n56

prehuman, hominin 69, 73, 78, 86, 128–29, 189, 193, 210, 214

prioritizing, as network governance principle 209–11, 213, 245, 248, 250–51

privacy, privacy paradox, contextual, instrumental, as fundamental right, as law, ontological theory of 3, 14n7, 61, 98n13, 102–5, 107, 111, 113–24, 127, 135, 141, 143–44, 149, 159, 163, 166, 168–69, 171–73, 175–77, 180, 182–84, 188, 191–93, 195–96, 203, 206–7, 215, 225, 233n41, 234n43, 244, 246, 248, 250

producing stakeholders, as network governance principle 208, 210–11, 213, 237–39, 240, 245–47, 251

Prometheus 240

property, private, public, common pool 6, 33, 37, 40, 70, 104, 113n33, 114, 189, 205–11, 213, 219, 236–37, 246, 248, 250–51, 254

public, vs. private, fragmentation of, public sphere 5–6, 55, 114n34, 116–17, 133–36, 138–42, 144, 160, 162–69, 178–81, 183, 188, 196–97, 203–7, 203n12, 224–25, 245, 248, 250

publicy 203, 203n12

rationality, pure reason 10–12, 15–16, 20, 26, 28, 30, 31, 34, 35, 35n32, 36, 38, 45, 89–90, 96, 100, 123, 128, 130–31, 243, 249

regulation, as law, as governance, by government 5, 7, 38, 40n35, 58, 62, 62n64, 71, 87, 101, 103, 117, 118, 120, 125, 133, 141, 148, 149n65, 156, 158, 169, 178, 179, 180–81, 183–85, 188, 201–2, 204–5, 207–8, 212–14, 235, 240, 244, 248, 250, 253, 255–56

relationing, selecting, steering as principles of systemic order 18, 21n16, 45, 51, 63, 66, 68, 80, 107, 210

religion, social subsystem 11n4, 16, 26, 34, 40, 53, 57, 63, 68n72, 126–27, 130

responsibility, moral, ethics of 4–5, 7–8, 14n7, 24, 85–86, 85n100, 101, 112, 122, 124, 176–77, 181–84, 194, 197–99, 202, 204, 215, 216–34, 238, 243–48, 254

robot, ethics of, humanoid 3, 13, 23n18, 24n20, 124, 237n49, 147–48, 175–78, 198n7, 218–19

Rowlands, Mark 111n29, n31

Rousseau, Jean-Jacques 156

rules, moral, social, non-moral 3, 8, 10–11, 13, 15–16, 15n9, 21–25, 27–30, 36, 40–42, 46, 61, 65–66, 68, 81, 92, 94n8, 96, 99, 118, 190, 204n15, 219, 235, 244–45

scandal, definition of, in media theory, and morality 5–6, 8, 132, 138, 149n65, 159, 160–69, 175, 178–79, 185, 188, 193, 202, 204, 243, 252, 255

skepticism, methodical 130, 188, 241

science, as social subsystem, science and technology studies 14–17, 20, 26, 33–35, 37–38, 40, 44–45, 49, 61–65, 68, 71–73, 83–84, 89, 91–92, 96, 119–20, 126–27, 129–31, 133, 175, 182, 189, 201, 212

selection, selecting as principle of systemic order (*see* relationing)

self, informational 95, 102–13, 115–16, 118–21, 183, 197, 203

semiotics 48, 55, 67n70, 76n87, 190

separating powers, network governance principle 40, 127, 212–13, 254

Simon, Herbert 214, 215

smart cities 145–46, 231

social science (*see* critique)

socialism 140

society, as a whole, as a system, as object of science, as domain of reality, as opposed to nature 2, 15–17, 15n9, 19–68, 71, 72, 81, 83–87, 109–11, 120, 126, 127–29, 131, 148, 168, 187, 188, 190, 194–99, 211–12, 216, 225, 244, 246, 251, 253

society, civil, modern Western, industrial, global, network, data-driven, digital, media, knowledge, platform 3–8, 12–14, 90–92, 100–102, 104, 114, 114n35, 122, 124, 126, 132, 133–35, 138–45, 149–50, 152–54, 156, 159–64, 167, 163, 168–69, 174–85, 188, 191, 193, 199–208, 213–14, 223–24, 242–43, 248, 250, 252, 254–56

sociology, perspective on morality, relational, as a science, as philosophy, of knowledge 14–16, 20–21, 26, 29n26

sociocracy 159, 252, 254n57, 32n30, 44–46, 59–61, 63–64, 71, 83–85, 130, 133, 164, 182, 211, 241
socio-technical network 7–8, 24n21, 70, 89, 91, 112, 120–21, 143, 178, 183, 190, 193, 193n3, 195–96, 199, 199n11, 221–22, 228–35, 240, 245–48, 250–51
Sorge 2, 75
Spencer-Brown, Georg 47, 83, 96n10
steering, principle of systemic order (*see* relationing)
stone ax 68–70, 73–74, 76–86, 94, 97, 99, 113, 115, 121, 128–29, 189–91, 193–94, 199, 201, 209–11, 214, 223, 241
structural coupling 28n25, 54–56, 58, 72, 110, 212
STS, science and technology studies 71, 148
subject, subjectivism (*see* autonomous rational subject)
substance ontology, philosophy of 6, 17, 19, 20, 29n27, 50, 74, 82, 85, 95, 98, 106, 112–13, 115, 120, 187, 195, 206, 215, 242, 244
sustainability, as value 3, 58, 176, 199–201, 209
symmetry, general symmetry, method of, with regard to agency 73, 73n81, 79n93
Symposium on Digital Ethics 174

taking account of, as network governance principle 208–9, 211, 213, 236, 245–46
The Royal Society 170
Thompson, John B. 160–62, 167n93
translation, as processes of network construction (*see* enrollment)
transparency, as ethical value, as network norm 7, 122, 136–37, 137n50, 141, 176–77, 195–97, 199, 202, 208, 213, 225, 231–32, 238, 243, 245–46, 248–52, 254
Twitter 164, 168

universal norms, rights, truths, reason 4, 10–11, 11n4, 15–17, 29–30, 34, 36–40, 42, 44, 60–64, 66, 84, 86, 89, 102–3, 124–25, 127, 130–31, 169, 175, 177, 184, 212–13, 245, 249, 253
Utilitarianism 10–12
Utopia 114n35, 256

Vallor, Shannon 9n1, 85n101
values, European, humanist, democratic, modern, private vs. public, network norms 4, 6–8, 13–14, 14n7, 16–17, 30, 32, 32n30, 33, 36, 38, 41–42, 44, 49, 61–62, 86, 100, 122–26, 132–35, 137–41, 143–44, 150, 156, 159, 162, 166, 168–69, 171, 173, 175–77, 179–80, 183–85, 188, 191–99, 201–4, 213, 224–26, 235–36, 239, 243–46, 250, 253, 255
van Dijck, José 133–42, 159, 192n2, 223–25
Verbeek, Peter-Paul 226–27, 244

Wark, McKenzie 1–3
Warren, S. Brandeis, I. D. 113, 122
Watzlawick, Paul 50, 110n28
Weber, Max 20, 38n34
WEF 172
Weinberger, David 136, 165
Wiener, Norbert 16n11, 82, 97
will, will to power, free choice, autonomy 2–3, 6–7, 10, 10nn2, 3, 11–16, 89–90, 98, 112, 118, 120, 130–32, 190, 198–99, 215, 217, 221n32, 222, 226–28, 234, 242, 243–44
Willke, Helmut 10n3, 31n28, 35n32, 40n35, 41, 49n48, 63n66, 156n77, 204n15, 228n38
Wittgenstein, Ludwig 25–27, 34, 45, 55nn55, 56, 57, 65n68, 110–11

Young, Kaliya 94n8
Youtube 168

Zuboff, Shoshana 142–60, 192, 192n2, 193, 231

www.ingramcontent.com/pod-product-compliance
Lightning Source LLC
Chambersburg PA
CBHW022010300426
44117CB00005B/120